PRACTICAL

D·I·Y

TECHNIQUES, PROJECTS AND MATERIALS

PRACTICAL

D·I·Y

TECHNIQUES, PROJECTS AND MATERIALS

SILVERDALE BOOKS

CONTENTS

This edition published in 2002 by
SILVERDALE BOOKS
An imprint of Bookmart Ltd
Registered Number 2372865
Trading as Bookmart Ltd
Desford Road, Enderby
Leicester LE9 5AD

© Little, Brown and Company (UK) 2000

Previously published by Orbis Publishing as
The Complete Home Carpenter,
The Complete Home Decorator,
The Complete Home Plumber,
The Complete Basic Builder.

ISBN 1-85605-668-6
Printed in Singapore

Little, Brown and Company (UK)
Brettenham House, Lancaster Place
London WC2E 7EN

PLEASE NOTE

Every care has been taken to ensure that the information in this book is accurate. However, the law concerning Building Regulations, planning, local bylaws and such related matters, differs from area to area, and is constantly changing. We strongly advise that you check with your local planning authority for advice about any major work you intend to make on your home. You are obliged to obtain the approval of local government authorities for certain developments such as building an extension, or changing the structure of a wall or fence. The planning authority will supply you with the relevant forms and information you may need.

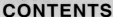

CONTENTS

HOME PLUMBING

HOME CARPENTRY

EXTERIOR MAINTENANCE

The publishers would like to thank the following companies for their help and advice in the preparation of this book.

PTS
MARSHALLS
RONSEAL LTD
C.S.D. ASSOCIATES
JOHN GUEST SPEEDFIT LTD
BLACK & DECKER
POLYPIPE PLC

PICTURE CREDITS

PTS - PAGES 101, 103, 146, 147, 151
MARSHALLS - PAGES 24, 63, 86, 91
JOHN GUEST SPEEDFIT - PAGES 127, 129, 131
C.S.D ASSOCIATES - PAGES 174, 175
BLACK & DECKER - PAGES 22, 225
POLYPIPE PLC - PAGE 129
RONSEAL LTD - PAGE 185

MATERIALS AND TOOLS

BRICKS

You may think bricks are all the same. They're not. There are thousands of different types available, and it really does pay to choose the bricks that are right for the job you're doing.

Faced bricks

Bricks are one of the most versatile of all building materials. To make the most of their qualities though, you must choose the right one for the job. Basically, two things affect your choice: how the brick is to be used and whether the final appearance is important.

For most do-it-yourself jobs, strength can be ignored. Even 'weak' bricks are more than adequate for, say, a garden wall, or a small outhouse. Similarly it's not important if bricks have slots, holes, or 'frogs' in them — unless the top face is visible. These are there to make the brick lighter and key with mortar better.

What you must not ignore if you're laying bricks outside is their weather resistance. Bricks are divided into various 'qualities' according to their ability to resist extremes of temperature.

Internal quality bricks have no weather resistance at all. As their name implies, they can only be used indoors — outside they would quickly disintegrate.

Ordinary quality bricks are suitable for exterior use, but will not stand severe exposure to the elements. This means they can be used to form the bulk of a free-standing wall, but not its coping. Ordinary quality bricks are also unsuitable for retaining walls and for brickwork underground. Here, the almost complete weather resistance of *special quality* bricks is required. These are very dense and very durable.

In terms of looks, if the brickwork is to be covered with rendering, plaster, or some form of cladding, it doesn't matter what they look like. Where appearance is important, you'll find a host of 'facing' or 'faced' bricks for use indoors or out.

Engineering bricks
Technically, engineering bricks are all special quality, but they are really more than that. They are extra special: very hard, very strong, regular in size and colour,

and almost completely impervious to water. Their major drawback is that they are expensive, so reserve them for situations where their virtues are really needed (eg, lining manholes, building an indestructible damp proof course into a wall, and so on). They come in two classes — A and B — which describe their exact strength and water resistance, but there are few DIY jobs where the choice is critical. You may also find bricks described as semi-engineering, but since there is no recognised definition of this type, you need to ask to find out what they are recommended for.

Commons
Bricks described as commons aren't meant to be beautiful. They are rough looking and vary considerably in colour, but they are relatively cheap and are normally either internal or ordinary quality. Some are sufficiently attractive to be left exposed (in which case they need protection by a coping). But in most cases they're used in situations where they will be covered up with some form of cladding which shields the bricks.

Faced and facing bricks
Both faced and facing bricks are designed to be put on display. The difference between them is that while faced bricks have only one or two sides that are presentable, facing bricks are attractive no matter which way you look at them.

Facing bricks made from clay are available in a variety of colours — reds, yellows, greys, blues, blue/greens, etc — and a combination of colours (called multi-coloured bricks). They also come in several textured finishes; some with commonsense descriptive names ('sand faced', 'rustic' and so on); some with names that indicate the methods of making ('hand mades', 'wire cut' etc). They offer the widest range and the best way to decide which you want is to go and look

at the bricks themselves — they are available in ordinary and special qualities.

Standard 'specials'
A wide range of these bricks is made to coordinate with standard bricks. They're designed to give either protection (eg, copings) or a finishing touch to the top of a wall or an end (eg, single, double or left and right hand bullnose). Radial headers and stretchers allow you to create a curve without cutting bricks or making the mortar joints thicker. These plus plinth headers and stretchers are the ones most useful in DIY work, and if not stocked can be ordered at builders' merchants. Most are available in ordinary or special quality; copings should always be special quality.

Calcium silicate bricks
These are made from either a mixture of sand and lime, or flint and lime. They're the same size and used in exactly the same way as clay bricks. Because of the way they're made, they are much more uniform in colour and size than clay bricks. There are a total of 6 classes available, but, as with classes of engineering bricks, most of them are to do with the bricks' strength. Basically, they fall into two categories: those designed to be on show (facing bricks), and those that aren't. Sandlime and flintlime bricks contain no soluble salts and efflorescence can only occur if salts come from the ground or materials stacked around them. For severely exposed places, specify class 3 or 4.

Concrete bricks
These are similar to calcium silicate bricks but are made from either portland cement or sulphate resisting cement. Concrete bricks are as uniform as calcium silicate bricks and are classified in exactly the same way. Good quality concrete bricks closely resemble the clay bricks they are designed to imitate.

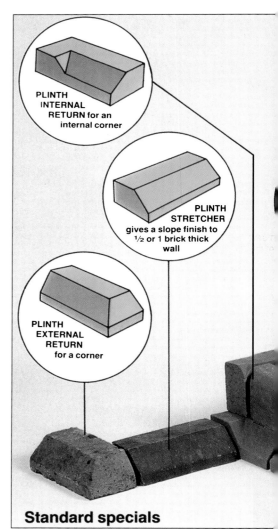

PLINTH INTERNAL RETURN for an internal corner

PLINTH STRETCHER gives a slope finish to 1/2 or 1 brick thick wall

PLINTH EXTERNAL RETURN for a corner

Standard specials

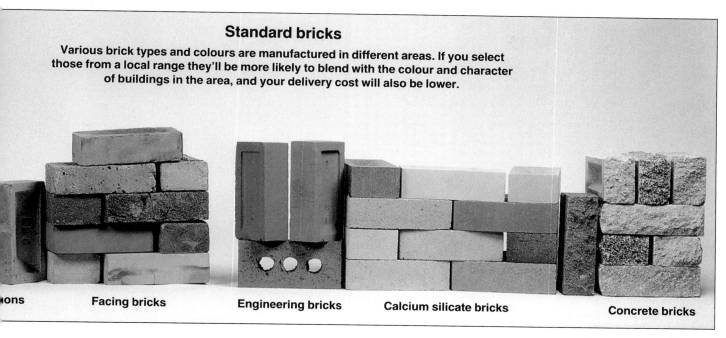

Standard bricks

Various brick types and colours are manufactured in different areas. If you select those from a local range they'll be more likely to blend with the colour and character of buildings in the area, and your delivery cost will also be lower.

ons

Facing bricks

Engineering bricks

Calcium silicate bricks

Concrete bricks

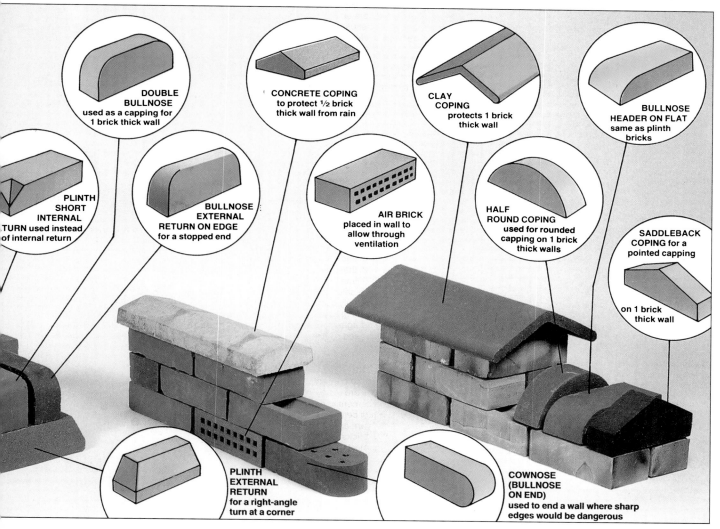

DOUBLE BULLNOSE
used as a capping for 1 brick thick wall

CONCRETE COPING
to protect ½ brick thick wall from rain

CLAY COPING
protects 1 brick thick wall

BULLNOSE HEADER ON FLAT
same as plinth bricks

PLINTH SHORT INTERNAL TURN used instead of internal return

BULLNOSE EXTERNAL RETURN ON EDGE
for a stopped end

AIR BRICK
placed in wall to allow through ventilation

HALF ROUND COPING
used for rounded capping on 1 brick thick walls

SADDLEBACK COPING for a pointed capping

on 1 brick thick wall

PLINTH EXTERNAL RETURN
for a right-angle turn at a corner

COWNOSE (BULLNOSE ON END)
used to end a wall where sharp edges would be dangerous

CEMENT, SAND AND AGGREGATE

Mortars and concrete are precise mixtures of cement, sand, aggregates and other additives. It's important to use the right ingredients for the best results.

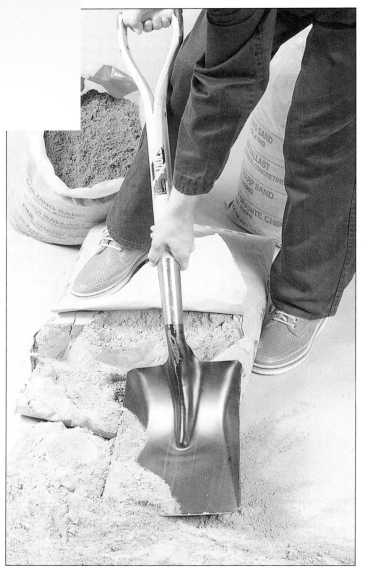

Y ou can't do much in the way of building work without having to mix up some mortar or lay some concrete, and if you're going to get good results you have to know the difference between the various types of cement, sand, aggregates and other additives you'll need. First, cement.

Cement
Cements are used to bind the sands and aggregates of a mortar or concrete mix together to give it strength. They set by the action of water, and for this reason they must be kept dry until they are used. Cement that has been stored in damp conditions and has partially hardened into lumps will not set properly and should not be used. Cements are usually sold in 50kg (1cwt) bags, but smaller sizes are available.

Portland cement is not a brand but a type of cement, and is made by several manufacturers. There are two commonly-used types.
Ordinary Portland cement (commonly abbreviated OPC) is the least expensive and most widely-used cement and is suitable for all normal purposes.

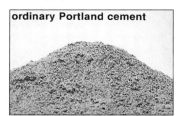

White Portland cement is made from white raw materials. It is used for making white mortars for pointing brick or stone walling, and for making white concrete for special decorative work. It is comparatively expensive.

Masonry cements are used for making bricklaying mortars, for bedding tiles and for backing renders for decorative wall finishes, including roughcast and pebbledash. They are not suitable for making concrete.
A masonry cement is not all cement; there are other materials added to improve the mix. It needs only the addition of sand to give a good mortar, and therefore it is simple to use. You can also add colouring pigments to change the mortar colour, but nothing else. Masonry cement is sold in 50kg (1cwt) bags.

Lime
Mortars and rendering mixes made with Portland cement and sand only are not ideal because they are too strong for general use and can be difficult to work with. Lime can be added to reduce the strength and to greatly improve the workability of the mix. It retains water well, which assists the proper hardening of the cement. The addition of lime to a mix also gives a degree of flexibility to the hardened material, making it less likely to shrink and crack.

Various mixes are recommended for different jobs, but in all cases the lime is similar. Builder's merchants sell 'white lime' for work where a light colour is required, or the cheaper 'grey lime' for all other work. Lime is sold in 25kg (1/2cwt) bags.

Plasticisers
Instead of adding lime to a mortar mix to make it workable, another additive, called a plasticiser, can be mixed in to produce minute air bubbles which act as a 'frictionless aggregate' in the mix.
Good-quality plasticisers are based on a resin that limits the

amount of air bubbles to a certain proportion. This improves the resistance of the hardened mix to frost damage.
Plasticisers are sold in liquid or powder form under various brand names. Liquids are easier to measure out and mix in than powders. They are available in 1 litre cans – enough to mix with four 50kg bags of cement.

Sands
Sand is the bulk material of mortars, renderings and floor screeds. It should be clean and well-graded. Sand is cleaned either by washing with water or by dry screening. Dry-screened sands are often better than washed ones, as they retain their finest particles and these can help to produce a more workable mix.

A well-graded sand is one that has particles of various sizes. The smaller particles fill the gaps between the larger ones, and so less cement is needed to bind them all together to make a strong material. Poorly-graded sands include a lot more air space and extra cement would have to be used.
Sharp sands are coarse and are generally washed. They are best suited for floor screeds and fine

concrete mixes. They can produce strong, durable mortars but they are slightly more difficult to work with. *Soft sands* (often called builders' or bricklayers' sands) contain large proportions of fine particles, including clay, which makes them unsuitable for good mortars. They are used for binding or filling hard-core sub-bases to floor slabs, drives and paths.

soft sand

Silver sand is a naturally-occurring and extremely pure white sand. It is used in work where appearance is important – for example, with white Portland cement to make white or light-toned pointing mortars and white concrete. Silver sands are fine and not well graded. Additional cement is needed to make a mortar with good strength and durability.

silver sand

Bulking is a factor that must be allowed for when using sand. The proportion of sand in a mix is given by volume, and this figure always refers to dry sand. In practice, all the sand you buy will be damp to some extent. Damp sand increases in volume – sometimes by up to 40 per cent – so you should measure out extra sand to allow for this.

Coarse aggregates
Coarse aggregates are mixtures of strong stones, not chippings, and are the main material forming concrete. They are usually graded by sieving to diameters of 5 to 20mm (about ¼ to ¾in). Grading of the particle sizes throughout the material is needed for strong concrete, but the range of sizes varies for different jobs. For this reason, always tell your supplier what you require the aggregate for.

All-in aggregates (commonly called ballast) combine sand and fine coarse aggregates, and are usually used where the precise strength of the concrete is unimportant.

Bulk-buying sand and aggregates
Large quantities of sands and aggregates are traditionally sold loose by volume, measured in cubic metres or parts of cubic metres. In some areas, builders' merchants now sell sand and aggregate by weight in 25kg (½cwt) bags, which you could collect yourself, and also in ½ tonne (approx 10cwt) and 1 tonne quantities which are delivered to the customer either

all-in aggregate

loose or in canvas bags off-loaded by a crane on the special delivery vehicle.

Buying small quantities
DIY shops now offer small bagged quantities of most of the commonly used sands and aggregates as well as ordinary Portland cement and lime. Sizes vary from 6kg (approx. 13lb) to 50kg (1cwt).

fine concrete mix

The range often also includes various general-purpose mixes for popular uses, including:
sand & cement mix – for floor screeds, laying crazy paving and repair work in damp locations;
bricklaying mortar mix – for general bricklaying and internal rendering;
coloured mortar mix – for bricklaying with coloured mortars;
fine concrete mix – for paths, steps, kerb surrounds, etc, where a fine

finish is needed;
coarse concrete mix – for foundations, setting fence posts and clothes line posts etc.

Most of the blended products do not state the exact composition of the mix. Read the application list printed on the bag carefully to make sure you have chosen the correct one for your job.

sand & cement mix

The range of mixes and pack sizes has been carefully worked out to provide a choice to suit commonly-occurring jobs around the home and garden. They save wastage and eliminate the trouble of buying and mixing together the separate ingredients. However, for some jobs it may be preferable to mix your own materials to the particular specification you require for the work.

coarse concrete mix

Special-purpose additives

The basic properties of standard mixes for mortars, renders and concretes can be modified by the inclusion of special-purpose additives. Here is a selection of the most common.

Colouring pigments are used to add colour to mortars and concrete. The pigments are stirred into the wet mix, and must be inert and colour-fast. Adding too much can weaken a mortar and reduce its

durability, so follow the instructions provided with the pigment.

Pigments are sold in powder form in 1kg and 5kg (2.2 and 11lb) tins. The maximum amount usually recommended is 5kg per 50kg bag of cement. The stockist will have colour charts indicating the effect of various proportions of the pigment. When using pigments, keep a record of the amount added to the mix and work with accuracy to keep the colour constant.

Waterproofing additives are used to make mortars and concretes waterproof. They come as powders or liquids, and can be used with Portland cement mixes, but some are not suitable for use with masonry cements. Check the manufacturer's instructions carefully when using these additives.

Well-compacted concrete is essential for waterproof work. Do not expect the additive to do the job at the expense of good workmanship.

Frost-proofers are additives used when working in cold weather. The frost resistance of a hardened

mortar, render or concrete is dependent on the strength of the basic mix; select a suitable specification and make sure that it is properly made up and used, and the work will be frost-resistant once is has set.

Frost-proofing additives are intended to give protection to work only during construction. Avoid working with mortars, renders and concrete when there is a risk of frost. Never start work in freezing weather, but if there is a risk of frost on new work or incomplete work, protect it with insulating covers such as hessian sacks, old blankets, or straw and the like, covered with polythene sheet or tarpaulins.

There is no effective frost-proofer to allow mortars and renders to be laid in near freezing conditions. However, concrete can be protected in low temperatures by the addition of an accelerator/hardener to the mix. This causes heat to be generated in the new-laid concrete, which should be covered as soon as practical in order to keep in the heat.

CONCRETE PAVING SLABS

Gone are the days when the local garden centre could offer you only paving slabs in dull grey or off-white. Today, a wide range is available in many colours and textures.

With slabs now made in an ever-increasing range of colours, textures and patterns, there's no longer an excuse for creating a concrete jungle in your garden. Your patio or path can have the mellow finish of old stone, the warm appearance of brick or cobbles, or the look of exposed aggregates.

What are concrete slabs?

Essentially concrete slabs, whatever appearance they might assume, are all made of the same material – cement. This reacts with water to form a hard, solid material. Crushed stone or gravel (coarse aggregate) and sand (fine aggregate) are added to form the body of the mix and provide strength and bulk. The cement-and-water paste coats the particles of aggregate and binds them all together into the dense mass known as concrete.

The cheapest slabs are simply cast in a mould of the required shape. A finish is then applied to the top face.

Pressed concrete slabs are stronger than cast slabs – although more expensive. They're hydraulically pressed during manufacture using many tonnes of pressure to compact and consolidate the fresh concrete. The result is a strong, double product.

Cast concrete slabs for garden use are generally 50mm (2in) thick, whereas pressed slabs are about 40mm (1½in) thick and a bit easier to lift and lay.

You might see concrete slabs described as made from 'reconstituted stone', the implication being that they are different from (and better than) concrete paving. All concrete is, in a sense, reconstituted stone. Manufacturers of this product, however, set out to simulate in concrete the appearance of a particular natural stone. Authentic stone is used for the aggregates, pigments are added and the product is made in moulds; themselves cast from an actual piece of stone in order to capture the correct texture.

Shapes and sizes

Most slabs are square or oblong, and come in a wide range of sizes, based on a 225mm (9in) or 300mm (12in) module. The most common sizes are:
225 x 225mm (9 x 9in)
300 x 300mm (12 x 12in)
450 x 225mm (18 x 9in)
450 x 300mm (18 x 12in)
450 x 450mm (18 x 18in)
600 x 300mm (24 x 12in)
600 x 450mm (24 x 18in)
600 x 600mm (24 x 24in)
675 x 450mm (27 x 18in).

Not all manufacturers make all of these sizes. The ones based on a 225mm (9in) module are the most useful, as they're appropriate in scale for most gardens. None of these sizes is too arduous to work with but normal precautions against back injury should always be taken. Bend the knees rather than the spine when lifting them, and watch your fingers and toes when stacking them: a 450 x 450mm (18 x 18in) slab weighs about 16.6kg (37lbs).

In addition to rectangular slabs you'll also find a wide range of other shapes – such as hexagons, and circles – although some are available only from specialist suppliers.

Hexagons, for instance, are particularly useful for making winding paths since you can change direction at 60° as well as at right angles. The commonest size measures 400mm (16in) in width between parallel sides. To obtain straight sides for a patio or path of hexagonal slabs half-hexagons are available.

Circular slabs come in various diameters and you can make a path of attractive stepping stones set in a lawn.

Estimating numbers

Estimating how many slabs you'll need to pave a given area is a matter of simple arithmetic with square and rectangular types. As a general rule, plan the size of your paved areas so that whole slabs are used when possible.

The easiest and most accurate way to work out how many slabs you'll need is to draw out the area you want to pave on squared paper, using one square to represent one slab.

Estimating the numbers of hexagonal slabs can be more difficult, although most manufacturers provide guides in their leaflets. When you're ordering your slabs it's wise to allow a few extra for breakages.

Colours and textures

Colour and texture must really be considered together. Relatively smooth, flat slabs can generally be found in the widest range of colours – from off-white, buff, yellow, brown and red to green, grey and dark slate.

With slabs designed to look like natural stone manufacturers naturally use stone colours. These include York stone in both buff and grey, Cotswold and a neutral stone grey. The most authentic looking slabs, however, are composed of two shades – a mixture of grey over buff to give a York – stone look and red with overtones of greys to simulate red sandstone.

Left: You can buy paving slabs with special cut-outs for paving around trees and all sorts of textured patterns that you can lay in swirling, interwoven designs.

Not all slabs are made to simulate natural stone; there's a wide range of other surface textures and patterns available. These range from a cobbled effect to more uniformly-patterned designs.

Slabs with relief patterns such as these are made in conventional sizes and shapes but you can also buy radius slabs to make a circular pattern contained within a square. Alternatively, some can be laid in such a way that they form interwoven swirling patterns or an overall herringbone effect.

A different approach to colour and texture is adopted with 'exposed aggregate' slabs.

Right: Surface finishes for square and rectangular slabs vary from smooth and riven to exposed aggregate.

Below: With pressed slabs you get patterns resembling brick, stone or mosaic in various shapes and sizes. With hexagonal slabs, two different edging slabs are available.

hints

Stacking slabs correctly
To prevent accidentally chipping the corners and edges of your slabs, and marking their faces, stack them on edge in pairs, face to face, against a wall, with their bottom edges on timber battens.

Handling slabs
Slabs are heavy and cumbersome to carry. The best precautions you can take are to wear heavy-duty shoes to protect your feet in case you should drop a slab on them, and gloves to protect your hands, especially if the slab has a rough surface. Grip the edges of the slab firmly and lift them with your knees bent and your back straight. Alternatively, you can hold the top corners of the slab and 'walk' it on its bottom corners.

Laying slabs in patterns
You've a lot of freedom in the way you lay your slabs. You can lay only one shape, size and colour or you can mix them to give various patterns.

GARDEN WALLING BLOCKS

If you're building walls in your garden, you don't have to stick to brickwork. There is a wide range of walling stone, natural or man-made, to choose from.

Many projects in the garden involve building free-standing walls, either for their decorative effect or to give shelter and privacy or to act as earth-retaining walls on sloping or banked sites.

In some areas, natural stone is still readily available at a price that makes it a worthwhile consideration for wall construction, but otherwise there is a good selection of reconstituted stone and high-quality precast concrete masonry blocks which come in a range of sizes and which offer an attractive alternative. In most areas the larger garden and DIY centres and builders' merchants keep good stocks. Stone merchants too, should not be overlooked as many offer quite an extensive range of reconstituted stone and precast concrete garden walling products as well as quantities of natural stone.

Reconstituted stone

Reconstituted stone blocks are made from concrete in which the aggregate is crushed natural stone and the sand and cement content is carefully selected so that the finished product closely resembles natural stone. They can be smooth, but most blocks have a texture intended to simulate traditional split stone walling.

These blocks are made in a co-ordinated range of sizes that can be laid in traditional stonework bonding patterns – either coursed or random. Precise sizes vary between makers and different brands are not generally interchangeable if regular bonding is to be maintained. But any size can be used on its own or together with others from the same co-ordinated range to produce the desired bonding pattern. The block sizes allow for joints 10mm (³⁄₈in) thick. There is a choice of about half a dozen natural stone colours; yellows, reds, greys and greens predominate. They can be used in mixtures to produce a multi-coloured walling.

Not all faces of the blocks are textured; often only one long face and one end is intended to be exposed, while the others are flat and smooth for neat bonding. Check this point when you are planning your wall and estimating quantities. If you want the wall to look good on both sides you may have to use two blocks back-to-back if the blocks themselves have only one textured face. Some ranges also include special blocks for corners and the ends, and also coping stones for finishing off the top of the wall.

Reconstituted stone can be used outside for the walls of buildings, extensions, garages and greenhouse bases, for boundary walls, retaining walls and barbecues; it is also ideal for use inside the house for fireplaces and decorative feature walls.

Simulated dry-stone walling

An interesting variation among reconstituted stone walling blocks is one which is moulded to give the appearance of eight or nine individual 'stones'. The false joints are deeply recessed, and for the best effect the 'real' joints should also be deeply recessed, and should be made with a mortar to match the colours of the block.

These blocks are faced on one long side and on both ends. They can be used to turn corners, but if

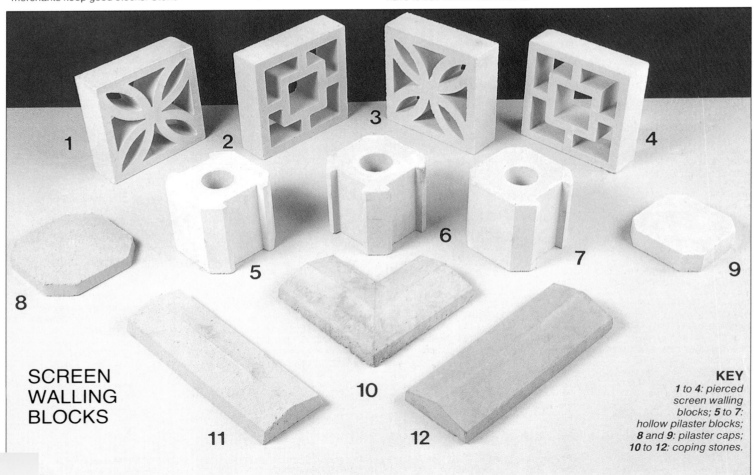

SCREEN WALLING BLOCKS

you want both sides of the wall to appear the same, then a double thickness wall will be required. The standard block size is 527 x 145 x 102mm (20¾ x 5¾ x 4in) which, allowing for a 6mm (¼in) thick joint, gives a work size of 533 x 152 x 102mm (21 x 6 x 4in). Half blocks are available for the half lap at the ends of the wall so that a soundly bonded wall can be built without cutting blocks. It is worth planning the work to suit the sizes of the block, as cutting will spoil the continuity of the pattern of false jointing. Special coping stones are made to suit single and double-leaf walls and square piers constructed from standard blocks.

These blocks are particularly suitable in the garden for retaining walls, boundary walls, piers for pergolas or pierced screen wall blocks, raised planting beds, seats and barbecues. As both ends are properly faced, a pierced screen or 'honeycomb' wall can be built with them as a design variation.

Concrete facing blocks

The lightweight concrete blocks used in houses for partitions and the inner leaf of cavity walls are not suitable for use in the garden, as they are not weather-resistant. Special concrete facing blocks should always be chosen for any outdoor work. They are walling blocks with a high-quality face intended to be left exposed. A wide variety of colours and textures are available, including sculptured, exposed-aggregate and split stone finishes. Usually they are made with dense concrete, but some types of lightweight blocks are made with dense weather-proof facing finishes. They are made in the standard work sizes of 450 x 225mm (18 x 9in) and 400 x 200mm (16 x 8in). Both sizes allow for 10mm (⅜in) thick mortar joints and they are made in several other thicknesses. Very thick ones are generally hollow to save weight. Other sizes are made to co-ordinate with these standard blocks for use at the ends or corners of walls. There are also other block sizes for special effects, including random course walling.

Facing blocks must be laid bonded – with vertical joints staggered – to give the wall strength. They can be cut with a bolster and club hammer, but it is best to set out the work to use whole block sizes as far as possible.

Decorative bricks

As an alternative to walling blocks of reconstituted stone, you could consider using specially coloured bricks – not the ordinary stocks or facing bricks used for house-building, although used these would often be suitable, but special types

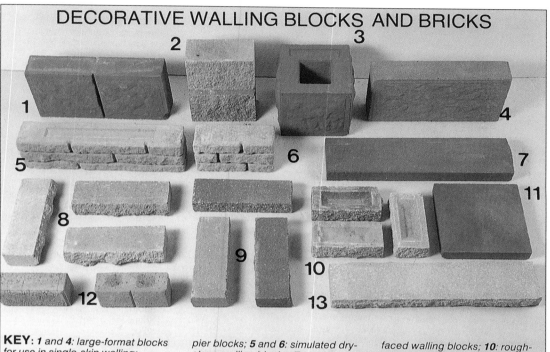

DECORATIVE WALLING BLOCKS AND BRICKS

KEY: *1* and *4*: large-format blocks for use in single-skin walling; *2*: rectangular 'jumper' blocks to course with 8 and 9; *3*: hollow pier blocks; *5* and *6*: simulated dry-stone walling blocks; *7*: coping stone; *8*: simulated split-stone walling blocks; *9* and *13*: smooth-faced walling blocks; *10*: rough-faced decorative walling bricks; *11*: pier capping stone; *12*: small-format walling blocks.

resembling dressed stone on their exposed faces and available in yellows, reds, greens and greys. The advantage these have over walling blocks is the presence of a frog (or indent) that helps to increase the bond strength – a useful bonus on exposed walls or earth-retaining structures. They are the same size as an ordinary brick.

Pierced screen wall blocks

Open screen walls made from pierced blocks can provide an attractive feature to give partial shelter or as a background for plants. They can be used to screen a patio, to build a carport wall or a porch screen, or to hide an unsightly area such as a compost heap or the dustbin.

The blocks are made from dense concrete, often white or near white, although some makers offer them in grey or other colours. Designs are generally based on geometric patterns. Some are laid in groups of four to give a larger interlocking design. Many manufacturers also make co-ordinating blocks which are not pierced; these can be incorporated in the pattern for special effects or they can be used where full screening is required in the general run of the decorative pierced walling.

Designs vary between manufacturers and different brands may not be interchangeable. Precise sizes may vary too, but they are generally a nominal

300mm (12in) square (including an allowance of 10mm (⅜in) for joints) and build a wall approximately 90mm (3½in) thick.

Pay attention to choosing the correct mortar mix for use with these blocks. White blocks should be laid either with a mortar made with white cement and silver sand to match, or else with a darker and deliberately contrasting mortar. The light grey colour of plain mortar made with ordinary Portland cement does not offer sufficient contrast and tends merely to look dirty. Take care to keep the mortar off the face of the blocks when laying them, so as to avoid the risk of staining. Align and level the blocks carefully and finish the joints neatly, as the square grid pattern will accentuate any irregularities.

Screen wall blocks are not laid with a lapped bond, but are 'stack-bonded', one on top of the other with the mortared joints aligning throughout. Stack-bonding is not as strong as lapped bonding, so a wall that is more than a couple of blocks high needs supporting piers. These piers should usually be every 3m (10ft), but follow the manufacturer's instructions for high walls or exposed locations. For extra strength, reinforcing mesh can be bedded in the horizontal mortar joints.

Piers can be built of bricks, or reconstituted stone or concrete walling blocks, but perhaps the simplest method is to use tailor-made screen wall pilaster blocks:

these are made to suit end, intermediate, corner and intersecting positions and have holes through the centre so that a steel rod can be threaded through, extending into the concrete foundation, to provide extra reinforcement for high walls; the hole is then filled with a weak concrete mix.

The tops of the pilasters are finished off with special caps, and copings are made to lay along the tops of the screen blocks. These strengthen the top of the wall, as the cappings each cover two or three blocks; they also help to shed rainwater, so minimising staining of the wall surface.

It is essential that this walling be laid on a flat base, so if you have a sloping site you will have to level it up in steps by building a dwarf wall in solid blocks or bricks. Even on a flat site this is often preferable, as two or three courses of bricks or stone walling is more practical next to soil than pierced blocks.

Mortars for garden walls

Never use mortars consisting of straight Portland cement and sand for building garden walls, since cracking is likely to result. The textbook mix is 1:1:6 cement:lime:sand, but other suitable mixes for this work include 1:4 masonry cement:sand and a 1:5 cement:sand mix with added proprietary plasticiser. In all cases the mix should be workable but not sloppy.

IRONMONGERY

There is a range of ironmongery designed for specific jobs, and using the right product can make your work go a lot more smoothly. Here are some of the things you're likely to find most useful.

F or most jobs around the house, buying what you need is usually quite straightforward. But some jobs need a special bit of hardware, and this may be hard to find unless you know exactly what you want. This list gives you an idea of what's available and gives you exact sizes so you can plan your work with confidence.

Ironmongery for building work
Concrete reinforcing mesh is used to strengthen concrete floors, paths, foundations, drives and so on. It is made from steel rods or 'wires' between 2 and 12mm (1/16 and 1/2in) in diameter, welded together to give a rigid mesh. The mesh sizes are 100mm sq (4in sq), 200mm sq (8in sq), 100x200mm (4x8in) or 100x400mm (4x16in). It is sold in sheets 2.4x6m (8x20ft), with some light meshes in 2.4m wide rolls up to 20m (60ft) long.
Brickwork reinforcing mesh is bedded in the mortar joins between courses of bricks or blocks to strengthen the bonding of the wall. It is made of 0.5mm (1/64in) thick galvanised steel and comes in widths ranging from 64 to 305mm (2½ to 12in) and in rolls either 22.8 or 82.4m (75 or 270ft) long.

Choose the width that leaves a 25mm (1in) gap between the edges of the mesh and the faces of the wall. Thus, for a half brick thick wall you'll need 64mm (2½in) wide mesh, and for a whole brick thick wall you'll need 178mm (7in) wide mesh.
Plaster laths and beads are used as a base when plastering across a gap, round a corner, or as reinforcement in positions where unprotected plaster is likely to crack.

Laths are made from 0.5mm (1/64in) thick galvanised steel mesh with a mesh size of 6mm (1/4in), and sold in sheets up to size 675x2440mm (2ft 3inx8ft).

Angle bead is used to reinforce corners, and there are two types available. The standard type is designed for 12mm (1/2in) thick plaster and comes in 2.4, 2.7 and 3m (8, 9 and 10ft) lengths. Thin-coat bead reinforces a 3mm (1/8in) thick skim coat of plaster and

comes in 2.3, 2.4m and 3m (7ft 6in, 8ft and 10ft) lengths.

Stop bead is used to finish and reinforce edges of plaster at openings, and there are types suitable for external use to provide a clean finish to the bottom edge of rendering on an upper floor. They come in 2.4 or 3m (8 or 10ft) lengths.

You can also buy prefabricated mesh arch formers, which you fix under the head of a rectangular opening to form the arch profile and then plaster over. They are made in a range of arch shapes, for openings of various widths.
Wall ties are used to bond together the two leaves of a cavity wall. There are four types available, though the first two types are the most common – and the cheapest.

The galvanised wire butterfly pattern is 203mm (8in) long and is made from 3mm (1/8in) wire twisted together to form a double loop.

The galvanised steel twisted pattern is 200mm (8in) long, by 20mm (3/4in) wide and 3mm (1/8in) thick.

Stainless steel ties look a bit like a propeller blade without the twist. The fins are embedded in mortar and are dimpled to improve the grip. They are available with insulation-retaining discs.

Finally, there are plastic ties. They are similar to the twist pattern and are available with insulation-retaining discs.
Door frame ties are used to provide fixing points for door or window frames in brickwork. They are built into the wall between courses in the same way as wall ties. There are two types.

The fishtail pattern is similar to the twist pattern wall tie, but with a 50mm (2in) pre-drilled and countersunk upstand for fixing to the wood. They are available in various sizes.

The second type is called a patent door and window frame holdfast. They have a sharp fishtail end which is driven into the wood so screws aren't required.

Profiles made of galvanised steel, are used to tie in a new wall without having to cut out joints. They are fixed to the existing wall with coach bolts and butterfly ties are clipped in to tie in to the new wall. They come in 2310mm (7ft 6in) lengths to suit 75 to 215mm (3 to 8½in) bricks or blocks.
Joist hangers are used to support the ends of the joists as an alternative to setting the ends in the masonry. Again there are two types.

One type of joist hanger has a fishtail lug which is keyed into mortar joints between courses of bricks, or set into concrete. It is made of galvanised steel and is available for 150 to 230mm (6 to 9in) deep joists, all 50mm (2in) thick. Other sizes (and different coloured finishes) are available if ordered specially.

The second type has two pre-drilled straight straps that you bend as necessary in order to hang one joist from another. It too is made of galvanised steel and is designed for nail fixing. It comes in a variety of widths from 38 to 100mm (1½ to 4in) and depths from 150 to 230mm (6 to 9in).
Herringbone joist struts are available, made of galvanised steel, and can be used as an alternative to constructing the struts from timber. They are designed for joists at 400mm (16in) centres, and various sizes are available according to the width and depth of the joists.

BUILDING & PLASTERING

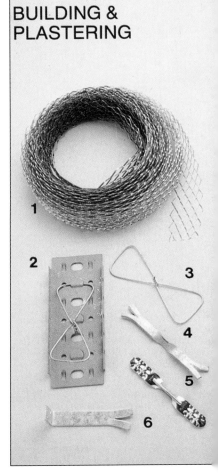

GUTTERS & FENCES

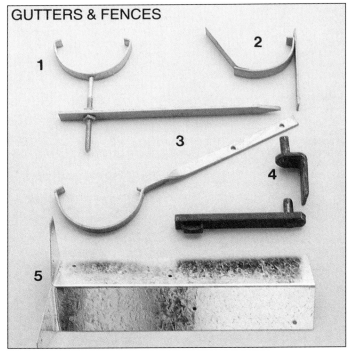

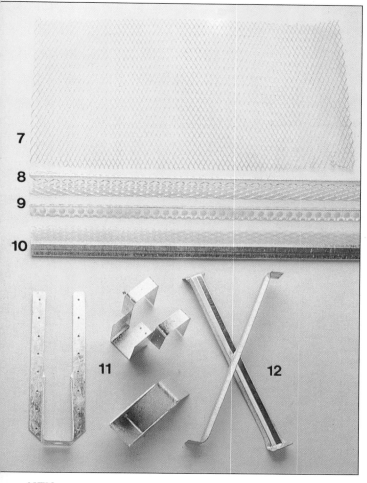

KEY

Building and plastering
1 Brickwork reinforcing mesh
2 Profile wall tie
3 Butterfly wall tie
4 Twisted wall tie
5 Stainless steel wall tie
6 Door frame tie
7 Plaster lath
8 Plaster-depth angle bead
9 Thin-coat angle bead
10 Stop bead
11 Joist hangers
12 Herringbone joist struts

Gutters and fences
1 Rise and fall bracket
2 Fascia bracket
3 Rafter bracket
4 Gate hangings
5 Arris repair bracket

Roofing and flashing
1 Lead flashing
2 Zinc flashing
3 Self-adhesive flashing
4 Copper crampons
5 'Jenny Twin' slate clips

ROOFING & FLASHING

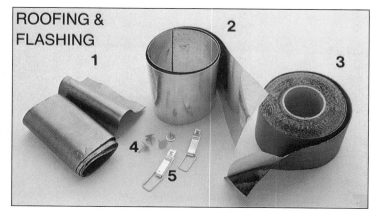

Ironmongery for carpentry and home repairs

Angle repair irons are used to reinforce butt joints in timber. They are available in four shapes – X, T, L and straight – and are screwed to the face of the timber or fitted into shallow recesses. They are made of bright steel or brass and are pre-drilled. Sizing is by leg length, which is normally between 50 and 75mm (2 and 3in).

Corner braces are also used to reinforce timber butt joints but are screwed to the inside of the angle. They are made from bright steel, with two pre-drilled countersunk screw holes per leg, with leg sizes of 50, 75 or 100mm (2, 3 or 4in).

Corner brackets are used to strengthen and square corners of cabinets and frames, etc. They are made from galvanised steel or plastic and there are two main types. One is for fixing to the face of the joint and the other for fixing in the internal angle. Both are triangular in shape and the latter has upstands on the sides to provide the fixing points.

Shrinkage plates are useful for reinforcing butt joints in natural timber where there is a possibility of shrinkage or swelling in the future. They are made from galvanised steel and have holes in one leg and slots in the other. The slot allows the timber to move without straining the joint. There are three main types – the angle bracket and the straight plates with either horizontal or vertical slots.

Fence repair brackets are used to reinforce damaged joints in fence posts. Normally made from galvanised steel, the most common type is used for joining arris rails to posts where the rail end has begun to rot away. There is an open socket to receive the end of the rail and a flange providing a screw fixing to the post.

Gate hangings are the large gate's equivalent of a hinge and consist of a bracket with an upright pin that locates in the hinge eye of the gate. There are four types – a bolt fitting for pre-drilled timber and concrete posts; a flange fitting for screwing to timber posts; a spike fitting for driving into timber posts; and lastly, a plain tail for bonding into masonry.

Gutter brackets support heavy cast iron guttering and are therefore handy for repair work. There are five main types, all made from galvanised steel. For screw fixing there are fascia brackets which fix to the surface of a wall or fascia, and rafter brackets that fix to either the top or side of a rafter. Other brackets have a long spike for bonding into masonry – 'drive' brackets have a horizontal spike and 'rise and fall' brackets have a vertical spike.

REPAIR BRACKETS

1 Repair plates
2 Corner brace
3 Shrinkage plate
4 Corner bracket

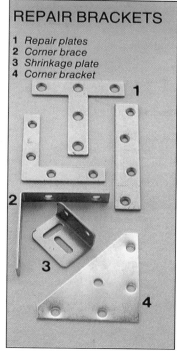

Sheet flashing is used to provide a waterproof join at junctions in a roof. It can be made from lead, zinc or aluminium.

Zinc is usually sold in 2440x915mm (8x3ft) sheets of various thicknesses and in strips 150mm (6in) wide. Lead is sold in 6m (20ft) rolls or by the metre, as a strip between 150 and 780mm (6 and 30in) wide. It comes in a variety of thicknesses, quoted as a code number from 3 to 8. Code 3 is for lightweight applications such as chimney flashings, but for general flashing code 4 is usually considered to be the minimum.

Aluminium flashing is soft, and easy to shape round any profile. It is also lightweight and much cheaper than lead or zinc. It is sold in 8m (26ft) rolls, 600 or 900mm (2 or 3ft) wide.

Self-adhesive flashing strip has a thin aluminium foil bonded to a bitumen base. It is useful for general flashing work as well as for repairing leaking gutters or old flashing. It comes in 100m (33ft) rolls with widths of 50 to 460mm (2 to 18in).

Slate clips, also known as tingles, are used to retain replacement slates. They are made of copper, 150mm (6in) long by 15mm (5/8in) wide. They are pre-drilled with a single hole to take the fixing nail.

A clever modern slate fixer called the Jenny Twin is also available. It's linked to the slate by a folding tab, and locks it onto the roofing batten as the slate is slid back into place.

Crampons made of copper are for securing asbestos-cement tiles.

SAFETY GEAR

Lots of jobs around the home can be dangerous, dirty, or just plain unpleasant. There's a wide range of protective clothing and accessories designed to help you get on with the job while keeping clean and reducing the risk of accidents.

There are times when you simply cannot avoid working in hazardous situations or with potentially dangerous materials and machines. And accidents will happen. The trick is to minimise the risk by following the safety rules appropriate to the job and by wearing the right gear.

This need not be anything elaborate. It all depends on what you are doing. If you are working with machinery, the 'right gear' may mean nothing more than buttoning your shirt sleeves and taking off your tie so they will not get tangled in the moving parts. If you are standing on a ladder for long periods, it may simply mean wearing comfortable 'sensible' shoes to reduce 'foot fatigue'. The right gear can even mean clothes which protect you from the weather, including warm gloves and sweaters, waterproofs or a sun hat. If you are too cold or too hot, your concentration will go, leaving you prone to errors. If you are extremely cold, you may actually injure yourself without knowing it.

But of course there are also times when only specialist equipment will give you the protection you need. The range available is detailed below.

Safety glasses/goggles
These will protect your eyes from dust, harmful liquids, and also from the flying debris produced by such jobs as chiselling masonry.

The cheapest are like ordinary spectacles, with impact-resistant plastic lenses. To stop things getting past them, more expensive types also have protective side screens, or curved main lenses. They are light and comfortable to wear, even for extended periods, but, like ordinary spectacles, have a tendency to slip if you are doing anything really active.

For greater protection, particularly against dust and liquids, safety goggles are better. To ease the problem of perspiration, the body of the goggles contains ventilation holes. Many can be worn over ordinary spectacles.

Protective masks/respirators
To stop you inhaling harmful dust, sprayed paint and so on you will need one of these.

The cheapest and most widely available consist of a simple replaceable cotton gauze pad mounted in an aluminium frame contoured to fit over the nose and mouth. For more demanding work, there are also moulded rubber and plastic masks (normally referred to as 'respirators') which accept more efficient replaceable cartridge filters. These filters are generally designed to filter specific substances, and it's important that you choose the right type. For example, some work against dust; others against the vapours produced by spray painting.

Heavy-duty gloves
If you want to avoid blisters, gardening gloves will probably do the trick. For some jobs though, you need far greater protection against abrasion on rough surfaces, cuts from sharp edges, and/or corrosive chemicals, and should wear purpose-made heavy duty gloves.

There are three common types. One is a chrome leather version, either with double thickness palm, or armoured with metal staples, to give good protection against cuts and abrasions.

Natural rubber gloves are the usual choice against corrosive chemicals. Unlike their domestic washing-up counterparts, these are not only proof against chemicals, but also have good resistance to tears, snags and abrasion. There are ordinary medium weight versions and also heavy gauntlets with extended cuffs to protect the forearms.

Then there are PVC gloves. Most are equivalent to medium weight gloves; some perform like chrome leather but give a degree of chemical resistance as a bonus.

Overalls
When tackling a dusty, dirty or potentially messy job, these simply stop your ordinary clothes getting in too much of a state.

They don't offer much more than splash protection though, particularly against oil, grease, paint and so on. If it's cold you will still have to wear old clothes underneath (if its warm, for many jobs you can just wear the overalls).

Work boots
If you have ever dropped a brick on your foot, or can imagine how it feels, the advantages of wearing a good strong pair of boots with steel-reinforced toe caps when carrying out general maintenance and building work are immediately obvious. They are not expensive, and since most have hard-wearing leather uppers and oil and alkali resistant rubber soles, they do represent very good value for money. Protective shoes made to the same standards are also available. The only thing they are not much good at is coping with mud and deep water, so, if you are digging trenches, wear your wellingtons.

Safety helmets
More commonly known as 'hard hats', these are really worth considering only if you are engaged in substantial demolition work, or intend to go clambering up professional type scaffolding. They can be hired. They are normally made from glass fibre or high density polythene and should have a fully adjustable harness allowing you to make them fit well enough not to fall off. The gap between harness and helmet also cushions any impact, so never wear a helmet without a properly adjusted harness. As an added safety precaution, make sure the helmet conforms to British Standards .

Ear protectors
These are designed to protect your ears from the damage that can result from prolonged exposure to high levels of noise.

Most are foam plastic filled plastic muffs mounted on a plastic covered sprung-steel headband. For the sake of general safety, when you are wearing the protectors you should still be able to hear moderately loud noises in your vicinity (so you can hear warning shouts for example) which is why they are preferable to ordinary ear plugs.

Knee pads
You will really appreciate these when tackling a job which means spending hours crawling about the floor. Some are simple cushioned rubber mats, others are strapped onto your knees. If you can't buy them, improvise with pads of cloth, or some old cushions.

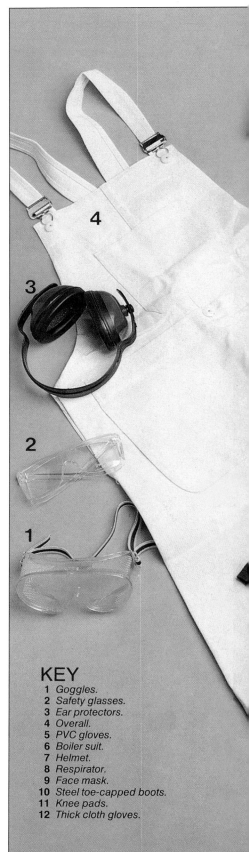

KEY
1 *Goggles.*
2 *Safety glasses.*
3 *Ear protectors.*
4 *Overall.*
5 *PVC gloves.*
6 *Boiler suit.*
7 *Helmet.*
8 *Respirator.*
9 *Face mask.*
10 *Steel toe-capped boots.*
11 *Knee pads.*
12 *Thick cloth gloves.*

MASONRY TOOLS

The term masonry can mean anything from a brick or piece of stone to a complete wall, so it is important to be specific when choosing the right tool for a cutting or shaping job.

The hardness of the material to be worked is, perhaps, the most important consideration when choosing masonry tools. Some stone-cutting tools are designed for use only on relatively soft stones such as sandstone, and to use them on a hard stone like granite could cause damage to the tool or workpiece. Most 'brick' tools are intended for use on ordinary, relatively soft bricks and tend not to cope with hard engineering bricks, which have to be treated more like hard stone. Some are tempered just to cut brick and nothing else, whereas others may cut a variety of materials; it is important to check. When dealing with mixtures of materials, the general rule is to pick a tool that will handle the hardest element in the mixture.

Cutting and shaping tools
The commonest tools for cutting and shaping masonry of all types are cold chisels. There are several general-purpose and specific versions.

The **flat-cut cold chisel** is frequently used on masonry for splitting, chopping out, cutting chases and, occasionally, rough shaping. Like the rest of the cold chisel family, it is a hexagonal steel bar with a cutting tip formed at one end – in this case a straightforward wedge-shaped tip a little wider than the bar. The other end has chamfered edges to prevent chipping when struck with a heavy hammer.

The **cross-cut cold chisel** also known as the Cape chisel, has a cutting edge very much narrower than the bar from which it is made, allowing it to cut slots and grooves with great accuracy.

The **half-round cold chisel** is a variation of the cross-cut chisel and may also be known as the round-nosed chisel. It has a single cutting bevel ground into the tip to produce a semi-circular cutting edge. Used mainly for cutting grooves, it can produce rounded internal corners as well.

The **diamond-point cold chisel** is yet another variation of the cross-cut chisel and is sometimes known as the diamond-cut chisel. It has a diagonally-ground single cutting bevel. Use it for making V-shaped grooves and neatly angled internal corners.

The **plugging chisel** is otherwise known as the seaming chisel or seam drill. It has a curious slanting head, and is used for removing the mortar pointing in brickwork. Two types are available: one with a plain head and the other with a flute cut into the side to help clear waste material.

The **concrete point** is a fairly rare cold chisel that tapers to a point rather than a normal cutting edge and is used for shattering concrete or brickwork in areas previously outlined with a flat chisel.

The **dooking iron** is intended for cutting holes through brickwork and stone. This extra-long, flat-cut cold chisel has a narrow 'waist' let into the bar just behind the head to help prevent waste from jamming it in the masonry.

The **brick bolster** has a extra-wide, spade-shaped head and is designed to cut bricks cleanly in two. Most have a 100mm (4in) wide cutting edge, but other widths can be found, and care should be taken not to confuse these with other types of bolster chisel such as the mason's bolster (see below) or even the floorboard chisel. They are not tempered in the same way and may be damaged if used incorrectly.

The **mason's chisel** comes in two varieties. Narrow versions look like ordinary cold chisels, but the wider versions are more like brick bolsters. They are intended for general shaping and smoothing of stonework. The very narrow types (sometimes called edging-in chisels) are used to make a starting groove for a bolster when splitting large blocks and slabs.

The **mason's bolster** is a much tougher tool than the brick bolster, being designed for use on stone or concrete. Use it to split blocks and slabs, or to smooth off broad, flat surfaces.

Breaking tools
When it comes to breaking up solid masonry, heavier-duty tools are needed. The **pickaxe**, usually known simply as a pick, is the tool most people think of for breaking up masonry. It has a pointed tip for hacking into hard material and a chisel or spade tip for use on softer material such as ashphalt. In practice, though, you may find it easier merely to crack the masonry with a sledge hammer (see below) and then use the spade tip of the pickaxe to grub out the debris. Neither tool is worth buying, hire them instead.

The **club hammer** is a double-faced hammer used for breaking up masonry and for driving chisels and bolsters. It is also known as the lump hammer.

The **brick hammer** is designed specifically for driving cold chisels or bolsters when cutting bricks. It has a head that incorporates a chisel end for trimming the brick after it has been cut.

The **sledge hammer** is used for directing heavy blows at masonry in order to break it up. For light work, it should be allowed to fall under its own weight, but for more solid material, it can be swung like an axe.

Electric hammers and hydraulic breakers
If you have a lot of demolition work to do or have to break through thick concrete, it is possible to hire an electric hammer to do the job. This will come with a variety of points and chisels.

Saws for masonry
For cutting blocks and slabs, or even masonry walls, a hand or power tool can help to achieve a neat finish.

Although the **masonry saw** resembles a normal woodworking saw, its extra-hard tungsten carbide teeth and friction-reducing PTFE coating are capable of slicing through brick, building blocks and most types of stone.

A large two-man version, which has a detachable handle at one end so that an assistant can help pull the saw through, will even cut through walls. Unfortunately, with the exception of small **chasing saws** used to cut electric cable channels in walls, using masonry saws is very hard work.

The **cut-off saw** is just another name for a heavy-duty circular saw which may be electrically or petrol driven. The key to cutting masonry, though, is not so much the power of the saw as the special cutting wheel – a rigid disc of tough abrasive that grinds its way through the stone. Various grades are available to match the material being cut.

Such saws are professional tools that can be hired if there is sufficient work to warrant it, or if a particularly deep cut is required. However, if you already own a circular saw, you should be able to buy a masonry cutting disc for it. Take care, though, to get the right grade for the job.

The **angle grinder** is usually used to cut and grind all types of metal – pipes, rods and sheets. However, fitted with the appropriate stone-cutting disc it can also be used to make cuts and shallow channels in brick, stone and concrete. It is extremely useful for cutting earthenware drainpipe sections.

Tools for drilling holes
When drilling holes in masonry of any type, it's vital to use a drill bit or other tool that is specially hardened to cope with the task. Never attempt to use ordinary twist drills.

Masonry drill bits allow you to drill into brick, stone, mortar and plaster with an ordinary hand or electric drill. Each has two small 'ears' at the end to help break up the waste, and is tipped with tungsten carbide.

Special long versions and extension sleeves are available for drilling right through walls.

Core drill bits are used for boring large-diameter holes – up to 50mm (2in). The bit is a hollow tube that cuts out a 'plug' of material much like a woodworking hole saw. A reduced shank allows it to be fitted into a normal drill chuck.

One thing that masonry drill bits cannot cope with is hard aggregate, such as that found in concrete. One solution is to break up the aggregate particles with a **jumping bit** as they are met. This is a hole boring tool that is driven in with a hammer and twisted by hand at the same time. Sometimes the bit is mounted in a special holder and is interchangeable with bits of different sizes. The **star drill** is a heavier-duty one-piece relation of the jumping bit, and has four tapered flutes to clear debris as the drill is hammered into the masonry.

Electric percussion drills look like normal electric drills and are used in the same way, but there is an important difference. While the drill bit rotates it is hammered in and out, offering the benefits of the twist drill and jumping bit in one.

If you intend buying such a tool, make sure the hammer action can be switched on and off as required and that it has a strong steadying handle. Also, check that it is powerful enough for your needs. This may be indicated by the wattage of the motor or by the chuck size; generally, the larger the chuck capacity, the more powerful the drill.

Finally, remember that safety goggles or glasses are essential when using masonry tools.

BREAKING AND SHAPING TOOLS

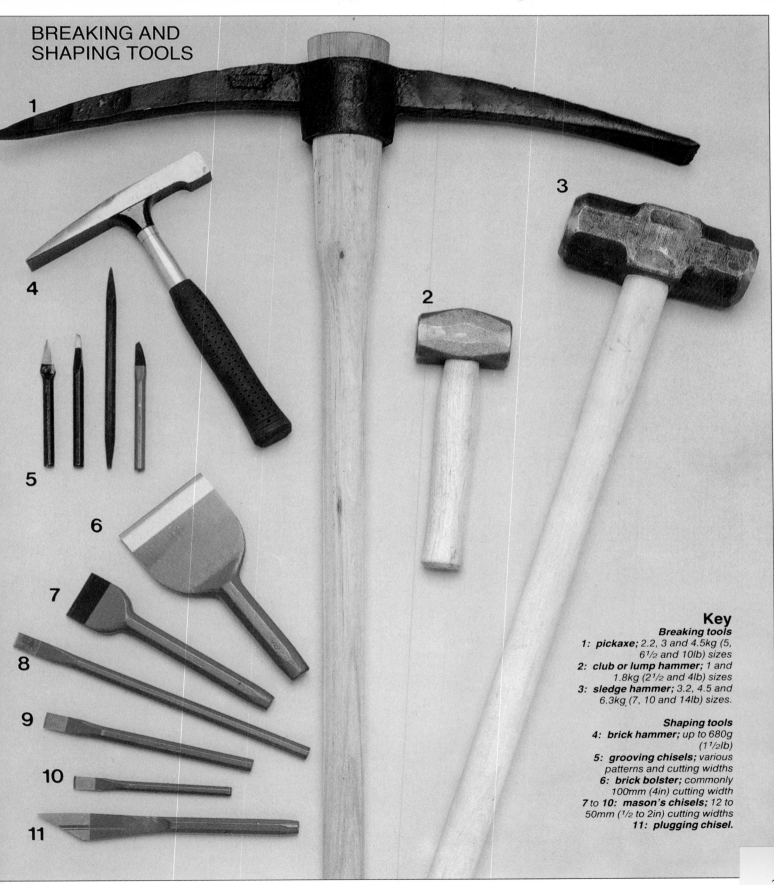

Key

Breaking tools

1: **pickaxe;** 2.2, 3 and 4.5kg (5, 6½ and 10lb) sizes

2: **club or lump hammer;** 1 and 1.8kg (2½ and 4lb) sizes

3: **sledge hammer;** 3.2, 4.5 and 6.3kg (7, 10 and 14lb) sizes.

Shaping tools

4: **brick hammer;** up to 680g (1½lb)

5: **grooving chisels;** various patterns and cutting widths

6: **brick bolster;** commonly 100mm (4in) cutting width

7 to 10: **mason's chisels;** 12 to 50mm (½ to 2in) cutting widths

11: **plugging chisel.**

POWER TOOLS

1. Angle grinder
2. Mouse
3. Cordless drill
4. Circular saw

BASIC BUILDING

BRICKS AND BRICKWORK

Successful bricklaying relies on three easily-mastered elements. The first is mixing mortar properly – like a cook's recipe, sloppy measuring and mixing spells disaster, while a correctly-mixed mortar will be as strong and long lasting as the bricks or blocks it bonds together. The second is laying a brick squarely and level. The third – and arguably the hardest – is laying all the other bricks square and true with their neighbours. Yet providing you can lay one properly, and you're prepared to check your work regularly as you proceed, a perfect wall will be the end result.

BASIC BRICKLAYING TECHNIQUES

There's a lot in bricklaying that you can only really pick up with practice. But there are some rules which can guide you every step of the way. Understanding bricks themselves, the right way to mix mortar and how to use a trowel correctly will help you achieve a result you can be proud of.

Brickwork is made up of two things: the bricks, and the mortar which forms the joints. Building a wall that's going to last needs careful attention to both, and the first thing is to choose the right bricks for the job.

Know your bricks

There are three groups of clay bricks:

1 Common bricks have no special finish because they are made to be used where they will not be seen or be subjected to major stress or load. They are mostly used in situations where they will be covered by paint, plaster, cladding, rendering etc. They are a relatively inexpensive brick and are usually a rather patchy pink in colour.

2 Facing bricks come in a variety of colours and textures for they are made to be displayed indoors and out. Also called *stocks,* they are capable of bearing heavy loads. If classed as *ordinary quality,* it means they can be used for most projects, but in very exposed conditions outdoors will need to be protected by a damp proof course at ground level (either a course of engineering bricks, see below, or a layer of bituminous felt) or with a coping above to prevent the bricks becoming saturated with rain. Without this protection they are liable to be affected by frost which would cause disintegration. *Special quality* facing bricks are suitable for use in exposed places or where great strength is needed, eg, for paving, retaining walls, garden walls and steps.

3 Engineering bricks are smooth and dense, designed to be used where strength and low water absorption is essential – for example in foundation courses (thus providing a damp proof course for a wall or planter) and load bearing walls.

Another type of bricks completely are the *calcium silicate bricks.* These are flint/lime bricks which are whitish when steam-hardened in an autoclave (they aren't fired like clay), but these are available in many colours because they take pigment well. They absorb moisture easily, so must never be laid with a mortar that doesn't contain a plasticiser. They can be used in just the same way as clay bricks. Like engineering bricks, they are also more regular in shape and vary less in size than ordinary bricks.

Brick types

Bricks also vary in their character as well as their composition: they may be solid, perforated or hollow, but most fall into the solid category. Even bricks with small or large holes in them (these are also known as cellular) are classed as solid so long as the perforations do not exceed 25% of the total volume. The same is true of bricks with a shallow or deep indentation known as a *frog.* As well as making the bricks lighter, perforations and frogs give bricks a better key(ie, the mortar is better able to bond them together).

Bricks are measured in two ways: when they come from the works the actual size is 215mm long, 102.5mm wide and 65mm deep; the format size, however, is the one used for calculating the number of bricks you need. This needs an allowance of about 10mm added to each of these dimensions for the mortar joints – ie, 225mm long, 113mm wide and 75mm deep. Bricks are also made in special shapes and sizes for particular uses (copings, bullnose and angles are some examples).

Storing bricks

As all bricks (except engineering bricks) are porous, they should be stacked on a level area away from damp, otherwise long after you've used them the mineral salts inside the clay will stain the surface with an unsightly powdery white deposit (known as *efflorescence*). In the garden, put bricks on planks or a metal sheet and cover them with plastic sheeting. Apart from anything else, bricks which are saturated with water (as opposed to just being wet) are hard to lay and will prevent a satisfactory bond between bricks and mortar.

Mortar for bricklaying

Cement and sand made into mortar with water will set quickly, but is liable to create a crack between the mortar and the brick if it shrinks during drying. The ideal mortar, in fact, doesn't set too quickly, doesn't shrink much and can take up settling movements without cracking. There are two ways of making a mortar like this:

● The first way is by adding hydrated lime to the mix. This makes the mortar more workable and smooth (or 'buttery' as the experts say).

● The second is by adding a plasticiser – a proprietary liquid or powder. Air bubbles are formed which provide spaces for the water to expand into, thus preventing cracks.

● Basic to mortar is cement. This acts as the adhesive, binding the particles of sand together. Ordinary portland cement is the one most commonly used.

● Fine sand is used for mortar to give it its correct strength. Use clean builder's sand (also known as 'soft' sand) which does not contain clay, earth or soluble salts (these can lead to efflorescence).

Buying the materials

Cement is usually sold in 50kg (112lb) bags, although you may also find smaller sizes. Sand is sold by the cu metre (1⅓ cu yd) and in parts of a cu metre. To give you a sense of scale, a cu metre of sand weighs about 1,500kg (1½ tons) — a very large heap. Both are usually bought from builders merchants, where you can also buy lime or

MIXING MORTAR

1 Unless you're using dry ready-mix (most suitable for small jobs) carefully proportion 1 part cement to 6 parts builders sand.

2 Thoroughly mix the cement into the sand so that you end up with an entirely consistent colour. Turn the mix over at least three times.

3 Adding a little plasticiser to the water (the amount will be specified on the container) will make the mortar easier to work with.

4 Form a crater and pour in half the water. In total you'll need about the same amount of water (by volume) as cement — but add the rest gradually.

5 Mix in the dry mortar from the inside walls of the crater. As the water is absorbed, add a little more. Turn the whole mix over several times.

6 The final mix should look like this. Check it by stepping the shovel back — the ridges should be firm and smooth, holding the impression of the shovel.

READY REFERENCE

BRICKLAYING GLOSSARY

Frog: the indentation in the top of a brick. Generally bricks are laid frog up except on the top course of a free-standing wall.

Header face: the small end of the brick. Bricks laid so this end shows on the face of the wall are called headers.

Stretcher face: the long side of a brick. Bricks laid lengthways are called stretchers.

Bed face: the underside of the brick which is set into a mortar bed.

Bonds: the patterns of bricklaying to give walls strength. Vertical joints (called perpends) in one course must be overlapped by bricks in the next so the joint doesn't run through.

Course: name for a single row of bricks. A course of stretchers is known as ½ brick thick, a course of headers 1 brick thick.

Joints: the average of 10mm of mortar between bricks.

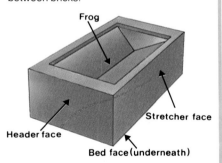

Frog

Stretcher face

Header face

Bed face (underneath)

BRICK SIZES

A standard brick is 215mm (8½in) long, 102.5mm (4in) wide and 65mm (2⅝in) deep. For estimating purposes the 'format size' is used instead. This includes 10mm in each dimension to allow for one mortar joint. Format size is 225 x 113 x 75mm (8⅞ x 4⅜ x 3in).

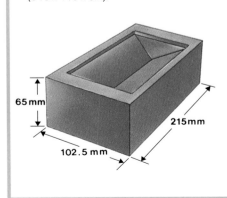

65 mm

215mm

102.5 mm

USING THE TROWEL

1 *Use the trowel to chop off a section of mortar (about the same size as the trowel) and separate it from the rest with a clean slicing action.*

2 *Shape the back of the mortar slice into a curve — so that it's pear-shaped. Sweep the trowel underneath to lift the mortar off the board.*

3 *Slide the trowel sharply backwards to lay the mortar in a 'sausage' shape. Spread it out by stepping the tip of the trowel down the middle.*

4 *When you've laid a brick in position, remove the mortar that squeezes out of the joint by sweeping the trowel upwards with its edge just scraping the brick.*

5 *To create the vertical joints between bricks, you 'butter' one end before you lay it. Scrape the mortar on by sliding the trowel backwards.*

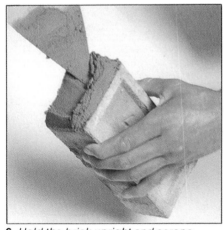

6 *Hold the brick upright and scrape down all four edges. Finally spread out the mortar evenly to a thickness of 10mm-12mm (about ½in).*

proprietary plasticisers. Alternatively you can buy special masonry cement which has a plasticiser already in it and only needs to be mixed with sand and water.

Proprietary plasticisers are available in 5kg containers and you will have more than you need if you're only doing a small job — only a capful or two for each bucket of cement. But always follow manufacturer's instructions for use. Hydrated lime is a powder bought in 25kg bags.

Dry ready-mix mortars are also available with all the necessary ingredients ready mixed — so you just add water. Although more expensive than buying the sand and cement separately, it's a convenient way of buying for small projects. Bags usually come in

10kg, 25kg, 40kg and 50kg sizes. Alternatively, you can buy bags in which the cement is packaged separately from the sand.

Remember that it's always better to have a little more than you need — so be generous in estimating (see *Ready Reference*). Also make sure that any surplus cement or dry-mix is well sealed. This is vital to prevent it going off.

Rules to remember
● When filling the cement bucket (proportions are by volume, not weight), tap it frequently to disperse any trapped air.
● Mortar that has begun to set is no use. Any not used within 2 hours of the wetting of the cement should be discarded – if used it would

dry too quickly and would not give the required strength to the brickwork.
● The sand and cement have to be thoroughly mixed before any water is added. Turn mixture over and over with the shovel until the pile is a consistent colour all through. The same rule applies to dry-mix mortar.
● When mixing in water, make crater on top of the pile, add some water and bring dry materials from sides to centre. Turn over whole pile several times, make another crater and repeat until mixture has a consistency which will hold the impression of the fingers when squeezed, or the impression of the trowel point.
● As builders' sand is rarely dry it is not possible to know how much water will be

needed to achieve the right consistency. Using a small container such as an empty tin will give you more control than using a bucket – and add water bit by bit.

The vital bricklaying tool

The trowel is the tool which makes the job, and no other tool can be substituted for it. A bricklayer's trowel is heavier and less flexible than any other trowel, and can be used to pick up and smooth down a required amount of mortar. Brick trowels can be bought in various blades sizes (from 225 to 350mm, or 9in to 14in) but the easiest to handle is the 250mm/10in one.

Brick trowels are roughly diamond shaped with a sharp point at the end opposite to the handle. The left side has a straight edge for scooping up mortar; the right side has a slight curve used for cleaning up the edges of bricks and for tapping the brick down into the mortar to level it. These are reversed in left-handed trowels.

Professional bricklayers use the curved edge of the trowel to cut bricks, but a more accurate and cleaner cut can be made with a brick hammer and bolster chisel. The trowel has a wooden handle raised slightly above the diamond, and at an angle to it to prevent you brushing your knuckles on the bricks as you are working. Getting the feel of the trowel and handling it properly is the key to good brickwork.

The trowel must be manipulated so that the mortar is scooped up in what's called a 'pear' or 'sausage' shape (see left) and placed on the bricks. This action is one that needs a lot of practice, for mortar that isn't compact is hard to manoeuvre and won't go where you want it to.

Practice routines

Make up a small amount of mortar (or 1 part of lime to 6 of sand, plus water to make it pliable) and practise combining it with bricks before you undertake a bricklaying project. The bricks can be scraped off within 2 hours (before the mortar sets). You have longer with

BRICK JOINTS

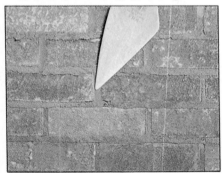

1 *The simplest brick joint is a 'struck' joint — do the vertical joints first, drawing the trowel upwards or downwards with a firm action.*

2 *Next do the horizontal joints — use the full length of the trowel and drawing it firmly backwards with a sliding action.*

Types of pointing

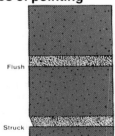
Flush

Struck

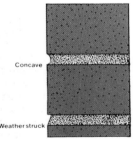
Concave

Weatherstruck

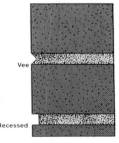
Vee

Recessed

There are lots of ways of finishing off the joints in brickwork. Above is a selection of six of the most common. The flush joint is finished flush with the brick surface, while struck, weatherstruck and vee joints are all formed with the point of the trowel. Concave or rounded pointing is formed by running the edge of a bucket handle or a piece of hose pipe along the joints, while recessed pointing is pressed back with a piece of wood planed to the same size as the brick joints.

HOW MANY BRICKS?

For a straight run of walling, remember
● One brick length + one joint = 225mm
● One brick height + one joint = 75mm
So for each metre of wall length you need 4.5 bricks; for each metre of wall height you need 13.3 bricks.

Example: a wall 4 m long and 2 m high needs 4 x 4.5 = 18 bricks in each horizontal course, and a total of 2 x 13.3 = 27 courses (to the nearest whole number). 18 x 27 = 486 bricks in total.

On more complex structures, dry-lay the first course of bricks and count how many are required. Then multiply this number by 13.3 for each metre of height required.

HOW MUCH MORTAR?

For small jobs: buy dry ready-mixed mortar, available in 10kg, 25kg and 50kg bags. A 50kg bag makes enough mortar to lay 50-60 bricks.

For larger jobs: it's more economical to buy materials separately and mix them up yourself. Here's how they are sold:
● Cement — usually in 50kg bags
● Lime — usually in 25kg bags
● Sand — by the ¼, ½ or whole cu m.
● Plasticisers — usually in 5kg containers

MORTAR MIX

Measure ingredients by volume, using a stout bucket or similar container. For general brickwork above ground level, mix:

   1 bucket ordinary Portland cement
   1 bucket hydrated lime
   6 buckets soft sand

● Replace lime with proprietary liquid plasticiser, added according to manufacturer's instructions, if preferred.
● One 50kg bag of cement mixed in the above proportions will give enough mortar to lay about 450 bricks.

TIPS: MORTAR MIXING

The amount of water you add to give the right consistency depends on how damp the sand is. As a rough guide allow 1 bucket of water for each bucket of cement. Remember:
● always add water gradually, never all at once, mixing after each addition
● always use mortar within 2 hours of mixing; it cannot be reconstituted once it has begun to set.

LAYING AND LEVELLING

1 Check layout by 'dry laying' the bricks, setting them a finger-width apart. Use string and pegs as a guide, fixing the ends with bricks, as shown.

2 Use your gauge rod — see **8** — to check that a corner is square. Measure 3 marks along one side, 4 along the other; if square, the diagonal will be 5 marks.

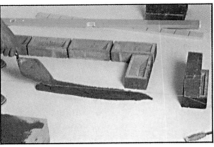

3 With the line and pegs still in position, lay the mortar on the base by drawing the trowel sharply backwards. Lay enough for at least 2 bricks at a time.

4 Tap the first brick into position, using the string as your guide. The mortar should make a joint 10mm (just under ½in) thick.

5 Lay the next 4 or 5 bricks, still following the line, making sure all mortar joints are the same thickness. Carefully scrape off the excess mortar.

6 Use the spirit level to check that the bricks are sitting perfectly level. If one is too high, tap it down. If too low, remove it and add mortar.

7 Each brick for the next course should straddle two on the first course. This creates the 'stretcher bond', evenly distributing the weight of bricks.

8 Check that the courses are rising correctly with a 'gauge rod'. The rod is marked at 75mm intervals — brick height plus a 10mm mortar joint.

9 With string and pegs removed, check each brick with the spirit level as you lay it. Tap the bricks gently with the trowel handle.

10 With each new course, check the corner with the gauge rod. With the first brick correctly positioned, other bricks are aligned with it.

11 Check that the faces of the bricks are vertical and aligned with each other. If not tap bricks back into position with the trowel.

12 Also check diagonally across the face of the bricks. Lay the bricks frog (the indentation in the top of the brick) down only on the final course.

lime mortar. The 'sausage' or 'pear' is the basic shape of mortar lifted onto the trowel. The following sequence is worth practising over and over until it becomes easy to do. Chop down into the mortar and draw a slice of it towards the edge of the board. Move the trowel to and fro, along the length of the slice, pressing the body of the trowel on to the mortar till you have shaped the back of the slice into a curve – the mortar should be smooth and have no cracks.

Now sweep the trowel underneath the curved slice and load it on to the trowel, it will either look like a sausage or a pear, hence the name. Put it back on the spot board, shape it again, then sweep it up ready for placing. This amount of mortar should give you a 10mm thick bed for two stretchers. Hold the trowel parallel to the course, then, as you draw it back towards you, lift and jerk it slightly so the mortar rolls off gradually in a smooth elongated sausage. Press the mortar along the middle with the point of the trowel so a furrow is made in the mortar. When you place a brick on it a small amount of mortar should ooze out.

Joints in brickwork
Bricks are laid with both horizontal and vertical joints to keep the bricks apart. After the excess mortar has been removed from the face of the bricks (and behind), the joints can be finished in various ways – for an attractive effect as well as for protection against the weather. Coloured mortar is a specially prepared dry mix to which only water needs to be added. Pigment can be bought to colour your own mix of mortar but it can be difficult to obtain the same colour for each batch.

Making a cross joint
Sometimes 'buttering' is used to describe the technique of coating the end of a brick with mortar to form the vertical joint. Sweep up enough mortar to cover about a third of the trowel. Now sharply flick the trowel so the mortar lifts up, then falls back onto the trowel, (this squashes out air and makes the mortar 'sticky'). Hold the brick at a slight angle, then scrape the trowel against the bottom edge. Use the trowel point to flatten and level the mortar on the header – it should be 10mm thick.

Cleaning off
The other important trowel action is removing excess mortar from the side of the bricks as you lay them. Cut the mortar off cleanly by firmly lifting the trowel upwards (if you do it horizontally it will smudge the bricks). This leaves a flush joint.

Tricks or bad habits?
Bricklayers will often add a few squirts of washing-up liquid to the water when mixing mortar. This on-site plasticiser, used instead of lime or a proprietary plasticiser, is not added in any precise manner. Although it might make the mortar more pliable it could also weaken it. And how much is a squirt anyway? If you want a pliable mix, buy a proprietary plasticiser additive, or ready-mix with it already added.

● The shovel is frequently used as a measuring stick when mixing mortar, and there's no doubt it's an easy way of proportioning the ingredients. It can, however, give wildly inaccurate results. A mound of powdery cement won't sit on a shovel in the same way as sand will. Measurement should always be by volume. A bucket is ideal for most quantities – although if you're only making a very small amount use a small metal container instead.

● The curved edge of the bricklayer's trowel will effectively cut bricks when wielded by a professional. Apart from doing a great deal of damage to the trowel (the edge of which is needed for the upward sweep required to remove mortar from brickwork), it is easier to cut bricks on a sandy or soft ground with a bolster chisel and a hammer.

Protecting brickwork from damage
As soon as you have finished bricklaying, and you've cleaned off and finished all the joints, it's worth taking a few simple precautions to protect your work until the mortar has set and it is able to take care of itself.

The biggest enemy is rain. A heavy downpour could wash mortar out of freshly-pointed joints – which you would then have to re-point – and stain the face of the brickwork. Such stains are particularly difficult to remove except by hosing and scrubbing. Furthermore, if your brickwork is set on a hard surround – a patio, for example, or alongside a path – rain could splash up from the surface onto your brickwork, again causing staining and erosion of mortar joints at or near ground level.

So on small projects it's a good idea to cover your work, at least for 24 hours or so, until the mortar has had time to set to something like its final hardness. Drape polythene or similar water-proof sheeting over the brickwork, anchoring it on top with several loose bricks, and drawing the sides of the sheeting away from the face of the brickwork before anchoring them at ground level a foot or so away from the wall. In windy weather, lay a continuous line of bricks, or use lengths of timber, to prevent the wind from whipping underneath the sheeting.

Remember that until the mortar has hardened any knocks will displace bricks and break mortar joints. Corners are particularly prone to knocks and accidental collisions. So it's well worth erecting some kind of simple barricade in front of the new work for a day or two.

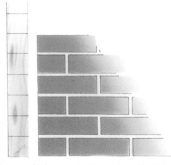

FORMING CORNERS AND PIERS

The techniques involved in making a brick wall turn a corner, or finish with a pier require an understanding of bonding, and how cut bricks might have to be used to keep a design symmetrical.

Building walls isn't simply a matter of arranging bricks in straight lines. You may have to include corners and, when you come to the end of the wall, it must be finished off properly. The techniques for doing this effectively are relatively easy once you know the basis of brick bonding.

Brick bonds are crucial to bricklaying; simply stacking bricks one above the other without any kind of interlocking would neither distribute the weight of the wall evenly nor provide the wall with any kind of strength, however strong the mortar between the bricks. And because the joints line up they would provide a perfect channel for water to get in and wash out the mortar.

The simplest way of bonding is to overlap the bricks, with no vertical joints continuing through adjacent courses. This kind of bonding can create numerous different patterns — some very simple, such as the stretcher bond used on pages 26-31 others much more complicated and requiring advance planning.

Exactly the same principle applies whether you're building a wall a half-brick thick (a single line of bricks) or one that needs to be one brick thick (two adjacent lines of bricks or one line laid header on). The difference is that instead of only overlapping the bricks lengthways as in a *stretcher bond* you can also overlap them widthways. With the *header bond*, for instance, all of the bricks are arranged header on to the face of the wall — and again the vertical joints only line up in alternate courses. In effect, the bricks overlap by half their width.

With any bonding pattern, there may be a need for cut bricks to maintain the bond. This may happen at the end of a wall built in stretcher bond where half bricks (called ½ bats) are needed in alternate courses. It may also occur where a new wall is being tied in to an existing wall (see below).

Similarly, with a wall built in header bond the ends need two three-quarter bricks (called ¾ bats) laid side by side in alternate courses to maintain the symmetry, the overlap and wall thickness. With other types of bond, the number and variety of cut bricks increases. The *English bond*, for instance, alternates a course of bricks laid stretcher face on with a

course header face on to make a one-brick thick wall — and it needs a brick cut in half lengthways (called a queen closer) in each header course or two ¾ bats laid side by side in the stretcher course.

Corners in brickwork

When it comes to turning a corner in brickwork (known as a *quoin*) the importance of correct bonding is even more apparent. Without it, you'd be building two walls which weren't interlocked and so lacking in real strength. In a half-brick thick wall in stretcher bond the corner is easy to make. Instead of cutting ½ bats for alternate courses, a whole brick is placed header face on at right angles to the front face of the wall.

The necessary 'tying in' of bricks with other bonding patterns, however, usually requires additional cut bricks and careful planning. In effect, the bond may change when you turn a corner. In header bond for example, which has alternate courses starting with ¾ bats, ¾ bats must be placed header on as well to create the corner. In English bond the stretcher course on one side of the quoin becomes the header course on the other.

MARKING OUT FOR A CORNER

1 *Bricks can be used to hold the string lines on already laid concrete but use profile boards if a trench has to be dug. Check with a builders square that all the lines cross at right angles.*

2 *Laying the bricks dry is the best way of checking your calculations after setting out is completed, the width of your finger being a good guide to the eventual thickness of the joint.*

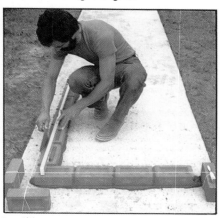

3 *After the first course is laid there are two things to check: the bricks must be horizontal (you can tap down any out of alignment) and their faces must be truly perpendicular.*

4 *From the first course onwards, the squareness of the corner must be checked so that any adjustments can be made immediately to prevent the wall leaning out (called an overhang).*

A bond may also have to be altered if the bricks don't fit the actual length of the wall. When this happens you have to break the bond as close as possible to the centre of the wall. If the length differs by 56mm or less don't use a ¼ bat (this is considered bad building practice) but use ½ and ¾ bats instead, making sure you place them so that no straight joints occur.

PROFILE BOARDS

These are placed to give accurate lines when digging the trench for the foundation. Strings attached to nails in the top of the boards define the width of the trench and must cross at perfect right angles where the corner is to be built.

The end of the wall
If you're building a wall as a boundary, or enclosing a corner of your garden, it may have to meet existing walls at one or even both ends. In such situations you have to tie in the bricks with the other wall(s), so this may affect your choice of bond for the new wall — it's always better if the new matches the old. It also means you have to match levels, and before you lay your first new brick you have to chip out bricks from alternate courses of the existing wall to provide for 'toothing-in'. Even if you can satisfactorily match the bond pattern, the old bricks may be a different size, so to make a proper connection expect to cut bricks to odd lengths to tooth in. More about this in another section.

If your wall comes to a free-standing end you must create what's called a *stopped end*. This requires careful checking for vertical alignment, and needs to be finished off to make a clean, neat face. But it is important to make sure the end is strong enough — and to do this you actually increase the width by a half brick to create a 'pier'. In effect, instead of cutting a ½ bat to finish off each alternate course, you lay the last brick in alternate courses at right angles to the wall face. By adding a ½ bat next to it you create a squared-off end — a simple pier.

Piers for support
It's not just at the end of a wall that you may need the added strength of a pier. To give a wall extra support, particularly on a long run, you need piers at regular intervals. For instance, walls of half-brick thickness need piers that project by at least half a brick every 1.8m (6ft). To do this in a wall built in stretcher bond, you will have to alter the bonding pattern to accommodate the pier, and add cut bricks to ensure the correct overlapping is maintained. If the wall is over 12 courses high, a more substantial pier is needed: three bricks are placed header on in the first course, and ¾ bats are used on the pier and either side of the middle stretcher in the second course.

One brick thick walls need piers at less frequent intervals — in fact every 2.8m (9ft) — but the pier has only to project by half a brick (see diagram).

Where piers occur, the foundation must be dug slightly wider at that point (about half a brick wider on both sides and beyond the end of the pier).

Method of building
Planning how you're going to lay the bricks is, of course, only the theoretical side of bricklaying. In practice, to make sure the wall stands completely perpendicular and the corners and ends are vertical it's most important to follow a certain order of work. Lay at least the first course of bricks dry so that you're sure they all fit in (see also pages

TURNING A CORNER

1 On each face of the wall check that it is perpendicular by holding the level at an angle. Tap bricks in or out.

2 As each course is laid use the gauge rod to check that the wall is rising evenly, with equal horizontal joints.

3 Check that the corner is vertical by using the spirit level straight. Hold it steady with your foot.

4 Lay the first course from the corner to the stopped end following a line and cutting bricks as needed.

5 Build up the stopped end so the courses are stepped by the correct overlap. This is called 'racking back'.

6 Raise the line to the next course between the racked corner and stopped end and fill in between.

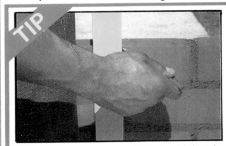

7 To make sure you get vertical joints in line, mark the position of each one on the whole brick above it.

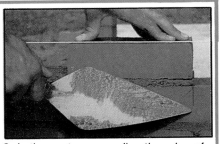

8 In the next course, align the edge of the brick with the mark. The joints will then be the right width too.

READY REFERENCE

A BUILDER'S SQUARE

Essential for checking that corners are 90°, this is simply three pieces of wood cut in the proportions of 3:4:5 (ie, a right-angled triangle). Nail them together with a half-lap at the right-angled corner and with the longest side nailed on top of the other two sides.

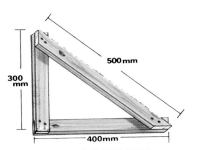

WHAT CAN GO WRONG

You can lose the horizontal because you didn't check often enough as the wall was rising. With every course
● use the spirit level
● use the gauge rod
The wall can lean out or in because you didn't check the vertical with the spirit level. Use it when
● racking back
● starting a new course
When laying to a line the last brick won't fit because the vertical joints further back along the course were not the same width. So make sure that in each course
● the joint width remains constant
● vertical joints line up in alternate courses – use the gauge rod for this.

LAYING TO A LINE

When you build up two corners at opposite ends of a wall, the process of laying bricks in between is called 'laying to a line'. To fix the line for each course use
● a bricklayers line and pins

● twine tied around two spare bricks

● triangular profile boards (good for beginners as you can see that the courses are rising evenly).

A PIER IN STRETCHER BOND

1 *In order to prevent any straight joints you have to break the bond. On the first course place two bricks header on, then place a ½ bat so it spans the joint equally.*

2 *On the second course to get the pattern right you have to lose a quarter from each of the stretchers on either side of the ½ bat. So cut and place two ¾ bats.*

3 *On the pier itself, the second course is not tied on but is merely a stretcher laid across the projecting two headers. This gives a pier the same width as the wall.*

26-52). Another big problem is that it is difficult to lay a line of bricks with each vertical joint exactly the same width — an inaccuracy of just 1mm in each joint between a line of 10 bricks will mean that the last brick at the corner or end will project over the one underneath by 10mm. The best way to avoid this happening is by 'racking back' — build up each corner or end first, stepping the bricks upwards and checking the vertical each time. When the bricks reach the required height, start filling in. Any slight inaccuracies can be accommodated by the joints in the middle part of the wall where they'll be less noticeable as long as you make sure the bricks overlap each other by as close to half a brick as possible.

Making the corner square

Marking out the corner for the foundation is the first priority—and it's vital that it is square. Using profile boards and strings—explained in Foundations, pages 48-52 —is the best way to start. Set the boards for each line of the corner about 1 metre (3ft) back from the actual building line (see diagram page 33). The strings must cross at right angles (90°) and to make sure that they do, use the 3:4:5 method (see *Ready Reference* page 34) to make yourself a builder's square. This is a large set-square made by nailing together three

75mm×38mm (3in×1½in) softwood battens cut into lengths of 450mm (18in), 600mm (2ft), and 750mm (2ft 6in) so that the sides are in the ratio 3:4:5. This is a manageable size but it can be made bigger if you prefer.

Laying out the corner

When you have the profile boards in position, dig the foundation trenches — see pages 48-52 — and lay the concrete. Allow it to 'cure' for at least 5 or 6 days before laying the first course of bricks. This gives it time to harden properly (although it needs about 3 weeks to reach its full strength). The next step is to mark out the actual building lines on the concrete, again using the profile boards and strings (see pages 48-52 again).

Lay the first course of the entire wall, starting at the corner and working outwards first along one wall line and then along the other. In building a half-brick thick wall in stretcher bond it is easy to turn the corner simply by laying two bricks to make a right angle. Check the angle using the builder's square.

Once the first course is laid, check again with the spirit level to make sure that all the bricks are sitting correctly. Add a little mortar or remove a little from underneath any bricks which are out of true. At the same time, check again that all the bricks follow your building line, and tap them into position if they don't.

CORNERS AND STOPPED ENDS

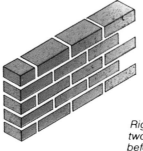

Left: At a stopped end in stretcher bond, the cut side of the ½ bats on alternate courses are hidden by the mortar joints.

Right: In a brick-thick wall in English bond, two ¼ bats or a queen closer are laid before the final header at a stopped end.

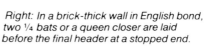

Below: At a corner in a stretcher bond wall, the header face is seen on one side while the stretcher shows on the other.

Below: The arrangement is the same at a corner, but to maintain the bonding the course on the other face becomes stretchers laid side by side.

FORMING CORNERS AND PIERS

Once this is done you can remove the lines and start building up the ends and corners.

Putting in the piers
If you're going to need piers at any point along the wall, don't forget to plan them in from the beginning. In a half-brick thick stretcher bond wall a pier is tied in by two bricks laid header on in alternate courses. The courses in between are not tied in but consist of a single stretcher laid parallel to the wall for the pier, and a ½ bat and two ¾ bats replacing two stretchers in the face of the wall.

A pier at a stopped end in a half-brick stretcher bond wall is made using a stretcher face at right angles at the end. The course is completed with a ½ bat and on the alternate course two stretchers are used parallel to the wall.

Checking as you build
One of the most useful checking tools you can make yourself is a gauge rod (see pages 26-31) and as you build up the corners and ends check each course with the rod to make sure the horizontal joints are consistent. If you're aiming for a wall of about 12 courses in total, build up the corners and ends to about 6 or 7 courses first before starting to fill in between them.

To step the bricks correctly, lay 3 bricks along the building line for every 5 courses you want to go up — so it's best to start by laying 4 bricks along each side of the corner and in from each end (see pictures 5 and 6 on page 34).

Filling in
Once you've built up corners and ends properly racked back (stepped with the correct overlap), the rest of the wall can be filled in course by course. Although you can lay the bricks normally, checking each time with the level and gauge, a good tip here is to string a line between bricks already laid at each end, then lay the bricks in between to this line. A bricklayer's line and pins (the pins are specially shaped to slip into a mortar joint) is ideal, but a string can be hooked around a brick at the correct height and then anchored under a loose brick to give a start line to follow.

If you over-mortar a brick and it protrudes above the level, gently tap it down with the end of the trowel handle and scrape off the excess mortar squeezed out of the joint. If a brick does not stand high enough, remove it and the mortar underneath, then replace it with fresh mortar.

Getting the last brick into the line can be quite tricky and a good tip is to scrape the mortar onto the end of bricks at each side — then squeeze the brick in.

PIERS

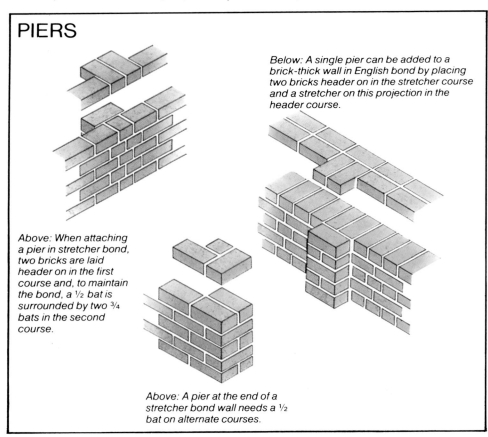

Below: A single pier can be added to a brick-thick wall in English bond by placing two bricks header on in the stretcher course and a stretcher on this projection in the header course.

Above: When attaching a pier in stretcher bond, two bricks are laid header on in the first course and, to maintain the bond, a ½ bat is surrounded by two ¾ bats in the second course.

Above: A pier at the end of a stretcher bond wall needs a ½ bat on alternate courses.

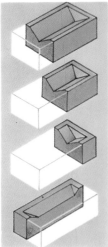

LAYING SPECIAL BONDS

Brick bonds are crucial to the strength of a wall, and they also provide a decorative face. With careful planning, even complex patterns are easy to make.

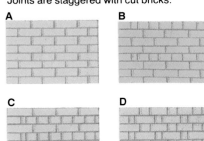

When you're building a brick wall it's vital that you lay each brick so that it overlaps and interlocks with its neighbours. You can't simply stack the bricks, one on top of the other; this would create vertical planes of weakness and, under load, the wall would soon collapse.

Instead, the bricks must be arranged so that the vertical joints (called perpends) in one course don't coincide with those in the course above and below. This arrangement, called a 'bonding pattern', ensures mainly that the weight of the wall and any load bearing on it is evenly distributed, but it can also be a decorative feature.

Types of brick bond
There are many bonding arrangements you can use, depending on the type of wall you're building, how strong it's to be, and whether its appearance is a consideration. They're basically all variations on the 'half-lap' bond, in which all bricks lap half a brick over the bricks in the course below, but there's also 'quarter-lap' bond, in which the bricks lap over a quarter of a brick length.

Stretcher bond
The most straightforward and common arrangement is called 'stretcher' or 'running' bond, which is used mainly for 112mm (4½in) thick – or half-brick thick – walls. Each course is identical; the bricks are laid end to end and each overlaps the one below by half its length, presenting its long stretcher face to the front face of the wall.

Header bond
The simplest type of bonding for a 225mm (9in) thick – or single brick – wall is 'header' bond, in which all the bricks are laid side by side with their ends (again often decorative) presented to the front face of the wall, and each course overlapping its neighbours by half its width. This type of bonding pattern, although attractive, is wasteful of bricks.

English bond
The strongest brick bond for 225mm (9in) thick or thicker walls – particularly if they're loadbearing – is called English bond. It consists of one course of parallel stretchers – to give the wall thickness – alternated with a course of headers laid across the thickness of the wall. In this tough, criss-cross bonding arrangement no straight joints occur within the thickness of the wall, which could weaken the structure.

Flemish bond
Where a highly decorative effect is needed in a single or half-brick thick wall, Flemish bond is often regarded as one of the most popular. The pattern consists of alternate headers and stretchers in each course – and the decorative effect can be increased by using contrasting coloured and textured headers, or even by slightly recessing some of the headers in the face of the wall, or allowing them to protrude fractionally.

Garden Wall bonds
Other common brick bonds you can use, mainly for their attractive appearance, but also because they're more economical, are really just modified versions of English and Flemish bonds. Basically they reduce the number of headers used, and introduce more stretchers yet still maintain the basic bonding patterns.

English Garden Wall bond, for example, originally used for boundary walls of one brick thickness, is one bond that reduces the

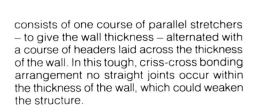

ENGLISH BOND WALL WITH END PIER

1 *English bond consists of a course of stretchers alternated with one of headers. Mark out the shape of the wall and pier and dry lay the first course.*

2 *Remove the bricks then re-lay them on a mortar bed. Lay the first course of the pier and the return wall first and check the level between them.*

3 *Make sure the end pier is laid perfectly square by checking with a builder's square. Note the brick that 'ties' the pier to the wall.*

6 *Work towards the pier using stretcher bond over the first header course then return to the corner laying the second half of the course.*

7 *Complete the second course then start the third course, which is a repeat of the first course. The return wall is laid as a row of stretchers.*

8 *Bond the pier with alternate courses of stretchers and headers spaced with queen closers. Lay the corners first and fill in with cut bricks.*

number of bricks that you'll need for headers; it usually consists of three or five courses of stretchers to one of headers.

Flemish Garden Wall bond is another decorative yet durable bond that consists of an arrangement of three, four or five stretchers to one header per course – each course being identical – and is especially attractive as the outer skin of a cavity wall. You can introduce headers of constrasting colour or texture, either inset or projecting, for a greater decorative effect.

When you're using these bonds in a half-brick thick wall you'll have to use cut bricks, called half-bats (see below and *Ready Reference*) for the headers.

Open bonding

Where load-bearing capacity isn't a vital consideration in your wall you can use an economical form of open' bond. It's especially good for screen walls for your garden or patio, giving a fairly solid appearance yet still admitting light and air.

Each course is laid as stretchers and the bricks are separated by quarter-brick spaces.

Using cut bricks

Any bonding pattern – except open bond – will need to include cut bricks in order to maintain the bond.

In a stretcher bond wall you'll have to include half bricks (called half-bats) in alternate courses at the end of the wall, or where you're tying a new wall into an original wall.

In a header bond wall you must insert two three-quarter bricks (called three-quarter-bats) laid side by side in alternate courses to maintain the symmetry of the pattern.

With the more complicated bonds the number – and variety – of cut bricks increases. English bond, for example, needs a brick cut in half lengthways (called a queen closer) in each header course, or two three-quarter-bats laid side by side in the stretcher course to maintain the bond.

You won't need to include cut bricks in an open-bond wall; you can maintain the symmetry by simply reducing the spaces between the bricks.

Turning corners

It's important to maintain the bonding arrangement throughout the wall for strength and symmetry, although when you come to turn a corner (called a quoin) you may have to vary the pattern over a small area (see pages 32-36). The most crucial point is to ensure both sides of the corner are interlocked, otherwise you'd end up with two separate walls lacking rigidity.

With some bonds, corners are fairly straightforward to make. If you're building a

4 Lay the bricks header on between pier and corner. The bond changes to stretchers on the return wall, with a queen closer spacer at the corner.

5 Start the second course at the corner; line up the first brick with the centre of the header next to the queen closer in the first course and the end brick.

9 Continue to lay alternate courses of stretchers and headers until you reach the finished height of your wall. Check the level frequently with a spirit level.

10 Check the 'plumb', or vertical level, of the wall, paying particular attention to the corners of the pier. Rack back the return wall if you're continuing next day.

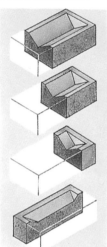

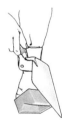
half-brick wall in stretcher bond, for example, you can simply turn a corner by placing a whole brick, header on, at the corner instead of filling in with half-bats at alternate courses. You can then continue to build the wall at the other side of the angle in exactly the same stretcher bond.

Other bonding arrangements, however, will require additional cut bricks so that you can tie-in the two leaves of the corner. In effect the pattern will change when you turn a corner, although it's re-established on the course above. In English bond, for example, the stretcher course on one side of the quoin becomes the header course on the other.

Piers for support

If you're building a particularly high or long wall you'll need to build in supporting columns called piers to give added strength to the structure. Build them at regular intervals

throughout the wall ('attached' piers) and at the ends. For a half-brick thick wall you'll need a pier that projects from the wall by at least half a brick every 1.8m (6ft). In a stretcher bond wall you must alter the bonding pattern by adding cut bricks to give the necessary overlap, which ensures that the pier is correctly tied into the wall. To form a minimum-sized attached pier in this type of wall, you must lay two bricks header-on in the first course and, to maintain the bond, a half-bat flanked by two three-quarter-bats in the second course. Repeat this arrangement.

For one brick thick walls you'll need piers at only 2.8m (9ft) intervals, but the pier must still project from the wall by at least half a brick. To form an attached pier of this size in an English bond wall you should lay two bricks header on in the stretcher course and a stretcher on the projection in the header course.

FLEMISH BOND WALL WITH ATTACHED PIER

1 *Flemish bond consists of alternate headers and stretchers in each course. Mark out the wall and dry lay the bricks, incorporating an 'attached pier'.*

2 *Lay the facing bricks of the first course on a mortar bed, including a queen closer at a stopped end. Fill in the second half of the course.*

3 *The first course of a single brick attached pier is bonded to the wall with headers for the sides and a stretcher brick between them for the back edge.*

4 *The second course is the same as the first, but the stretchers are laid over the headers and vice versa. Lay the facing bricks first.*

5 *The second course of the pier is laid using ³/₄-bats at the back corner to keep the shape of the pier, with a ¹/₄-bat to fill the gap that's left inside.*

6 *A stopped end – one without a pier – is formed by the inclusion of a queen closer and a brick header-on in alternate courses; then continue normally.*

7 *Build the wall as high as you'd like it, repeating the rows of headers and stretchers in alternate courses. Check the level across the face of the wall.*

8 *Check that the mortar joints are constant using a gauging rod marked off in 75mm (3in) intervals – brick height plus a 10mm (³/₈in) mortar joint.*

9 *If you leave the wall overnight, rack back the end in steps so that your continuation can be bonded correctly. Finally, check the plumb of the pier.*

FINISHING BRICKS FOR WALLS

*There are many ways you can finish off
your wall neatly and decoratively, using a
selection of special-shaped bricks made
to co-ordinate with standard bricks
Some of the bricks you can
use for a straight run of walling include:*

1 Double bullnose as a stopped end
2 Bullnose header on flat
3 Plinth header (stretcher also available)
4 Bullnose double header on flat
5 Half round coping
6 Saddleback coping

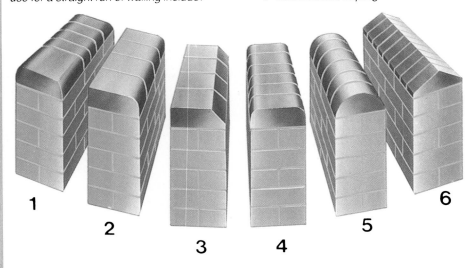

*There's also a variety of special-shaped
bricks for use at right-angled corners,
both in left- and right-hand versions. You
can use them in conjunction with the
straight-run bricks above for a neatly
finished effect. They include:*

A Bullnose external return on flat
B Bullnose external return on edge
C Plinth external return
D Cant external return
E Single cant (for half-brick walls)
F Single bullnose

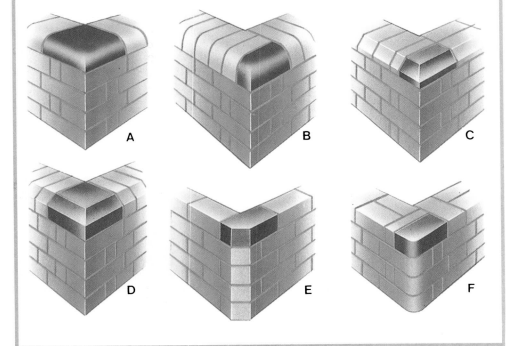

TIP: DRY LAY BRICKS

To help you work out complex bonding arrangements accurately, and to calculate the number of whole and cut bricks you'll need, lay the first few courses, or until the pattern repeats, without mortar, maintaining finger-width joints throughout.

DECORATIVE PATTERNS

For a greater decorative effect:
● lay a random or regular pattern of coloured, textured stretchers and headers so they protrude slightly from the face of the wall (A)
● lay some cut stretchers or headers in different colours and textures so they're recessed slightly from the face of the wall (B).

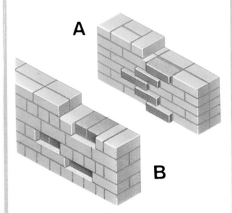

USING A LINE AND PINS

To ensure your brick courses are laid level:
● insert the flat blade of a pin into an upright mortar joint at one corner or end of your wall
● stretch the line attached to the pin to the other end of the wall
● secure the line taut with a second pin so that it's 10mm (³⁄₈in) clear of the wall but in line with the top edge of the next course
● move line and pins up at each course.

USING
CONCRETE

Concrete is perhaps the do-it-yourselfer's most versatile building material. It's cheap, easily mixed from readily available ingredients and capable of forming floors, walls, paths, and drives, bases for outbuildings and many other things besides. As with mortar, half the skill is in proper mixing of the correct ingredients for the job; the other half is the laying, and different techniques are used for different needs. Master these techniques and you'll have no problems, whether you're working with a small bag of dry concrete mix from the corner shop, or a lorry-load of ready-mix from the local depot.

TOOLS FOR MIXING AND LAYING CONCRETE

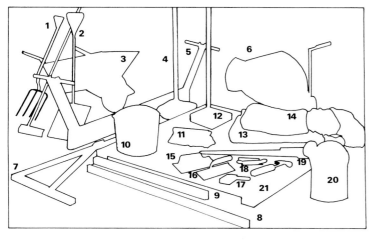

Mixing and laying concrete involves a surprising number of tools. Many of them you will have, some you can hire and others you can make. Always scrub tools well after each work session.

1 Fork For digging out foundations. You will also need a spade.

2 Shovel You will also need a rake to spread the concrete slightly proud of the formwork timbers.

3 Wheelbarrow

4 Ramming tool For compacting the subsoil or hardcore if a roller is unavailable. Fill a timer mould (about 200 x 150 x 100mm/8 x 6 x 4in) with concrete, insert a broom handle and keep it supported until the concrete has set.

5 Tamping beam. For levelling large areas. Make it from 150 x 50mm (6 x 2in) timber. Strong handles help you move the tamper more easily.

6 Hand-operated concrete mixer. The machine is pushed along a hard level surface to rotate the drum and mix the concrete.

7 Builder's square To check the corners of the form. Make one by joining three lengths of wood with sides in the proportions of 3:4:5. A good size is 450 x 600 x 750mm (18 x 24 x 30in). Use an L-shaped bracket and screws to make rigid joints.

8 Spirit level

9 Timber straight-edge For setting out fall of concrete if drainage is required. You can also use it for levelling: a 100 x 50mm (4 x 2in) straight-edge is sufficient.

10 Buckets You will need two for measuring and two shovels of equal size for mixing. Keep one bucket and shovel for measuring out and adding cement. The second set can be used for adding ballast and water and for mixing.

Using equal sized buckets gives an easy guide to quantities: a 1:5 mix needs one bucket of cement and five buckets of ballast.

11 Coarse brush You can give a textured finish to concrete by sweeping the surface with a coarse brush.

12 Punner For compacting concrete. Nail together several layers of timber and attach a broom handle.

13 Polythene sheeting Use to protect concrete from the elements.

14 Straw and sacking Either can be used to protect new concrete from frost.

15 Wood float For a textured finish.

16 Steel float For finishing concrete.

17 Measuring tape

18 Pegs and string For marking out the site.

19 General purpose saw and claw hammer For making formwork.

20 Watering can To control the rate at which water is added.

21 Mixing platform Use where there is no suitable solid area for mixing concrete. Nail boards together for the base and add side pieces to keep the concrete in place. Or fix sides to a larger sheet of 18 or 25mm (¾ or 1in) plywood.

BASIC CONCRETING TECHNIQUES

One of the most versatile of all building materials, concrete is also one of the easiest to work with. The techniques for laying anything from a garden path to a patio are much the same – once you know the basic rules for mixing up the ingredients, making formwork, laying and levelling.

Concrete is made of cement, aggregate and water. Cement itself is quite a complex chemical formed by burning chalk, limestone and clay at high temperatures and then grinding the resulting clinker to a fine powder. Added to the water it becomes an adhesive and coats and binds the aggregate (clean, washed particles of sand, crushed stone or gravel — never brick — for the clays can react against the cement).

The strength or hardness of any concrete simply depends on the proportions of these ingredients. Only a small part of the water you add is used up in the chemical reaction — the rest evaporates.

Ordinary portland cement is used for most concreting work. (The name doesn't refer to the manufacturer or where it is made, it's simply that when invented in the 1820s it was thought to resemble Portland stone.)

Aggregates are graded according to the size of sieve the particles can pass through — anything from 10-20mm. Coarse aggregate has the largest stones (20mm) while fine aggregate, often described as shingle, can be 10-15mm. Sand, the third part of concrete, is also considered aggregate. (The cement holds the sand together and the combination of sand and cement holds the stones together.) In concreting the sand used is known as 'sharp' sand and graded by the sieve method. All-in aggregate is a combination of both sand and stones.

Choosing your mix

Different projects require different mixes of concrete. Three are most commonly used.

Mix A (see ESTIMATOR below and *Ready Reference* overleaf) is a general-purpose mix for surface slabs and bases where you want a minimum thickness of 75mm-100mm (3-4in) of concrete.

Mix B is a stronger mix and is used for light-duty strips and bases up to 75mm (3in) thick – garden paths and the like.

Mix C is a weaker mix useful for garden wall foundations, bedding in slabs and so on, where great strength is not needed.

The amount of water needed depends very much on how wet the sand and stones in the aggregate are. A rough guide is to use about half the amount (by volume) of cement. But add it gradually. Too much will ruin the mix and weaken the concrete.

How concrete works

New concrete hardens by chemical action and you can't stop it once it's started. The slower the set the better and it is important that after laying, exposed surfaces are covered with wet sacks, sand or polythene (and kept wet) for the first 4-6 days. Concrete also gives off heat as it sets — a useful property in very cold weather, although it would still need covering to protect it from frost.

Freshly mixed concrete will begin to set within 1-2 hours — in dry hot weather it will be faster. It takes 3-4 days to become properly hard — you can walk on it at this stage. To reach full strength, however, may take 28 days or more.

How to buy concrete

For small jobs it's best to buy the cement, sand and aggregate dry-mixed together, in

What to buy for mixing concrete

The quantities given here for sand and aggregate are rounded up to the nearest fraction of a cu metre that can be ordered. The mixes are made up by volume (see **Ready Reference**) so some sand and aggregate may be left over.

To make 1 cu metre eg 10m x 1m x 100mm	Cement 50kg bags	Sharp sand plus aggregate	OR	All-in aggregate
MIX A (1:2½:4)	6 bags	½ cu metre + ¾ cu metre		1 cu metre
MIX B (1:2:3)	8 bags	½ cu metre + ¾ cu metre		1 cu metre
MIX C (1:3:6)	4 bags	½ cu metre + ¾ cu metre		1¼ cu metre

MIXING

1 *Unless you're using dry ready-mix, first spread the cement over the aggregate and gradually mix by heaping into a 'volcano'.*

2 *Add about half the water to start with. Form a crater and mix in from the inside walls. Add the rest of the water gradually — not all at once.*

3 *When the concrete is about the right consistency shovel it into heaps again. Turn it into a new pile 3 times to ensure thorough mixing.*

4 *The finished concrete should look like this. When you draw the shovel back in steps, the ridges should be smooth and firm and not 'slump'.*

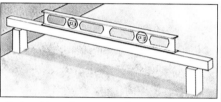

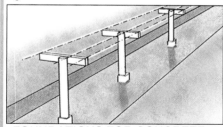
either 10kg, 25kg or 50kg bags. All you have to do is add water.

For larger projects, this can work out to be very expensive. Here it is better to buy the materials separately. The cement is normally sold in 50kg (just under 1 cwt) bags, though smaller (again more costly) quantities – 10kg and 25kg – are available. Both sand and aggregate are sold in 50kg bags, but it is more common to buy them loose by the cubic metre or fraction of a cubic metre. The combined or 'all-in' aggregate is available in the same way.

For really large work, however, (patios, long drives and the like) mixing the amount of concrete required by hand is extremely hard work. You could hire a powered mixer, but generally it is more convenient to buy it ready-mixed and have it delivered to the house. Check with the supplier on the minimum amount they are prepared to deliver — for quantities close to that minimum you could find it prohibitively expensive and you should consider sharing a load with a neighbour who is also carrying out building work. With ready-mix remember that you

have to be prepared to lay it fast and if there is no direct access to the site and the concrete can't be tipped directly into your prepared formwork, you must have plenty of able-bodied help with heavy-duty wheelbarrows (you can hire these) standing by.

Dry-mixes have the amounts that made-up concrete will cover printed on the bag. For mix-at-home quantities, see the ESTIMATOR.

How to store materials
Under normal conditions cement will start to harden after about 30 days simply because it'll be absorbing moisture from the air. However, older cement that's still powdery inside can still be used where great strength or a high quality finish is *not* essential – but mix in a higher proportion of cement than usual, ie 1:1:2.

Cement should always be stored under cover and raised well off the ground — on a platform of wood, for example. Stack the bags closely, keep them clear of other materials and cover them to help keep the moisture out. If a bag has been part used, the remainder can be stored for a while inside a well-sealed plastic bag.

Loose sand and aggregate should be piled on a flat, dry and hard area and covered with heavy-duty plastic sheeting. It's most important to avoid the aggregate being contaminated by soil or other foreign materials. Any organic matter would decompose in the concrete leaving 'voids' which weaken it.

Site preparation

This is a major stage before you begin to erect any formwork, mix or lay any concrete. For accurate marking out, use pegs and strings to give yourself guide lines to follow. The area should be dug out and made as level as possible (see *Ready Reference*).

The big question is, how deep should you dig and how thick should you lay the concrete? To some extent this depends on how firm the soil is. For a path or patio a 75-100mm/3-4in thickness of concrete is usually enough — add a layer of hardcore of the same depth if the soil is very soft. If, however, you're building a driveway where there'll be a lot more weight on top, then 125-150mm/5-6in of concrete on top of hardcore would be advisable.

Some soils can lead to unsuccessful concreting. If your site is *clay* for example you have to concrete it as soon as possible after it has been revealed. The reason? Clay dries out quickly and then contracts. Because it will absorb water from the concrete mix, it makes an unreliable base.

Peaty and loamy soils will sink under a heavy load. Use good hardcore (see below) in the prepared area.

Made-up ground is another way of describing land that's been reclaimed. There's no knowing what was used as the in-fill, and it should always be assumed that it has minimal load-bearing capacity. Any concreting here will need good reinforcement such as hardcore, well compacted and the same thickness as the concrete you're laying on top.

Soft pockets

After you've prepared a site for laying a path or patio you could find pockets of soft soil which will cause any concrete to sink.

Large areas of soft pockets or made-up ground need something solid as a base — and this is where hardcore (broken concrete), rubble (broken brick) or a very coarse aggregate is essential. Tamp it into the ground until well consolidated — a must for areas such as drives or structural foundations taking a lot of weight.

If necessary small areas can be reinforced with a steel mesh set into the concrete. For most purposes 7mm diameter rods formed in a mesh of 150mm squares is quite adequate, and this is readily available at most builders' merchants. Rest the rods on small pieces of broken brick before you lay the concrete; make sure that the ends of the rods don't protrude from the area you're concreting, and that the mesh is completely covered.

Creating the work area

Using formwork boards to create a kind of box in which to lay your concrete has two big advantages. Firstly, it contains the concrete neatly, and secondly it gives you levels on either side to guide you in levelling the concrete itself. Although this is the most usual method of containing concrete, a brick

LAYING AND LEVELLING

1 *Shovel the concrete well into the corners and only lay as much as you can finish off in one go. It's important that there are no hollows.*

2 *Roughly level the concrete with your shovel to a height about 6mm /¼in above the sides of the formwork. This will allow for compaction.*

3 *The 'tamping' board fits neatly across the formwork. First use a sawing action to level the mix, then a firm chopping action to compact it.*

4 *With the surface level, tap sides of formwork with hammer. This helps to compact the concrete. Fill in any hollows that result and level off again.*

5 *For an expansion joint use a piece of softboard the same depth as the concrete you're laying. Support it with pegs on one side.*

6 *Finish the concrete off on one side before you start laying on the other. Once the board is supported, hammer the pegs in deeper.*

FINISHES

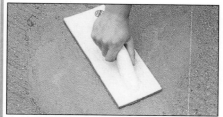

1 Using a wooden 'float' gives you a smooth finish. Press the float down firmly as you 'scrub' the surface with circular movements.

2 A brushed finish leaves a much rougher surface by exposing the small stones in the aggregate. Use a stiff brush to create a pattern of straight lines.

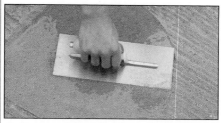

3 For a polished finish, use a steel 'float' at a slight angle to the surface, drawing it towards you with a sweeping semi-circular action.

surround can be used just as well — and this has the added advantage of not having to be pulled up. With bricks, however, it's more difficult to establish a completely straight and level line to follow.

For formwork use sawn (unplaned) softwood — it's called carcassing in the trade — for concrete that's to be placed below ground. It should be as wide as the depth of concrete you intend to lay and 25mm (1in) thick. Don't skimp on the thickness for it must be firm and rigid to support the weight of concrete.

Pegs are used to keep the formwork in place. They must be sturdy, not less than 50mm (2in) square and long enough to go well into the ground. Place pegs every 1 metre (3ft) against the *outside* face of the boards.

If building a raised path, formwork will give a finish to the concrete edge so you should use a timber that's planed. Unplaned timber can be used if the formwork is lined with 6mm (¼in) plywood, or if you intend finishing off the edges with more concrete after the formwork has been removed.

If you want to curve a corner in the formwork, use hardboard cut into strips as wide as the concrete is deep. This will need to be supported with pegs at more frequent intervals than softwood boards.

If you have difficulty driving the pegs into the ground (which may happen if you've put down hardcore) use lengths of angle iron instead. Alternatively drive the pegs in further away from the formwork and put timber blocks between the peg and formboard.

Expansion joints

Any large area of concrete needs expansion or movement joints to control cracking. A one-piece slab shouldn't be more than 3 metres (10ft) in any direction without a joint being included; a path should have joints at intervals of 1½ times the width of the path.

The simplest way of doing this is to incorporate a length of flexible plastic movement joint as you're laying the path. The material can be bought at most builders' merchants. Alternatively, use a piece of softboard impregnated with bitumen – it should be the same depth as the concrete and about 12mm (½in) thick.

Drainage slopes

With a wide expanse you should have a gentle slope (1 in 60 is the general rule) so that rainwater can drain away. This is achieved by setting the forms on one side slightly deeper into the ground. To check that the slope is the same all along the formwork, set a small piece of wood (about 12mm/½in for a 1m/3ft wide path) thick on the lower side and use your spirit level to check across to the other side.

To keep the formwork on each side of a path rigid, place a length of softwood across the width at the peg points, but not so that it will make an impression on the concrete. This can be used as a guide for levelling as well.

Whether you are building a concrete path, a base for a shed or garage, a hardstanding for a car or even a large patio, the principle of formwork is the same — only the number of boxes or bays you divide the area into varies. With each stage of the job you should mix only enough concrete to fill one bay or box at a time.

As the concrete starts to dry (after 2 hours) cover the surface with plastic sheeting or damp sacking to stop it drying too quickly.

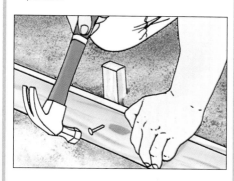

FOUNDATIONS FOR GARDEN WALLS

Even if it's only for a wall to grace the garden, building a solid foundation is a must. But how deep should you dig? How wide? And what's the right thickness of concrete? Here's an easy to follow explanation of why foundations are so important, how they differ and which one to choose.

All walls need foundations to give them stability, and free-standing garden walls are no exception. The foundation is like a platform, helping to spread the weight of the bricks in the wall onto the earth base below.

Most foundations are made of concrete laid in a trench, and for a garden wall where there's no additional weight for it to carry (unlike a structural wall, for example, which may also carry part of the weight of a roof) the concrete itself doesn't need to be very thick — between 100mm (4in) and 150mm (6in) of concrete is quite enough for a wall up to a metre in height. But the thickness of the concrete is not the only thing you have to consider. How deep in the ground you place it is just as important.

For a concrete foundation to provide an effective platform which won't allow the brick wall to crack, it has to be laid on firm 'subsoil'. And you won't find this until you get below the topsoil. The depth of topsoil varies enormously from place to place, so there can be no hard and fast rules about how deep you must dig — but expect anything between 100mm and 300mm (4-12in). Once you're through to the harder subsoil, you've then got to dig out enough for the depth of concrete — at least another 100-150mm (4-6in).

In practice the other big variable is the nature of your soil. Different subsoils have different load-bearing capacities — for instance hard chalky soils can support more weight than clay (see Choosing your foundation, page 52), but sandy soils can take less. The weaker the subsoil, the wider you have to build the foundation — consult your local building inspector for advice on soil conditions in your area.

There's another important reason for digging down so deep and that is the effect the weather has on soil. In clay subsoils, for example, a prolonged dry spell will cause the clay near the surface to shrink; then, when it rains, the clay will swell. All this causes considerable movement of the ground and unless a concrete foundation has been laid deep enough it'll crack up under the stress of constant expansion and contraction. To counteract this, the foundation has to be laid *below* the point at which the weather can cause movement. Again, in different soils, this varies from 150mm (6in) to 500mm (20in) or more down, but it's advisable to consult your local building inspector to get a more precise figure for soil conditions in your area.

Foundation design

All foundations have to be designed so that they evenly transfer the weight of the wall above to the earth base below. Because of the way the wall's weight spreads out onto

The weight of a wall spreads at an angle of 45° from its base into the foundation and then on into the subsoil.
This is called the angle of dispersion.

MARKING OUT

1 Set the pegs for the profile board outside the line the foundation will follow. First hammer the pegs in, then nail a cross-piece on top.

2 You'll need profile boards at each end of the foundation trench so that you can string guide lines for digging out between the two.

3 Fix nails in the cross-pieces to establish the width of the trench. Normally this is a minimum of 300mm (12in).

4 Tie the line to one of the nails, then string up to the others. Loop the line round each nail and keep it taut. Don't cut the line.

5 The lines now mark the edges of the trench. At a later stage the building line for the wall is marked out in the same way.

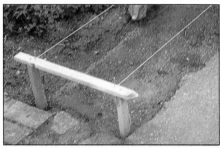

6 To give you an accurate line to follow for digging out, sprinkle sand beneath the lines. After this remove the strings, but not the profile boards.

the foundation – called the angle of dispersion – the foundation is built so that it is wider than the wall. In fact this 'load spreading' follows an angle of 45° (see page 59) and means that the width of the foundation on each side of the wall has to be at least equal to the depth of the concrete. This is a simple rule of thumb which will help you decide how wide your foundation has to be for different wall widths. Of course, if you're building on a relatively soft subsoil, your building inspector may recommend that you build a wider foundation. Like a raft floating on water, the bigger it is the more stable it will be.

Once you've dug your trench, you'll be faced with another decision: do you just lay the minimum thickness of concrete or lay enough concrete to fill up the trench so you have fewer bricks to lay? In fact, there can be quite a difference in the amount of work involved. If your trench is 500mm (20in) deep and you only lay a 150mm (6in) depth of concrete, it means that just to get back to ground level you've got to lay some 5 courses of bricks which ultimately won't even be seen. Nevertheless, it makes no difference to the strength of the foundation – it

LAYING THE CONCRETE

1 Once the trench is dug out, check the depth at 1 metre (3ft) intervals. The actual depth depends on the nature of the soil — see page 52 .

TIP

2 Hammer in pegs at 600mm intervals down the middle of the trench. These can be adjusted to act as an accurate depth guide for laying the concrete.

3 Use a spirit level to check that the tops of the pegs are level. This marks the top of the foundations, and accuracy is essential. (Continued overleaf)

49

simply depends on whether you prefer laying more concrete (and it'll be quite a lot more) or more bricks. Engineering bricks are recommended for any work below ground, though any special quality brick will do almost as well.

Marking out

Digging a trench foundation to a depth of about 500mm (20in) is probably the safest rule of thumb to follow if you're building a wall that's going to be more than 5 or 6 courses above ground level. (For smaller walls see Foundations for low brick walls).

And to make sure that the line of the trench is straight and the width constant, you have to mark out accurately. For this you need to set up what are called 'profile boards' at each end of the trench. All you do is string lines between the boards in the position you want for the foundation.

To make profile boards, use lengths of 50mm x 25mm (2in x 1in) timber cut a little wider than your trench. For pegs, use 50mm square (2in square) timber about 600mm (2ft) long. You'll also need nails and string.

Hammer two pegs into the ground at each end of the wall line, and nail the cross-pieces onto them. Next drive nails into the tops of the boards – to mark the outer edges of the foundation – and string lines between them, pegging the string into the ground beyond the profile boards.

These strings are then the guide lines for digging the trench, and can be transferred down to the ground using a spirit level. When the trench is dug and the foundation laid, these same profile boards can be used to create the building lines for the wall – you just add more nails and string up as before.

Constructing the trench

Remove the topsoil and dig a trench according to your marking up. To give you a guide for laying the concrete, you'll need pegs about double the depth of concrete required. These

FOUNDATIONS FOR LOW BRICK WALLS

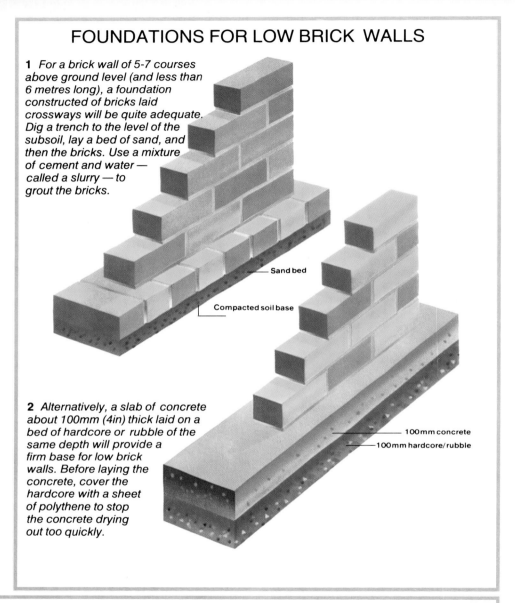

1 For a brick wall of 5-7 courses above ground level (and less than 6 metres long), a foundation constructed of bricks laid crossways will be quite adequate. Dig a trench to the level of the subsoil, lay a bed of sand, and then the bricks. Use a mixture of cement and water — called a slurry — to grout the bricks.

Sand bed

Compacted soil base

100mm concrete

100mm hardcore/rubble

2 Alternatively, a slab of concrete about 100mm (4in) thick laid on a bed of hardcore or rubble of the same depth will provide a firm base for low brick walls. Before laying the concrete, cover the hardcore with a sheet of polythene to stop the concrete drying out too quickly.

LAYING THE CONCRETE

4 Fill the trench with concrete to just above the level of the pegs. Make sure it's well compacted before you roughly level it with the shovel.

5 Use a large piece of timber as a 'tamping' beam to finally level off so that the tops of the pegs are just visible. The surface doesn't need to be smooth.

6 Check the level of the foundation using a spirit level placed across a straight edge. If necessary make adjustments by adding more concrete.

should have tops cut square and should be driven into the centre of the trench at intervals of 600mm (2ft). The tops should all be precisely levelled using a builders level or a straight-edge and spirit level. Soak the trench with water and allow it to drain before the concrete is poured in. This should then be well 'rodded' (with a broom handle, for example) to ensure that the entire volume of the trench is filled and the concrete is as high as the tops of the pegs (these don't have to be removed and will eventually rot). Use a wooden float or suitable piece of timber to level the surface. It needn't be perfectly smooth as a fairly rough surface provides a good key for the mortar. Cover the concrete with plastic sheeting or damp sacking and leave for 6 days to 'cure' – longer if the wall is more than 12 courses high. The slower the curing the stronger the concrete, so don't try and build a wall on the foundations too soon.

Concrete foundations

Concrete is ideal for foundations for no other material can take up the precise shape of the subsoil surface at the bottom of the trench and transfer the load so evenly. It should be made of 1 part cement to 3 parts sand to 6 parts aggregate (see Working with concrete,

pages 44 - 47) with just enough water to produce a pliable consistency.

Trench foundations can be reinforced with rods or mesh – either will increase the strength of the foundation and whatever is built upon it. Both kinds of reinforcement are actually quite simple to add – you just have to make sure that the steel rods or mesh are bedded in the lower part of the concrete and not exposed at the sides or ends. In some cases, reinforcement is essential – for example, if you're laying a foundation over a drainpipe. For most garden brick walls, however, going to the trouble of reinforcing a foundation just isn't necessary – the weight of the wall doesn't justify it. What is important is that the wall doesn't crack because the ground underneath moves slightly.

Raft or slab foundations

For small walls of 7 courses or less the simplest concrete foundation is a raft or 'slab'. This is cast just below ground level (after the topsoil has been removed) in much the same way as you'd lay a concrete path. First dig out to a depth of about 200mm (8in), then add a layer of compacted broken brick or hardcore to provide drainage. Cover this with light polythene sheeting just before concret-

ing – this will prevent the concrete drying out too quickly because of water being absorbed by the base. Then lay your concrete about 100mm (4in) deep and tamp to a level surface (see pages 49 - 50). Once the wall is built the concrete foundation can be hidden by soil and grass.

Brick foundations

For low walls under 7 courses high you could even avoid the expense and trouble of mixing concrete altogether, because a foundation strip of bricks laid cross-ways can be perfectly adequate. Lay the bricks on a thin layer of sand which has been well compacted and levelled in a shallow trench. This should be dug to below the level of topsoil – anything between 100mm (4in) to 300mm (12in) below ground level. Grout these together with a 'slurry' – a creamy mixture of cement and water. This is called a 'footing' course and you can lay bricks on top in the usual manner even before the slurry is hard.

Earth retaining walls

Sometimes walls built in the garden may not be free-standing but used to retain earth on one side – for example, as terraces on a sloping site or to enclose flat areas of lawn or

MARKING BUILDING LINES

1 For a half brick thick wall (a single line of bricks) position nails on the profile board 100mm in from each side of the trench and string up between them.

4 A piece of scrap wood held diagonally against the spirit level gives a bit of extra support as you mark down vertically and score the mortar bed with a trowel.

2 These strings give you clear guidelines to follow, but it's usually worth double-checking that the building lines are positioned centrally on the concrete.

5 Lay the bedding mortar for the first course of bricks alongside the marked line. Furrow the mortar with the tip of the trowel.

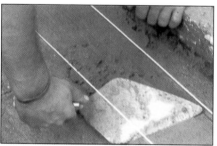

3 Lay a thin bed of mortar directly underneath the building lines and smooth it out with the trowel. This is for marking down from the line.

6 Lay the first three bricks, and then check them with the spirit level. Once the first course is complete, remove the profile lines.

FOUNDATIONS FOR GARDEN WALLS

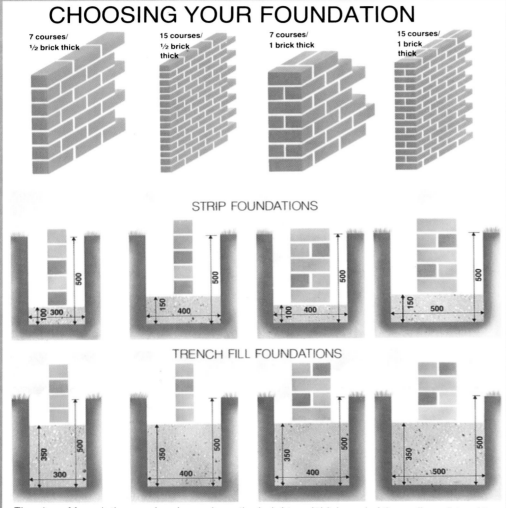

CHOOSING YOUR FOUNDATION

7 courses/ ½ brick thick

15 courses/ ½ brick thick

7 courses/ 1 brick thick

15 courses/ 1 brick thick

STRIP FOUNDATIONS

TRENCH FILL FOUNDATIONS

*The size of foundation you lay depends on the height and thickness of the wall you intend to build, and on the load-bearing capacity of the subsoil. The chart above gives recommended dimensions for strip and trench-fill foundations for half-brick and one-brick thick walls, below 7 courses or up to 15 courses high, on a typical clay subsoil. On crumbly, loose soils the recommended widths should be doubled. See also **Ready Reference.***

See also **Ready Reference.**

READY REFERENCE

PROBLEM SOILS

● clay subsoils are prone to shrink and swell so make the foundation trench at least 500mm deep, and lay the concrete to the width and thickness shown in the chart
● loose, poorly-compacted subsoils need foundations double the normal width to help spread the load of the wall, and should be laid as trench-fill foundations
● if the sides of your trench tend to collapse, use timber to shore them up before pouring in the concrete, or cut them wider than necessary and slope the sides.

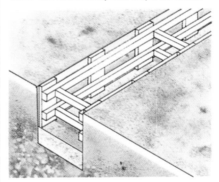

TIP:
LET CONCRETE DRY SLOWLY

● first soak the trench with water and allow it to drain away
● cover concrete with damp sacking or plastic sheet
● Allow concrete to 'cure' for at least 6 days before building on it.

UNEXPECTED HAZARDS

● if the trench fills with water it must be drained before you lay the foundation concrete. Water in a small trench can be emptied with a bucket; in a large trench you may have to hire a pump
● if you discover underground pipes as you're digging the trench, dig soil away around them to the required depth. Lay the foundation as normal on either side of the pipes, then 'bridge' them with a short reinforced concrete lintel or, for narrow gaps (300mm/12in or less) lengths of paving slab laid two courses deep.

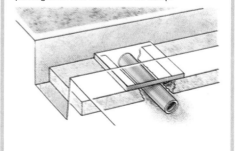

flower beds. In such cases the soil behind the wall is constantly trying to push outwards, completely changing the pattern of stress involved.

The simplest solution is to make the structure strong enough to withstand this extra pressure. With a 4 or 5 course wall this can usually be done by building the wall one brick thick (instead of ½ brick thick) and by providing 'weepholes' at regular intervals to drain excess water. These are made by removing mortar from a number of the vertical joints before it sets.

If you find that the surface of an earth-retaining wall is marked by white crusty deposits – called 'efflorescence', and caused by water carrying salts through the wall from the soil behind – dig away the earth

and coat the inner surface of the wall with bituminous emulsion to create a damp barrier.

Building on a slope

It is visually unsettling and structurally unde-sirable to lay bricks running parallel to a slope. So, to build a wall that 'steps' down a slope, the trench foundations also have to be stepped or 'benched' into the slope. Level-ling, pegging, pouring and finishing are all carried out in the same way as with a horizontal trench, but in stepped sections. You'll need form boards to frame the outer edge of each step, but otherwise the width and depth of the foundation is exactly the same as for an ordinary wall. Only the length of each step varies.

LAYING CONCRETE SLABS

Concrete is the ideal material for laying a slab for a shed, patio or driveway. Once you've mastered the techniques of mixing and casting it, you can provide a hard durable surface that will last for years.

A concrete slab can be a tough, hard-wearing base for a variety of uses in your garden, but its success is only as good as the preparation you've put into making it. Concrete consists of stone particles called 'aggregate', bonded with a Portland cement and water mix (see Working with concrete). You must mix the ingredients carefully, cast the slab on specially prepared foundations, apply a finishing texture, and allow the concrete to set properly, if your results are to be long-lasting.

Planning a concrete slab

After you've decided exactly where you want to put your square or rectangular slab, you'll have to mark out the ground accurately and prepare the foundations before laying the concrete. But if you're laying a more complex shape or a much larger concrete base, you'd be wise to make some preliminary sketches and transfer them to squared paper, to help in calculating the material required.

Before you start to lay your slab it's sensible to check with your local authority whether you're infringing any bye-laws. One of the main objections they might have is the position of your planned slab in relation to existing drains and pipe runs; as a result, you might have to re-route some of these to keep them out of harm's way.

Access to the site and the time you'll have available for laying your slab are important considerations, particularly if you're laying a large concrete drive or a garage floor, for example. With work on this scale you should use ready-mixed concrete, which is delivered in bulk ready for casting. If you go for this method, it's vital that you provide access for the lorry and space for the load to be dumped as close as possible to your site. You must have your foundations prepared so that you can cast the mix as soon as it's delivered. Any delay could mean that the mix starts to set rendering it useless.

Calculating the size of slab

Before you can mark out your slab on the ground and prepare its foundations you'll have to work out its dimensions and calculate how much concrete you're going to need. As

a basic guide, the larger your slab the thicker it must be.

For an ordinary garden shed, for instance, you'll need a slab about 75mm (3in) thick, except where the ground is soft clay, when you should increase its depth to 100mm (4in) If your slab is to form the floor of a workshop, or a drive leading to your garage, a thickness of 100mm (4in) is appropriate on ordinary soils, 125mm (5in) on soft clay or other poor sub-soils.

Once you've decided on the dimensions of your slab you can estimate how much concrete you'll need and how you're going to mix it (see *Ready Reference*).

Marking out the slab

Before you start to mark out your slab on the ground, dig out and remove the top-soil, including any grass and the roots of shrubs, from the area you're going to concrete. Allow a margin of a few feet all round your proposed slab for working space.

Use strings stretched between wooden pegs driven into the ground just outside the area you're going to concrete to mark out the shape of your slab (although, for a very small slab it's possible simply to mark it out using planks positioned squarely on the ground – see photographs). Use a builder's square (see *Ready Reference*) to set the corners of your slab accurately. If you're

READY REFERENCE

SETTING UP FORMWORK

Formwork is needed to mould and retain the concrete while it sets. To set up a frame for a small square or rectangular slab:
● drive 50x50mm (2x2in) softwood pegs 300 (1ft) long into the ground just outside the slab perimeter at 1m (3ft) centres
● nail lengths of sawn softwood 25mm (1in) thick and as wide as the concrete depth to the pegs, making sure they're level and square
● butt joint the corners. Alternatively, make up the formwork to size elsewhere, and then carry it into position (see page 54).

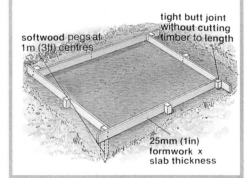

tight butt joint without cutting timber to length

softwood pegs at 1m (3ft) centres

25mm (1in) formwork x slab thickness

53

making strip foundations for a wall you can use 'profiles' to set the levels (see Working with concrete, pages 44 - 47).

Once you've positioned your string lines you can dig out the sub-soil to roughly the depth of your foundation, taking it about 150mm (6in) beyond the strings to leave space for setting up 'formwork', which moulds and retains the concrete while it's hardening.

Setting the levels

While the base for a shed should be virtually level, a concrete slab patio or garage drive should be laid with a slight slope to allow rainwater to run off quickly. And of course, if the slab is near a wall you'll have to ensure that the fall drains away from it. You must allow for the slope when you're preparing the base. A gradient across the site of about 1 in 60 is about right.

You'll also have to make sure when laying a drive leading to a garage that the drive doesn't drain into the garage. If the ground is naturally sloping in that direction take it to a level below the garage floor and lay a short section of slab sloping away from the garage. Where the two slopes meet you'll have to include a channel leading to a suitable drainage point.

To establish the level of your slab over its entire area hammer 50x25mm (2x1in) softwood pegs into the ground at about 1.5m (5ft) intervals. The first peg must be one that establishes the level of the others, and its called the 'prime datum'. If your slab is to adjoin a wall you can fix the level of this peg at the second course of brickwork below the dpc, (damp-proof course) or some other fixed point of reference.

Drive in some more pegs and check across their tops from the first peg with a spirit level on a straight-edged length of timber to check their level.

You can allow for a drainage fall by placing a wedge of timber called a 'shim' under one end of the straight edge.

Once you've set the datum pegs, measure down them whatever thickness of concrete you'll need for your slab and excavate the ground, or fill in, where necessary.

Fixing the formwork

Wet concrete tends to spread out as it sets and so you'll have to fix a timber frame called 'formwork' at the perimeter of the foundations to retain it and support its edges. It must be strong enough to withstand heavy tamping, which compacts and strengthens the mix. Use straight lengths of stout timber a minimum of 25mm (1in) thick, set on edge and nailed to pegs of 32x32mm (1¼x1¼in) timber driven into the ground at the perimeter of the slab at 1m (3ft) centres. Fix the pegs outside the area that's to be con-

PREPARING THE FOUNDATIONS

1 You can mark out a small concrete slab on the ground with scaffold boards and pegs at the corners, then start to remove the topsoil or turfs.

2 Continue to dig out the topsoil or turfs until you've accurately marked out the shape of your slab. Then dig down to the depth you want the slab.

3 To fix formwork around your base butt joint four lengths at the corners. Nail battens at each corner to hold the angle; then saw off the waste.

4 Position the formwork within the foundations and check across the top with a long spirit level to ensure that it's level, or sloping for drainage.

5 Tamp or roll the base of the foundations firm. If the soil is soft, add some hardcore and compact this into the surface with a sledge hammer.

6 Add as much hardcore as you need to give a firm base for the concrete. You may need to add a layer of sand to fill any voids in the surface.

creted, with their tops flush with, or slightly below, the top edge of the formwork.

You can use your string lines as a guide to positioning the formwork and a builder's square to ensure that the corners are set perfectly at right angles.

The top edge of the formwork must be set so that it's flush with the top of your finished slab; it's best to use timber that's the same thickness as your slab, otherwise you'll have to recess it into the ground. You can use your intermediate datum pegs as reference points when levelling the formwork with a builder's level, making sure you incorporate the drainage falls.

The corners of the formwork must be tightly butt-jointed (see *Ready Reference*) to prevent the wet concrete from seeping through. If you have to join two planks together end to end in order to make the required length you should again use butt joints, but back both planks at the joint with a short section of timber nailed in place and wedged with a peg at this point.

Movement joints
You can cast a slab in one piece if it's no longer than about 3m (10ft) in width or length. But if it's bigger than this, or if its length is greater than twice is width, it's usual to divide the overall slab into 'bays' that are as square as possible – or equal in size – and to include a gap called an 'expansion joint', which prevents the slab from cracking due to expansion or contraction. Fill the gap with a length of softwood 10 to 12mm (3/8in to 1/2in) thick, the depth of the slab, and cut to fit between the formwork at the sides of the slab. Treat the fillet with preservative before fitting it within the slab.

Each bay is cast separately so it's best to back up the jointing timber with a piece of formwork temporarily pegged in place for support. When you've cast and compacted the first bay, remove the formwork behind the jointing timber and cast the second bay, leaving it permanently in place.

Mixing the concrete
If your slab is too small to justify a load of ready-mixed concrete or you wish to lay it in stages over several weekends, you'll need to buy all the ingredients and mix them yourself. To decide on the volumes of cement and aggregates you'll need for your particular slab, you must first decide on the concrete mix proportions to use. *Ready Reference* gives a basic guide to proportioning, which you can relate to your own needs. Following these guidelines and using the example of the car port base given in *Ready Reference*, the volume of concrete you'd need is $1.8m^3$ (63 cu ft). Materials needed are therefore going to be in the order of 1.8mx6 = 10.8 bags of cement; $1.8x0.5 = 0.9m^3$ of sand; $1.8x0.8 = 1.44m^3$ of coarse aggregate.

$1.8x0.8 = 1.44m^3$ of coarse aggregate.

Allow a 10 per cent margin for wastage to the cement to the nearest whole bag and buy 12 bags of cement. Round up quantities of aggregates to the nearest whole or half cubic metre and buy $1m^3$ (36 cu ft) of sand and $1.5m^3$ (53 cu ft) of coarse aggregate. Your calculations, though, should always be regarded as a guide only; exact amounts needed for a job will depend on the care you take in storage and handling and on the accuracy with which you prepare the base for the slab.

When you've an idea of the amounts of materials you'll need, you must decide on what method to use to mix them: by hand or by power mixer. Many different types of electric- petrol- and diesel-powered mixers are available for hire, and take much of the hard work out of mixing.

To get the correct consistency of concrete using a mixer, add half the coarse aggregate needed for the batch and half the water first. Then add all the sand and mix for a few minutes. Next you can add the cement and the remainder of the coarse aggregate. Finally add just enough water to achieve a workable mix. Most beginners add too much water; when it's of the right consistency the concrete should fall off the blade of your shovel cleanly without being too sloppy.

If you have to break off your work for a while, add the coarse aggregate and water you'll need for the next batch and leave the mixer running, while you are away, to keep the drum clean.

For how to mix concrete by hand (although it's really only viable for small jobs), see pages 44 - 47.

If you're mixing the concrete yourself you can store the aggregates indefinitely on a hard surface covered with a polythene sheet to keep it clean. Cement, however, must be kept dry: moisture in the air can penetrate the paper sacks and cause it to harden. Stack the sacks, under cover if possible, flat on a raised platform of planks on bricks and cover them with polythene.

Using ready-mixed concrete
Ready-mixed concrete is delivered by mixer lorry, usually in minimum loads of $3m^3$ (105 cu ft). If you need this amount, or more, ready-mixed concrete is worth considering as it takes a lot of hard work out of concreting and enables you to complete fairly large projects quickly.

Your supplier will want to know the volume of concrete you'll need, at what time you want it delivered, what it'll be used for, and how you're going to use it on delivery. This information will enable him to determine an appropriate mix and give you a price. You'd be wise to seek several quotations and try to choose a depot close to your home: much of

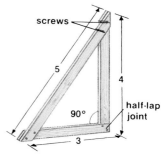
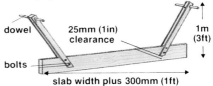

CASTING THE CONCRETE

1 Lay a path of scaffold boards from the concrete mix to the slab so you can take the mix by wheelbarrow without harming the ground.

2 Spread out the first barrowload of concrete over your foundations, using a shovel to work it into the hardcore and to avoid air bubbles.

3 Continue to tip barrowloads of concrete into your foundations until you've half-filled the area, just proud of the tops of the formwork.

6 Compact the wet concrete by lifting and dropping the tamping beam onto the concrete as you work across the slab. Repeat using a sawing action.

7 When you've filled the entire slab and have tamped the mix thoroughly tap the outside edge of the formwork with a hammer to settle the concrete.

8 You can produce a non-slip finish of fine swirls on your slab by running the back of your shovel over the wet surface.

the cost of the concrete is in its transportation.

To receive your concrete you'd be wise to lay down a large polythene sheet to make clearing up easier afterwards. If you need to transport it any distance from the point of delivery get together as many wheelbarrows – heavy-duty ones, not light garden types – shovels and helpers as you can. It's sensible to lay a pathway of scaffold boards or planks from the pile to your site if you have to cross areas of lawn or go up or down steps.

Laying the concrete

When your formwork has been positioned you can remove the levelling pegs from within the areas, and the string lines from the perimeter, but if you're going to lay the concrete on a hardcore base you should add the ballast at this stage. Compact it well with a sledge hammer, fence post tamper or a garden roller, and leave the levelling pegs in

place until you've set the foundations at the correct level.

When the base is ready, tip in the concrete from a barrow, or by the bucketful: if you're making a big slab you might even be able to get the delivery lorry to tip the mix straight into your prepared base.

Spread the concrete evenly with a garden rake to level it to just above the tops of the formwork. This allows an excess for compacting the mix. When all the concrete has been cast, compact it, using a tamping beam (see *Ready Reference*) made from a straight-edged length of 175x25mm (7x1in) softwood about 300m (1ft) longer than the width of your slab. For very large slabs use 150x50mm (6x2in) timber to make the beam, with handles fitted at each end so that you can work from a standing position rather than crouching (see *Ready Reference*).

Use the beam with a chopping action, lifting

it then dropping it to compact the concrete and force out any air bubbles. Work along the slab in this way and, after a few passes, change to a sawing action, which levels any high spots and fills depressions as you move down the formwork. Continue to tamp until the concrete is even and flush with the top of the formwork.

Finishing the concrete

You can apply a variety of finishes to your concrete slab to suit its purpose. For a garage drive you can simply leave the fairly rough, non-slip, texture created by the tamping beam or you could brush the fresh concrete across its width with a stiff-bristled broom to give a more regular, but still non-slip, finish.

A smoother finish is easier to keep clean for a shed or garage floor, and you can produce this with a wooden float used in a wide, sweeping action. For a more polished effect,

4 *Draw a stout timber tamping beam across the tops of the formwork to spread the concrete roughly and to flatten any high spots.*

5 *Fill any indents left behind after you've drawn the tamping beam over the top with shovelfuls of concrete, then draw the beam across again.*

9 *Run the blade of a steel trowel along the perimeter of the concrete to prevent the edges crumbling when you remove the formwork.*

10 *After about 24 hours, when the concrete has set, remove the formwork by tapping it away from the slab with a hammer.*

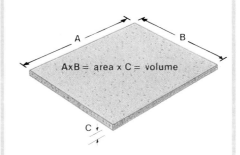
you can smooth over the surface with a steel trowel after you've treated it with the wooden float, and once more when the concrete has almost set.

One of the simplest finishes to apply is to go over the surface with the back of a shovel, producing fine swirls.

Curing the concrete

After you've applied the finishing texture to your slab you should 'cure' the concrete by leaving it to set without drying out too quickly, which could cause it to crack.

Although you shouldn't attempt to lay concrete at all during frosty weather (as this can affect the strength of the slab) it's possible that a cold spell will strike when you're least expecting it. If this happens you can protect your freshly cast concrete by insulating it with a quilt of straw sandwiched between two layers of heavy gauge polythene, or you

can shovel a layer of earth, sand or compost on top of your conventional curing sheet, which has the same effect.

Once you've cured the concrete properly, which normally takes about three or four days (ten in winter), you can remove the polythene. It's perfectly alright for you to walk on the slab, and you can even start to build onto it, but be very careful at the edges, which will still be weak and susceptible to chipping.

Don't put the base to full use for about ten days, when you can remove the formwork. To do this, tap it downwards with a hammer in order to release it from the slab, then knock it away from the face of the concrete edges by releasing the nails securing the butt joins at the corners.

Once you've removed the formwork you can fill in the gap it occupies with soil or lay turfs to continue your lawn.

LAYING READY-MIX CONCRETE

Ready-mix concrete takes a lot of the hard work out of laying a large slab for a drive or patio, or as the base for a garage. It's delivered to your house and takes only a few hours to place.

Concrete is a tough, hardwearing material that is ideal for laying as a base for a shed or garage, or as a durable surface for a patio, path or driveway. Once you've mastered the basic techniques of mixing, casting and curing the concrete (see Laying concrete slabs, pages 53-57) it's quite straightforward to make a fairly small square or rectangular slab, mixing the ingredients by hand or portable mixer. But if you're covering a much larger area the amount of concrete you'll need makes mixing your own impractical – unless you plan to lay the base in stages over several weekends.

Ready-mix concrete, which is sold in bulk and delivered to your home by mixer truck ready for casting, takes a lot of the hard work out of mixing large quantities of concrete and enables you to complete substantial projects quickly. Ready-mix has a number of other advantages over mixing your own: because the cement, sand, coarse aggregates and water are all correctly proportioned by the supplier and mixed for you, there's less likelihood that your mix will be too weak or brittle, or that you'll run out before you complete the slab. Also, you don't need to store large quantities of materials or hire mixing equipment

Casting concrete in bulk
Laying a large area of ready-mixed concrete follows the same sequence of operations as laying a small slab – you simply have to spread the mix to an even thickness over prepared foundations (see 'Foundations and formwork' opposite), apply a finishing texture and leave it to harden.

But there are some important details you should be aware of before you go ahead and order your concrete. You must provide sufficient access for the mixer truck and space for the mix to be dumped (see *Ready Reference*). If you can't arrange for the concrete to be dumped direct onto your foundations, try to get it as close as possible to your site. You must be sure that you'll be able to handle such a large amount of concrete, as well as cast it, compact it and cure it in one session, because you won't have a second chance once it has set.

Slab dimensions
The first consideration is what your slab will be used for, as this helps you decide on the correct thickness of concrete and allows your supplier to determine the correct strength of mix you'll need. Basically, the greater the load on the slab the thicker it must be. If your slab is to form the floor of a workshop or garage, or a driveway, for instance, a thickness of about 100mm (4in) is appropriate on ordinary soils. But on soft clay or other poor soils allow 125mm (5in).

On normal soils you may be able to lay the concrete direct onto the well-compacted ground, but on loose or soft soils you should include a 75mm (3in) layer of well-rammed hardcore. This can be of broken bricks or concrete, and should be topped with a 'blinding' layer of sand to fill in any voids that would be wasteful of concrete.

When you've decided on the position of your slab, and its dimensions, draw a scale plan of it on squared paper to help you estimate how much concrete you'll need.

Planning a drive
If you're altering the position of an existing vehicle access on to your property to make a new drive, you'll have to apply for permission to do so from your local authority; they'll need to make a dropped kerb and a cross-over of the pavement from the road, for which there's usually a charge.

Pay particular attention to the slope of the ground when you're planning a drive. Acute changes from one gradient to another within the drive can cause your car to hit the ground at either end or underneath.

Check also that your proposed drive allows sufficient clearance for an up-and-over garage door or that there's plenty of room for side-hinged doors to open without binding on the ground.

Draining the slab
Your slab must incorporate a slight slope to allow rainwater to run off quickly and you must allow for this when you're preparing your base.

A minimum fall of 1 in 60 to one side is adequate for a large slab, although you can form a high point along the centre of the slab with falls to both sides.

If the ground slopes naturally and your slab would drain towards a garage or house wall you should excavate it to a level below that of the floor of the building, and make a short slope away from the wall, with a gully or gutter at the lowest point to ensure run-off of rainwater to a suitable drainage point (see *Ready Reference*, page 61).

Excavating and setting out
When you've decided where you're going to lay your slab you'll have to prepare the foundations (see Laying concrete slabs). Dig out and remove the top-soil and any grass or roots within this area. Allow a margin

FOUNDATIONS AND FORMWORK

Before you take delivery of your ready-mix you must prepare the base. On firm ground simply roll the surface and cast the concrete direct; on soft ground first add about 75mm (3in) of well-rammed hardcore topped with sand to fill any voids. Set up a frame of timber formwork to mould and retain the mix while it hardens.

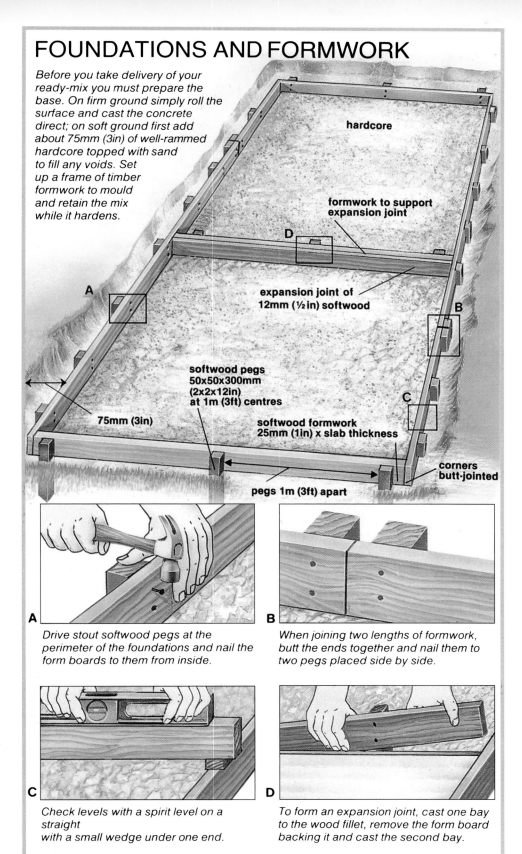

hardcore

formwork to support expansion joint

D

expansion joint of 12mm (½in) softwood

A

B

softwood pegs 50x50x300mm (2x2x12in) at 1m (3ft) centres

C

75mm (3in)

softwood formwork 25mm (1in) x slab thickness

corners butt-jointed

pegs 1m (3ft) apart

A
Drive stout softwood pegs at the perimeter of the foundations and nail the form boards to them from inside.

B
When joining two lengths of formwork, butt the ends together and nail them to two pegs placed side by side.

C
Check levels with a spirit level on a straight with a small wedge under one end.

D
To form an expansion joint, cast one bay to the wood fillet, remove the form board backing it and cast the second bay.

READY REFERENCE

ORDERING READY-MIX

To enable your ready-mix supplier to work out an appropriate concrete mix and give you a price quotation, he'll need to know:
● the volume of your proposed slab
● what you plan to use the slab for
● what time you'd like it delivered
● how you'll handle it on delivery
● what access to the site there is.

ACCESS FOR THE TRUCK

You can have your load of ready-mix dumped direct onto the foundations or as close as possible to the site, depending on access. To help you decide if you have enough room, a typical truck measures:
● about 8m (26ft) long
● 3m (10ft) tall
● 2.5m (8ft 6in) wide.
It features:
● a 2m (6ft) long chute for discharging concrete anywhere in a semi-circle behind the truck
● a 1m (3ft) extension chute for delivery to awkward or more distant sites.
Be particularly careful if you have any overhead electrical or telephone cables, which could easily be damaged as the truck manoeuvres.

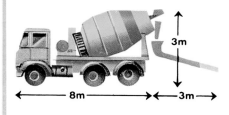

3m

8m 3m

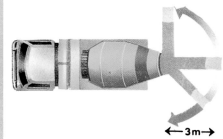

3m

TIP: LAYING ON A SLOPE

If you're laying your slab on a slope:
● tell your supplier so that he can give you a stiff mix
● work up the slope when you're tamping, keeping a close watch on levels so that the mix doesn't bulk up below the beam
● if you're working down the slope make sure the mix doesn't slump downwards from the formwork.

CASTING READY-MIX CONCRETE

1 *Try to have your load of ready-mix concrete dumped direct onto your foundations. As soon as it's been unloaded, transfer it to barrows.*

2 *Transport the concrete to the far end of the slab, tip it onto the hardcore then spread it out. A sheet of hardboard will protect doors from splashes.*

3 *Spread out the concrete using a garden rake or a shovel. Work the mix well into the corners of the formwork and at the sides to avoid air pockets.*

6 *Fill any depressions in the concrete with shovelfuls of fresh mix, then pass over the area again with the tamping beam to level the surface.*

7 *Continue to tamp with a chopping action then work back with a sawing action to level the surface, drawing along a ridge of excess concrete.*

8 *When you've compacted the slab you can apply a finishing texture. For a polished surface, trowel over the concrete using a steel float.*

of about 600mm (2ft) around your proposed slab so you've enough room to work.

Mark out the shape of your proposed slab on the ground with strings stretched between wooden pegs, and use a builder's square to set the corners accurately.

Next, dig out the sub-soil to roughly the depth of the foundation and take it about 150mm (6in) beyond the string lines to leave space for setting up the timber formwork, which you use to mould and retain the concrete while it's hardening.

To ensure that your finished slab will be perfectly level over its entire area use 50x25mm (2x1in) wooden 'datum' pegs, taken from a 'prime datum', or fixed point that establishes the level (see pages **53 - 57** and **82 - 85**).

Drive the pegs into the ground at 1.5m (5ft) intervals and check across their tops from the prime datum with a spirit level on a

straight-edged length of timber to check their level. Remember to incorporate a slight slope for drainage; you can allow for this by placing a 25mm (1in) wedge of timber called a 'shim' under one end of the straightedge (see 'Foundations and formwork', page 59).

Measure down the pegs whatever thickness of concrete you'll need for your slab, plus about 75mm (3in) for hardcore, and excavate or fill in the ground where necessary.

If there's a drainage pipe within the area of your proposed slab it must be at least 150mm (4in) below the underside of the concrete; if it isn't you'll either have to divert the pipe run or alter the level of your slab. If you don't need to move the pipe you should, nevertheless, dig out the soil about 150mm (6in) at each side of it and fill in with pea shingle. Lay shingle rather than hardcore directly over the pipe too.

Where there's a manhole within your slab

you'll have to remove the frame and cover, then reset them at the new level, perhaps even raising the manhole brickwork itself by one or more courses (see also step-by-step photographs, page 62).

The original cover may be a lightweight one that's unsuitable for supporting heavy loads, such as your car, and you may have to buy a new, stronger one.

Fixing the formwork

A timber frame called 'formwork' (see 'Foundations and formwork', page 59) is used to retain and support the edges of the wet concrete, which tends to spread out as it sets. Use straight lengths of 25mm (1in) thick sawn timber as wide as the depth of the slab, set on edge and nailed to 50x50mm (2x2in) pegs driven into the ground at the perimeter of the slab at 1m (3ft) centres.

Position the formwork using your perimeter

4 *If you're laying your slab adjoining the house you'll have to cast it in easily manageable 'bays' and compact the mix with a tamping beam as you work.*

5 *Work along the slab using the tamping beam in a chopping action to compact the concrete. This flattens high spots and reveals depressions in the surface.*

9 *The easiest finish to apply is to smooth over the surface of the fresh concrete with the back of a clean shovel, producing fine swirls.*

10 *For a more regular, yet still non-slip finish, draw a stiff-bristled broom gently across the slab to produce a finely ridged texture.*

READY REFERENCE

DRAINING THE SLAB

Your slab must slope slightly to one side, or both sides, for drainage of rainwater. If the slab slopes naturally towards a garage or house wall:
● excavate the foundations to a point below the floor level
● slope the slab upwards to the building
● make a gutter or gully at the lowest point to drain water to one side.

COMPACTING THE CONCRETE

To compact and level a large concrete slab you'll need a tamping beam. Make one from a straight-edged length of 150x50mm (6x2in) timber, with handles bolted on at each end. To use the beam:
● work across the slab with a chopping action
● work back with a sawing action.

For more information about laying concrete see pages 44 - 47 and 53 - 57.

strings as a guide and make sure their tops are flush with the finished level of your proposed slab, using a spirit level and shim to incorporate a drainage fall, as previously described. Set the corners at right angles using a builder's square (see *Ready Reference*, page 53). All lengths of timber should be tightly butt-jointed to prevent the concrete seeping out.

Movement control joints

A slab that's longer than about 3m (10ft) in length or width must include a 'movement control' joint, which prevents the slab from cracking due to expansion or contraction.

To make the joints, divide the slab into equal-sized bays and fill the gap with a length of preservative-treated softwood fillet 10 to 12mm (3/8 to 1/2in) thick, matching the slab depth, and cut to fit between the formwork. Back up the fillet with temporary formwork

and pegs and cast each bay separately: once you've cast and compacted the first bay, remove the temporary formwork and cast the second bay, leaving the fillet permanently in position, and so on along the slab.

If the slab is to abut a wall or existing paving use a length of bituminous felt as a dpc and movement joint instead of timber.

Estimating and ordering ready-mix

Ready-mix is usually sold and delivered in minimum loads of 3cu m (105cu ft) and in 1/4cu m increments above that volume. To calculate how much concrete you'll need you must work out the volume of the proposed slab: multiply its length by its width (both in metres) to get the area; then multiply this figure by the slab thickness in mm, and divide the answer by 1000 to give the volume in cubic metres. For example a slab measuring 5x4m = 20sq m in area; at a thickness of 150mm the volume is 20x150 = 3000 ÷ 1000 = 3cu m.

Ordering ready-mix is straightforward: you can, in fact, leave most of the calculations to the supplier, although you should make sure you'll receive a little extra in case of mis-calculations. He'll want to know the volume of concrete you'll need, at what time you want it delivered, what it'll be used for – hard standing for a car, for instance, or simply garden furniture or foot traffic – and how you're going to handle it on delivery. With this information he'll be able to determine an appropriate mix and give you a price. Obtain several quotations and try to choose a local depot because much of the cost of ready-mix is in its transportation.

You'll also need to discuss with the supplier access for the lorry and whether the load can be discharged directly into the formwork. If this isn't possible you'll have to arrange for a suitably sized space for dumping which won't cause an obstruction either to you or others. In this case you should lay a large sheet of thick-gauge polythene on the ground first to make clearing up easier afterwards.

Coping with delivery

If your ready-mix is going to be dumped some distance from the proposed site – or if the slab is very long – you'll need to gather as many helpers with heavy duty wheelbarrows as you can to transport the wet mix (it takes 40 barrow loads to move 1 cu m). Lay down scaffold boards as runways for the barrows if you've to transport the mix up steps or across rough or soft ground. Wear old clothes or overalls, Wellington boots and gloves, when laying the concrete.

Placing and compacting concrete

Casting the concrete is a job for at least two people. But you'd be wise to enlist further aid as timing is critical.

Barrow the concrete to the furthest end of the foundations and tip it in. Work it well into the corners and around the edges with your boot or shovel to avoid air pockets. You can use your shovel or a garden rake to spread out the concrete to about 12mm (½in) above the level of the edge boards; this allows for settlement during compaction.

Try to organize your helpers as a team, using some to cast the concrete while two others follow along compacting the mix. Compaction is essential for the strength and durability of the mix; and it's done using a tamping beam (see *Ready Reference*). Position the beam so that it spans the edging formwork; and move along the slab about half the beam's thickness each time with a chopping action in a steady rhythm.

This tamping action will show up any high spots in the mix, which you can disperse by changing to a sawing action across the slab.

CASTING ROUND A MANHOLE

1 *If there's a manhole within your new slab you'll have to reset the lid at the new height. Remove its temporary cover when the mix has stiffened.*

2 *Build up the level of the manhole using bricks or, if the difference isn't too great, mortar. Set the lid frame in mortar, checking that it's level.*

3 *Once you've set the frame of the manhole lid accurately you can cement it into place so that it's flush with the new surface of your slab.*

4 *Remember to choose a manhole cover strong enough to support your loads. Apply a finishing texture to the slab and leave it to set hard.*

Use this excess to fill in any depressions that are left by the tamping beam, and go back over the surface to level it off. Repeat the tamping process until the concrete is level with the top of the formwork.

If you're unable to stand at each side of the slab to use the tamping beam – if it's against a wall, for example – you can cast and compact the concrete in narrow strips.

Finishing the concrete

There are a number of finishes you can apply to the concrete slab. The final pass with the tamping beam can, for example, make a slightly ridged non-slip surface texture for a drive. Alternatively, you could brush the fresh concrete across its width with a stiff bristled broom to give a finer, more regular but still non-slip finish.

A smoother, polished effect is easier to keep clean for a shed, workshop or garage floor and you can achieve this texture by trowelling the surface with a wooden or steel float in a wide, sweeping action.

One of the simplest finishes, however, is to go over the surface with the back of your shovel, which produces a swirling pattern.

Curing the concrete

Together with thorough compaction, curing is essential for a durable concrete slab. This means that it shouldn't be allowed to dry out too quickly, when it could crack. As soon as the surface has set enough not to be marked easily, cover the entire slab with a polythene sheet, tarpaulins, wet hessian or sacking.

Curing will take about three to four days (ten in winter, though you shouldn't really attempt concreting then unless there is no risk of frost), after which you can remove the covering. You can remove the formwork and use your slab after about ten days.

PATHS, STEPS AND PATIOS

One of the best areas to practise your building skills is in the garden. Absolute perfection won't matter so much, it doesn't matter if you make a mess and to begin with you only have to work in two dimensions. Garden paths and patios can be laid extremely quickly using prefabricated slabs or bricks, and once you've mastered the art of laying them level you can move on to building simple free standing or built-in steps.

LAYING PATHS WITH PAVING SLABS

Of all the materials you can use to build a path, slabs are among the simplest to lay. The large size of the individual units means a path should not take long to complete and the range of slabs available gives you a wide choice when deciding how your path will look.

Paths are made for going places and while their function might be to prevent mud being trampled into the house or to get a wheelbarrow to the garden shed without making furrows in the lawn, how they look in relation to the garden and your house is also important.

A wide range of attractive paving materials is available for you to choose from. This section deals with the techniques for laying pressed concrete slabs. Techniques for the smaller shapes such as bricks and concrete blocks (pavers) are covered on pages 68 - 71. and crazy paving on pages 79 - 81.

Planning a path

Any path should have a purpose. There's little point, for example, in laying a path that skirts the garden and then seeing it ignored as short cuts are taken across the lawn.

You should also make sure your choice of material blends with the surroundings. Concrete slabs, for instance, can look out of place if you have a lot of brick walls, whereas crazy paving might complement them. If the lawn is large and you want a path straight across it, an unbroken length of slabs might look too prominent and it might be preferable to use stepping stones with areas of grass in between (remember to relate the spacing of the stones to a normal walking pace or you will defeat the purpose of the path). If the garden is dotted with trees and shrubs it might be more eye catching to curve the path around them so that it doesn't dominate the setting.

When you're designing, think of the width as well as the length — a path that's too narrow to walk on easily will remain a source of irritation. If you make it too wide it might give the garden an unbalanced look, though a wide path can look very good if flanked on both sides with an array of shrubs or flowers.

PREPARING A HARDCORE BASE

1 Set up string lines to mark the trench edges about 50mm (2in) wider than the finished path.

2 Dig out the trench so it is just a little deeper than the thickness of the slabs you are going to use for paving.

3 Using a stout timber pole, tamp the dug-out area to compact the ground and provide a firm foundation on which the path can be built.

4 Use a timber straight-edge and a builder's level to check that the trench is flat. Inset: If the ground is still soft, dig down another 75mm (3in).

5 Fill the extra depth with a layer of broken brick (rubble) or concrete (hardcore) and compact this so it is firmly bedded down.

6 Fill gaps in hardcore with sand. You can then move string lines in to mark path edges. To lay slabs on sand, add an extra 25mm (1in) thick sand bed.

LAYING ON SAND

1 For butt joining, place edge of slab against other slabs, lower it into place and tap it into position (inset) with the shaft of a club hammer.

2 Check the horizontal with a builders' level and make sure the slight drainage fall is even. Over several slabs use a timber straight-edge.

3 Fill the gaps left between the top surfaces of the slabs by carefully brushing a mixture of soil and sand into the cracks.

4 To complete the job, fill the gaps at the path sides with soil and let the grass grow back, or infill with soil and then replace turf on top.

The best way to start planning is on paper. Use graph paper to make a scale plan of the garden, marking in any fixtures such as established trees and a shed or greenhouse and obvious targets for the path such as a gate or the washing line. Draw them in ink and use pencil to plan in path shapes — they can always be rubbed out if you change your mind.

The plan will give you something to work to as well as a method of calculating the number of slabs and the amount of sand and cement you'll need. But first you'll have to decide on the pattern you want and the type of slab (home-made or bought), whether you want grass to grow between the cracks or whether you prefer the overall look that formal pointing will give.

Paving shapes

The most common concrete paving slabs are square or rectangular in shape, though you can also buy them circular or as parts of a circle (called radius slabs). These are useful for curved or meandering paths which are difficult to make with formwork. Hexagon-shaped slabs look good, too, and these can be married up with half hexagons which give a straight edge for the path's borders.

Concrete slabs can be bought in a variety of colours — anything from red, green and yellow to brown and the ordinary 'cement' grey. Some concrete slabs which are patterned to look like brick or natural stone are finished with a blend of two colours — grey over deep red and grey over buff. But the important thing to remember about any coloured slabs is that the colours won't always last. The pigments are added to the concrete during manufacture, and in time they will fade with the effect of sun and rain. In damp shady spots under trees, lichen will grow on the surface and diminish the original colours. Some slabs may also show signs of staining as a result of efflorescence — white powdery deposits brought to the surface as water dries out of the concrete. Brushing will remove the deposits temporarily.

WHAT SIZE SLABS?

Square and oblong slabs come in a range of different sizes. The commonest are:
- 225 x 225mm (9 x 9in)
- 450 x 225mm (18 x 9in)
- 450 x 450mm (18 x 18in)
- 675 x 450mm (27 x 18in)

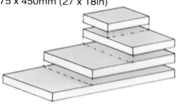

Some slabs are based on a 300mm (12in) unit, so squares are 300 x 300mm or 600 x 600mm (24 x 24in), and rectangles 600 x 300mm (24 x 12in) or 900 x 600mm (36 x 24in). Slabs over 450 x 450mm (18 x 18in) are very heavy.

Hexagonal slabs are usually 400mm (16in) or 450mm (18in) wide. Half slabs are also made, either cut side to side or point to point, and intended to be laid as shown in the sketch.

Both rectangular and hexagonal slabs are generally 38mm (1½in) thick.

LAYING METHODS

Light-duty paths — for walkers only — can be laid with slabs bedded on sand about 25mm (1in) thick. The joints should be filled with sand or soil, not pointed with mortar.

Heavy-duty paths — for wheelbarrows, rollers and heavy mowers — should have slabs bedded in stiff mortar (1 part cement to 5 parts sand) and mortared joints.

TIP: STACKING SLABS

To avoid chipping corners and edges and marking the slab faces, stack slabs on edge in pairs, face to face, against a wall, with their bottom edges on timber battens.

LAYING ON MORTAR

1 *For heavier duty use, lay slabs on pads of mortar. Place the fist-sized pads on the path bed ready to take the slab.*

2 *Lower the slab into place so there are 19mm (³/₄in) wide gaps between it and neighbouring slabs. Use timber spacers to give correct joint width.*

3 *Use the shaft of a club hammer to tap the slab into position – a builders' level will tell you if the surface is even or needs adjusting.*

4 *With a timber straight-edge and a builders' level check the level across the path, making sure the drainage fall is not too abrupt.*

5 *Brush a dry 1:5 cement:sand mix into the joints and sprinkle them with water, or* 6 *Mix up a crumbly mortar and use a pointing trowel to press this into the joints (inset). Then draw the trowel at an angle along the mortar surface.*

Patterns of laying

You may decide on a simple chequerboard pattern using one size of slabs or a pattern with staggered joints as in stretcher bond brickwork. Alternatively you can create a more decorative path using different sized slabs. Riven surfaced slabs can be particularly effective if two sizes of slabs are used with the larger slabs set to radiate around the smaller ones, producing a square which is repeated down the length of the path. For further suggestions on laying patterns see the slab manufacturers' literature.

Cutting slabs

If the pattern you've worked out requires cut slabs (it's helpful and certainly more easy if they're half sizes), the cutting is relatively easy. After you have marked the cutting line all round the slab you place it on a bed of soft sand or even on the lawn (anything to absorb the shock) and cut a groove along the cutting line, using a bolster chisel and a club hammer. You can then split the slab by tapping the bolster with the hammer along the groove.

Cutting sections out of paving slabs is not

so easy. Chipping to shape is time consuming and cast slabs are likely to fracture anyway. It's worth considering filling L-shaped gaps with two separately cut pieces, or leaving out the paving slab altogether and infilling with pebbles, stones or even cobbles set in mortar, or simply finishing off with bricks.

If you want a perfect finish for cut pieces and have a lot of cutting to do, it is worth hiring a masonry saw from a plant hire shop. Although it's possible to fit masonry cutting discs to an ordinary drill, with a lot of cutting you run the risk of burning out the motor.

Buying paving slabs

Visit local garden centres and builders merchants to see what sizes, colours and textures they have in stock. It's always worth shopping around. Your supplier should be able to give you helpful information — for example, some coloured slabs are more colour-fast than others, and he should know which ones. If local suppliers don't have what you want, remember that the cost of transporting heavy slabs over a long distance is high, so it may be better (or at least cheaper) to choose from what is available.

Prices will obviously vary depending on the type of slab — for example, hydraulically pressed slabs are more expensive than cast slabs. And when ordering, allow for a few more than the exact number required for the path; you may crack one or two during laying so it's better to have spares handy.

Preparing the base

Making a flat base is the single most important step in laying the path. And to do this you will usually have to dig out a shallow trench along the line you want the path to follow.

Digging out the topsoil, roots and any organic matter needs to be done carefully

CUTTING SLABS

1 *Mark the cutting line right round the slab with chalk; use a straight-edge so you can mark a straight line the right distance from the sides of the slab.*

and you should dig the trench to a depth just a little deeper than the slab thickness. As well as being flat, the laying surface must be firm and compacted. At this stage, an easy way of checking that the trench is flat is to use a length of straight-edged timber — a plank or a fence post, for instance — to indicate hollows or bumps which might not be obvious to the eye.

Once the trench is dug you may find that because of the type of soil, the surface is still soft. The answer is to dig out another 75mm (3in) or so and then fill the extra depth with a layer of broken brick (rubble) or broken concrete (hardcore). This layer has to be well compacted before a layer of sand or fine ash (called a 'blinding' layer) is spread on it to provide a smooth surface. If you don't want anything to grow up through the path, saturate the trench with a powerful weed-killer.

Laying paving slabs

The easiest way to control the line of a path as you begin to lay the paving slabs is to set up string lines to mark out the edges. How the slabs are bedded — whether on sand or pads of mortar — depends on the weight of traffic the path will carry and whether you intend to point the gaps between the slabs with mortar.

As you lay the slabs, use a timber straight-edge to check that each slab sits flush with its neighbours across and along the path. On level ground, you must lay them so that there is a slight slope across the width of the path — a drop of about 25mm (1in) across 1 metre (just over 3ft) will be sufficient. Check the slope by placing a 25mm thick block of wood under one end of your spirit level or batten; the bubble should then be in the 'dead level' position. On sloping ground, the slabs can be laid dead level across the path width to achieve the same effect.

Slabs can sometimes be butt jointed tightly together. However, because there is often some slight variation in the sizes of slabs, it makes sense to allow for a joint of about 9mm to 12mm ($^3/_8$in to $^1/_2$in) to take up these minor inaccuracies. It's important that the joints be kept even — for they act as a frame for the slab shape. Spacers cut from board will give you the desired joint thickness and will also prevent the newly laid slabs closing up as you lay adjacent ones.

Finishing off

When you have positioned all the slabs you can fill the joints. If you are not pointing them, simply brush a mixture of soil and sand into the gaps. Where you want a pointed finish there are two methods you can use — and both require care or mortar stains will mar the slabs.

One method is to mix the cement and sand dry — the sand needs to be very dry — and pour or brush this into the joints. You then sprinkle the joints with a watering can fitted with a fine rose, or wait until it rains.

A better method is to mix up dry crumbly mortar and press this into the joints with a pointing trowel. Any mortar crumbs falling onto the face of the slab can easily be brushed away without staining. You can also use a piece of wood or a trowel to finish the joint so it is slightly recessed.

After pointing is completed don't walk on the path for a few days — if you tread on an edge of a slab you may loosen it and you will have to lift it (using a spade) and lay it again on fresh mortar.

To finish off the gaps at the edges you can point them where they adjoin masonry or a flower bed; where they run alongside a lawn, fill them with soil and let the grass grow back, or fill space with gravel which will drain away excess water.

2 With the slab on a surface which will absorb the shock, use a bolster chisel and club hammer to cut a groove along the line, including the slab edges.

3 Place the slab face up and work the bolster back and forth along the groove, tapping it with the hammer as you go, until the slab splits in two.

LAYING PATHS WITH BRICKS

Paths need to be functional but they should also contribute to the overall appearance of their surroundings. Brick and concrete pavers come in a variety of natural colours and can be laid in patterns to suit your style of garden.

When you want to build a path with a small-scale pattern you can use bricks or concrete block paving. They can also be used to break up the larger scale pattern of a slab path. Because they are small units you can lay them to gently rolling levels and in restricted spaces where it would be awkward to lay larger slab materials.

Buying bricks and concrete pavers
These materials should be obtainable from a good builders' merchant but, with such a variety on the market, they may have to be ordered. If you live near a brickmaker who makes paving bricks it may be worthwhile enquiring direct – be sure to make it clear you want bricks of paving quality.

Clay brick pavers are produced in a variety of colours from dark red through buff to dark blue/black and a range of finishes both smooth and textured. Calcium silicate are not recommended for paving as their edges are likely to chip. Concrete bricks come in a good range of colours with smooth and textured surfaces while concrete paving blocks tend to be light in tone. Colours include buffs, greys and light reds.

Planning the path
As with paths made from other types of materials, a path of brick or concrete pavers needs to meet functional and design requirements so it will serve its purpose and be an attractive feature of the garden.

Draw up a scale plan of the garden and work out where the path will go. You can also use this to assist you in working out the quantities of materials you will need. Work out patterns that will avoid unnecessary cutting of the pavers. For dry-laid paving, interlocking is an important feature and patterns which avoid continuous straight joint lines are preferable.

When deciding on your design remember that these small units of paving can be used on their own. You may feel, for example, that the bond pattern, colour and textural patterns of clay bricks give sufficient surface interest without recourse to mixing brick types – you might, in fact, find laying rather difficult if bricks were intermingled.

Preparing the base
The foundations on which the paving is laid must be properly prepared to ensure a long-lasting path. You will have to dig out grass, soil and roots – since there will be a granular sub-base topped with a bed of sand plus a layer of pavers, you should dig down to at least 225mm (9in) below the finished level to allow for the thickness of construction.

When you are calculating the depth, remember that if the path runs next to your house the finished level should ideally be two courses of brickwork below the dpc (damp proof course) in the wall. If it's alongside a lawn, make sure its surface is below that of the grass for convenient mowing. Don't forget that on a level path you will have to allow for a drainage fall to one side of the path. Where the path adjoins a wall, the slope should be away from the wall.

To set out the levels, slopes and edge lines you can use timber pegs and string lines. To work out slopes and levels you will need a length of straight-edged timber and a builder's level.

The sub-base should consist of hard-core, which is available through sand and gravel suppliers or builders' merchants. The levels and gradients should be formed in this material so the bed of sand in which the pavers or bricks are laid can be spread evenly over the whole area.

Laying paving dry
For an even, firm path you must take care when you lay the sand base to ensure consistent compaction and perfect level. To give a regular finished surface the sand should be exactly the same throughout the work so allow it to drain before use. Cover it over during storage to minimise variation in moisture content.

You'll also have to include edge restraints for dry-laid paving at both sides of the path. These can be of creosoted or preservative-

PREPARING THE BASE

1 Stretch strings between pegs to mark the edges of the path. Include a margin for the timber edge restraints on dry-laid paths.

2 Cut along the string lines using a spade or, if making a path across a lawn, a turfing iron. Use this tool to lift thin rectangles of turf.

3 Dig down to a level that will take a 50mm (2in) sand bed and, if the soil is spongy, a hardcore base. Compact the base using a fence post tamper.

4 Set creosoted boards at the sides of the trench as edge restraints. On loosely packed earth, nail the boards to stakes driven into the ground.

5 Check the level of the boards across the path using a builder's level. On a lawn, lower the path slightly to make mowing the grass easier.

6 When you have levelled the base of the trench and set the edge restraints, shovel in washed sharp sand, which forms a level bed for the bricks.

7 Spread out the sand over the path using a garden rake. Work only a small area at a time to avoid walking on newly-levelled base.

8 Make a timber spreader to level the sand bed by drawing it along the path, resting on the edge restraints and fill any hollows and level again.

READY REFERENCE

PAVING MATERIALS

Brick pavers are made in a variety of sizes up to 225mm (9in) square and up to 65mm (2½in) thick. Some are shaped to interlock; other have chamfered edges to reduce chipping.

Clay building bricks must be paving quality (frost-resistant when saturated). Standard size is 230 x 110 x 76mm (9 x 4½ x 3in).

Concrete building bricks are the same size as standard clay bricks.

Concrete paving blocks are rectangular (200 x 100 x 65mm) or square (225 x 225 x 65mm) and edges of face side are chamfered. Special interlocking shapes are about the same size overall.

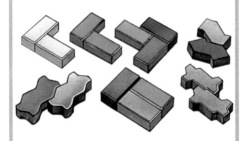

LAYING METHODS

Dry-laid (without mortar) is best for interlocking brick and concrete pavers. Needs sub-base of hardcore 100mm (4in) thick and 50mm (2in) thick bed of sharp sand.

For 1 sq metre you'll need
● 40 brick-size units laid flat
● 60 brick-size units laid on edge
● 50 small concrete pavers

Mortar bed and jointed technique can be used for standard bricks. Needs a 75mm (3in) compacted hardcore sub-base, a blinding layer of sand or fine ash under 50mm (2in) thick mortar bed (1:4 cement and sand) with 10mm (⅜in) mortar joints. To lay and point 3 sq m (105 bricks laid flat) or 2.5 sq m (120 bricks on edge) you'll need:
● 40kg bag of cement
● 17 2-gallon buckets of damp sand

TIPS: STOPPING WEED GROWTH
● under bricks place plastic sheeting on top of the hardcore
● under concrete use a long-term weedkiller

LAYING BRICKS DRY

1 *Begin by laying the bricks in your chosen pattern – a basketweave design is shown here – butting up each brick to the next one.*

2 *Tap the bricks into place using the handle of your club hammer but don't exert too much pressure or you risk making the sand bed uneven.*

3 *If any of the bricks are bedded too low, remove them and pack more sand underneath, then level again.*

4 *Bed the bricks level using a stout timber batten held across the path, which you can tap with a club hammer, then check with a spirit level.*

5 *Hold your spirit level on top of the batten and check that the path is bedded evenly, incorporating a drainage fall to one side.*

6 *Brush sand over the surface of the path when fully laid, using a soft-bristled broom to fill the crevices between the bricks.*

treated timber, or of bricks or kerb stones set in mortar.

The base should be no less than 50mm (2in) thick. When the finished surface is bedded in some of the sand will be forced up into the joints from below so the depth of the sand layer will be effectively reduced. And to complicate matters, moist sand 'bulks' in volume – the moisture acts on the sand particles to give them a fluffy texture – so the thickness of the sand may seem more than it will, in fact, be when the bricks or blocks are firmly bedded down in place. In this case you may have too little sand and will have to compensate. However, you can have too much sand – a layer which is too thick may cause surface undulation.

It's a good idea to add an extra 6mm ($\frac{1}{4}$in) to 15mm ($\frac{5}{8}$in) of sand to the 50mm (2in) thickness to accommodate any unevenness. After you have levelled the first few metres of sand you can check to find out if you have added too much or too little and compensate if necessary. You should check again at frequent intervals as you continue levelling.

You will need a stout timber straight-edged board with notched ends to level the sand surface. The ends fit over the existing edge restraint and you draw the board along

over the sand so that it is evenly spread over the area to be paved. This also ensures that the surface is properly compacted.

You should find laying the paving units quite simple provided you take care how you position the first few pavers. Each paver should be placed so it touches its neighbour – be careful not to dislodge a laid paver from its position – accidental and unnoticed displacement will have a multiplying effect. Similarly, don't tilt any of the laid pavers by kneeling or standing on them as the depressed edge will distort the level of the sand.

Where whole bricks or pavers do not fit at the edges, fill the spaces by cutting whole units to the required size. Gulley entries and manholes can also be dealt with by cutting bricks or pavers to fit. Alternatively, very small areas with a dimension of less than 40mm ($1\frac{1}{2}$in) can be filled with a 1:4 cement:sand mortar.

When all the bricks or pavers are in place you will have to bed them securely in the sand. For this you can use a stout timber straight-edge and a club hammer or, particularly useful where you are paving a large area, you can hire a mechanical plate vibrator. Once the bricks or pavers are bedded, you brush fine sand over the

paving and again go over the surface with the machine to vibrate sand into the joints or re-tamp the surface with the straight-edge to ensure settlement. Once all the joints are filled you can brush the surplus sand away. The path will be ready for immediate use.

Laying bricks on mortar

This method of laying bricks is more permanent than using a sand bed, and no edge restraint is needed. Again, when you are digging out the trench, remember to allow for the drainage fall and the level of the path in relation to the dpc or lawn, and dig down deep enough to allow for the thickness of construction.

The sub-base should be a layer of hard-core which is tamped down or rolled to provide a firm foundation for the path and topped with a blinding layer of fine sand or ash. The bricks are bedded in a fairly dry, crumbly mortar mix and with spaces between them to allow for grouting. Dry mortar is brushed into the joints and then the whole path is sprayed with water. With this method, you should not use the path until a week has passed after laying the pavers. In hot, dry weather the paving should be protected against drying out prematurely by covering it with polythene sheets or damp sacking.

LAYING BRICKS ON MORTAR

1 To bed bricks on a mortar base, trowel a fairly stiff mix in dabs onto the sand bed. No edge restraints will be needed when a mortar bed is used.

2 Press the bricks onto the mortar in your chosen design – here you can see a herringbone pattern – and adjust the mortar thickness so they are level.

3 Leave a 10mm (³⁄₈in) gap between each brick to allow for a mortar joint, which is added afterwards. Use timber offcuts as spacers for the joints.

4 Check the level of the brickwork using a straight-edged length of timber and a spirit level. Adjust the thickness of the mortar if necessary.

5 Brush a dry mortar mix, in the same proportions as the bedding mix, into the joints until they are flush with the surface of the path.

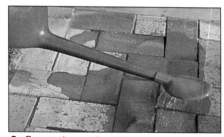

6 Spray the path with clean water from a watering can fitted with a fine rose, then leave the path for about one week before using.

CUTTING A BRICK

1 Mark a cutting line in chalk around the bricks to be cut; place them on a sand bed and mark the line by hitting it with a bolster chisel and club hammer.

2 Turn the brick over and score lines on each face (inset). Return to the first line and hit it sharply with the chisel until the brick breaks cleanly.

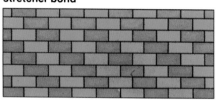

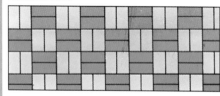

BUILDING FREE-STANDING STEPS

A garden composed of different levels will look disjointed unless there is some visual link between parts. A flight of steps not only serves the practical purpose of providing access to the various levels, but also gives a co-ordinated look to a scheme.

The main purpose of steps is to provide access from one level to another and they're an important factor in the landscaping of a garden, bringing otherwise detached areas into the overall scheme. Wide, shallow steps can, for example, double as seating for a terrace bordering a lawn, or as a display area for plants in containers, while narrow, angular steps will accentuate interesting changes of ground level.

This section deals with freestanding steps, which are designed to rise from flat ground level to a slightly higher level, such as a path to a terrace or raised lawn. Built-in garden steps describes how to construct steps which are not freestanding, but built into a bank or slope.

Types of materials
For a good visual effect, the steps should be constructed from materials that complement the style of the garden. If you've built a path, for instance, continue the run by using the same materials for the steps. Where you're building up to a wall, match the two structures, again by using the same materials.

For a formal flight, bricks can be used as risers (the vertical height of the step). Decorative walling blocks with 'riven' or split faces, or natural stone, used in the same way give a softer, more countrified look. You can top these materials with either smooth- or riven-faced slabs or even quarry tiles to form the treads (the horizontal part of the step on which you walk). Or, if you prefer, you can use other combinations of building materials for the steps; bricks and blocks, for example, make attractive treads as well as risers.

You can choose from a wide range of coloured bricks, blocks and slabs, mixing and matching them to best effect. Pre-cast or cast in situ concrete can be used as a firm base for these materials or makes a durable surface in its own right.

Planning the steps
There are no building regulations governing the construction of garden steps so you have a lot of flexibility in deciding how they will look. Sketch out possible routes – you can build them parallel to the side of the terrace so they don't extend too far into the garden. This is particularly suitable where the ground slope is steep. Decide whether the steps will be flanked by flower beds, rockeries or lawn, or linked at the sides to existing or new walls. You could build steps with double-skinned side walls and fill the gap between with soil to use as a planter.

Bear in mind the dimensions of the completed steps when choosing materials. Treads and risers should measure the same throughout the flight to ensure a constant, safe, walking rhythm. (If they are not constant, the variations must be made

PREPARING THE BASE

1 *Fix pairs of string lines so they are level and square over the centre of the concrete strip foundations to mark the height and width of the first riser.*

2 *Lay mortar along the front of the foundation and scribe a line parallel to the inside string to indicate the back of the first course of blocks.*

3 *Lay the first course of blocks on the mortar, checking the surface is even with a spirit level. Tap the blocks in place with the handle of a club hammer.*

4 *Position the first course of the side walls in the same way and check that the angle at the corners is at 90°, using a builder's square.*

5 *Start laying the second course of blocks at one corner, aligning them with the strings. Tap the blocks into place with the handle of your trowel.*

6 *When two courses of blocks are laid allow the mortar to set partially, then shovel in hardcore. Use a fence post to compact the hardcore.*

visually obvious for safety reasons.) Make provision, also, for drainage of rainwater from the steps by sloping the treads slightly towards the front.

Steps should be neither too steep nor too gradual – steepness can cause strain and loss of balance while with too shallow a climb you run the danger of tripping on the steps. Steep steps, and those likely to be used by children and elderly people, require railings on one or both sides to aid balance. These can be of either tubular metal or wood and should be set at a height where your hand can rest on top comfortably – this usually

works out at about 850mm (2ft 9in) high measured from the nose of the steps. Alternatively, you can build small brick, block or stone walls at each side of the flight. There should be no hand obstructions along the length of the railings or walls, or other projections on which clothing could snag. Railings should also extend beyond both ends of the flight by about 300mm (1ft); they might, in fact, continue an existing run of railings along a path.

Treads should be non-slip for safety. However, this is difficult to achieve outdoors, where they are subjected to ice, rain

READY REFERENCE

STEP ESSENTIALS

To ensure comfortable, safe walking, garden steps must be uniform in size throughout the flight, and neither too steep nor too shallow.

Risers are usually between 100mm and 175mm (4in and 7in) high. The shallower the slope the shallower the risers.

Treads should not be less than 300mm (1ft) deep – enough to take the ball of the foot on descending without the back of the leg hitting the step above. They should be about 600mm (2ft) wide for one person; 1.5m (5ft) for two people.

Nosing is the front of the tread, which projects beyond the riser by about 25mm (1in) to accentuate the line of the step in shadow.

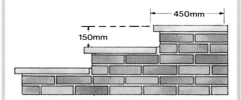

HOW MANY STEPS?

To calculate the number of steps:
● measure the vertical distance between the two levels
● divide the height of a single riser (including the tread thickness where relevant) into the vertical height to determine the number of risers.

TYPICAL TREAD/RISER COMBINATIONS

For comfortable walking combine deep treads with low risers, shallower treads with high risers.

Tread	Riser
450mm (1ft 5½in)	110mm (4½in)
430mm (1ft 5in)	125mm (5in)
400mm (1ft 4in)	140mm (5½in)
380mm (1ft 3in)	150mm (6in)
330mm (1ft 1in)	165mm (6½in)

MORTAR MIX

Bed treads and risers in a fairly stiff mortar mix: 1 part cement to 5 parts sand.

HOW MUCH MORTAR?

50kg cement mixed with 24 two gallon (9 litre) buckets of damp sand will be sufficient to lay about 7sq m of slabs – around 35 slabs 450 x 450mm (18 x 18in) – on a 25mm (1in) thick bed. Don't mix this much mortar at once or it will set before you can use it all.

CONSTRUCTING THE STEPS

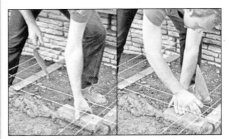

1 Move the front strings back the depth of the tread to the second riser position, then lay the blocks on a mortar bed as described previously.

2 When the third and fourth courses are laid, in-fill with more hardcore and compact it thoroughly so it's flush with the top of the blocks.

3 After laying each course, you should check with a gauge rod at the corners that the mortar joints are of the same thickness throughout.

4 The slab treads can be laid on either a bed of mortar around their perimeter or on five dabs of mortar – one at each corner and one centrally.

5 Position the slabs squarely on the risers but projecting forward by about 25mm (1in) and sloping forward slightly to allow for drainage of rainwater.

6 When the slabs have been laid, fill the gap behind with a mortar fillet – but be sure not to spill wet mortar on the slabs, as this may stain them.

and formation of moss. Proprietary liquids are available for painting on treads so they won't be slippery but a more practical solution is to use hydraulically-pressed slabs, which come with a variety of surface textures or relief designs that are both attractive and non-slip.

When you've decided on the basic appearance and route of the steps you must calculate the quantity of bricks, slabs or other material you'll need. It's best to work out your design taking into account the sizes of slabs, blocks or bricks available. Make a scale plan (bird's eye view) and a side view on graph paper to help in planning and construction.

Building methods

In order to support the steps. concrete trench foundations must be formed underneath the retaining walls. Mark out these foundations using strings stretched between pegs (see foundations. pages 48 - 52). Construct the flight one step at a time. When the first courses of the retaining walls have been built. a hardcore filling is used to provide a firm base for the treads. When this is rammed down. lay a blinding layer of sharp sand to fill

gaps and provide a level bed for the treads. Subsequent levels are built on top in the same way and the treads laid on mortar.

When tamping down the hardcore backfilling in each level take care not to dislodge any bricks or blocks. Concentrate on the areas that will support the next risers and the back edges of the treads because these parts are subject to the most pressure.

This method of construction is suitable only for freestanding units up to five steps high. If you want larger steps, you'll have to make substantial foundations in the form of a cast concrete slab about 75mm (3in) thick, covering the entire area of the steps, and build intermediate supporting walls the width of the flight under each riser – a hardcore back-filling alone is simply not firm enough to support the extra weight. These walls can be laid in a honeycomb fashion, with gaps between the bricks in each course; this allows for drainage through the structure and uses less bricks than a solid wall. Each section formed by the intermediate walls should contain a rammed-down hardcore back-filling topped with a blinding layer of sand.

Alternatively, you can cast a solid concrete flight in timber formwork and lay the surface materials on top, bedded in

mortar, but this will involve large quantities of concrete.

Larger flights built up to a wall should be joined to the wall or there's the risk of them parting company after time. 'Tooth-in' alternate courses to the brickwork or blockwork of the terrace by removing a brick from the terrace wall and slotting in the last whole brick from the side walls of the steps. On smaller flights you can tie in the steps by bedding a large 6in (150mm) nail in a mortar joint between the two structures for added rigidity.

Brick bonds

The type of brick bond you use in the construction of the retaining walls depends upon the size of the materials you use for the risers. You should, though, try to keep the perpends consistent throughout the flight for strength and for best visual effect.

It's wise to dry-lay bricks or blocks first to make sure you get the best – and strongest – bond: perpends that are very close together mean a weaker construction and you should try to avoid this if possible (see Bricklaying. pages 26-31). When choosing materials. you should take note of typical, 'safe tread/riser combinations (see *Ready Reference*).

ARRANGING THE BONDING

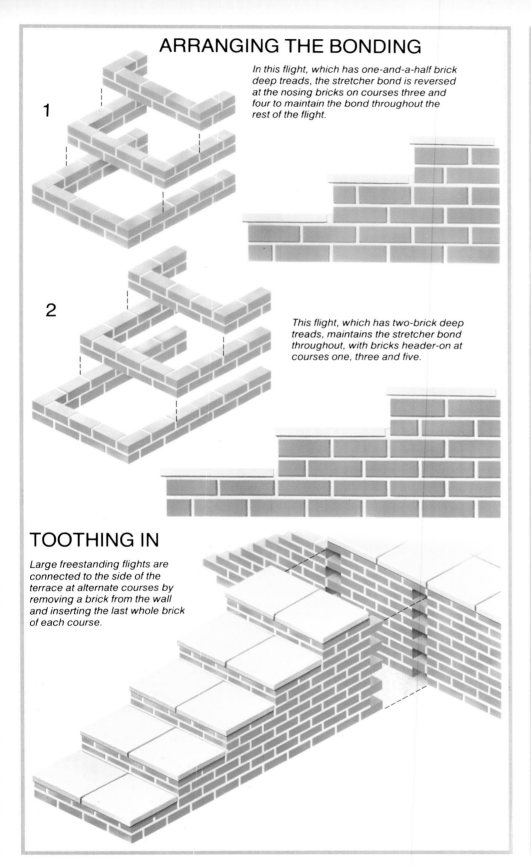

1

In this flight, which has one-and-a-half brick deep treads, the stretcher bond is reversed at the nosing bricks on courses three and four to maintain the bond throughout the rest of the flight.

2

This flight, which has two-brick deep treads, maintains the stretcher bond throughout, with bricks header-on at courses one, three and five.

TOOTHING IN

Large freestanding flights are connected to the side of the terrace at alternate courses by removing a brick from the wall and inserting the last whole brick of each course.

READY REFERENCE

MASONRY STEPS

A simple freestanding flight consisting of five treads requires:
● a concrete-filled trench about 100mm (4in) deep and twice as wide as each retaining wall
● broken brick or concrete back-filling
A flight larger than five treads requires:
● substantial foundations in the form of a cast concrete slab about 75mm (3in) thick, covering the entire area of the steps
● intermediate supporting walls the width of the flight under each riser
● rammed-down hardcore back-filling topped with a blinding layer of sand
● or a concrete base flight cast in timber formwork, on which the surface materials can be laid, bedded in mortar.

DRAINAGE

Rainwater must not be allowed to collect on the steps. Provide drainage by:
● allowing for a fall of about 12mm ($\frac{1}{2}$in) to the front of each tread or, where the steps abut a wall:
● make concrete gullies about 50mm (2in) deep by 75mm (3in) wide at each side of the flight to drain from the top.

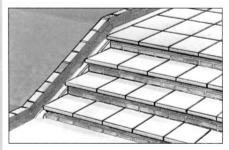

If the flight drains towards a house wall:
● make a channel at the foot of the steps, parallel to the wall, to divert water to a suitable drainage point.

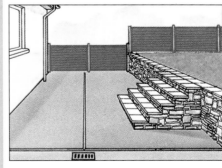

CREATING BUILT-IN STEPS

Steps can be used to great effect in the garden. They not only enable you to get from one level of the garden to another with ease, but draw together otherwise separated features of the landscape.

On pages 72 - 75 you'll find details of the techniques for freestanding unit steps, which lead from flat ground level to a slightly higher level and have their own support. It is also possible to incorporate steps into an existing slope or bank by using the shape and structure of the slope as the base.

The rough shape of the flight is dug into the bank and the steps are then bedded in mortar on a hardcore base. With some soils, well-compacted earth alone can make a firm enough base for the treads and risers. On a soft crumbly soil you may find it necessary to build low retaining walls at the sides of the flight before you lay the treads, to prevent the soil from spilling onto the treads.

Planning the site

When planning you should consider the site as a whole or the steps might end up looking out of place. You have a considerable amount of freedom in the design of your steps as construction rules are more relaxed outdoors than they are for buildings, but you should adhere to the design principle that the new element should fit into its setting. Because you're using the lie of the land as your foundations it's as well to plan the flight so that it traces existing gradients or skirts flower beds, trees or other features.

Make a sketch of the garden, plotting possible locations for the steps and transfer this information to a more detailed plan on graph paper, including a cross-section of the ground slope. With this plan you can calculate quantities of materials – always try to design the steps with particular sized bricks, slabs and blocks in mind to avoid having to cut them or alter the slope dimensions unduly.

Match materials that have been used elsewhere in the garden – as boundary walls or raised flower beds for instance – for a feeling of continuity. Also remember the basic rules of step design: although you should avoid creating steep steps, which can cause strain, shallow flights are also not recommended because you can easily trip on them.

Bricks, blocks and natural stone come in sizes that are suitable for building risers in

one or more courses. Riven- or smooth-faced concrete slabs or quarry tiles make convenient, easy-to-use and non-slip treads for these materials. You can also use the smaller-scale materials such as bricks and blocks for the treads as well as the risers, although they'll need a much firmer base than slabs.

The colour of the steps is also important and most materials are available in a range of reds, greens, browns and greys.

Whatever combination of materials you choose, keep the dimensions of the steps constant throughout the flight – a jumble of sizes not only looks untidy but also upsets a comfortable walking rhythm and so can be dangerous.

Where your flight is larger than 10 steps it's wise to build in a landing. This will visually 'foreshorten' the flight, provide a broad resting place and more practically, will serve to 'catch' anyone accidentally falling from the flight above. You should also include a landing when changing the direction of a flight at an acute angle.

Include railings to aid balance on steep or twisting flights, or those likely to be used by children and elderly people. They can continue the run of existing fences or walls along a path for a sense of unity.

You should also allow for a slight fall towards the front of each tread so that rainwater will drain quickly away. Don't slope the

READY REFERENCE

STEP ESSENTIALS
Steps should conform to the following dimensions to ensure comfortable, safe walking:

- **risers** between 100mm and 175mm (4in and 7in)
- **treads** not less than 300mm (1ft) deep; a minimum of 600mm (2ft) wide for one person, 1.5m (5ft) wide for two
- **nosing** projecting beyond risers by 25mm (1in)
- **flights** not more than 10 steps without a landing.

MORTAR MIX
Bed treads and risers in a fairly stiff mortar mix: 1 part cement to 5 parts sand.

HOW MUCH MORTAR?
One 50kg bag of cement mixed with 15¾ 3-gallon (14-litre) bucketfuls of damp sand will be sufficient to lay about 7sq m of slabs on a 25mm (1in) thick mortar bed. Don't mix all the mortar at once or it will set before you can use it all – mix about a quarter at a time.

AVERAGE DIMENSIONS

PREPARING THE SLOPE

1 To measure the vertical height of the slope stretch string between a peg at the top and a cane at the base; check that it's level with a spirit level.

2 Set string lines from the top to the bottom of the slope to indicate the sides of the flight, ensuring they are parallel and that the flight is straight.

3 Mark the nosing for each tread with string lines stretched across the slope; check that they are level and that the angle with the side strings is at 90°.

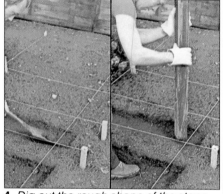

4 Dig out the rough shape of the steps, taking care not to dislodge the nosing markers and compact the earth using a fence post as a tamper.

5 Continue to dig out the steps, working up the slope. Use each cut-out as a standing base for excavating the next, but be careful not to crumble the edges.

6 Dig below and behind the nosing strings to allow for the depth of the slab treads and the thickness of the block risers, thus defining the step shape.

treads to one side as this can give the flight a lopsided look.

Planning awkward slopes

Your plans for building in steps will seldom run true, as your slope probably won't be regular in shape. If the riser height doesn't divide equally into the vertical height of the slope your steps will have inconsistent dimensions – not only unattractive but also likely to upset constant walking pace. One solution is to remodel the slope. Use earth from another part of the garden placed at the top to increase the slope's height; remove earth from the top to decrease its height. Any extra earth must be compacted before it can be 'stepped'.

You can often use any undulations to your advantage: because you're using the firmed ground as your foundations you're able to build much longer and twisting flights. So base your plan on the shape of the ground rather than vice versa.

Marking out the flight

Before you can mark out the flight on the slope you must calculate the number of steps you'll need by measuring the vertical height of the bank.

To mark out the steps stretch strings between pegs from the top to the bottom of the slope to indicate the width of the flight. You can then set other strings across the slope to indicate the top edges of each step's nosing. You should check the level of these nosing strings using a spirit level.

Constructing the flight

Starting at the base of the slope, excavate the rough shape of the first step, digging behind and below the nosing marker to a depth that will allow for a hardcore filling and the thickness of the tread and riser.

Compact the earth, then use the cut-out as a standing base for excavating the next step. Work in this way up the slope. When the whole flight has been excavated in this way, and compacted, lay a hardcore base (if necessary) followed by the treads and risers. Use the back of each tread as a base for the next riser and back-fill with hardcore, which should be well compacted with a fence post tamper, taking care not to dislodge the newly-laid riser.

The first riser should ideally be laid on a cast concrete footing to support the weight of of the flight, preventing it from 'slipping', although on small flights where the soil is firm this might not be necessary. The footing should be about 100mm (4in) deep and twice the thickness of the riser.

An alternative way to build steps into a slope is to cast a concrete slab flight in timber formwork and either face it with bricks, blocks, slabs or tiles, or leave it bare.

LAYING THE STEPS

1 Lay any slabs at ground level where a path run continues then add hardcore under the first riser position. Compact and lay mortar on top.

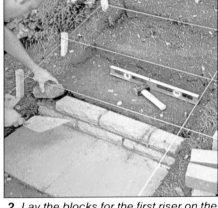

2 Lay the blocks for the first riser on the bed of mortar, making sure they're level and square. Tap down into place with the handle of your club hammer.

3 Fill the gap between the blocks and the soil with hardcore, then compact to the top level of the riser. Take care that you don't dislodge the blocks.

4 Shovel hardcore onto the first tread position and compact well using a fence post. Check the level of the foundation, incorporating a fall to the front.

5 Lay the first two slabs on mortar and check that they are level. Set them forward by about 25mm (1in); the nosing marker should align with their top edge.

6 Bed the next course of blocks for the second riser in mortar on the back of the first tread; try not to splash mortar on the slabs as this will stain.

7 Back-fill with hardcore and tamp down thoroughly, then lay the next two slabs; a bed of mortar at the perimeter of each slab makes a firm and level bed.

8 Continue in this way to the top of the flight, bedding each riser on the tread below it. Set the last tread level with the ground at the top of the slope.

9 Brush a dry mortar mix into the gaps between the slabs, point all the joints and brush off any debris. Leave the steps for 7 days before using.

LAYING CRAZY PAVING

Garden paving doesn't have to be all squares and rectangles. With crazy paving you can have a more informal look in any shape you fancy, and you can use it on wall surfaces too.

Crazy paving is a versatile material that can be used as a resilient and attractive surface for patios, driveways, garden paths or steps, or as a decorative feature in an otherwise plain paving scheme.

It's simply broken paving slabs and you can often buy it quite cheaply, by the tonne, from your local as demolition material. Slabs bought in this way will usually be a heavy duty variety used for pavements and have a rather dull grey colour and a relatively plain finish, but you can add interest in the way you lay the pieces. Local building contractors can often supply broken slabs of various textures in greens, pinks, reds and buff tones in sufficient quantities for use in paving. Natural stone can also be bought to make up crazy paving.

Planning crazy paving

Before you can begin to lay your paving, sketch out some ideas for its overall shape, size and, in the case of paths, its route through the garden. Transfer your final design to graph paper so that you can use this to estimate the total area to be covered and place an order for the correct quantity of paving. You can also use your plan as a blueprint for ordering and laying the slabs.

Because of its irregular profile crazy paving, unlike conventional square or rectangular slabs, can be used to form curves, such as a winding path, a decorative surround to a pond, or an unusual-shaped patio. Although you have a lot of freedom in your creative design you mustn't allow the paving to appear out of place with its surroundings. If your garden is strictly formal, for instance, avoid complex curves or too 'busy' a surface texture — the mix of angles could clash. Small areas of random paving can, on the other hand, give a plain scheme a visual 'lift'.

Although crazy paving has an overall random design, it must be placed with some precision to avoid an unbalanced look. The best way to plan out an area of paving when you've decided upon a basic site is to dry-lay it when the base is complete.

Separate the pieces that have one or more straight sides for use as edging and corners and lay these first, choosing only the largest pieces — small ones tend to break away.

You can lay the paving with a ragged outline to achieve an informal look, but you will still have to use the largest pieces for the edging. When plants have been introduced into the irregular edges and allowed to trail over the slabs you'll find that your path soon assumes an established air.

It's not important to make a regular joint width between the pieces — in fact, the paving will probably look much more natural if the joints vary. Fit the smaller inner pieces together like a jig-saw puzzle, mixing colours to best effect. When dry-laying the slabs avoid a continuous joint line across the path as this can be jarring to the eye and weakens the structure.

Laying the paving

The methods of laying crazy paving are similar to those using regular paving slabs (see pages 64 - 67 and 82 - 85 — with a firm base being the first requirement.

To prepare the base remove the topsoil and compact the area using a roller or tamper. If the ground is soft or crumbly add a layer of hardcore and compact this into the surface. A blinding layer of sand added to the top accommodates any unevenness in the hardcore base and acts as a firm bed for the slabs.

Lay the slabs on generous mortar dabs under each corner or, with smaller pieces, on an overall mortar bed.

Work your way across the dry-laid surface,

READY REFERENCE

PATH LAYING

When laying a path in crazy paving:
● place the larger straight-sided slabs first as the path edging, if these are to be straight
● place the largest irregularly-shaped slabs down the centre of the path, fill in between the edging and centre slabs with small broken fragments.

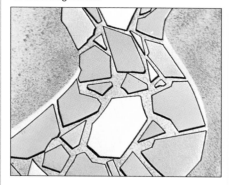

SLAB THICKNESS

Remember when laying crazy paving that the slabs might be of different thicknesses and you'll have to accommodate these variations in the thickness of the mortar bed.

PREPARING THE BASE

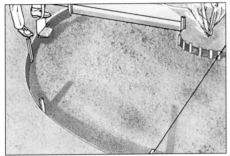

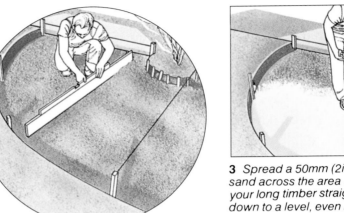

1 Mark out the area to be paved using pegs and string, and remove the topsoil (above). Then tamp the subsoil down all over (below), adding hardcore if needed.

2 Having thoroughly compacted the surface and filled any hollows, check that it is flat in both directions using a long timber straight edge. Allow for a slight drainage fall in one direction across the paved area by scraping away soil from the base so that your spirit level bubble is slightly off centre.

3 Spread a 50mm (2in) thick layer of sand across the area (above). Then use your long timber straight edge to tamp it down to a level, even bed (below).

bedding each stone in turn and checking the level frequently using a builder's level — don't forget to incorporate a slight drainage fall to one side of a path or to the front of a patio or step treads. Tap the paving in place using the handle of your club hammer: as you do this some mortar will be squeezed up into the joints, which can be anything up to 25mm (1in) wide. You needn't scrape out this mortar from the joints: it actually makes for a stronger bond.

After you've laid the slabs point between them with mortar (see *Ready Reference*). Be careful not to smear any on the faces of the slabs otherwise they will stain. Alternatively you can leave the joints mortar-free and brush in soil later in which to plant low growing plants or herbs.

If you have used crazy paving for patio or path surfaces, you may also want to give your garden a unified look by cladding steps and low walls.

On steps, start at the bottom of the flight and clad the lowest riser first. Build up the cladding 110m ground level, buttering mortar onto the back of each piece of paving and pressing it firmly into place against the riser. Finish cladding the riser with pieces that fit flush with the existing step surface, and then lay paving on the surface of the tread so that those at the front overlay the riser by about 25mm (1in). Clad all the risers and treads, then point between the pieces. Clad low walls in the same way as step risers.

DRY-LAYING THE SLABS

1 When you've marked out the shape of your paved area and dug out and prepared the foundations, start to dry-lay the slabs in one corner.

2 Separate the straight-edged slabs from the irregular-shaped ones and dry-lay the largest pieces at the perimeter of your marked-out area.

3 Fill in small gaps between the perimeter slabs with straight-edged fragments, but avoid a run of small pieces, as it makes a weaker edge.

4 When you've placed all of the perimeter slabs you'll be able to see what the overall effect will be: swap them about for the best-looking plan.

LAYING THE PAVING

1 When you're satisfied with the positions of the slabs you can start to bed them on a fairly stiff mortar mix; lay the large ones on five dabs of mortar.

3 Bed each slab level with the ones next to it by tapping it gently with the handle of your club hammer. Allow mortar to squeeze out between the joints.

5 Check at intervals across the tops of the slabs with a builder's level to ensure they're bedded evenly. Tap them in place with the handle of a club hammer.

7 If you want to make a feature of the joints fill them with soil rather than mortar and add some low-growing plants to give a natural, established look.

TIP

2 You can lay smaller pieces on a continuous mortar bed. Trowel ridges in the mortar: this aids levelling and provides a stronger bond.

4 Mortar in the perimeter slabs first then start to in-fill with smaller, irregular-shaped pieces, using different colours for a more varied pattern.

6 Mortar joints can be up to 25mm (1in) wide. Make the joint flush with the slabs but don't spill mortar on the slab faces, or it will stain them.

8 After you've pointed the joints, or filled them with soil, brush over the surface of the paved area with a stiff-bristled broom to remove any debris.

READY REFERENCE

POINTING PAVING

There are three ways to treat the joints between crazy paving:
- Flush pointing — fill the joints with mortar flush with the tops of the slabs.
- Bevelled pointing — form bevels in the mortar about 9mm (³/₈in) deep at each side of the joint to outline the shape of each slab.
- Soil joints — fill the joints with soil and plant low-growing plants or herbs to blend in the paving with the rest of the garden.

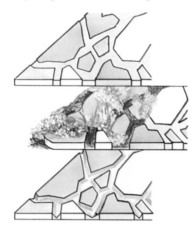

TIP: BREAKING LARGE SLABS

A delivery of crazy paving might include some pieces too large to lay. Break them by dropping them on any hard surface — easier than using a bolster chisel and club hammer. Use these tools for trimming smaller pieces.

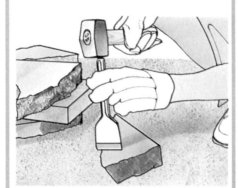

COLOURED POINTING

Make a feature of the joints in crazy paving by colouring the mortar. Additives are available for adding to the mix but you should follow the maker's instructions precisely — too great a proportion of colouring can upset the strength of the mortar.

For more information on laying paving slabs see pages 64 - 67 and 82 - 85.

BUILDING A PAVED PATIO

Building a patio close to the house is one way of transforming a dull and featureless garden into a durable paved area that's geared especially for outdoor living.

A patio makes a versatile summertime extension to the house, providing space for dining, entertaining, or merely for relaxing and soaking-up the sun. You must plan your patio to take advantage of the best aspect and construct it from materials that are both in keeping with the house and garden and durable enough to withstand harsh weather conditions.

Siting the patio

Patios are usually sited as close to the house as possible – ideally adjoining it – or at least nearby for easy access. The best aspect is south-facing, but whichever way your garden faces, you should examine the proposed site at different times of the day during the summer to see how shadows fall. Neighbouring buildings, or your own house, might obscure the sun and this will severely limit the use of the patio. Unfortunately there's nothing you can do about this, but if the obstruction is just a tree or tall hedge you might be able to prune it.

Some shadows can be used to your advantage: although you might want to lie sun-bathing at certain times of the day, you'll appreciate the shade while you eat. If there's no natural shade, you could attach an awning to the house wall, which can be folded away when not needed. A pergola or trellis on which you can train climbing plants will also provide shade where you need it. Or you might prefer simply to allow enough space for a table with an umbrella or a swing seat with a canopy.

What size patio?

In theory a patio may be as large or small as you wish, but in practice you'll be limited by available space. Try to relate the dimensions of the patio to the needs – and size – of your household. Measure your garden furniture and allow enough space around it so that you won't be cramped: the patio must measure at least 2.4m (8ft) from front to back to enable you to position furniture and allow free passage. In general a patio measuring about 3.7m sq (12ft sq) is big enough to take a four-seater table or four loungers.

To work out the size and position of the patio make some preliminary sketches of the garden with the proposed patio in various locations. When you've decided upon a suitable scheme transfer your ideas to a scale plan on graph paper. Cut out a paper template of the patio and use it in conjunction with the plan to help you decide upon the best position.

What type of surface?

There is a wide range of paving materials available in various shapes, sizes and colours and you should choose those which blend with materials used around the house exterior and garden for a sense of unity. The main requisites are that the surface is reasonably smooth, level and free-draining. Whatever your choice of paving, avoid too great a mix – two types are usually sufficient to add interest without making the surface look cluttered. You can, however, include confined areas of small-scale materials such as cobblestones and granite setts to add a textural change to an otherwise flat scheme composed of larger slabs.

Cobblestones – oval pebbles – can be laid in three ways: on a continuous mortar bed over hardcore foundations; on a bed of dry mortar 'watered in' by watering can; or loosely piled on top of each other on compacted earth. Granite setts are durable square-shaped blocks with an uneven

PREPARING THE BASE

1 Set a long prime datum peg in a hole 300mm (1ft) deep at one side of the patio. Its top should be 150mm (6in) below the house dpc.

2 Set a second peg at the other side, level with the first. For a very wide patio use intermediate datum pegs set 1.5m (5ft) apart.

3 Use a string line to set timber pegs accurately in line with each other so that they outline the proposed perimeter of the patio.

4 Check with a builder's square to make sure that the corners of the patio are perfectly square. Adjust the peg positions if they are not.

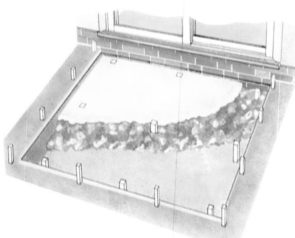

5 Dig out the site to a depth of about 230mm (9in), saving the top-soil and turf. Then compact the earth with a garden roller.

6 Drive in pegs 1.5m (5ft) apart over the entire area. Check that they are level with the datum peg and each other using a spirit level.

7 Fill the hole with hardcore, then compact it thoroughly to a depth of about 125mm (5in) using a tamper. Don't disturb the pegs.

8 Rake out and roll a 50mm (2in) layer of sand over the hardcore. The peg tops should be level with the sand surface.

LAYING THE SLABS

1 Start to lay the slabs at the corner marked by the prime datum peg. You can lay them dry on the sand bed, without using any mortar.

2 As you progress across the patio you should check frequently with a builder's level that the slabs are bedded evenly on the sand.

3 Lift up any slabs that are unevenly bedded and trowel in some more sand until the bed is filled out and the slabs are flush with their neighbours.

4 Alternatively you can lay the slabs on dabs of fairly stiff mortar, one placed under each corner of the slab and one under the centre.

5 Position the slab carefully on top of the mortar dabs. Space out the slabs using offcuts of timber 9mm (³⁄₈in) thick for pointing later.

6 Bed down the slabs using the handle of your club hammer. If any of the slabs are too low, remove them and add more mortar to the dabs.

7 Stretch the string lines across the patio every second course to help you align the slabs accurately.

8 When all the slabs are laid, brush a dry mortar mix between the joins and remove any excess from their faces. This will form a bond when watered in.

9 Water in the dry mortar mix with clean water from a watering can fitted with a fine rose. Avoid over-watering or you'll wash away the mortar.

surface texture, and can be laid on sand or mortar.

Other small-scale paving materials that can be used in large or small areas include concrete blocks, brick pavers and paving-quality bricks. They're available in various colours and the blocks also come in a range of interlocking shapes. Lay these materials in patterns for best effect and use coloured mortar joints as a contrast.

You can also use special frost-proof ceramic tiles for a patio surface but they are very expensive and need a perfectly flat base if they are to be laid correctly. Consequently, they're really only suitable for very small patios.

Probably the simplest of surfaces is one made of a solid slab of cast concrete. Although the concrete can be coloured with pigments, many people find its surface appearance unattractive.

Concrete paving slabs are probably the best materials for a simple rectangular patio. Made with reconstituted stone, they're available in a range of reds, greens, yellows and buff tones with smooth, riven or patterned faces. Square, rectangular, hexagonal and half-hexagonal shapes are also made and they're easy to lay on a sand bed. Broken concrete slabs, known as crazy paving (see pages 79 - 81 for details), can also be used as a patio surface, laid on a mortar bed.

Link the patio to the rest of the garden by building walls, paths and steps (see pages 64 - 78 inclusive) in matching or complementary materials.

Marking out patterns
Whatever paving materials you choose you have enormous flexibility in the design of your patio. There's no reason why, for instance, it should be square or rectangular – most of the materials previously described can be laid in curves or can be cut to fit other shapes and angles.

Sketch out some patterns and dry-lay the paving in both width and length to test how the designs work in practice. Adjust the pattern or the dimensions of the patio to minimise the number of cut pieces you use. This will ensure the surface looks 'balanced'.

Concrete slabs can be laid in various grid and stretcher bond patterns but, for a more informal effect, whole and half slabs can be used together in a random fashion. Crazy paving should be laid with larger, straight-edged pieces at the borders and smaller fragments inside. You can lay bricks in herringbone or basket-weave designs.

Setting the levels
Draw your plan on graph paper, then use it to transfer the shape of the patio onto the site. Use strings stretched between pegs to mark

out the perimeter of the patio. You must also drive pegs in to represent the surface level of the patio, so to ensure they're accurately placed you have to drive a 'prime datum' peg into the ground against the house wall (if the patio is to abut the house). The peg should indicate one corner of the patio and should be set in a hole about 300mm (1ft) deep with its top 150mm (6in) below the level of the house damp-proof course. If the soil is spongy you may have to dig deeper in order to obtain a firm enough surface on which to lay the foundations.

Set a second peg in the ground against the wall to mark the other side of the patio, and check that the level corresponds to that of the prime datum peg by holding a long timber straight-edge between the two and checking with a spirit level.

All other marking-out strings and pegs should be taken from the base line formed between these two datum pegs. Indicate squares and rectangles by stretching strings from the two pegs and checking the angle with a builder's square. Plot out curves by measuring from the base line at intervals and driving in pegs at the perimeter, or use lengths of string or a long hosepipe to mark the curves. Circles and half-circles can be marked out by taking a string from a peg placed as the centre of the circle: you place the first slabs or other paving along the string, then move it around the radius and set the next row.

If size permits, you could incorporate planting areas in your patio by leaving sections un-paved, or simply place tubs of plants on the perimeter.

Laying the paving
When you've marked out the shape of your patio, remove the topsoil (which you should save for use elsewhere in the garden) from within your guidelines and set intermediate datum pegs at 1.5m (5ft) intervals over the entire area of the excavation. These pegs have to be sunk to the level of the prime datum peg, using a spirit level on a batten between the pegs. Now is the time to set the drainage fall away from the house.

When you've set the levels, fill the hole with hardcore, which you must compact thoroughly by rolling and tamping. Then a layer of sand rolled out flat over the hardcore brings the level of the foundation up to that of the peg tops, and provides a flat base for the paving.

On a site that slopes away from the house you'll have to build a low retaining wall of bricks or blocks; the ground behind it can be filled with hardcore and then paved. However, where the ground slopes towards the house you must excavate the patio site in the bank (forming a drainage fall away from the house), and build a retaining wall.

READY REFERENCE

PREPARING THE FOUNDATIONS
Patio paving requires foundations of compacted hardcore covered with a blinding layer of sand. The excavation should be:
● about 150 to 200mm (6 to 8in) deep to allow for 75 to 125mm (3 to 5in) of hardcore plus the sand and paving
● about 230mm (9in) deep if the patio is to be built up to a house wall, so the paving can be set 150mm (6in) below the dpc.

ALLOWING FOR DRAINAGE
To ensure run-off of rainwater the patio surface must slope by about 25mm in 3m (1in in 10ft) towards a suitable drainage point, which might be an existing drain or soakaway.

On ground sloping away from the house: construct perimeter walls for the patio from brick, block or stone, to form a 'stage'. Infill with hardcore and a blinding layer of sand and gravel, then pave. The walls must be set on 100mm (4in) deep concrete footings.

On ground sloping towards the house: excavate the site for the patio in the bank, forming a fall away from the house. Build a retaining wall to hold back the earth.

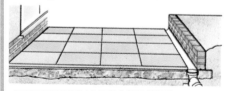

INSPECTION CHAMBERS
The patio must not interfere with access to drainage inspection chambers. If drain covers are within the patio area:
● build it up to the level of the new surface
● cover it with loose-laid slabs for access.

TIP: PAVING ROUND TREES
If you're paving around a tree or shrub to make a garden feature, keep the paving at least 300mm (1ft) from the trunk to allow rainwater to reach its roots.

For more information on laying paving slabs see pages 58-67.

LAYING BLOCK PAVING

Concrete block pavers can be used to make a durable and decorative surface for a drive, path or patio. They're quick and easy to lay in an interlocking pattern on a sand bed – and no mortar is needed.

A path or patio must be durable enough to withstand fairly heavy traffic – from people, wheelbarrows, other garden equipment and furniture; and a drive has the additional weight of a car to contend with. So the surface must be tough and long-lasting.

But traditional surfacing materials – commonly cast concrete, asphalt and paving slabs – tend to give a plain, slab-like appearance, which often detracts from other features. 'Flexible' paving, however, is a method of making a hard surface that's both attractive and easy to lay.

Using concrete pavers

This type of surface uses concrete paving blocks, small-scale units that are very tough and can be laid in numerous patterns. Each block interlocks with its neighbours to form a solid, firm and decorative surface capable of supporting fairly heavy loads.

Concrete paving blocks are made in a variety of shapes (see 'Types of block') some with a rough texture for a more natural effect, others with smooth faces for a formal setting. They're also made in a choice of reds, blues, greys, charcoal and buff tones, and some have a mottled effect that resembles old brick. The simplest types of blocks are rectangular – usually about 200 x 100mm (8 x 4in) and about 65mm (2½in) thick. Some have a bevel or 'mock joint' on their top edge so that the shape of each block – and the bonding pattern – is accentuated when laid in a large area.

Other types – approximately the same size overall as the rectangular ones – incorporate zig-zag edges, some sharp, some gently rounded, which mate together when laid. There are basically three bonds in which you can lay concrete blocks: herringbone, stretcher and parquet (see 'Forming patterns with blocks').

By using the irregular-shaped blocks you can also create a rippling effect across the area of paving.

Herringbone is the strongest bond and ideal for drives, where the wearing and load from cars is considerable; stretcher and parquet bonds aren't as tough and so they're better for areas that will receive lighter traffic.

It's also possible to create variations on standard bonds, by laying blocks in pairs, for example, or mixing two bonds in an area of paving.

Laying the blocks is straightforward: they're simply positioned on a layer of sand between permanent edge restraints (see 'Site preparation') and are bedded down by vibration, using a special machine which you can hire. Suitable edge restraints are: existing paving, kerbstones set in concrete, a house or garden wall, pegged boards or a row of bricks. In most types of flexible paving no mortar is needed, either to bed the blocks or to point the joints between them. For this reason it's quite simple to remove the blocks whenever you like and reposition them on a new sand bed in a new bonding pattern.

Preparing the base

The base for your paving must be firm and level. Firstly, clear all weeds, and loose materials from the area. Dig out any soft spots and fill the holes with firmer soil – or even broken rubble – then compact the surface thoroughly using a garden roller.

If you're making a drive or other area that's to be used for vehicular traffic you should excavate the site and lay a firm base of at least 100mm (4in) of clean, fine hardcore, which you should also compact thoroughly.

Areas that are only to be used for foot traffic, such as paths and patios, will probably only need a base of compacted soil, unless the surface is clay or soft, peat soil; here, the base should be the same as for drives.

The base must be at least 115mm (4½in)

TYPES OF BLOCK

Block paving may be fired clay (A) or concrete (B, C and D – like small paving slabs). The clay ones are usually rectangular, but the concrete types come in a range of interlocking shapes as well. The surface texture is fairly coarse, and most have chamfered top edges to give the effect of a mock joint when laid.

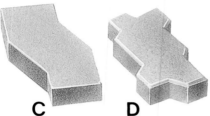

A **B** **C** **D**

Forming patterns with blocks

1 Interlocking blocks such as type D above look highly attractive when laid in a parquet bond of alternating pairs. They can also be laid in a herringbone pattern.

2 So-called 'fishtail' blocks (type C above) look best when laid in stretcher bond. The effect is of undulating lines in one direction, aligning joints in the other.

3 The simplest way of laying rectangular blocks is in stretcher bond, with successive rows having their joints staggered by half the length of a block.

4 An alternative to stretcher bond that looks very attractive with the rectangular block format is a simple herringbone pattern. Half-blocks form the edging.

READY REFERENCE

CONCRETE BLOCK FORMAT
Concrete block pavers are available in a variety of shapes, colours and textures (see 'Types of block'). They measure:
● 200 x 100mm (8 x 4in) overall
● 50, 60 or 65mm (2, 2¼ or 2½in) thick.

FOUNDATIONS FOR BLOCK PAVING
Concrete block paving must have firm, level foundations. These should consist of:
● a well-compacted sub-base of soil for light use
● 110mm (4½in) of well-compacted hardcore for heavy traffic
● plus 50mm (2in) of sharp sand levelled and smoothed over the sub-base
● suitable edge restraints.

EDGE RESTRAINTS
To retain the edges of your paved area:
● fix creosoted timber formwork at the perimeter
● bed kerb stones or bricks in concrete
● or lay the paving against an existing wall or fence.

DRAINAGE FALLS
Your paved area must slope away from house walls. To allow for this:
● fix timber 'datum' pegs into the sub-base at 1.5mm (5ft) intervals so their tops are level with the sand bed
● check across the pegs with a spirit level on a straightedge
● incorporate a fall of about 1 in 50 with a 25mm (1in) thick wedge of timber (shim) under one end of the level.

TIP: LAYING BY HAND
For small, decorative, non-loadbearing areas of paving it's not really worth hiring a plate vibrator. Instead:
● lay the blocks as normal on sand
● bed each in place using an offcut of wood just larger than the block and a wooden mallet.

TIP: CUTTING BLOCKS
To cut paving blocks:
● chop along the cutting line with a club hammer and bolster chisel, or
● use a hydraulic stone splitter or guillotine.

LAYING BLOCK PAVING

SITE PREPARATION

Bed the blocks on sand over a levelled hardcore base. The area can be bounded by a wall (A), kerbstones set in concrete (B), pegged boards (C) or bricks (D).

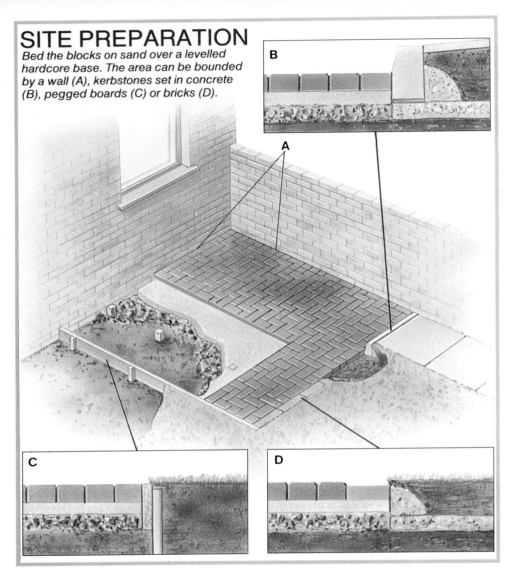

edging stones or a row of bricks on edge can be used, bedded in a strip of concrete, or you could use creosoted lengths of 38mm (1½in) thick softwood screwed or nailed to stout 50 x 50mm (2 x 2in) pegs driven into the ground outside the area you're going to pave. The depth of these battens should equal the thickness of the blocks plus the sand bed.

The sand bed
When you've levelled and compacted the sub-base and have set up the formwork you can lay the bedding sand directly on top. For this you'll need sharp (concreting) sand. As a rough guide to amounts, 1 tonne of sand is ample for 10 sq metres (110sq ft) of paving.

Although the final thickness of the sand bed should be 50mm (2in) you'll have to add more to allow for compaction of the paving.

You'll find it more convenient to work if you divide the load of sand into separate piles and position them at intervals along the site, away from the point at which you want to start laying the blocks.

Spread out the sand evenly over the sub-base, between the edge restraints, using a garden rake, then 'screed' or smooth the surface to the correct level with a straight-edged length of timber that spans the width of the area you're paving. The top of the sand bed should be levelled to about 50mm (2in) below the finished paving (and therefore the level of the edge restraint) when you're using 65mm (2½in) thick blocks, and about 45mm (1¾in) below when using 60mm (2¼in) thick blocks. To allow for this depth you can cut notches in the straightedge to form 'arms' that rest on the formwork; the body of this 'spreader' should be the thickness of the blocks plus about 15mm (½in) for compaction of sand (see 'Site preparation' for more details).

Where you're using an existing wall or fence as an edge restraint you'll have to set a temporary screeding batten on the sub-base, which you can remove after levelling. Fill the groove left by the batten with more sand and level the surface.

Screed the sand in areas only about 2m (6ft) ahead of the blocklaying for convenience and avoid walking on the sand during or after you've levelled the surface.

Laying the blocks
Start to lay the blocks in your chosen pattern against the edge restraint nearest to your pile of blocks. Bed each block up to its neighbours, without any gaps. The blocks can be fairly rough, so you'd be wise to wear thick gloves.

As your area of paving enlarges you should work from a plank laid across the blocks as a kneeling board, to spread the load. Lay plank runs also for transporting barrowloads of blocks from the main pile to the laying edge

below the level of the completed paved surface. The top surface, in turn, must be at least 150mm (6in) below the house damp-proof course (dpc) to prevent moisture rising in the walls or rain splashing up above the dpc.

Setting levels
Unless there's a natural slope to the site you'll have to excavate the base so that the finished surface will slope to one side – or at least away from the house walls – with a fall of about 1 in 40, to ensure efficient drainage of rainwater.

To set the levels over the area of the base drive 300mm (1ft) long timber pegs into the ground at about 1.5m (5ft) intervals and set them at the correct level, taken from a 'prime datum', or fixed point of reference: two bricks below the dpc is adequate, for example. Use a long timber straightedge with a spirit level

on the top edge to check that the pegs are set at the correct depth. Place a small wedge or 'shim' of timber under one end of the spirit level to incorporate an adequate drainage fall (see 'Site preparation').

Edge restraints
The edges of your concrete block paving are best retained, by the walls of your house, garden walls or existing paving: simply setting them against earth won't prevent eventual spreading of the blocks. If your dpc is lower than 150mm (6in), however, you must leave a 75mm (3in) wide channel between the wall and the paved surface to stop rainwater from splashing up and soaking the wall above the dpc. In this case you'd need to fit an edge restraint.

If there isn't a natural or existing edge restraint you'll have to install permanent formwork. Precast concrete, concrete path

LAYING THE BLOCKS

1 Unless the blocks abut a wall, you'll need some sort of edge restraint. Here preservative-treated boards are nailed to stout timber pegs.

2 Start placing the blocks by hand in the pattern you want (here, a herringbone pattern). Leave gaps at the edges to be filled later with cut blocks.

3 As laying proceeds, kneel on a board to spread your weight. This avoids pressure on individual blocks, which could bed them too deep in the sand.

4 If you find that occasional blocks are obviously sitting proud of their neighbours, lift them and scrape away some of the sand beneath before replacing them.

5 Then tap the offending block back into place using the heel of a trowel or club hammer. Similarly, if a block is sitting too low, lift it and add more sand.

6 To avoid having to traipse to and fro for more blocks, fill a barrow with blocks and park it nearby. Use boards to spread the barrow's weight.

7 With stretcher and herringbone patterns, you will have to cut blocks to fill the edge gaps. Hold a block over the gap and score the cutting line on its surface.

8 You can cut paving blocks by hand with a brick bolster and club hammer, but if you have many to cut a hired hydraulic splitter will make light work of the job.

9 Finish off the laying sequence by placing the half blocks in position round the edges of the area as you cut them. Set them level with their neighbours.

to avoid disturbing the blocks you've already laid but haven't compacted.

Cutting the blocks

Although you should use whole blocks wherever possible for maximum strength, you'll certainly need to cut some to size and shape where the paved area contains obstacles such as drains or inspection covers, and where it meets the edge restraints.

It's possible to mark the individual blocks to size and cut them using a club hammer and bolster chisel but you can hire a hydraulic stone splitter or guillotine, which will make the job much easier. Keep the guillotine close to the edge of the paving for convenience. If you must stand it on the paving, rest it on a board so you don't mark or upset any of the blocks. If you use a hammer and chisel be sure to wear gloves and goggles to protect your eyes from flying fragments.

Compacting the blocks

When you've laid a large enough area of blocks bed them firmly into the sand using a plate vibrator fitted with a rubber sole plate. This will settle the blocks into place and force sand up into the joints, without damaging them.

The plate vibrator should have a plate area of 0.2 to 0.3sq metres (2 to 3sq ft), a frequency of 75 to 100 Hz and a centrifugal force of 7 to 20kN, to ensure the blocks will be bedded correctly. Most machines of this type will fit easily into the boot of a car.

Make two or three passes over the paving with the plate vibrator in order to bed the blocks to the correct level, but avoid lingering in one place or you might sink them too low. Also, don't take the machine closer than 1m (3ft) to the unrestrained edge you're laying or you're likely to form a dip in the surface.

Finishing the paving

Finally, simply brush sand onto the paved surface and make a few more passes with the plate vibrator to force the sand down between the blocks.

If you're laying a very small, mainly decorative, area of blocks that won't be used for vehicles – a narrow border around a flower bed, for instance – it's acceptable to lay them without using the vibrator, although the job is more laborious and the results won't be as durable

Instead lay a thinner sand bed, moistened with water from a watering can fitted with a fine rose, and level and compact this with a straight-edged tamping board. Lay the blocks as previously described but bed each as level as possible using a wooden mallet with an offcut of timber just larger than the block (see *Ready Reference*). Water more sand into the joint, again using your watering can, to complete the area of paving.

COMPLETING THE JOB

1 *Vibrate the blocks into the sand bed with a hired plate vibrator. You can avoid marking the blocks by running the machine over some old carpet.*

2 *After the first passes with the plate vibrator, scatter sand over the surface and brush it well into the gaps between the individual blocks.*

3 *Run the plate vibrator over the surface again, making two or three passes over each area, to compact the sand between the blocks thoroughly.*

4 *Finish off the paving by brushing off excess sand with a soft-bristled broom, taking care not to brush out the joints. The paving is ready for immediate use.*

Immediately you've laid the blocks and vibrated them into place, your paved area is ready for use. Inspect the surface after a few months to make sure there aren't any areas that have subsided fractionally. If there are uneven areas you may simply be able to lever out the relevant blocks and re-bed them on more sand.

Paving irregular areas

Because of the small size of the blocks, you can use them to good effect to pave irregularly-shaped areas. Where necessary the blocks can be cut at an angle to form neat edges, and circles can be formed by laying the blocks with wedge-shaped joints instead of parallel-sided ones – rather like forming a brick arch. To achieve perfect curves, lay the blocks using a string line attached to a peg at the centre of the curve, so that by holding the string taut you can align them accurately.

Coping with steps

If you have used blocks for a path or patio, you may want to link these areas with steps paved in the same way. Because of the small size of the blocks it is vital to bed them on mortar rather than on sand, particularly at the edges of the treads. You can still use sand to fill the joints between the blocks and so maintain the overall sense of unity.

Building with blocks

Similarly, you may want to build dwarf walls at the edges of your paved area, and while you could use any garden walling blocks for this there is nothing to stop you using two or three courses of paving blocks instead. The rectangular ones are laid just like bricks with pointed mortar joints between, but the interlocking and fishtail types can also be built up into walls if they are overlapped by half a block and aligned carefully.

WALLS AND WALLING

Using the basic techniques of bricklaying, it's a short step to tackling simple garden walls. Perhaps the simplest type to build is the screen block wall, using square blocks available in a range of attractive pierced designs. Earth-retaining walls must be built more sturdily with an allowance for water drainage. Decorative arches can top off your handiwork.

BUILDING RETAINING WALLS

Regardless of whether your garden is flat or sloping, earth-retaining walls are an ideal way of remodelling it to create interesting features such as a raised lawn, a sunken patio or terraced flower beds.

A sloping garden, although it may be an attractive, natural-looking feature of your property, can be hard work to keep in good order. You'll probably find it tiresome to work on, especially if you have to carry heavy tools and equipment such as the lawnmower to the top.

You can, however, landscape the shape of the bank into a series of flat terraces, connected by steps which not only offer easier access when gardening but also give you greater flexibility in planning your planting arrangements.

But you needn't only alter the shape of a sloping plot; it's also possible to re-style a flat, featureless site by building a raised flower-bed, lawn or patio. By digging out areas of your garden you can even create sunken features.

However you design your new scheme you'll have to incorporate in it a solid, load-bearing barrier called a retaining wall, which must be strong enough to support your re-modelled earth and prevent the soil from spilling onto the lower level.

Planning a retaining wall
The scale of your wall largely depends on the amount of earth it's to retain and the steepness of the bank. But if it's to be over about 1.2m (4ft) high, you should consult your local authority. They may demand that you include some form of safety measures for the structure or that you adhere to certain building standards, especially if it's part of a boundary wall, where it could affect public access.

Start planning by sketching out your landscaping ideas, and try to keep your terraced or sunken features in scale with the rest of the garden. If you simply want to border a shallow sunken patio or path, for instance, or create a raised lawn or flower-bed in a level garden, you could build a fairly low wall, 300 or 600mm (1 or 2ft) high, and lay flat coping stones on top to use as informal seating, or as a display for garden ornaments or plants in containers.

A gradual sloping site with two or more terraces will allow you more scope for varied planing than a single, high 'platform' would, and also forms a much stronger structure because there's less weight bearing on the individual walls.

Where you're building a flight of steps in a bank (see section on page 76) to connect your terraces, you may need to include 'stepped' retaining walls at each side to stop the earth from spilling onto the treads.

When you're remodelling your ground don't forget to set aside any topsoil and re-use it for any new planting beds. The remaining areas that you excavate for foundations must be well consolidated or compacted, then levelled, on a layer or hardcore, so that they're firm enough for normal traffic without danger of subsiding.

Laying the foundations
The prime requirement for your wall, whatever building material you use, is to build it on adequate foundations set below the frost line (see *Ready Reference*).

In effect, your foundations should be a cast concrete strip or 'raft' foundation (see section on page 48-52) the length of the wall and about twice its width. For example, for a typical 225mm (9in) thick brick wall 1.2m (4ft) high, built on clay soil, you'll have to lay your concrete 500mm (20in) wide and 150mm (6in) thick. Set the entire foundation in a trench about 500mm (20in) below soil level. In very loose soil you'll have to increase the width of the strip, or build a 'key', which projects down at the toe, or outer edge of the

(see section on page 76)

(see section on page 48-52)

READY REFERENCE

PARTS OF THE WALL
A retaining wall must have enough mass and sufficiently solid foundations to resist the lateral, or sideways, pressure of piled earth and the water that builds up within it. A typical retaining wall up to 1.2m (4ft) high should consist of:
● cast concrete strip foundations (A) the length of the wall, 500mm (20in) wide, 150mm (6in) thick, and set in a trench 500mm (20in) below soil level
● rigid construction using bricks (B), blocks or stone
● adequate drainage from the back of the wall (C).

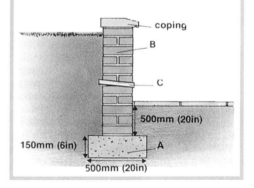

BUILDING UP TO GROUND LEVEL

1 Start laying the first bricks at a corner if one is planned, at one end of the wall otherwise. Bed down the bricks in the outer 'skin' first.

2 Having laid several bricks on each side of the corner, lay the first course of the inner 'skin' alongside them. Note how the bond is arranged.

3 With the first course complete at the corner, check with a builders' square that there is a perfect right angle inside and outside the corner.

4 Return to the corner, and start to lay the second course of brickwork in the outer skin, scraping off excess mortar with the side of the trowel.

5 After laying two or three courses of stretchers, lay the next course as headers – a bonding pattern known as English Garden Wall bond.

6 As you add each course to the wall, check that it is level, that the faces of the wall are truly vertical and that the corner is a true right angle.

TIP

7 When the footings reach ground level, form drainage holes in the wall by bedding short lengths of plastic waste pipe in a generous mortar bed.

8 Check that the pipe slopes down towards the outer face of the wall at a slight angle so that it will drain water away efficiently.

9 With the piece of pipe in place, you will have to cut the bricks in the inner and outer skin of the wall to maintain the bonding pattern.

10 *Continue building up the wall above ground level, alternating three to five courses of stretchers with a course of headers.*

11 *As an alternative to building in short lengths of pipe to provide drainage, you can form weep holes – simple gaps left between the bricks.*

12 *Where you have left weep holes in the ground-level course, lay the next course as stretchers to bridge them and maintain the wall's strength.*

foundation, to help prevent the wall sliding forwards under pressure from the retained earth (see *Ready Reference*).

Choosing walling materials

Your earth-retaining wall must have enough mass, as well as sufficiently solid foundations, to resist the lateral, or sideways, pressure of the retained soil and the rainwater that collects in it (see *Ready Reference*). So long as you provide this strength, you can build your wall from most common building materials – bricks, concrete or stone blocks, cast concrete, and even timber. Which you choose depends on the visual effect you want to achieve and on the conditions you're building in.

Bricks must be dense and durable to withstand the damp conditions to which your wall will be exposed, and can give a neat, formal appearance in a garden that has rigidly defined areas, such as lawn, patio and rockery. Choose 'special quality' or special engineering bricks which are quite impervious and ideal in wet surroundings. Ordinary quality or common bricks are far too porous and susceptible to frost damage, although if your wall's going to be fairly small and in a sheltered situation you can use the more attractive second-hand ordinaries in conjunction with a water-proofing treatment (see below).

The strength of a brick wall is in its bonding and the mortar mix used. A brick retaining wall, therefore, must be built a minimum of 225mm (9in) – or one whole brick – thick in a tough bond such as Flemish, English, or English Garden Wall bond (see pages 26-31) for strength.

Concrete blocks, which are much larger than bricks and much lighter to handle enable you to build a high wall relatively quickly. They're available either solid or with hollow cavities to take reinforcement (see *Ready Reference*, page 97). Make sure you choose dense quality blocks that are suitable for use underground.

If you don't like the plain, functional look of concrete blocks you can clad the completed wall with a cement render, or coat it with a textured masonry paint. A rendered finish, though, is likely to crack eventually in damp conditions. Alternatively you can just use the blocks underground and continue the wall above ground with bricks. Concrete blocks should be laid in stretcher bond to give the strongest structure.

Decorative concrete walling blocks are suitable for low retaining walls; they're available both in brick size and in the larger 215x440mm (9x18in) size, and usually have a split-stone or riven face for a more natural, softer look. They also come in a range of reds, greens, and buff tones for a more attractive finish. You should only use this

READY REFERENCE

DRAINING THE BANK
To prevent a build-up of rainwater behind the retaining wall:
● leave vertical joints free of mortar every 1m (3ft) just above lower ground level to act as weep holes, or
● bed 75mm (3in) diameter drainage pipes in the wall every 1m (3ft) just above lower ground level
● additionally, bury lengths of pipe in pockets of gravel behind the wall to drain water to the sides of the wall
● include a trench 200mm (8in) wide, filled with layers of compacted bricks, pebbles or gravel for rapid drainage.

TIP: WATERPROOF THE WALL
Although it's impossible to waterproof an earth-retaining wall totally, you can reduce the risk of serious damp penetration by:
● painting the back face of the wall with two coats of bituminous paint, or
● tacking a 250-gauge thick polythene sheet to the back face of the wall.

PREVENTING LANDSLIDES
In loose soils your wall may tend to be pushed forward by the weight of the retained earth. To prevent this:
● form a 'key' at the toe of your strip foundation
● set your wall and foundation at an angle or 'batter' – no more than 1 in 5 – into the bank
● build the bank side of the wall in steps, becoming narrower at the top.

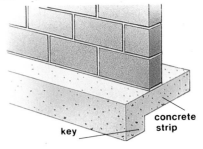

key   concrete strip

INSTALL MOVEMENT JOINTS
A long retaining wall will need a break in the bond, called a movement joint, which allows for seasonal expansion or contraction and prevents the masonry from cracking. Joints should be:
● the height of the wall
● filled with strips of expanded polystyrene
● pointed with a weak mortar mix to conceal the polystyrene filling.
In a brick wall:
● leave joints every 3.6m (12ft)
In a block wall:
● leave joints every 1.8m (6ft)

COMPLETING THE WALL

1 Instead of English Garden Wall bond, you can use Flemish bond; each course has alternate stretchers and headers laid as shown.

2 When your wall has reached the height you want, finish it off with a soldier course – a course of bricks laid on edge to form a coping.

3 Since the top of the wall is the most exposed, ensure that a complete layer of mortar is 'chopped' down between each of the soldiers.

4 Complete the soldier course by pointing neatly between the bricks. Rounded joints, formed with a piece of metal or hosepipe, look neatest.

5 Finish the job by brushing down all the wall surfaces with a soft brush to remove any excess mortar that could stain the brickwork.

6 Leave the wall to stand for a few days, then start to back-fill behind it, tamping the soil down gently but firmly as the level rises.

type of block above ground. Use the same bonding patterns as bricks for a stronger structure.

A cast concrete retaining wall is tough and durable. but it has a drab. slab-like appearance and calls for the construction of sturdy timber formwork to mould the mix while it hardens. If you think you'll need such a robust structure you can make it look a little more attractive by adding a pigment to the mix.

You can even build a dry stone retaining wall for an unobtrusive cottage-style garden wall, although it's not suitable for holding high banks or heavy soil weights. The irregular soil-filled gaps between each stone make ideal places for introducing creeping plants to mellow the overall look of the wall. In this type of wall, each stone must be tilted downwards into the bank, forming a slanted or 'battered' wall. This will increase the strength of the structure, and will also give it a much less formal appearance.

Naturally rot-resistant hardwoods or pre-servative-treated timber can be used to make a wooden earth retaining wall, or you can use it as cladding for a concrete or blockwork wall. Railway sleepers, for instance, which you can often buy from specialist suppliers, can be used to make sturdy retaining walls if you pile them on top of each other, or stick them in the ground vertically, and support them with steel rods or stout fence posts set in concrete foundations. You could even stack concrete or wooden fence posts in this fashion, or in a dove-tailed design, to leave small soil-filled gaps between each post for planting.

Reinforcing the wall

Brick walls and walls made of small-scale block materials are susceptible to bulging outwards under pressure. You can reinforce them by setting hooked metal rods in their mortar joints, which project through the back of the wall into the bank where they're 'tied' to blocks of cast concrete called 'deadmen', which act as stabilisers. Timber retaining walls can be reinforced with a similar arrangement of sturdy timber braces set in the bank.

In a hollow concrete block wall you can lay a wider strip foundation on the downhill or outer side of the wall and set in it L-shaped steel rods on which you can slot the blocks for extra reinforcement (see *Ready Reference*), then fill in the block cavities with concrete.

A tall wall over about 1.2m (4ft) high must incorporate supporting columns called 'piers' (see *Ready Reference*) at each end, and also at intermediate positions along its length if it's very long. You may, though, just want to include piers in a smaller wall purely for visual effect, where the wall breaks at each side of a flight of steps, or where the wall must support a heavy gate.

In a brickwork wall you should bond the piers into the structure for strength but in solid block walls you can simply tie a stack-bonded pier to the wall by setting galvanised expanded metal mesh in the horizontal mortar joints.

A wall of hollow concrete blocks can be similarly tied to a matching pier with special metal cramps, and the hollow cavities can then be filled with concrete for extra rigidity.

Another means of reinforcing an earth-retaining wall is to build it thicker at its base, stepping back the courses from the earth side to the final thickness at the top (see *Ready Reference*, page 94).

Long walls must also incorporate breaks in the bond called 'movement joints', which allow for seasonal expansion and contraction. Joints should run the full height of the wall and can be packed with a compressible material such as expanded polystyrene which can then be pointed with a weak mortar mix to conceal the gap. You should leave movement joints at every 3.6m (12ft) in brick walls and at every 1.8m (6ft) in block walls.

Drainage and damp-proofing

Because of their location, buried in the ground and holding back a large amount of earth, retaining walls are susceptible to dampness. It's vital, therefore, that you include adequate drainage in the structure so that the earth behind doesn't become waterlogged and heavy. In the long run this would weaken the wall and could even cause it to collapse. Freezing water trapped behind the wall could also cause the masonry to crack.

You can provide drainage in two areas: at the back of the wall and actually through its face. To drain the back you can set pipes of porous, unglazed terracotta or plastic – slightly sloping and surrounded by gravel to quicken the rate of drainage – behind the wall, just above the foundation. Take the pipe run along the wall to each end, where the rain-water can drain into a soakaway or other suitable drainage point.

To drain the retained bank through the wall you can simply leave 'weep holes' – open mortarless joints – every one metre (3ft) just above ground level, or set short lengths of 75mm (3in) diameter drainage pipe in the wall at these intervals, tilted slightly downwards to the outside.

In very wet areas, or where you're building a high wall, you'd be wise to dig out the earth behind the wall and make an infill trench of well-rammed broken bricks topped with gravel. This will help to relieve the pressure on the wall from expansion as the soil soaks up water in winter.

Where there's an excessive amount of water draining from your wall you should

make a shallow gutter or gully at its base to carry the water to a suitable drainage point.

In addition to providing drainage for the bank you can further protect your wall from damp by applying two coats of bituminous paint to the back face, or by tacking on a sheet of thick 250 gauge polythene. Take care not to damage this membrane when you back-fill behind the wall.

It's not usual to incorporate a damp-proof course (dpc) in a garden wall, but for greater protection from rising damp you can bed a layer of slate between courses, or lay a course of water-resistant engineering bricks at this point instead. If the wall adjoins the house, and rises above the house damp course level for any reason, a vertical dpc must be included between house and wall to prevent any moisture from rising into the house structure.

Finally, you should bed sound copings of concrete or brick on top of your wall, to keep water out of the mortar joints. Precast concrete copings usually have a bevelled top for drainage, project beyond the face of the wall, and have channels called 'drip grooves' under the front edge to prevent water trickling back onto the surface of the wall. You can also buy a variety of special coping bricks with shaped edges for a softer, decorative effect.

Supporting the excavated earth

Where you're building your earth retaining wall in a steep bank, or in loosely-packed earth, you might have to construct a type of 'dam' from temporary timber struts and braces to shore up a series of vertical boards or planks called shuttering. This should be laid directly against the face of the soil to hold it in place while you can dig and lay your concrete strip foundations and build your wall.

On very high walls you might find it easiest to build the shuttering in stages as you excavate the site. You should leave about 300 to 600mm (1 to 2ft) between your proposed retaining wall and the face of the shuttering to allow you plenty of access when laying foundations and building the wall.

Once the foundations have been laid and you've completed the lower courses of bricks or blocks you should start to lay your drainage pipes. Set some actually in the wall, draining to the front, and lay others at the back of the wall, set in gravel or hardcore, to drain the sides.

Continue to build the wall in the normal way and, when it's completed, and you've pointed the joints, you should leave the structure for at least 24 hours to set before removing the shuttering.

Back-fill the wall with well-compacted soil or a porous filling (see *Ready Reference*) and top the wall with concrete or brick copings to complete the structure.

READY
REFERENCE

BUILDING PIERS

Retaining walls over about 1.2m (4ft) high need supporting columns called 'piers' at each end, and at intermediate positions if they're very long. Piers should be:
● a brick or decorative block column bonded into a brickwork or blockwork wall (A)

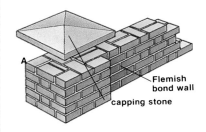

Flemish bond wall

capping stone

● a hollow concrete-filled blockwork column tied alongside a hollow block wall with metal cramps (B)
● a column of blocks tied to a solid block wall with galvanised expanded metal mesh (C).

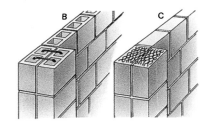

REINFORCING A LARGE WALL

High, heavy-duty walls will require reinforcement to hold back the weight of the earth. Hollow concrete blocks are the simplest to reinforce. To do this:
● set L-shaped steel rods (A) the height of the wall in a wide concrete strip foundation (B)
● slot hollow concrete blocks (C) onto the rods as you build the wall
● fill the cavities in the blocks with concrete (D).

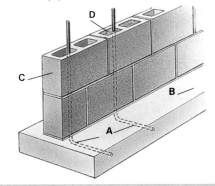

BUILDING ARCHES IN BRICKWORK

An arch can make a decorative feature of your door and window openings – or even give a grand treatment to your garden gate. Here's how to build a basic brick arch.

If you're making a large opening in a wall for a new door, window or serving hatch – or where you're knocking two rooms into one – you must include adequate support for the masonry above, and any load that bears on it. The usual way to span an opening such as this is to bridge it with a rigid horizontal beam called a lintel, or, for very large openings, a rolled steel joist, or RSJ. But this limits you to a square or rectangular opening, which you may not think is really suitable for a more decorative effect.

In the past, arches – although there were many complex, elegant variations on the basic shape – were used for more practical reasons: wider openings could be spanned than was possible with timber or stone lintels, and they were also used in conjunction with lintels or in long stretches of wall to relieve the pressures on the structures.

Nowadays, however, with the development of lightweight steel lintels, RSJs and reinforced concrete lintels – which can be used to span much wider openings – arches aren't a really practical or cost-effective proposition. Consequently they're used mainly for their decorative effect on smaller-scale structures.

How an arch works

An arch works in virtually the same way as a lintel, by transmitting the weight of the walling above, and its load, to solid masonry at each side of the opening.

The individual components of your arch – usually bricks, reconstituted stone or natural stone blocks – are laid on a curve, forming a compact, stable beam.

Types of arch

The type of arch you choose to build depends on whether you simply want a decorative effect or a load-bearing structure.

You can use arches on internal walls as conventional doorways, to create an open-plan scheme between two rooms, or as a serving hatch. On external walls you can form arches above doors and windows, and outdoors they can make an attractive feature of your garden gate, connected to your boundary walls or even to the house.

Decorative arches

If your arch is to be a purely aesthetic feature indoors you don't necessarily have to build a sturdy structure from masonry. Instead you can make a decorative arch to your own specification from plasterboard, hardboard or chipboard panels cut with a curved edge and fixed to the masonry at the sides of the opening underneath the lintel of a conventional doorway. You can use hardboard, which can be bent, for the underside of your arch. You don't need to alter the structure of the wall in any way.

To finish off your arch, if you're careful to conceal the join between it and the wall, you can simply decorate it with wallpaper or textured paint.

Prefabricated arch formers made of galvanised steel mesh offer a ready-made choice of arch profiles. They come in various widths of opening – and you can even buy simple corner pieces to turn an ordinary doorway into an arched opening. The preformed mesh frames are simply attached to the masonry, under the lintel, then they're plastered over to match the rest of the wall. You can even use them outdoors for a rendered arch finish.

Structural arches

However, where your arch is to form an integral and load-bearing part of a wall its construction is rather more complicated. Brick

READY REFERENCE

SIMPLE ARCH SHAPES

Medieval stonemasons arrived at the shape of the perfect arch by trial and error, and went on to develop many elegant and complicated variations on the basic shape. Three simple types are in common use today, and are easy to construct. They are:

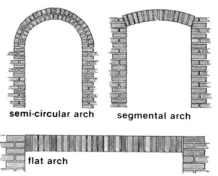

semi-circular arch   segmental arch

flat arch

Flat arches are nowadays usually supported by a steel lintel and so are not truly load-bearing. On spans over about 1.8m (6ft) a flat arch should have a very slight upward curve to counter the optical illusion that it is sagging in the centre.

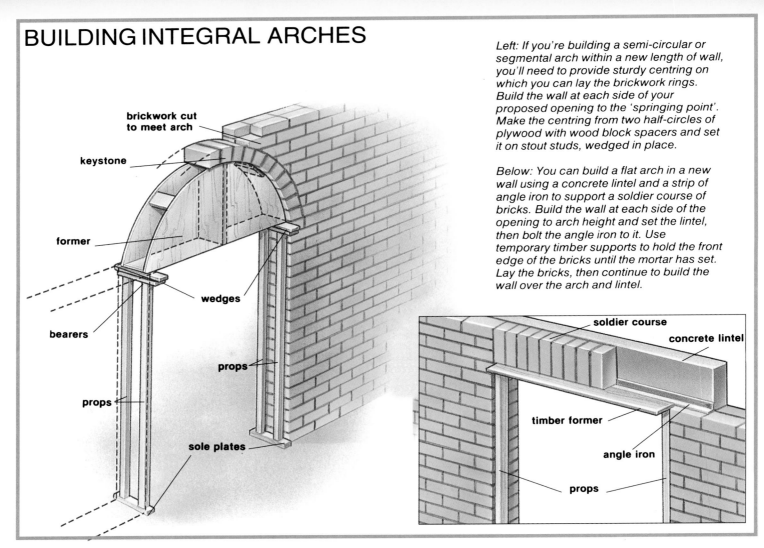

BUILDING INTEGRAL ARCHES

brickwork cut
to meet arch

keystone

former

wedges

bearers

props

props

sole plates

Left: If you're building a semi-circular or segmental arch within a new length of wall, you'll need to provide sturdy centring on which you can lay the brickwork rings. Build the wall at each side of your proposed opening to the 'springing point'. Make the centring from two half-circles of plywood with wood block spacers and set it on stout studs, wedged in place.

Below: You can build a flat arch in a new wall using a concrete lintel and a strip of angle iron to support a soldier course of bricks. Build the wall at each side of the opening to arch height and set the lintel, then bolt the angle iron to it. Use temporary timber supports to hold the front edge of the bricks until the mortar has set. Lay the bricks, then continue to build the wall over the arch and lintel.

soldier course

concrete lintel

timber former

angle iron

props

is probably the best material to use for this type of arch; you can either leave it exposed as a feature or clad it with render outside or plaster inside for a smooth finish.

Arch profiles

There are various types of arch profiles you can make. One of the commonest is the 'flat' arch (see *Ready Reference*). It's suitable for narrow spans up to about 1.2m (4ft) and the bricks – usually special wedge-shaped types – are set to radiate from a central, vertical point, called the 'keystone'. You can make large flat arches by laying conventional-shaped bricks vertically in a 'soldier' course on a steel or concrete boot lintel or resting on a length of angle iron used in conjunction with a concrete lintel (see 'Building integral arches'. above).

On openings wider than about 1.8m (6ft) the brickwork may look as if it's sagging fractionally and you can remedy this optical illusion by laying the bricks so that the centre

of the arch is about 12mm (½in) higher than the ends. One way you can do this is to set the bricks on a curved strip of flat iron instead of the angle iron.

Simpler types of arch, which don't need the use of specially-shaped bricks, or the additional support of a lintel, are the 'semi-circular' (see *Ready Reference*) or 'segmental' types. Both of these arches form part of a circle. The centre of the circle in a semi-circular arch is on the imaginary line between the highest bricks on each side of the opening, from which the arch starts to curve inwards. Its diameter equals the distance between the sides of the opening. For a segmental arch the centre line of the much larger circle which the arch follows is some way below this point.

Because the bricks used for these arches are the conventional format the 'wedging' effect necessary to spread the load of the wall sideways is achieved by shaping the mortar joints between each brick. However, if you are contriving a solid wall above the arch,

you'll have to cut the bricks at each side to fit the arch shape.

Building piers

The base of your arch, called the 'springing point', or the point at which it starts to curve inwards, must be supported on sound brickwork at each side, for it's here that the load of the structure is transferred.

If you're building an arch into an existing wall, or if you're building a new wall containing an arch, the load will be taken on solid bearings at each side. But if you're building a freestanding arch between two walls, such as a surround for a garden gate, you'll have to build separate supporting columns called 'piers' at each side. Build up your piers from 225mm (9in) thick brickwork on concrete foundations (see pages 48-52) making sure that they're set perfectly vertical and that each course matches that of the opposite pier, (see step-by-step photographs on page 99).

BUILDING UP THE PIERS

1 Mark guide lines on the foundations to indicate the line of the arch, and start to build up the first pier – in this case measuring 1½ x 1 bricks.

2 As the first pier rises, check at intervals with your spirit level that it is rising vertically. Tap any out-of-line bricks gently into place.

3 Measure out precisely the separation of the two piers, and start to build up the second pier. Check continuously that the two piers align accurately.

4 When you have laid six to eight courses in each pier, go back and point up the mortar joints while the mortar is still soft.

5 Continue to build up the piers one course at a time, checking at every stage that the courses are level and the pier separation is constant.

6 When the piers have reached the desired height – about 1.5m (5ft) for a garden arch – check the measurements accurately on each pier.

MAKING THE FORMER

1 Using the pier separation to give the diameter of the semi-circular former, draw the curve out on plywood and cut it out with a jig-saw.

2 Nail the first semi-circle to a stout piece of softwood just narrower than the wall thickness, and cut a number of spacers to the same length.

3 Nail on the second semi-circle, and then add the spacers at intervals round the edge of the former to hold it rigid when it's in place.

BUILDING THE ARCH

1 Set timber props at each side of the arch opening. If the brickwork will be continued above the arch, use two props and wedges at each side.

2 Position the former on top of the props, and use a spirit level to check that it is level. Lay the first brick of the inner ring on top of one of the piers.

3 Measure the curve length at each side and divide this by the brick width to indicate how many whole bricks will fill the ring. Mark their positions.

4 Continue adding bricks until you reach the top of the inner ring. Then butter mortar onto both faces of the keystone and tap it into place.

5 Build up the second ring in the same way as the first, trying to avoid aligning the mortar joins in the two rings. Add the second keystone.

6 Leave the former in place for at least 48 hours (and preferably longer) before carefully removing the props and allowing the former to drop out.

Supporting the arch

Semi-circular or segmental arches are usually built on a timber former or support called 'centring'.

If you're building a simple freestanding arch between two piers you can make a fairly lightweight frame from two sheets of plywood cut to the profile you want for your arch (see *Ready Reference* and step-by-step photographs, page 99). Set the former perfectly level at the springing point on timber studs wedged against the piers at each side. You can then build your arch over the former.

If you're building an arch within an existing wall – or if you're building a new wall – you'll have to provide much sturdier centring (see page 98). You'll also need temporary support for the existing walling above the opening. You can do this by setting up adjustable metal props and timber needles which will support the masonry while you build the arch.

Building the arch

With your formwork in position you can start to lay the brickwork for your arch. The best way to do this accurately is to lay the bricks alternately from each side, finishing with the central, topmost, keystone brick.

So that you can keep the mortar joint thicknesses constant throughout the arch you'd be wise first to mark out the positions of each brick on the side of the plywood former as a guide to laying. When you're spacing out the bricks on your 'dry run', remember that the mortar joints will be thicker at the top than at the bottom and that the narrowest point shouldn't be less than 6mm (¼in) thick.

Your arch can have one, two or three 'rings', or courses, of bricks. But you must ensure that as few vertical joints as possible coincide with those on adjoining courses, or this will weaken the arch. Point the joints as you go, while the mortar is still soft.

Finishing the arch

Once you've laid the rings of the arch you can fill in the wall surrounding it, unless your arch is freestanding, and has a curved top. Follow the bonding pattern used for the rest of the wall, cutting the bricks next to the arch to fit the curve.

When you've completed the arch leave the structure for about one week so the mortar hardens then remove the centring. You'll have to rake out the joints underneath the arch and repoint them to match the rest of the brickwork.

HOME PLUMBING

WATER SUPPLY AND DRAINAGE NETWORKS

Very few people are aware of what is involved in supplying clean, drinkable water to their homes, or indeed what happens to waste water when it disappears down a drain. Yet beyond the taps and the waste outlets is a vast network of underground pipes, drains and sewers, pumping stations, reservoirs, water towers and treatment works, all designed to ensure an efficient and constant supply of fresh water and the swift removal of waste.

UNDERSTANDING WATER SUPPLY

Each one of us uses about 160 litres (35 gallons) of water a day, and takes it for granted. Only in a long spell of dry weather comes an awareness that we should use it carefully. Our use is controlled by the supply system - this is how it works.

In the last 50 years the consumption of water has almost doubled. Rising standards of living have given rise to increased consumption, and a greater awareness of the need for hygiene has also played a large role in increasing the demand. Faced with this high demand, supply sources have been hard pressed to keep up.

Where it comes from

Water is supplied by the local water authority (or the 'Undertaking' as it is known in the plumbing trade). After falling as rain it is collected in reservoirs which are fed by streams and rivers, or is pumped from underground wells. Water varies a lot in its chemical makeup since it picks up minerals and gases as it flows. If it picks up calcium, magnesium and sodium salts it will be 'hard' – the menace of pipe systems. Before being distributed it is usually filtered through sand and pebble beds to remove solids and organisms, and may have chlorine added to it to ensure that it is 'potable' – drinkable. Fluoride is also sometimes added for the protection of teeth.

Distribution is carried out by a network of pipes starting with 'trunk mains' which may be as much as 610mm (24in) in diameter. These split into mains and sub-mains which run underneath streets and side streets. It is these sub-mains which are tapped by individual houses for their supply.

The house system may be 'direct' in which all cold water supplies are piped direct from the rising main, with the cistern only being used to supply the hot water tank. Or it may be an 'indirect' system in which all cold-water supplies are taken from the cistern, with the exception of a direct supply to the kitchen sink for drinking purposes.

For water to flow through the trunk mains – and eventually into your house – it must be under a certain amount of pressure. This pressure is assisted by pumps but it is vital that somewhere in the mains system the water should reach a height in a reservoir or water tower, higher than any domestic system it has to supply. The vertical distance through which the water 'falls' is known as the 'pressure head' and without it our

cisterns would never fill up without a lot of expensive additional pumping. The storage cistern also provides a pressure head inside the house, which is why it's preferable to have it in the roof space.

The house system

The sub-main underneath the road is tapped by the 'communication pipe' which ends at the authority's stop-valve. This is usually situated under the pavement about 300mm (1ft) outside the boundary of your property. The stop-valve is located at the bottom of a vertical 'guard' pipe – about 1 metre (39in) deep – which is covered at the surface by a hinged metal cover. It should only be operated by the water authority and requires a special key to turn it. But in a real emergency you may be able to turn it yourself. In old houses it may be the only way of turning off the water supply. After this stop-valve the water enters the service pipe and from then on all pipes become your responsibility.

The service pipe continues under the wall of the property at a depth of at least 750mm (2ft 6in) to protect it from frost – though some water authorities insist that it should be 900mm (3ft) deep. As it travels under the house wall or foundation it usually goes through an earthenware pipe to protect it

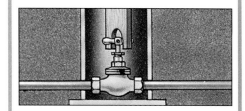
103

INDIRECT COLD SUPPLY

The most common system of water supply in the UK is called 'indirect' because most taps take water from the storage cistern in the roof and not direct from the mains. The cistern is fed by the rising main which in turn is fed by the distribution pipe from the mains.

Water input to the cistern is controlled by a high pressure ball-valve. If this valve jams open the water level rises to flow out of the overflow or 'warning' pipe which should stick well out from the wall.

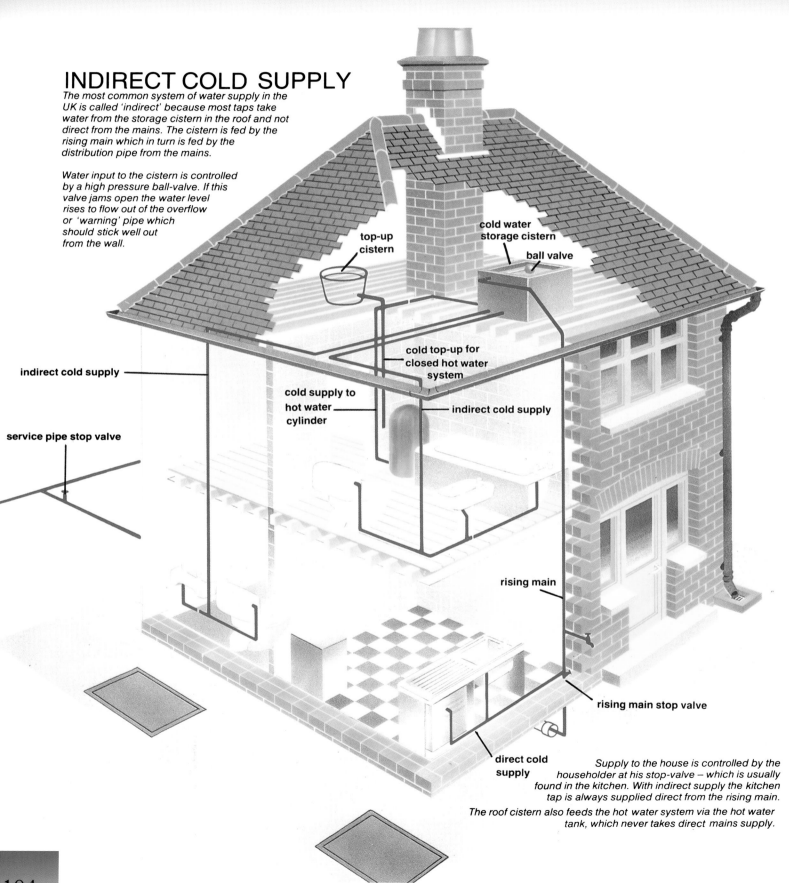

top-up cistern

cold water storage cistern

ball valve

cold top-up for closed hot water system

indirect cold supply

cold supply to hot water cylinder

indirect cold supply

service pipe stop valve

rising main

rising main stop valve

direct cold supply

Supply to the house is controlled by the householder at his stop-valve – which is usually found in the kitchen. With indirect supply the kitchen tap is always supplied direct from the rising main.

The roof cistern also feeds the hot water system via the hot water tank, which never takes direct mains supply.

from possible settlement which might cause it to fracture. To prevent any risk of freezing in cold weather the service pipe should not emerge above ground level until it is at least 600mm (2ft) inside the inside wall surface.

Up to about 40 years ago, service pipes were usually made of lead (in fact the word plumbing originally stemmed from the Latin word for lead – *plumbum*). Today copper and polythene are used instead. The latter is particularly good as it is a poor conductor of heat and is less prone to freezing and fracture.

The service pipe

The service pipe continues under the wall near the kitchen sink, which means that it is often attached to the inner face of the outside wall. This is contrary to the recommendation that it should be attached to an inside wall, and so such a pipe should be lagged with insulation material. The pipe should also be insulated if it comes through any sub-ground floor cavity where it would be subjected to the icy blasts of winter from under-floor ventilation. Again these precautions are both intended to minimise the risk of frost damage.

When the service pipe rises above the ground floor it is called the 'rising main' and it eventually terminates in the supply cistern, which is usually in the roof cavity. The householder's main stop-valve is usually found on the rising main a little way above floor level. This is the most important 'tap' in the house. In any plumbing emergency – when bursts or leaks occur, for example, your first action should be to turn this tap off, thus isolating the house system from the mains water supply. The stop-valve should always be turned off when you go away if the house is going to be empty. In old houses the location of the stop-valve may vary considerably, it may be in the cellar, under the stairs, or even under a cover beneath the front path – or it may not exist at all, in which case the authority's stop-valve is the only control.

Branch supply pipes

At least one 'branch' supply pipe leaves the rising main close above the stop-valve and drain tap – this is to the tap over the kitchen sink. This tap must be supplied direct from the main supply as it is supposed to provide all drinking and cooking water. Water which has been in a storage cistern is no longer considered drinkable, sometimes termed 'potable', as it may be slightly contaminated by debris in the storage cistern.

Other branches may be taken at this point to an outside tap, or to a washing machine or dishwasher.

The rising main continues upwards and while its ultimate destination is the cold water storage cistern the pipework in between will vary from house to house, depending on

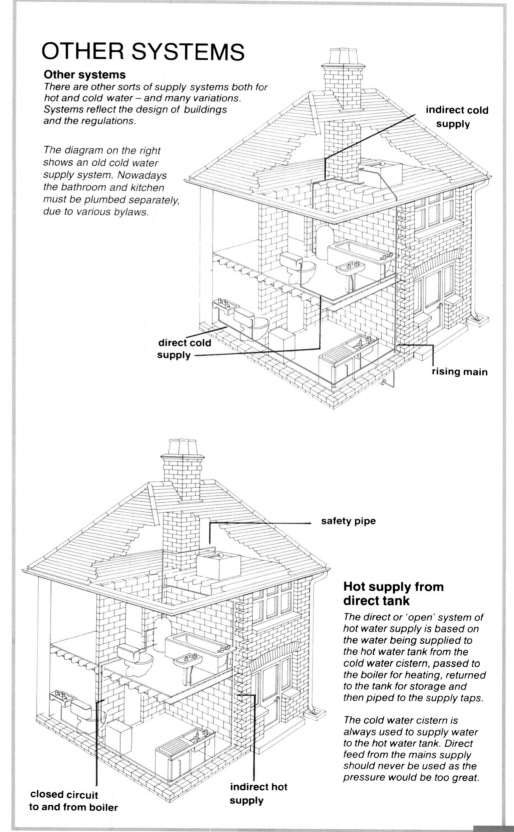

OTHER SYSTEMS

Other systems

There are other sorts of supply systems both for hot and cold water – and many variations. Systems reflect the design of buildings and the regulations.

The diagram on the right shows an old cold water supply system. Nowadays the bathroom and kitchen must be plumbed separately, due to various bylaws.

indirect cold supply

direct cold supply

rising main

safety pipe

Hot supply from direct tank

The direct or 'open' system of hot water supply is based on the water being supplied to the hot water tank from the cold water cistern, passed to the boiler for heating, returned to the tank for storage and then piped to the supply taps.

The cold water cistern is always used to supply water to the hot water tank. Direct feed from the mains supply should never be used as the pressure would be too great.

closed circuit to and from boiler

indirect hot supply

INDIRECT HOT WATER SUPPLY

In an indirect or 'closed' hot water system a closed pipe runs from the boiler, through a heat exchanger in the hot water tank and back to the boiler again. This closed system contains water which never comes into contact with the hot water used by the household. The closed circuit between boiler and hot water cylinder loses water very slowly, and is topped up automatically by water from a small reservoir cistern in the loft. A safety pipe returns over-heated water to this or the main cistern.

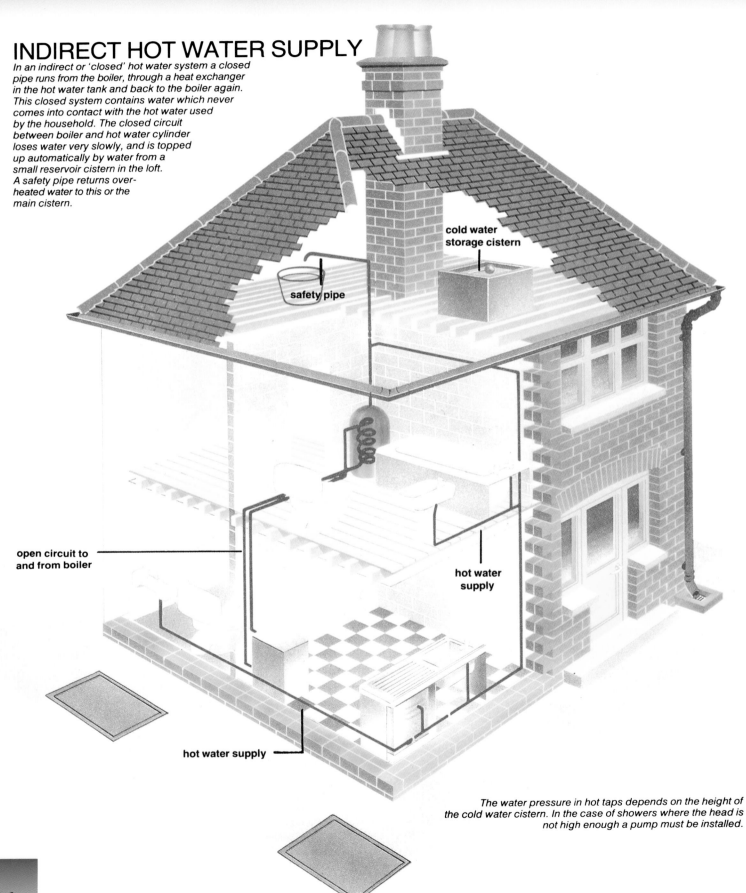

cold water storage cistern

safety pipe

open circuit to and from boiler

hot water supply

hot water supply

The water pressure in hot taps depends on the height of the cold water cistern. In the case of showers where the head is not high enough a pump must be installed.

whether a 'direct' or 'indirect' system has been installed.

In many areas indirect systems must be installed in new buildings, yet in Western Europe direct systems are the rule. Indirect systems have been encouraged because of the difficulty in maintaining constant mains pressure particularly at times of peak demand. Routing of most supplies through the storage cistern evens out fluctuations, and it also rules out the risk of 'back siphonage' whereby dirty water could be sucked back into the mains supply – though this rarely occurs. The 1976 drought in the UK provided good reason for indirect systems, since each house had an emergency supply in the storage cistern if the mains water had to be shut off.

Cisterns

The 'tank' in your loft or attic is in fact a 'cistern'. Cisterns are not sealed – though they should be covered – and so are subject to atmospheric pressure. Tanks are completely sealed – as with a hot water storage tank – and are not subject to atmospheric pressure.

Cold water cisterns ,have traditionally been made of galvanised mild steel and it is quite likely that you will find one like this in your loft. They are still available, but are not usually installed in new houses. Other materials used have been asbestos, cement, copper and glass fibre, but today the most common material is plastic, of which glass fibre reinforced polyester (GRP), polythene and polypropylene are the most common varieties.

The advantages plastics have over all other cistern materials are their lightness in weight, resistance to corrosion and flexibility. Galvanised steel is heavy and liable to corrode, while asbestos and cement are not only heavy but can become porous and are prone to accidental damage. Don't forget the capacity of a typical cistern is 227 litres (50 gallons), and this water alone weighs nearly 0.25 tonne (¼ ton), so all cisterns must be fully supported on the joists. With rigid materials such as steel the cistern can rest across the joists, but with plastic and glass fibre a platform should be installed to support the whole area of the bottom, otherwise the material may develop local weaknesses.

Cisterns should be covered to prevent any contamination of the water. Where the underside of the roof is exposed dust and dirt are liable to fall in. The top and sides should also be insulated to minimise the risk of freezing. The bottom is left uncovered to allow rising warm air from rooms below to keep the water above freezing point, and so you shouldn't insulate the roof space under the cistern.

Cisterns were often installed before the roof was put on and if you want to replace yours, perhaps because it's made of steel and is corroding, you may not be able to get it through the trap door. While it is sometimes suggested that a cistern should be cut up to get it out this is in fact a very heavy and arduous job in such a confined space and it would be better to manoeuvre it to one side and leave it in the loft, installing a new cistern alongside. Modern plastic cisterns can literally be folded up so they can be passed through small loft hatches.

Pipes and taps

Water leaves the storage cistern in distribution pipes which are usually 22mm (¾in) or 15mm (½in) in diameter. In a direct system, supply from the cistern will usually only be to the hot water tank, and in an indirect system this link must also be direct – but other distribution pipes are used with branches to supply the other appliances – basins, baths and WC cisterns. Distribution pipes usually end in taps but in the case of a WC a low pressure ball-valve controls the flow.

The WC in an indirect system has a low pressure ball-valve because when the water leaves the storage cistern it is no longer at mains pressure but at normal atmospheric pressure which is pressing down on the surface of the stored water. This means that the higher up the house a tap or other outlet is situated the lower will be the water pressure. In practice this means that you can't have a tap in an indirect system which is above the level of its distribution outlet from the cistern. Showers are particularly affected by this difference of pressure, and if there is not sufficient 'head' to 'drive' the shower a special pump may have to be installed.

Cold water supplied to the hot water tank is heated in two different ways again called indirect and direct systems – or, respectively, closed and open. In the latter the cold water is circulated through the boiler, where it is heated, and returned to the tank from where it flows to tapped outlets. In the indirect system the cold water supplied never actually goes to the boiler, instead it is heated in the tank by a coiled pipe or jacket containing hot water which is continuously circulating through the boiler. In either case a pump often helps the water flow through the boiler, and supplementary or alternative heat may come from an immersion heater. If there is no boiler but only an immersion heater in the tank the system is essentially direct with the heating of the water taking place in the tank rather than in the boiler.

Draining the system

Just above the rising main stop-valve should be a drain cock. With the stop-valve turned off the drain cock can be used to drain part of the cold water system when repairs are necessary – the hot water system has its own drain cock.

Ready Reference

PIPE SIZES AND THEIR USES

Distribution pipes
● 22mm (¾in) pipe – water supply to bath and hot water cylinder
● 15m (½in) pipe – WC, basin, bidet and shower supplies
● 28mm (1in) pipe – for use with multiple appliances, but usually unnecessary.

Warning pipes (Overflows)
● these must have a diameter greater than that of the inlet pipe to prevent cold water cisterns and WC cisterns from overflowing.

CONNECTIONS AT COLD WATER CISTERN

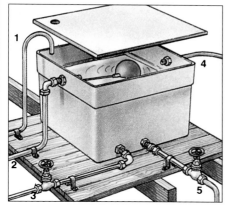

1 safety pipe	**3 cold supply to taps**
2 rising main	**4 overflow**
	5 cold supply to hot water tank

DRAINING THE SYSTEM

To drain the system from the mains stop-valve to cistern, turn off the stop-valve and attach one end of the hose to the drain cock, which should be just above the stop-valve, and run the other end to a drain. Then open the drain cock.
Drain remainder of system by turning off

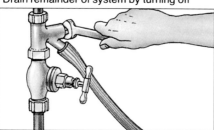

mains supply and opening cold water taps. The hot water system has its own drain cock, usually found close to the boiler.

WASTE WATER SYSTEMS

A waste water system must be able to dispose of used water from the kitchen and bathroom efficiently and hygienically, and also have to cater for rainwater falling on the roof. Here's how it's done.

The supply of hot and cold water to the taps in your house is really only half the domestic plumbing story. You also need a waste system to remove what you've used or don't want. And besides coping with the dirty water from the bath, basin and sink and the waste from the WC, the system also has to deal with the rainwater which falls on the roof.

The drainage system therefore has to be efficient and durable, and for obvious reasons of hygiene, self-cleansing. Waste matter mustn't be allowed to remain in the pipes and if blockages occur it should be possible to remove them easily.

How the drainage system works
There are several domestic drainage systems but each of them can be broken down into five separate sections. When waste water leaves an appliance of any sort, it will go immediately through a 'waste trap' – a 180° bend containing a water seal which fills the trap whenever the waste pipe empties. This keeps drain smells out of the room and prevents insects and the like from entering the home. With WCs it also makes self-cleansing easier. WC traps are cast as an integral part of the WC pan, but on other appliances they are separate, and are attached to the outlet pipe by a large retaining nut.

From the trap, waste water enters a branch pipe which leads to the main vertical drainage 'stack'. This takes it below ground level to the first underground section of the drainage system where it flows through at least one inspection chamber (covered with a manhole cover) and into the public sewer, which is usually situated underneath the road. The sewer is provided by the public health authority and it is their responsibility to remove all waste running into it.

Often rainwater from the roof is fed into the drainage system to flow into the public sewer. But some authorities provide a separate street drain for it or insist on the provision of soak-aways (pits filled with rubble and gravel which allow the water to soak into the surrounding earth) near the house. Tanks and cisterns rarely overflow, but when they do they discharge clean water, so it's not necessary for the overflow pipes to be located over a drain.

The water can fall directly onto the ground.

The cost of laying public sewers in rural areas means that the waste from many houses in these parts flows into a cess pool or septic tank. These are specially constructed pits for storing effluent (and in the case of a septic tank, for breaking it down into harmless matter). Both of these require periodic pumping out, cess pools much more often as they store all the waste. If you're buying a house with one of these systems, check how often this has to be done, who does it and how much you may have to pay.

How it all began
Proper plumbing systems have only been around for about 100 years. The large urban expansion which took place during the Industrial Revolution lead to squalid housing conditions, and disease was rife. Eventually, enclosed sewers were introduced along with piped water supplies and pottery WC pans. By the 1870s many homes were equipped with a basin, a WC and a sink; but an acute shortage of qualified plumbers lead to ridiculous installations which often produced as great a health threat as before. The London County Council took the lead in sorting things out by laying out a set of rules in 1900, establishing the 'two-pipe' system – one stack for waste water from basins and sinks, another for 'soil water' from WCs.

The amount of pipework needed with the two-pipe system, and the increased siphonage problems on tall buildings, led to the introduction of the 'one-pipe' system. This system was the forerunner of the modern 'single stack' system and abandoned the distinction between the soil and the waste pipe stacks. It was only used extensively on multi-storey buildings.

On the one-pipe system all discharges flowed into a single stack which had an open-ended outlet at roof level. All traps had deep seals and each branch pipe was also connected to a vent pipe which rose to eaves level.

The single stack system was developed in the UK in the late 1940s to overcome the drawbacks and complications of the two-pipe systems, and to simplify the installation – everyone must be familiar with the untidy cluster of pipes on the outside walls of houses with these systems.

The advent of light plastic piping helped in this development, as it made the production of accurate mouldings easier, and cut down the installation time because plastic was quicker to join than the old metal piping.

The single stack system
This consists of a single waste stack into which all the branch pipes discharge. However, ground floor waste doesn't have to go

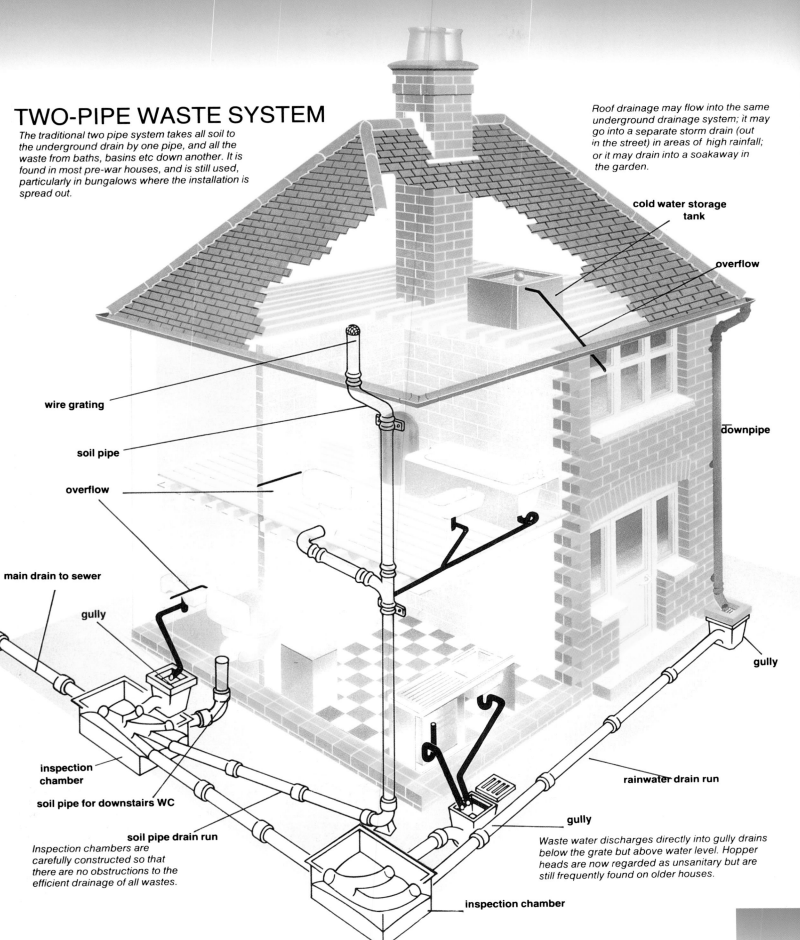

TWO-PIPE WASTE SYSTEM

The traditional two pipe system takes all soil to the underground drain by one pipe, and all the waste from baths, basins etc down another. It is found in most pre-war houses, and is still used, particularly in bungalows where the installation is spread out.

Roof drainage may flow into the same underground drainage system; it may go into a separate storm drain (out in the street) in areas of high rainfall; or it may drain into a soakaway in the garden.

cold water storage tank

overflow

wire grating

soil pipe

overflow

downpipe

main drain to sewer

gully

gully

inspection chamber

soil pipe for downstairs WC

rainwater drain run

gully

soil pipe drain run

Inspection chambers are carefully constructed so that there are no obstructions to the efficient drainage of all wastes.

Waste water discharges directly into gully drains below the grate but above water level. Hopper heads are now regarded as unsanitary but are still frequently found on older houses.

inspection chamber

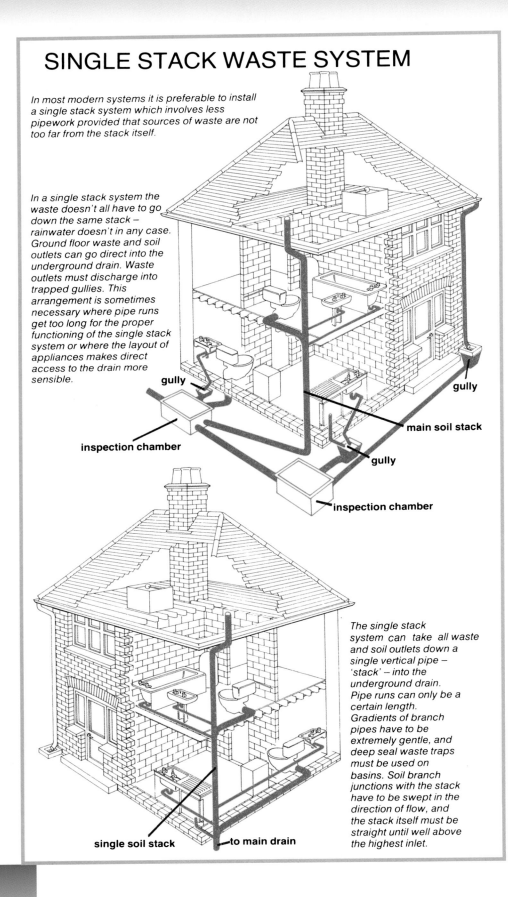

SINGLE STACK WASTE SYSTEM

In most modern systems it is preferable to install a single stack system which involves less pipework provided that sources of waste are not too far from the stack itself.

In a single stack system the waste doesn't all have to go down the same stack – rainwater doesn't in any case. Ground floor waste and soil outlets can go direct into the underground drain. Waste outlets must discharge into trapped gullies. This arrangement is sometimes necessary where pipe runs get too long for the proper functioning of the single stack system or where the layout of appliances makes direct access to the drain more sensible.

gully

inspection chamber

gully

main soil stack

gully

inspection chamber

The single stack system can take all waste and soil outlets down a single vertical pipe – 'stack' – into the underground drain. Pipe runs can only be a certain length. Gradients of branch pipes have to be extremely gentle, and deep seal waste traps must be used on basins. Soil branch junctions with the stack have to be swept in the direction of flow, and the stack itself must be straight until well above the highest inlet.

single soil stack   **to main drain**

into the stack. Sink waste water may flow into a trapped gully and ground-floor WCs may be connected directly into the underground drain. This avoids any risk that a blockage at the base of the stack (where it bends to join the underground drain) could lead to waste water being forced back along the waste pipes to ground-floor appliances.

In appearance the single-stack system is the simplest waste system of all and the most economical to install. As a result it is incorporated in the majority of new houses. But because the branches have to be comparatively short, the system is less useful in bungalows where appliances are likely to be spread out. Usually all the pipework is sited indoors, which means a neater appearance for the house exterior; it also reduces the possibility of frost damage. All you'll see of the system is a tell-tale vent pipe poking up through the roof.

In order to make the system work properly a number of technical regulations have to be taken into account when it's being installed. These relate to the length, diameter, bend radii and angles of bend of the branch pipes, the use of P-traps and S-traps on waste pipes other than WCs (see *Traps for each appliance*), the positioning of the stack connectors, and the dimensions of the stack itself. While the system may look simple, considerable research has been done to ensure that problems of siphonage aren't likely to occur.

The two-pipe system

The principles of the two-pipe system were based on a belief that all kinds of disease were caused by the 'bad air' in drains, and the system aimed to keep this out of homes. The basic principle was that the 'soil' discharge from WCs went directly down one stack into the underground drain. All other discharges, termed 'waste', went down another stack which led into a trapped gully (a cast drain incorporating a water trap) at ground level and from there joined the soil discharge under-ground. Sometimes waste had to fall into a channel at ground level before running into the drain.

All waste and soil pipework had to be fixed to the outside of the building. The soil pipe was continued upwards to eaves level where it terminated open-ended in a wire cover to keep nesting birds from causing a blockage. This allowed free passage of air from the underground drain.

When the two-pipe system came into existence, most homes only had an outside WC (quite often shared) and a kitchen sink, so discharge was entirely at ground level, but when upstairs bathrooms became popular waste was directed into hoppers attached to stand-pipes, which caused new problems. Hoppers were not self-cleansing and soapy water drying on the inside could start to smell; draughts could also blow up the pipe to the hopper, bringing smells from the drain at the bottom. This led to some authorities banning hoppers and insisting on discharge direct into another stack which meant installing an eaves-level vent as with the soil stack.

On buildings over two storeys high this created another problem known as 'induced siphonage'. When water flowing down the waste stack from one outlet passed another outlet where it joined the stack, it could cause a partial vacuum in the second pipe which could suck out the contents of the water trap. To cure this problem the upper part of each trap had to be connected to a branch vent pipe which either connected to a separate vertical stack to eaves level, or joined the vented waste stack at least 900mm (3ft) above the level of the highest waste connection. If you live in a tall house you may have this system, and any repairs to vent pipes should follow the existing system. The alternative is to take out the entire system and replace it with a single stack arrangement.

Traps for each appliance

The traditional trap was a simple U-shaped bend attached to a horizontal branch outlet – today called a 'P' trap. If the branch outlet is vertical this trap bends round again into a double 'U' or 'S' outlet. In systems with lead pipes, the traps were often formed from lengths of pipe, while with modern plastic waste systems the traps are separate and easily detachable. The plastic bottle trap, which performs the same function, is also now widely used, and this is more compact and neater in appearance.

The depth of the water-filled part of the trap is known as the 'depth of seal'. Shallow traps have a seal depth of around 50mm (2in), 38mm (1½in) or 19mm (¾in), while 'deep-seal' traps have a 75mm (3in) seal.

Lead traps usually allow access for clearing blockages, and this is obtained by unscrewing an access cap or 'eye'. Modern plastic traps are connected by screwed collars at both ends and can be completely removed for cleaning if blocked. The lower part of bottle traps likewise completely unscrews. Adjustable plastic traps are available for fixing to existing pipework where access is difficult and special adaptors are used to link to copper and iron pipes.

Traps must remain filled with water and it is against the bye-laws if they don't. This is the most important and lasting principle handed down from the waste disposal thinking of the last century.

The water seal can be lost from traps for lots of reasons. Siphonage is the worst problem and where it occurs it's usually due to a badly designed system. Simply, if the air pressure beyond the trap is slightly less than the normal atmospheric pressure acting on the surface of the water in the trap, the water will drain away. This is more likely with 'S' traps than 'P' traps, and with shallow rather than deep traps. The problem of siphonage led to the introduction of venting systems and dictated the dimensions in the single stack system (and also excluded the use of 'S' traps).

Overflow pipes

There are two sorts of overflow pipes – those which are connected to storage cisterns and WC cisterns, and those which are attached to or form a part of appliances such as basins and baths. They are known in the trade as warning pipes. Both sorts should be fitted to avoid the risk of overflows damaging your home. This may be caused when you forget to turn off the bath, or by mechanical failure when the ball-valve on the water storage tank jams open.

In sinks, basins and baths the overflow must discharge into the branch waste pipe between the trap and the appliance, or into the trap above the water level of the seal, and must be able to cope with the flow of water from one tap turned full on.

Sink and basin overflows are usually built into the design of the appliance, while those for baths are supplied as part of the plumbing and connect to a slot in the waste outlet casting.

Overflows from tanks and cisterns consist of a length of pipe of a minimum 22mm (⅞in) internal diameter, capable of discharging water as quickly as any incoming flow. They usually emerge through the outside wall and stick out far enough to avoid any water flow sluicing down the wall surface, which could be a potential source of damp.

Pipe and trap materials

All waste and soil pipes are today mainly manufactured in plastic. Branch pipes were made of lead or copper, stack pipes of cast iron, traps of lead or brass and underground pipes of vitrified clay. Only the latter still predominantly utilize the traditional material.

Your legal position

Drainage regulations fall under the Public Health Acts as well as the Building Regulations, so it's important to know where you stand. The householder is responsible for the entire drainage system until it enters the public sewer – even though this is usually beyond the boundary of the property. While blockages beyond the lowest inspection chamber are rare, any clearance work can be very expensive – particularly if you use a '24-hour' plumbing service. The public sewer is provided by the public health authority and is their responsibility.

If your house was built as one of a group of houses, then it's quite possible that you'll have shared drainage facilities. This means there is one drainage pipe collecting the waste of several homes before it discharges into the public sewer. The system was adopted because it saved installation costs. If your house was built before 1937, it's still the responsibility of the local authorities to cleanse the shared drainage runs, although you're responsible for clearing blockages and for maintenance. But if you live in a post-1937 house then the responsibility for the shared drains rests collectively on all the owners concerned and if a blockage is caused by someone else you will have to pay a proportion of the bill. It is therefore important when moving house to check out the exact position. If this is difficult to ascertain, try the Environmental Health Officer for advice; he should also be consulted if you want to change the system.

PLASTIC WASTE TRAPS

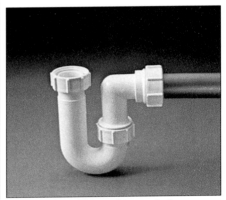

The modern U-bend *is made from one of several plastic materials.*

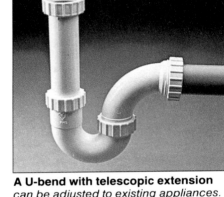

A U-bend with telescopic extension *can be adjusted to existing appliances.*

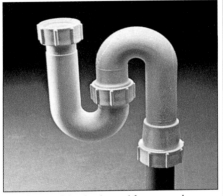

An S-bend *is designed for use where the outlet is vertical.*

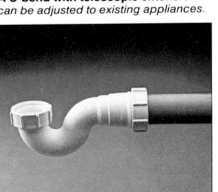
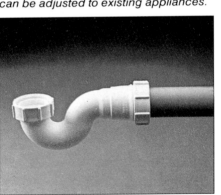

A bottle trap *gives a neater appearance, but is less efficient.*

A shallow trap *is used beneath a bath or shower where space is crucial.*

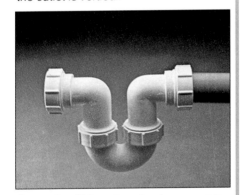

A running U-trap *handles two or more untrapped appliances piped together.*

A dip partition bottle trap *has a base which unscrews.*

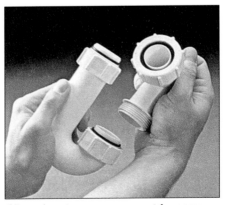

All modern traps come apart for easy cleaning and installation.

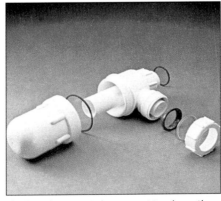

A dip tube trap taken apart to show the O rings and washers.

BASIC SKILLS AND TOOLS

There is no doubt that a professional plumber is a highly skilled person and matching his expertise would take you many years of study and training. However, you can acquire sufficient skills without too much trouble, allowing you to carry out most of the plumbing jobs you will come up against, providing you take care in what you are doing.

JOINTS FOR COPPER PIPE

Joining copper pipe is one of the basic plumbing skills. Compression and capillary joints are easy to make and once you've mastered the techniques, you'll be prepared for a whole range of plumbing projects.

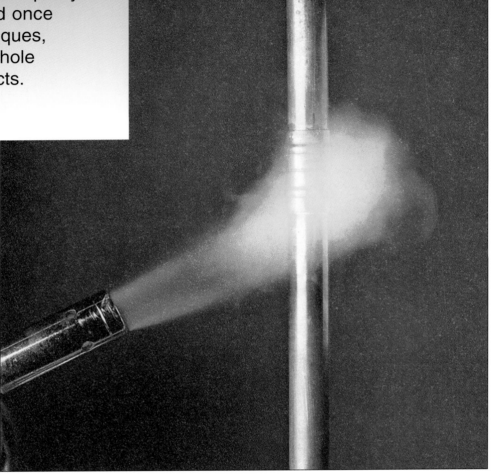

Connecting pipes effectively is the basis of all good plumbing as most leaks result from poorly constructed joints. For virtually all domestic plumbing purposes you will only have to use compression or capillary joints. Compression joints are easy to use but expensive, while capillary joints are cheap but need some care in fitting.

If you are making a join into an existing pipe system remember to make sure the water supply has been turned off at the relevant stop-valve (see EMERGENCY PIPE REPAIRS, pages 170 and 171) and the pipe completely drained.

Preparing the pipes

Before joining pipes together, check that the ends are circular and have not been distorted. If they have been dented, cut back to an undamaged section of the pipe using a hacksaw with a sharp blade or a wheel tube cutter (see pages 119 to 121).

The ends should also be square and a simple way of checking this is shown on page 117 (see *Ready Reference*). Use a file to make any correction and remove ragged burrs of metal. If you're using a capillary joint clean up the sides of the pipe with abrasive paper or steel wool.

Compression joints (friction joints)

A compression joint, as its name implies, is made by compressing two brass or copper rings (known as olives or thimbles) round the ends of the pipes to be joined, so forming a watertight seal. There are two main types of compression joint – the non-manipulative fitting and the manipulative fitting.

Although not the cheapest means of joining a pipe, a non-manipulative joint is the easiest to use and requires only the minimum of tools. It comprises a central body made of brass or gunmetal with a cap-nut at each end which, when rotated, squeezes the olive tightly between the pipe end and the casing. This is the most commonly used type of compression joint suitable for most internal domestic plumbing purposes.

A manipulative joint is now rarely used in indoor domestic water systems. Because it

cannot be pulled apart it is sometimes used for underground pipework, but capillary joints will do equally well in these situations.

The joint usually comprises a male and a female union nut. These are slipped over the pipe ends which are then flared ('manipulated') using a special steel tool called a *drift*. Jointing compound is smeared on the inside of the flares and a copper cone is inserted between them. The nuts are then screwed together to complete the seal.

How a compression joint works

The olive (thimble) is the key part of a non-manipulative compression joint. When the cap-nut is rotated clockwise the olive is forced between the casing and the pipe and is considerably deformed in the process.

A watertight seal is dependent upon the pipe ends having been well prepared so they butt up exactly to the pipe stop in the casing. This forms a primary seal and ensures that the pipe is parallel to the movement of the rotating cap-nut. An even pressure is then

applied to the olive so that it does not buckle under the strain of tightening.

What size of pipework and fittings?

Pipework is now sold in metric dimensions, but plumbing in your home may be in imperial sizes. The metric sizes are not exactly the same as their imperial equivalents – check the table *(Ready Reference,* right) which shows the different ways pipe can be bought.

These differences can cause problems. With capillary joints you have to use adaptors when converting pipe from one system to another. Adaptors are also needed for some compression joints although the 12mm, 15mm, 28mm and 54mm sizes are compatible with their imperial equivalents. This means if you already have imperial compression joints you can connect in new metric pipework, without replacing the joints.

Adaptors are made with different combinations of metric and imperial outlets to fit most requirements. A supplier will advise on what replacements to use.

HOW OLIVES MAKE A WATERTIGHT SEAL

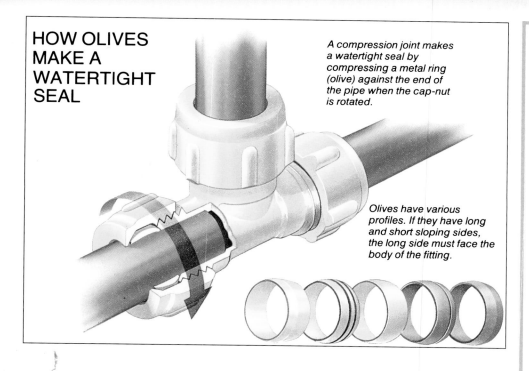

A compression joint makes a watertight seal by compressing a metal ring (olive) against the end of the pipe when the cap-nut is rotated.

Olives have various profiles. If they have long and short sloping sides, the long side must face the body of the fitting.

Capillary joints

A capillary joint is simply a copper sleeve with socket outlets into which the pipe ends are soldered. It is neater and smaller than a compression joint and forms a robust connection that will not readily pull apart.

Because it is considerably cheaper than a compression joint it is frequently used when a number of joints have to be made and is particularly useful in awkward positions where it is impossible to use wrenches.

Some people are put off using capillary fittings because of the need to use a blow-torch. But modern gas-canister torches have put paid to the fears associated with

paraffin lamps and are not dangerous.

How a capillary joint works

If two pipes to be joined together were just soldered end to end the join would be very weak because the contact area between solder and copper would be small. A capillary fitting makes a secure join because the sleeve increases this contact area and also acts as a brace to strengthen the connection.

Molten solder is sucked into the space between the pipe and fitting by capillary action, and combines with a thin layer of copper at the contact surface thus bonding the pipe to the fitting. To help the solder to

What happens when solder melts

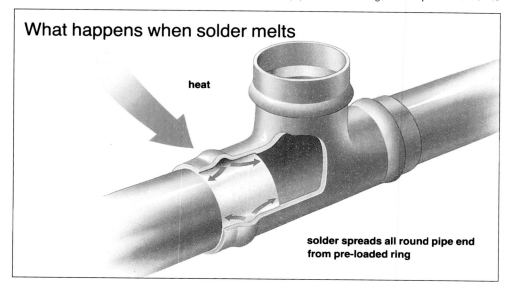

heat

solder spreads all round pipe end from pre-loaded ring

MAKING A COMPRESSION JOINT

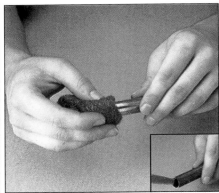

1 Check that the end of the pipe is square using a file to make any correction and to remove burrs. Clean pipe end and olive with steel wool.

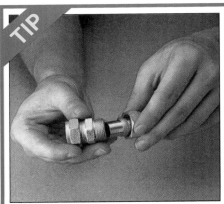

2 The olive goes on after the cap-nut. If it has both long and short sloping sides, make sure the long side faces the main body of the compression fitting.

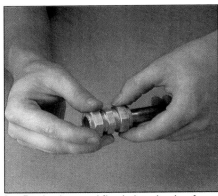

3 Push pipe end firmly into body of fitting so that it rests squarely against pipe stop. Screw up cap-nut tightly with your fingers.

4 Make pencil mark on cap-nut and another aligning on body of fitting to act as guide when tightening cap-nut with wrench.

5 Use one wrench to secure body of fitting and the other to rotate the cap-nut clockwise. About 1½ turns is sufficient to give a watertight seal.

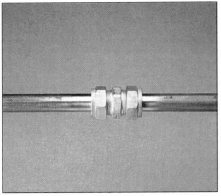

6 Repeat operation to join other pipe to fitting. If water seeps through when supply is turned on, tighten cap-nut further by half a turn.

'take' the copper needs to be clean and shining. Therefore flux is applied to prevent oxides forming which would impair the solder-copper bond.

Types of capillary joint

The most common type of capillary joint has a ring of solder pre-loaded into the sleeve. It is known as an integral ring or 'Yorkshire' fitting – the name of a leading brand.

The 'end feed' type of capillary joint is virtually the same as an integral ring fitting, but you have to add the solder in a separate operation. The sleeve is slightly larger than the pipe and liquid solder is drawn into the space between by capillary action.

Flux and solder

Essential in the soldering operation, flux is a chemical paste or liquid which cleans the metal surfaces and then protects them from the oxides produced when the blow-torch heats the copper so a good metal-solder bond is formed. Mild non-corrosive flux is easy to use as it can be smeared onto the pipe and fitting with a clean brush or a sliver of wood. Although it is best to remove any residue this will not corrode the metal. There is an acid-corrosive flux which dissolves oxides quickly, but this is mostly used with stainless steel. The corrosive residue must be scrubbed off with soapy water.

Solder is an alloy (mixture) of tin and lead and is bought as a reel of wire. Its advantage in making capillary joints is that it melts at relatively low temperatures and quickly hardens when the heat source (blow-torch) is removed.

Blow-torches

A blow-torch is an essential piece of equipment when making capillary joints. It is easy, clean and safe to use providing you handle it with care. Most modern torches operate off a gas canister which can be unscrewed and inexpensively replaced (larger cans are relatively cheaper than small). Sometimes a range of nozzles can be fitted to give different types of flame, but the standard nozzle is perfectly acceptable for capillary joint work.

Using a blow-torch

When using a blow-torch it's most convenient to work at a bench, but you'll find most jointing work has to be carried out where the pipes are to run. Pipework is usually concealed so this may mean working in an awkward place, such as a roof space, or stretching under floorboards. However, always make sure you are in a comfortable position and there's no danger of you dropping a lighted blow-torch.

MAKING A CAPILLARY FITTING

1 Make sure the pipe end is square, then clean it and the inner rim of the fitting with steel wool or abrasive paper until shining.

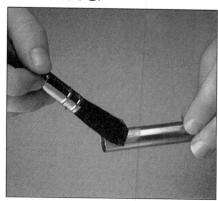

2 Flux can be in liquid or paste form. Use a brush, rather than your finger, to smear it over the end of the pipe and the inner rim of the fitting.

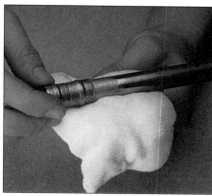

3 Push pipe into fitting so that it rests against pipe stop, twisting a little to help spread the flux. Remove excess flux with a cloth.

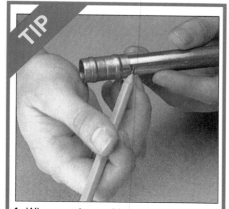

TIP

4 When you're making up a whole pipe run, it helps to make corresponding pencil marks on pipe ends and fittings as a guide for correct lining up.

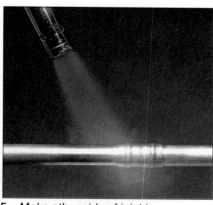

5 Make other side of joint in same way, then apply blow-torch. Seal is complete when bright ring of solder is visible at ends of fitting.

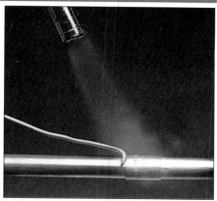

6 For an end feed fitting, heat the pipe, then hold the solder to mouth of joint. A bright ring all the way round signifies a seal.

Ready Reference

WHICH TOOLS?

For cutting pipe:
● hire a **wheel tube cutter** (which ensures perfectly square pipe ends)

or use a **hacksaw**
● use a **metal file** for removing ragged burrs of metal and for squaring ends of pipe that have been cut with a hacksaw. A half-round 'second-cut' type is ideal.

For compression joints:
● use two adjustable **spanners** or **pipe wrenches** (one to hold the fitting, the other to tighten the cap-nut)

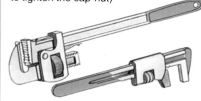

● **steel wool** to clean the surface of pipes before assembling a joint.

For capillary joints:
● a **blow-torch** to melt the solder
● **steel-wool** for cleaning pipe surfaces
● **flux** to ensure a good bond between the solder and copper
● **solder** because even if you're using integral ring fittings (which already have solder in them) you may need a bit extra
● **flame-proof glass fibre** (or a ceramic tile) to deflect the torch flame from nearby surfaces.

TIP: CUTTING PIPE SQUARELY

For a perfect fit, pipe ends must be cut square. If you're using a hacksaw, hold a strip of paper round the pipe so its edges align and saw parallel to the paper edge. Use the same trick if you have to file an inaccurately-cut end.

TIP: PROTECT NEARBY JOINTS

With capillary fittings, the heat you apply could melt the solder in nearby fittings. To help prevent this, wrap them in wet cloths.

When working near to joists and floor-boards, glass, paintwork and other pipework with capillary joints it is important to shield these areas with flame-proof glass fibre matting.

Applying the heat

When making a capillary joint gradually build up the temperature of the copper by playing the flame up and down and round the pipe and then to the fitting. When the metal is hot enough the solder will melt and you can then take away the flame. The joint is complete when a bright ring of solder appears all round the mouth of the fitting. Stand the torch on a firm level surface and turn it off as soon as you have finished. Where two or more capillary joints are to be made with one fitting, for example the three ends of a tee, they should all be made at the same time. If this is not possible wrap a damp rag round any joints already made.

Repairing a compression joint

If a compression joint is leaking and tightening of the cap-nut doesn't produce a watertight seal you'll have to disconnect the fitting and look inside – after turning off the water supply. If a cap-nut is impossible to move, run a few drops of penetrating oil onto the thread. If that doesn't do the trick, you'll have to cut it out and replace the fitting and some piping.

Once you have unscrewed one of the cap-nuts there will be enough flexibility in the pipe run to pull the pipe from the casing. Usually the olive will be compressed against the pipe. First check that it is the right way round (see page 115) and if it isn't replace it with a new one making sure that it is correctly set.

Sometimes the olive is impossible to remove and needs to be cut off with a hacksaw – make the cut diagonally. Reassemble the joint following the procedure on

page 116 and repeat the operation for the other end of the pipe. Turn on the water supply to check that the repair is watertight.

Repairing a capillary joint

Poor initial soldering is usually the reason why a capillary fitting leaks. You can try and rectify this by 'sweating' in some more solder but if this doesn't work you'll have to remake the joint.

Play the flame of the blow-torch over the fitting and pipe until the solder begins to run from the joint. At this stage you can pull the pipe ends out of the sockets with gloved hands. You can now reuse the fitting as an end feed joint or replace it with a new integral ring capillary connection.

If you reuse the fitting clean the interior surface and the pipe ends with abrasive paper or steel wool and smear them with flux. Then follow the procedure for making an end feed capillary joint.

REPAIRING A COMPRESSION JOINT

1 *Unscrew cap-nut using wrenches. There's enough flexibility in pipe run to pull pipe from casing. Check that olive fits, and isn't damaged.*

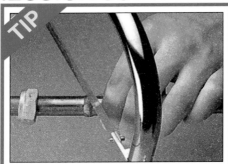

2 *A damaged olive must be removed. Use a hacksaw and to make it easier make the cut on the diagonal – but take care not to cut into the pipe itself.*

3 *Prepare end of pipe with steel wool or abrasive paper. Slip on new olive and finger tighten cap-nut. Rotate cap-nut 1 1/2 turns using wrenches.*

REPAIRING A CAPILLARY JOINT

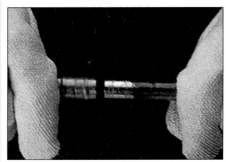

1 *Drain pipe and wrap a damp cloth round nearby joints. Play flame on fitting and pull pipe from rim using gloved hands.*

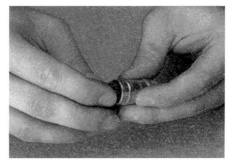

2 *If you remake both sides of joint use a new fitting. A spent integral ring fitting, thoroughly cleaned, can be used as an end feed joint.*

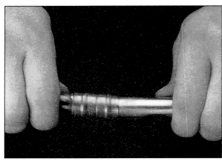

3 *Use steel wool to clean end of pipe and inside of fitting. Brush with flux and push pipe into socket. Apply blow-torch to melt solder.*

CUTTING AND BENDING COPPER PIPE

One of the advantages of domestic copper pipe is that it's easy to cut and bend. Few tools are required and even if you've only a few bends to make in a pipe run, it makes sense to know how it's done. Making accurate bends may need some practice, but it's cheaper than buying specially-shaped fittings.

In all plumbing water has to be carried from a source to a fixture and often then to some type of exit where it can disperse as waste. Basic to all of this is that water must run smoothly with nothing causing resistance to the flow — an important factor when the pressure is low.

Generally the best plumbing practice is to make pipe runs as straight and direct as possible. But sometimes bends are unavoidable (like, for example, when pipe has to go around a room or to turn down into an area below) and if available fittings are neither right for the angle nor attractive to look at, then you'll have to bend the pipe to suit.

Copper piping, because it is both light and resistant to corrosion, is a popular choice for home plumbing work. It can be joined with either capillary or compression fittings (as described on pages 114 to 118) and when bends are needed you can create the angles in several ways.

The first essential is to accurately work out the pipe lengths you require. Once you've made the measurement double check it — it's quite easy to forget to allow for the pipe that will fit into the socket ends of the joints. You can make the actual marks on the pipe with pencil as this is clearly visible on copper and is a good guide when you come to cutting.

Cutting pipe accurately

For smaller pipe sizes, a sharp-bladed hacksaw is the best tool to use to make the cut. You'll need to hold the pipe firmly, but if you use a vice be careful not to over-tighten the jaws and crush the bore of the pipe (see *Ready Reference*, on page 121).

It's important to cut the pipe square so that it butts up exactly to the pipe stop in the joint. This will ensure the pipe is seated squarely in the fitting which is essential for making a watertight seal. It will also help to make that seal. It's surprising how near to square you can get the end just cutting by eye. But the best way to make a really accurate cut is to use a saw guide. This can be made very easily by placing

a small rectangle of paper round the pipe with one long edge against the cut mark. By bringing the two short edges of the paper together and aligning them you effectively make a template that's square to the pipe. All you then have to do is hold the paper in place and keep the saw blade against it as you cut. Any burr that's left on the cut edges can be removed with a file.

If you intend to carry out a lot of plumbing, or are working mainly in the larger pipe sizes, it may be worthwhile buying (or hiring) a wheel tube cutter. Of course using one of these is never absolutely essential, but it does save time if you've more than, say, half a dozen cuts to make. And once you have one you'll use it for even the smallest jobs. It's quick to use and will ensure a square cut without trouble every time. You simply place the pipe in the cutter and tighten the control knob to hold it in place. The cutter is then rotated round the pipe and as it revolves it cuts cleanly into the copper. This circular action automatically removes burr from the outside of the pipe, but burr on the inside can be taken away with the reamer (a scraping edge) which is usually incorporated in the tool.

Bending copper pipe

If a lot of changes of direction are necessary in a pipe run it's cheaper and quicker to bend the pipe rather than use fittings. This also makes the neatest finish particularly if the pipework is going to be exposed. Under a pedestal wash-basin, for example, the hot and cold supply pipes rise parallel to each other in the pedestal before bending outwards and upwards to connect to the two tap tails.

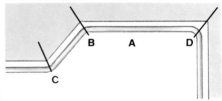

Using fittings in this situation would be more costly as well as possibly being unsightly, while the cheaper alternative, making bends, means the pipework is less conspicuous. The pipe can also be bent to the exact angle required so this method of changing direction is not limited by the angles of the fittings. And with fewer fittings in a pipe system there are fewer places where leaks can occur.

The smaller sizes of copper pipe, those most commonly used in domestic plumbing (15mm, 22mm and 28mm), can be bent quite easily by hand. The technique of annealing — heating the pipe to red heat in the vicinity of the bend to reduce its temper (strength) and so make bending easier — is unnecessary when working in these pipe sizes. But you will need to support the pipe wall, either internally or externally, as the bend is made. If you don't you'll flatten the profile of the pipe. Using it in this condition would reduce the flow of water at the outlet point.

For small jobs a bending spring is the ideal tool, supporting the pipe internally. It is a long hardened steel coil which you push into the pipe to the point where the bend will be made. It's best used for bends near the end of the pipe, since the spring can be easily pulled out after the bend is made. However, it can be used further down the pipe if it is attached to a length of stout wire (which helps to push it into place, and is vital for retrieving it afterwards).

Bending techniques

You actually bend the pipe over your knee, overbending slightly and bringing back to the required angle. The spring will now be fixed tightly in the pipe and you won't be able simply to pull it out. However, its removal is quite easy. All you have to do is to insert a bar — a screwdriver will do — through the ring at the end of the spring and twist it. This reduces the spring's diameter and will enable you to withdraw it. It's a good idea to grease the spring before you insert it as this will make pulling it out that much easier (also see *Ready Reference* page opposite).

Slight wrinkles may be found on the inside of the bend, but these can be tapped out by gentle hammering. It's wise not to attempt this before taking out the spring. If you do you'll never be able to remove it.

Bending springs are suitable for 15mm and 22mm diameter pipe. But although it is possible to bend 28mm pipe as well, it's advisable to use a bending machine instead. This is also preferable if you have a lot of bends to make. And if you don't want to go to the expense of buying one, you can probably hire a machine from a tool hire shop.

A bending machine consists of a semi-circular former that supports the pipe externally during the bending operation and a roller that forces the pipe round the curve when the levers of the machine are brought together. The degree of bend depends on how far you move the handles.

Flexible pipe

This is a kind of corrugated copper pipe which can be bent easily by hand without any tools. You can buy it with two plain ends for connection to compression joints or with one end plain and one with a swivel tap connector for connection to a tap or ball-valve.

As it's the most expensive way of making a bend, it's not cost effective to use it when you have to make a number of changes of direction in a pipe run. It's not particularly attractive to look at so it is best used in places where it won't be seen. As such it's most commonly used for connecting the water supply pipes to the bath taps in the very confined space at the head of the bath. And it can make the job of fitting kitchen sink taps easier, particularly when the base unit has a back which restricts access to the supply pipes.

CUTTING COPPER PIPE

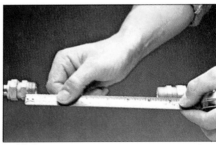

1 Make an accurate measurement of the proposed pipe run. Don't forget to allow extra for the pipe that will fit inside the joints.

2 Use a simple paper template to help you cut pipe squarely. Wrap the paper round the pipe and align the edges.

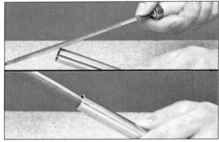

3 Use the flat side of your file to clean any burr from the outside of the pipe. The curved side of the file can be used to clean the inside.

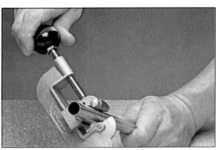

4 When using a wheel tube cutter, position the cutting mark on the pipe against the edge of the cutting wheel, then tighten the control knob.

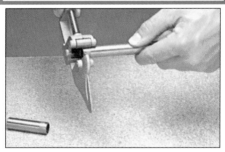

5 Once the pipe is clamped in place, rotate the cutter so it makes an even cut. The rollers on the tool will keep the blade square to the pipe.

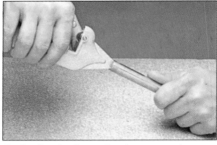

6 A wheel tube cutter leaves a clean cut on the outside of the pipe, but any burr on the inside can be removed with the reamer (an attachment to the tool).

BENDING COPPER PIPE

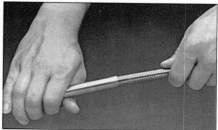

1 *Always use a bending spring which is compatible in size with the pipe. Smear it with petroleum jelly.*

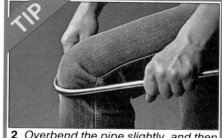

2 *Overbend the pipe slightly, and then bend it back to the required angle.*

3 *Put a screwdriver through the ring at the end of the spring. Twist it, then pull the spring out.*

4 *To use a bending machine, open the levers and position the pipe as shown, then slide the straight former on top.*

5 *Raise the levers so the wheel runs along the straight edge and the pipe is forced round the circular former.*

6 *Bend the pipe to the required angle, then remove by opening the levers, and taking out the straight former.*

FLEXIBLE COPPER PIPE

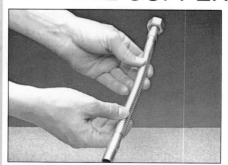

1 *Although relatively expensive, flexible pipe is ideal for making awkward bends in the pipe run to connect to taps.*

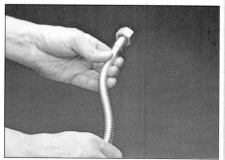

2 *It's easy to hand bend the pipe to the required shape, but don't continually flex it or the thin wall will split.*

Ready Reference

PIPE LENGTHS

Draw a rough sketch plan of the complete pipe run, then work out:

● how many 2 metre lengths you'll need
● where to join them in on the straight (not at a bend)
● how many fittings you'll need to connect the pipes to each other.

TIP: CUTTING PIPE

Copper pipe can be crushed in the jaws of a vice so use a bench hook when cutting with a hacksaw. Pin a scrap of wood beside it to hold the pipe snugly.

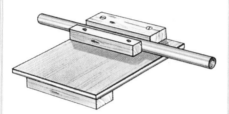

BENDING AIDS

For 15mm and 22mm pipe use a *bending spring* to match the pipe size. It's a flexible coil of hardened steel about 600mm (2ft) long.

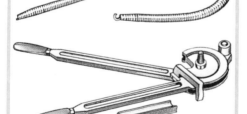

For 28mm pipe hire a *pipe bending machine* which supports the outside of the pipe wall as it bends.

TIP: REMOVING BENDING SPRINGS

For bends over 600mm (2ft) from the pipe end use a wire coathanger with a hooked end to turn and withdraw the spring.

CONNECTING NEW PIPES TO OLD

Improvements or additions to a domestic plumbing system inevitably involve joining new pipework into old. How you do this depends largely upon whether the existing pipework is made of lead, iron or more modern materials - copper, polythene or even unplasticised PVC.

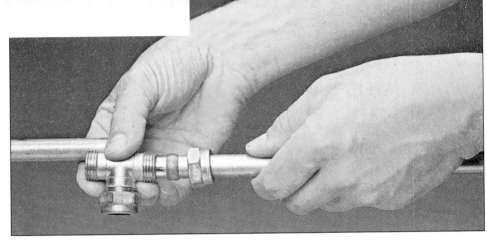

The principle of joining into existing pipework is quite straightforward. You decide where you will need your new water supply – at a bedroom basin or an outside tap, for example – and then pick a convenient point on the plumbing system to connect up your 'branch line'. At this point you have to cut out a small section of the old pipe and insert a tee junction into which the branch pipe will be fitted. That's all there is to it: laying the branch pipe will simply involve routine cutting, bending and joining of new pipe, and final connection to the new tap or appliance at the other end.

Before you can begin the job, however, you have to do some reconnaissance work to identify what sort of existing pipework you have. You might be tempted to relate the plumbing to the age of the house, thinking that an old house will have an old system with lead or iron pipework. But this isn't a reliable guide. Many old properties have been modernised and so may actually have a more up-to-date system than a house built relatively recently.

Until the 1950s the only types of pipe used in domestic plumbing were lead and iron, but then these were superseded by thin-walled copper piping. Today there are other alternatives too: stainless steel is sometimes used as an alternative to copper, and polythene and UPVC (unplasticised polyvinyl chloride) pipes can be installed for cold water supplies only.

Check the table (see *Ready Reference*, right) for the type of pipe you can use. While copper is the most common one for new work, it must *never* be joined to galvanised iron because of the severe risk of electrolytic corrosion of the iron if the galvanising is not in perfect condition.

First things first

Before cutting into a pipe run you'll first have to turn off the water supply to the pipe and then drain it by opening any taps or drain cocks connected to it (as described on pages 143 to 145). But this need not be too inconvenient if you make up the complete branch line before you turn the water off so you are without water only while you make the final branch connection.

Connecting into copper pipe

When taking a branch from a copper pipe it's probably easier to use a compression tee fitting rather than a capillary fitting. A compression fitting can be made even if there is some water in the pipe run – capillary joints need the pipe to be dry – and you won't have to worry about using a blow-torch and possibly damaging other capillary joints nearby (if they are heated up, their solder will soften and the joint will leak).

It's quite easy to work out how much pipe to cut out of the main run in order to insert a tee junction (of either compression or capillary fittings). Push a pencil or stick into the tee until it butts up against the pipe stop. Mark this length with your thumbs, then place the stick on top of the fitting so you can mark the outside to give a guide line. Next you have to cut the pipe at the place where the branch has to be made and prepare one of the cut ends (see the pictures on page 124). Now connect to the pipe the end of the tee that doesn't have the guide line marked on the casing and rest the tee back against the pipe. You will now be able to see where the pipe stop comes to and you can then mark the pipe to give you the second cutting point. Remove the section of pipe with a hacksaw and prepare the pipe end.

With a compression fitting put on the other cap-nut and olive. If you gently push the pipe and tee sideways to the pipe run this will give you more room to position the body before you allow the pipe end to spring into place. When this is done the cap-nut can be pushed up to the fitting and can be tightened with your fingers. Both sides of the tee can then be tightened using your wrenches to give the cap-nuts about one-and-a-half turns.

Remember that you must use a second wrench to grip the body of the fitting so it stays still as the cap-nut is tightened. If it should turn, other parts of the joint which have already been assembled will be loosened or forced out of position, and leaks will result. The connection into the main pipe run is now complete and you can connect up the branch pipe.

If you are using a capillary tee fitting there are a number of points to bear in mind. It's easiest to use one with integral rings of solder (this saves the bother of using solder wire) and after the pipe ends and the inside rims have been prepared and smeared with flux the fitting can be 'sprung' into place. The branch pipe should also be inserted at this stage so all the joints can be made at the same time.

When using the blow-torch, it is important to protect the surrounding area from the effects of the flame with a piece of flame-proof glass fibre matting or the back of a ceramic tile. It's also worthwhile wrapping damp cloths round any nearby capillary joints to protect them from accidental over-heating and thus 'sweating'.

IDENTIFYING OLD PIPEWORK

Below are some examples of pipework that you may find in your home. Most plumbing these days is done with plastic pipes and fittings, but it is still important to be able to recognise the type of plumbing you have in your home before work can begin. It is also worth noting, that although it is not illegal to still have in your home, lead pipes should be replaced with modern plastic pipework. If you find lead pipes in your home, we strongly reccommend that you contact a reputable plumber for advice.

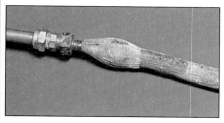

1 *Lead pipes are grey and give a dull thud when knocked. You can nick the surface with a knife. Look for smooth bends and neat even swellings – these are 'wiped' soldered joints. Repairs are now made using copper pipe.*

2 *Iron pipes have a grey galvanised or black finish and give a clanging sound when knocked. A knife will only scrape along the surface. Look for the large threaded joints which appear as a collar on the pipe or at a bend.*

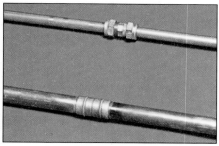

3 *Copper pipes are recognised by their familiar copper colour. Changes of direction are often made by bends in the pipe itself or by using angled fittings. The joints will be either the compression or capillary type.*

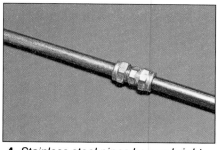

4 *Stainless steel pipes have a bright silvery surface. They come in the same sizes as copper and can be joined in the same way. Bends are only found in sizes up to 15mm. These pipes are not commonly used in the home.*

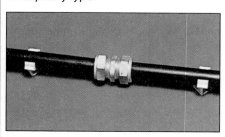

5 *Polythene pipes are usually black and are soft enough to be slightly compressed between the fingers. Joints are made with metal compression fittings which require special gunmetal olives and liners.*

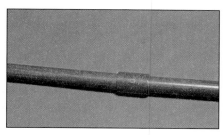

6 *UPVC pipes are grey and rigid. Connections and changes in direction are made by angled joints which fit like slim collars over the ends of the pipes. These are fixed in place using solvent weld cement.*

Ready Reference

WHAT JOINS TO WHAT?

Use this table as a guide to choosing new pipework – the first material mentioned is the best or most usual choice.

Existing pipe	New pipework
copper	copper, stainless steel, polythene
lead	copper, stainless steel, polythene
iron	iron, stainless steel, polythene
stainless steel	stainless steel, copper, polythene
polythene	polythene, copper, stainless steel
UPVC	copper, stainless steel, polythene

CONNECTING OLD TO NEW

Fitting metric to imperial pipework can be complicated by the slight differences in pipe diameters. The problem connections are:

copper to copper (compression fittings)
● some metric fittings can be used directly with imperial-sized pipes (eg, 15mm fittings with 1/2in pipe and 28mm fittings with 1in pipe)
● with other sizes you need to buy special adaptors or larger olives to replace those inside the fittings, so to connect a 15mm branch into existing 3/4in pipe you'll need a tee 22 x 22 x 15mm with special olives for the 22mm ends of the tee.

copper to copper (capillary fittings)
● metric capillary fittings with integral solder rings are not compatible with imperial pipes, but straight adaptors are available to connect the two sizes of pipe
● use these to join in short lengths of metric pipe, the other ends of which are connected to opposite ends of the metric tee
● with end-feed type fittings, extra solder can be added to make a good joint with imperial-sized pipe.

copper to stainless steel – as for copper to copper connections, but usually compression fittings only.

stainless steel to copper – as above for copper to stainless steel.

stainless steel to stainless steel – as for copper to copper.

Connecting into lead pipe

Inserting a tee junction into lead pipe involves joining the run of the tee into two 'wiped' soldered joints. Join short lengths of new copper pipe into opposite ends of a compression tee. Measure the length of this assembly, and cut out 25mm (1in) less of lead pipe. Join the assembly in with wiped soldered joints – a job that takes a lot of practice, and one you may prefer to leave to a professional plumber until you have acquired the skill. You then connect the branch pipe to the third leg of the tee.

Connecting into iron

Existing iron pipework will be at least 25 years old, and likely to be showing signs of corrosion. Extending such a system is not advisable – you would have difficulty connecting into it, and any extension would have to be in stainless steel. The best course is to replace the piping completely with new copper piping.

Connecting into polythene pipe

If you have to fit a branch into a polythene pipe it's not a difficult job, especially if you use the same material. Polythene pipes are joined by compression fittings similar to those used for copper. Polythene hasn't yet been metricated in the UK and each nominal pipe size has a larger outside diameter than its copper equivalent. So you'll have to use either special gunmetal fittings for polythene pipe (still made to imperial sizes) or else an ordinary metric brass fitting a size larger than the pipe – 22mm for ½in polythene.

You also need to slip a special metal liner inside the end of the pipe before assembling each joint to prevent the pipe from collapsing as the cap-nuts are tightened. In addition, polythene rings are used instead of metal olives in brass fittings. Apart from these points, however, inserting a tee in a length of polythene pipework follows the same sequence as inserting one into copper.

Connecting into UPVC pipe

As with polythene it's an easy job to cut in a solvent weld tee – a simple collar fitting over the ends of the pipe and the branch. After you've cut the pipe run with a hacksaw you have to roughen the outsides of the cut ends and the insides of the tee sockets with abrasive paper and then clean the surfaces with a spirit cleaner and degreaser. Solvent weld cement is smeared on the pipe ends and the insides of the sockets, and the pipe ends are then 'sprung' into the sockets.

You have to work quickly as the solvent begins the welding action as soon as the pipes meet. Wipe surplus cement off immediately, and hold the joint securely for 15 seconds. After this you can fit your branch pipe to the outlet of the tee.

CUTTING INTO METRIC COPPER PIPE

1 *On one side of the tee, push a pencil or piece of dowelling along the inside until it butts against the pipe stop. Mark this length with your thumb.*

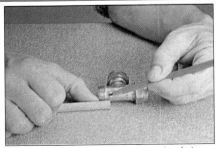

2 *Now hold the marked length of dowel against the outside of the fitting so you can see exactly where the pipe stops. Mark this position on the fitting.*

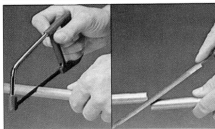

3 *Having turned off the water and drained the supply pipe, cut it at the place where you want the branch to join in. Clean one of the ends with steel wool.*

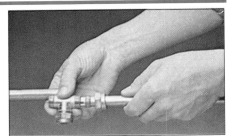

4 *Now slip a cap-nut and then an olive over the cleaned pipe end and connect up the unmarked end of the tee fitting to the pipe.*

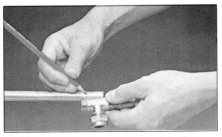

5 *Allow the tee to rest alongside the pipe run. The mark on the front of the fitting is your guide to where the pipe has to be cut again.*

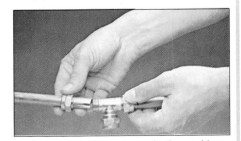

6 *Cut the pipe at this mark, thus taking out a small section. Clean the end and slip a cap-nut and olive into place. Spring the pipe end into the tee.*

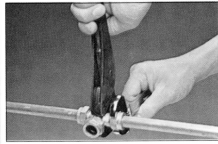

7 *Support the fitting with a wrench while tightening the cap-nuts on both ends of the tee with an adjustable spanner or wrench.*

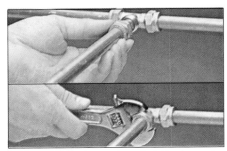

8 *Insert the cleaned end of the branch pipe into the tee and tighten the cap-nut 1½ turns with a wrench, holding the fitting to stop it from twisting.*

JOINING METRIC TO IMPERIAL PIPE

1 *Cut two short lengths of metric pipe and prepare the pipe ends, the metric/imperial adaptors and also the tee junction.*

2 *Smear flux over the ends of the pipe, inside the rims of the adaptors and each opening on the tee. Then assemble the fitting.*

3 *With the water turned off and the pipe drained, cut it where you want to make the connection. Prepare one of the ends with steel wool.*

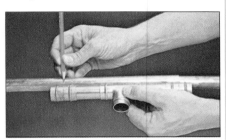

4 *Hold the fitting so the pipe stop of one adaptor rests against the cut. Now you can mark the other pipe stop position on the pipe run.*

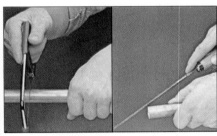

5 *Cut out the section of pipe and prepare the newly-cut end. Don't forget to apply the flux, smearing it on the outside of both pipe ends.*

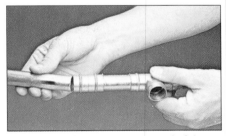

6 *Push the fitting onto one end of the supply run, then gently spring the other end into place so that the tee junction is correctly positioned.*

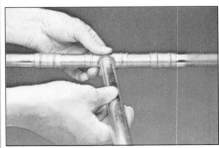

7 *Prepare the end of the branch pipe and push it into the tee. Make sure that all the pipe ends are butting up fully against the pipe stops.*

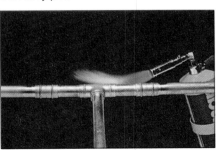

8 *Make all the joints at the same time. Rings of solder round the mouths of the fittings indicate that sound, watertight connections have been made.*

Ready Reference

CONVENIENT CUTTING

Try to join into existing pipework at a point where you have room to manoeuvre.
If space is very tight
● use a junior hacksaw instead of a full-sized one, or
● use a sawing wire for cutting pipes in corners

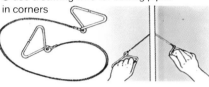

THE RIGHT TEE

Your branch line may be the same diameter as the main pipe, or smaller (it should never be larger). Tees are described as having all ends equal (eg, 15 x 15 x 15mm), or as having the branch reduced (eg, 22 x 22 x 15mm).

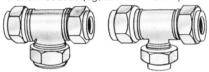

SUPPORTING THE PIPEWORK

All pipework needs supporting at intervals along its length with pipe clips (usually plastic or metal). Fit them at
● 1.2m (4ft) intervals on horizontal pipe runs
● 1.5m (5ft) intervals on vertical pipe runs.

TO SAVE TIME AND TROUBLE

● hold the body of a compression fitting securely with one wrench or spanner while doing up the cap-nut with another
● wrap nearby capillary fittings in damp cloths when soldering in new ones
● make up the entire branch line before cutting in the branch tee
● have cloths handy for mopping up when cutting into existing pipework
● if you're using compression fittings on a vertical pipe run, stop the lower cap-nut and olive from slipping down the pipe by clipping a clothes peg or bulldog clip to it
● keep a replacement cartridge for your blow-torch in your tool kit so you don't run out of gas in the middle of a job.

JOINING INTO PLASTIC PIPES

1 Polythene pipe is joined by a compression fitting with a larger olive than usual (right hand) and pipe liners to support the pipe walls.

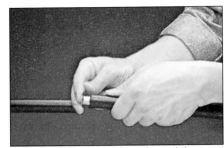

2 Turn off the water supply and then cut the pipe. Use a file to remove any rough edges and then insert a liner into one end of the pipe.

3 Undo the compression fittings and slip a cap-nut over the pipe end containing the liner; then slip on the olive.

4 Mark the pipe stop on the outside of the tee, join the tee to the prepared end, then mark across the pipe stop to show where the pipe is to be cut.

5 Cut out the section of pipe and connect the other end of the tee. Hold the fitting securely while you tighten the cap-nuts 1¹/₂ turns.

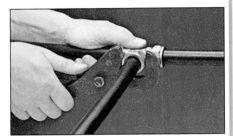

6 Insert the branch pipe into the tee fitting and again use a wrench or adjustable spanner to give the cap-nuts 1¹/₂ turns.

7 With UPVC pipe, mark the pipe stops on the outside of the tee. Use these as a gauge to cut out a small section of pipe with a hacksaw.

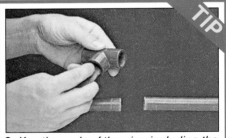

8 Key the ends of the pipe including the branch and the inside of the tee with abrasive paper. This is essential when using solvent-weld cement.

9 Thoroughly clean the ends of the pipes with a degreaser, which you apply with a brush, and leave until completely dry.

10 Once you've done this, spread solvent weld cement on the contact surfaces. Take care not to inhale the fumes as you work.

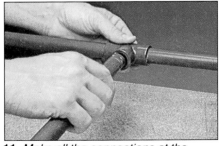

11 Make all the connections at the same time, and check to ensure that all the pipes are pushed right into the tee. Hold for 30 seconds.

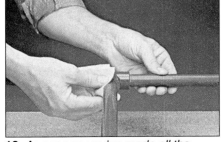

12 As soon as you've made all the connections, use a cloth to remove any surplus cement from the pipes. Water shouldn't be turned on for 24 hours.

USING PLASTIC PIPE AND FITTINGS

Plastic pipe and fittings can now be used for hot water supplies and central heating. They are easy to work with, and allow the DIY plumber to tackle a wide range of jobs.

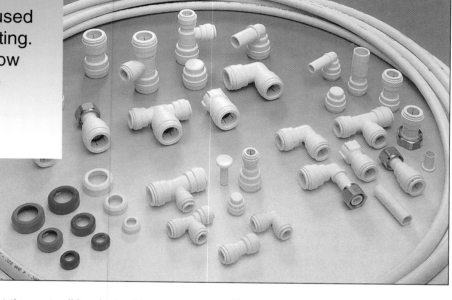

Over the last twenty years plastic has become the most popular plumbing material for above and below ground drainage, for rainwater collection and disposal, and for subsoil drainage. In the form of black polythene tubing it has also become a material widely used for water transportation on camping sites and farms. In the home, however, it has not proved popular. Although this lack of interest can partly be attributed to the conservatism of plumbers and householders, the main reason has been that up until now the plastic pipes that have been available have been suitable for cold water supplies only. This has meant that plumbers, who have had no choice but to use copper or some other metal for the hot water or central heating system, have almost always tended to use the same material when dealing with the cold water system. Householders have doubted the ability of plastic pipework to do a good, life-long job, and have also tended to resist its use on grounds of taste: quite simply, in places where pipework is exposed to view the combination of plastic and copper (or stainless steel or iron) is not one that is very pleasing to the eye.

Now, however, all this has changed. Recently the National Water Council (NWC) gave its approval to two proprietary systems of plastic plumbing, one made out of polybutylene and the other of chlorinated polyvinyl chloride (CPVC), both of which can now be used for cold *and* hot water supply as well as for wet central heating systems. These two rival plumbing systems should hold a special appeal for the DIY enthusiast and – now that they have gained the NWC's approval – there is nothing to prevent them gaining widespread acceptance.

The advantages of plastic pipework

The most obvious advantage is the lightness of the pipework, which makes for ease of handling, but the most important benefit is the ease with which plastic can be cut and joined. This means that the level of skill you require to undertake a particular plumbing task is greatly reduced, as is the amount of time you require to carry it out. Both systems are also strong and durable, more resistant

to frost than a traditional plumbing system and, unlike the latter, not subject to corrosion. Last but not least, they are competitively priced.

Plastic pipes are less vulnerable to frost because plastic is a poor conductor of heat compared to metal (which means that, unlike metal, it provides a certain amount of insulation), and because it has greater elasticity. This means that plastic pipes are not only less likely to freeze than metal ones, but also that in the event of their doing so they are much less likely to burst. The greater degree of insulation that plastic provides also brings other benefits: it results in less heat being lost from pipe runs between radiators (or between the hot water cylinder and the hot taps), as well as meaning that less insulation is necessary for pipework that needs to be protected against the cold.

Plastic pipes aren't subject to corrosion for the simple reason that plastic isn't attacked by the water supply. Electrolytic corrosion, which results in the build up of hydrogen gas and black iron oxide sludge (magnetite) and can ultimately lead to leaky radiators and early pump failure, is therefore far less of a problem when a central heating system is fitted with plastic pipes.

This also means that plastic is a safer material to use for your drinking water supply pipes than metal, the use of which can, under some circumstances, present a health risk.

One final point to be borne in mind before you replace metal pipes with plastic ones is that plastic is a non-conductor of electricity. This means that all-plastic plumbing systems cannot be used to earth a domestic electricity supply (see *Ready Reference*).

You can obtain both polybutylene and CPVC tubing in the 15mm (½in), 22mm (¾in) and 28mm (1in) diameters commonly used in domestic hot and cold water supply and in small-bore central heating. However, in other respects – particularly as regards the flexibility of the two different types of tubing and methods of cutting and jointing – the two systems differ. So, before you undertake a plumbing task using plastic pipes and fittings, you'd do well to consider which system best suits your particular application.

Polybutylene tubing

Polybutylene tubing is brown in colour and naturally flexible; in this respect it differs from CPVC tubing, which is rigid. As well as being available in 3m (10ft) lengths in all three diameters, it is also obtainable as a 100m (325ft) coil in the 15mm (½in) size, and as a 50m (162ft) coil in the 22mm (¾in) size. This flexibility, and the long lengths in which the tubing is available, is particularly useful as it cuts down the time you need to spend on installation, and reduces the number of fittings necessary (which means less cost). You can thread polybutylene pipes under floors and between joists with minimal disturbance, their flexibility also allowing you to take them through apertures and round obstacles that would otherwise present serious difficulties. You can bend the tubing cold to easy bends with a minimum radius of eight times the pipe diameter; 15mm (½in) tube can therefore be bent to a minimum radius of 120mm (4¾in) and 22mm (¾in) to a minimum radius of 176mm (7in). You must, however, provide a clip on either side of the bend to secure it. The flexibility of polybutylene tubing means that

POLYBUTYLENE PIPE AND FITTINGS

1 The best way to cut polybutylene pipe is with the manufacturer's shears. Alternatively, you can cut polybutylene pipe with a hacksaw or a sharp knife.

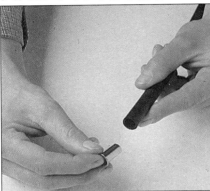

2 Before jointing the pipe, insert a stainless steel support sleeve into the pipe end. This prevents the tube end getting crushed within the fitting.

3 Polybutylene pipe can be used with ordinary compression fittings. Within a polybutylene fitting a grab ring holds the pipe in place, while an 'O' ring ensures a watertight seal.

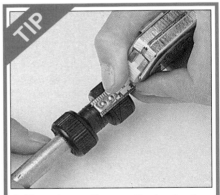

4 The witness lines on the body of the fitting indicate the length of pipe hidden within it when the joint is assembled. Remember to allow for this.

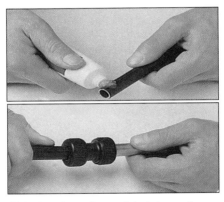

5 Before inserting polybutylene pipe into a polybutylene fitting, apply a special lubricant to both the pipe end and the interior of the socket.

6 The pipe can be withdrawn only if you unscrew the cap-nut. To re-use the joint, crush and discard the grab ring, and then replace it with a new one.

CPVC PIPE AND FITTINGS

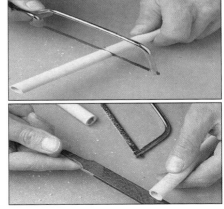

1 You can cut CPVC pipe with either a fine-toothed saw or an ordinary pipe cutter. Use a file or a knife to remove the swarf from the pipe end.

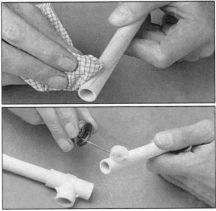

2 Before making a joint with CPVC the surfaces to be solvent-welded must first be cleaned. Immediately afterwards, apply the solvent weld cement.

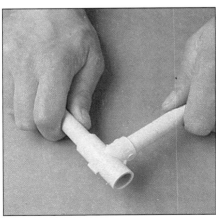

3 The solvent-weld cement goes off fairly rapidly, so you must make the joint as soon as you've applied it. Push the pipe home with a slight twisting motion.

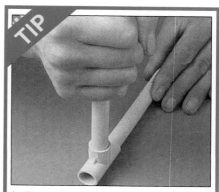

4 The solvent-weld cement's rapid setting time also means you must make adjustment for alignment immediately. Do not remove surplus cement.

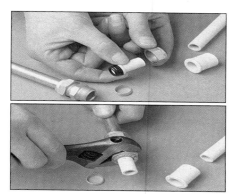

5 You can join CPVC pipe to copper using a compression fitting and a two-part adaptor. Discard the olive as the first part of the adaptor is self-sealing.

6 Having solvent-welded the two parts of the adaptor together, complete the fitting by solvent-welding the CPVC pipe to the second part of the adaptor.

PLASTIC PIPE AND FITTINGS

1 Push the 2 pipe removal shims along the pipe, fully into the socket of the fitting. Hold them in place with one hand and pull the pipe out of the socket with the other hand.

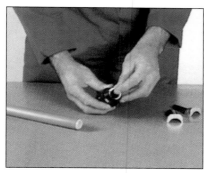

2 Remove the grab-ring by pulling one end out of the socket and then turning the grab-ring with a helical motion. The grab-ring must be discarded and replaced with a new grab-ring.

3 Insert a new 'O'-ring, if necessary and fit a new grab-ring by pushing one end down and entering it into the socket with a helical motion ensuring that the grab-ring is fitted the correct way.

SPECIAL FITTINGS

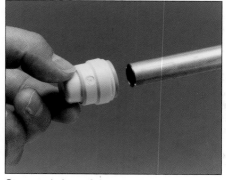

Stop end. A useful gadget for a temporary leak proof seal. It can be readily removed to allow work to be continued or extended.

The simplest way to connect taps, is to use a tap connector, available from most DIY stores.

Monobloc fitting. Getting behind sinks and basins is now much easier with push-in fittings, avoiding trying to use spanners in restricted spaces.

you will have to give continuous support to any visible horizontal pipe runs in order to eliminate the possibility of unsightly sagging (see *Ready Reference*).

You can cut polybutylene tube with a sharp knife or a hacksaw. However, for speed of operation and to ensure an absolutely square cut pipe end every time, the manufacturers recommend that you use their specially designed pipe shears. It would certainly be worthwhile investing in a pair of these shears before embarking on a major project that involved the making of a large number of joints.

You can join polybutylene tubing by using either non-manipulative (Type 'A') compression joints (as used with copper), or else the manufacturer's own patent push-fit connectors. One of the advantages of being able to use Type 'A' compression joints with tubing is that it enables you to replace a length of copper pipe with polybutylene tubing using the existing compression tee or coupling.

When using polybutylene tubing with this type of joint the procedure you follow is identical to that which you adopt with copper pipe (as described on pages 114 to 118). But in order to prevent the collapse of the tube end when the cap-nut is tightened, you must insert a purpose-made stainless steel support sleeve into it. And if you use jointing compound to complete a threaded fitting connected to polybutylene pipe, make sure none comes into contact with the polybutylene.

The patent polybutylene joints and fittings are available in the usual range of straight couplings, tees, elbows, reducing fittings and tap and tank connectors, and in appearance they resemble their brass compression counterparts. But there is one important difference – you don't have to loosen or unscrew the cap-nuts to make a joint. To make a connection you simply have to push the prepared pipe end into the fitting (see step-by-step photographs). Polybutylene fittings have one further advantage in that they allow you to rotate a pipe that has been inserted into one of them, even when it is filled with water. This means, for example, that a polybutylene stop-valve can rest neatly against a wall until you need to use it. You then pull the handle away from the wall so you can open and close it easily.

CPVC tubing

CPVC tubing differs from the polybutylene type in two basic ways. First, it is rigid rather than flexible, which means that it is only available in relatively short lengths of 2m (6ft 6in) or 3m (9ft 9in). Secondly, it is joined by a process known as solvent welding, a slightly more involved procedure than making a push-fit or compression connection (see

step-by-step photographs). Superficially, CPVC tubing can be distinguished from polybutylene by its off-white colour. An hour after the last joint has been made you can flush through the system and fill it with cold water; before filling with hot water you need to wait at least four hours.

CPVC pipe does expand when hot water passes through it, but this won't cause a problem in most domestic systems unless one of the pipe runs exceeds 10m (33ft), which is unlikely. In this case you will have to create an expansion loop using four 90° elbows and three 150mm (6in) lengths of pipe.

The manufacturers of CPVC tubing provide an exceptionally wide range of fittings to meet every eventuality. There are 90° and 45° elbows, equal and unequal tees, reducing pieces, tap and ball-valve connectors, stop-valves and gate-valves, and provision for connection to existing copper or screwed iron fittings. The connectors for copper tubing have a solvent-weld socket at one end and a conventional Type 'A' compression joint at the other. Those for iron fittings have a solvent-weld fitting at one end and either a male or female threaded joint at the other. If you are connecting a fitting to an existing iron socket, make sure that you render the screwed connection watertight by binding plastic PTFE tape round the male thread before screwing home.

What system to use

Neither system is 'better' than the other, and each has its merits and its drawbacks. The polybutylene tubing is flexible and available in extremely long lengths which reduce the number of joints you will have to use, as well as enabling you to get through or round obstacles that might prove difficult were you using the CPVC system. On the other hand the push-fit polybutylene joints are bulkier and more obtrusive than those used with the CPVC system.

Bearing in mind this, and the fact that the rigid CPVC pipes will be less prone to sagging than the flexible polybutylene tubing, the CPVC system is probably the more acceptable one in situations where plumbing is exposed to view. The more complex construction of the polybutylene joints – the cause of their bulkiness – also makes them relatively expensive: which means that the smaller number necessary for carrying out a given plumbing task won't always cost you less than the greater number necessary with CPVC. However, polybutylene joints, unlike CPVC ones, can be used more than once.

Lastly, in case your decision to opt for one system or the other is influenced by the colour of the material out of which it is made (dark brown for polybutylene and off-white for CPVC), you can paint both systems with ordinary household paints.

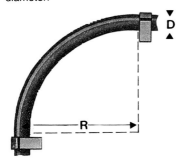

COMPARING THE SYSTEMS

To show how the two plastic systems look in use, here is the pipe run involved in teeing off a spur to a washing machine, assembled using the appropriate fittings in each case. For comparison the same run has been assembled using copper pipe with capillary and compression fittings too.

Key to fittings

1 *Male iron socket adaptor 22mm x3/4in BSP*
2 *Staight connector 22x22mm*
3 *Socket reducer 22x15mm*
4 *Stop-valve 15x15mm*
5 *90˚ elbow 15x15mm*
6 *Polybutylene pipe clip 15mm*
7 *Equal tee 15x15x15mm*
8 *Straight coupling copper x male iron*
9 *Stop-valve 15x15mm*
10 *Elbow copper x copper 15x15mm*
11 *Tee for copper 15x15x15mm*
12 *Tank connector 15mm x $^1/_2$in*
13 *Straight tap connector 15mm x $^1/_2$in*
14 *Male iron socket adaptor 15mm x$^1/_2$in BSP*
15 *Female iron socket adaptor 15mm x$^1/_2$in BSP*
16 *Pipe clip for copper 15mm.*

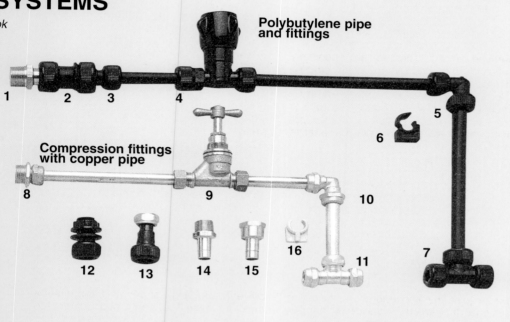

Polybutylene pipe and fittings

Compression fittings with copper pipe

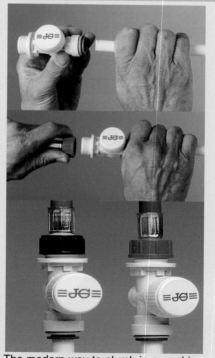

The modern way to plumb in a washing machine is with plastic push-fit fittings, as above.

Key to fittings

1 *Equal tee adaptor 15x15x15mm*
2 *90˚ elbow 15x15mm*
3 *Coupler with copper spigot 15mm*
4 *Washing machine valve 15mm*
5 *CPVC pipe clip 15mm*
6 *Stop-valve 15mm (alternative to 4)*
7 *Tee for copper 15x15x15mm*
8 *Elbow copper x copper 15x15mm*
9 *Washing machine valve 15mm*
10 *Pipe clip for copper 15mm*
11 *Tank connertor 22mm x $^3/_4$in*
12 *Straight tap connector 15mm x$^1/_2$in*
13 *Connector to famale iron 15mm x $^1/_2$in BSP*
14 *Connector to male iron 15mm x $^1/_2$in BSP*

CPVC pipe and fittings

Capillary fittings with copper pipe

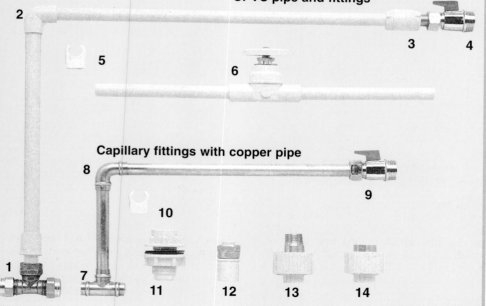

JOINING PLASTIC WASTE PIPES

Most waste pipes installed today are made of plastic, which is cheap, lightweight and easy to work with. A little practice and careful measuring will enable you to replace all parts of your system. Here's how to join them together.

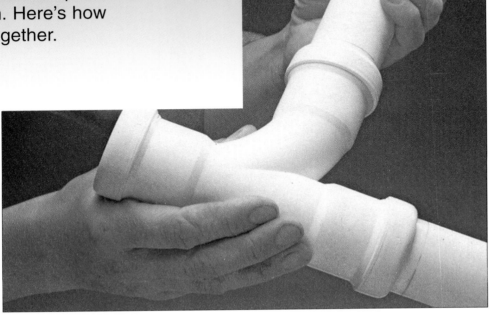

Waste systems draining baths, basins and sinks used to be made of lead, heavy galvanised steel with screwed joints, or copper. Soil pipes from WCs were traditionally cast iron, as was all the outside pipework for both waste and soil disposal. Nowadays waste and soil pipes are made of one or other of a variety of plastic materials, which may be used for repairs, extension work or complete replacement of an existing system.

These plastic pipes are lightweight and easily cut, handled and joined. They are made of materials usually known by the initials of their chemical names – UPVC (unplasticised polyvinyl chloride), MPVC (modified polyvinyl chloride), ABS (acrylonitrile butadiene styrene) and PP (polypropylene). CPVC (chlorinated polyvinyl chloride) is usually used for hot and cold water supply pipes. Pipes and fittings are available in white, grey or a copper colour, depending on type and manufacture.

All these materials are satisfactory for domestic waste systems and – with one exception – can all be joined in the same way: either by push-fit (ring-seal) jointing or by solvent welding.

The exception is PP pipe. This was first developed because of its good resistance to very hot water and chemical wastes, and was therefore extensively used in industry. Nowadays, however, it is frequently used in the home for waste or rainwater drainage. The big difference between PP and other plastic pipes used in waste drainage is that it cannot be solvent-welded. All joints must be push-fit. In most situations this is no great disadvantage but it does make it important to be able to distinguish PP from other plastics. It has a slightly greasy feel and, when cut with a fine toothed saw, leaves fine strands of fibrous material round the cut edges.

Sizes

When buying plastic pipe and components it is wise to stick to one brand only. Pipes and fittings from different makers, though of the same size, are not necessarily interchangeable. Most suppliers stock the systems of only one manufacturer, although the same

PREPARING THE PIPE ENDS

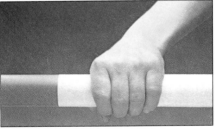

1 To make sure that you cut the pipe squarely, hold a sheet of paper around it so that the edges meet and overlap each other. This is your cutting line.

2 Hold the pipe firmly and cut it with a hacksaw, using gentle strokes. You may find it easier to use a junior hacksaw, which gives a finer cut.

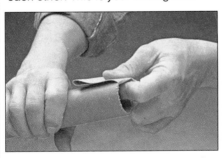

3 When you've cut the pipe, use a piece of fine glass paper to clean off the burr left by sawing.

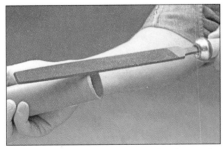

4 Now take a file and chamfer the end of the pipe all round the edge to a 45° angle. Try to keep the chamfer even.

SOLVENT-WELD JOINTING

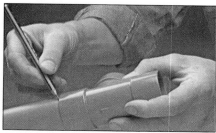

1 Push the end of the pipe into the socket of the fitting as far as it will go. Mark the pipe at this point with a pencil as a guide to the length within the joint.

2 Take the pipe out of the fitting and, with a file, roughen the whole of the end surface that will be inside the fitting up to the pencil mark.

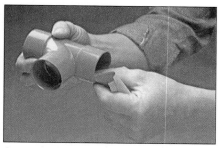

3 Take the fitting itself and roughen the inside of the socket with fine glass paper. This will provide a key for the solvent cement.

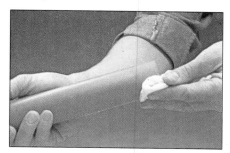

4 Now clean off the roughened surface of the pipe and socket with spirit as recommended by the manufacturer to remove all dust and debris.

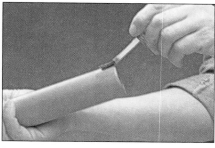

5 Apply the solvent cement to the roughened end of the pipe, making sure that the whole roughened area is covered. Try and keep it off your fingers.

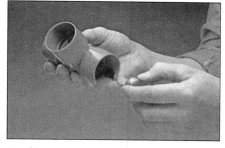

6 Also apply solvent cement to the socket of the fitting. Try to use brush strokes along the line of the pipe.

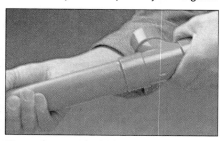

7 Gently push the pipe fully home into the socket. Some manufacturers suggest a slight twisting action in doing this but check their instructions first.

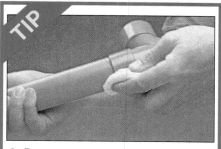

TIP

8 Remove any excess solvent at the edge of the socket with a clean cloth, hold the joint in position for 30 seconds.

Ready Reference

THE TOOLS YOU'LL NEED

● hacksaw – a junior or larger – for cutting the lengths of pipe as you need them
● piece of paper – to help cut the pipe truly square
● tape measure
● file – for chamfering the pipe ends
● fine glasspaper – to abrade pipes and sockets for solvent-welding, and for cleaning up the ends of pipes where you have cut them
● pencil – for marking the cutting points and socket depths to find the working area of the pipe.

VITAL ACCESSORIES

● solvent cement – for solvent-welding
● cleaning fluid – for cleaning the pipe ends and socket fittings when making solvent-weld joints
● petroleum jelly – for lubrication when inserting the pipe into the socket in push-fit joint assemblies
● tissues or rag for cleaning off excess solvent or petroleum jelly.

TYPES OF PIPE

Unplasticised PVC (UPVC) is used for all waste pipe applications.
Modified PVC (MPVC) has rubber or some other plasticiser added to make it more resistant to shock.
Chlorinated PVC (CPVC or MUPVC) is used where very hot water discharge occurs, such as washing machine out-flows.
Polypropylene (PP) is an alternative to PVC and can withstand hot water – but it expands a lot and is only suitable on short runs.
Acrylonitrile butadiene styrene (ABS) is stronger than UPVC and is used for waste connection mouldings.

SAFETY TIPS

● don't smoke when you are solvent-weld jointing – solvent cement and solvent cement cleaner become poisonous when combined with cigarette smoke
● don't inhale the fumes of solvent-weld cement or cleaning fluid – so avoid working in confined spaces
● don't get solvent-weld cement on any part of the pipe you're not joining as this can later lead to cracking and weaknesses, especially inside sockets where the solvent cement can easily trickle down
● hold all solvent-weld joints for 15 seconds after joining and then leave them undisturbed for at least 5 minutes – if hot water is going to flow through the pipe don't use it for 24 hours.

PUSH-FIT JOINTING

1 Cut the pipe squarely as in solvent-weld jointing and remove the burr, then take the fitting and clean the socket out with the recommended cleaner.

3 Now chamfer the end of the pipe to an angle of 45°, and smooth off the chamfer carefully with fine glass paper so that no rough edges remain.

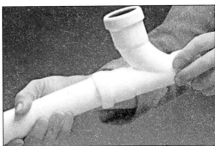

5 Push the pipe into the socket gently but firmly. Then push it fully home and check that all is square, otherwise you may damage the sealing ring.

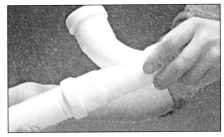

7 Gently pull the pipe out from the fitting so that your pencil mark is about 10mm (³/₈in) away from the fitting to allow for expansion when hot water is flowing.

2 Check that the rubber seal is properly seated in the socket. You may find seals are supplied separately and you will have to insert them.

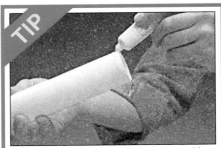

4 Lubricate the end of the pipe with petroleum jelly over a length of about 5mm (³/₁₆ in).

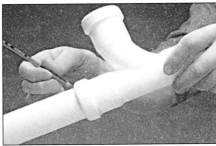

6 Now make a pencil mark on the pipe at the edge of the socket – you can easily rub it off later if you want to – to act as a guide in setting the expansion gap.

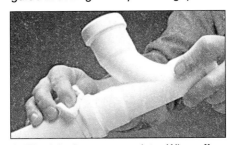

8 The joint is now complete. Wipe off any excess petroleum jelly. Don't lose the expansion allowance when joining the other side of the fitting.

manufacturer may make both PP and either PVC or ABS systems.

It is worth asking the supplier if there is an instruction leaflet supplied by the maker. There are slight variations in the methods of using each particular make of pipe and fitting. The manufacturer's instructions, if available, should be followed to the letter.

Buying new pipe

Existing waste pipe is likely to be imperial in size – 1½in internal diameter for a sink or bath and 1¼in internal diameter for a wash basin.

Metric sized plastic pipes are normally described – like thin-walled copper tubes – by their external diameter, though at least one well-known manufacturer adds to the confusion by using the internal diameter. Both internal and external diameters may vary slightly – usually by less than one millimetre between makes. This is yet another reason for sticking to one make of pipe for any single project.

The outside diameter of a plastic tube that is the equivalent of a 1¼in imperial sized metal tube is likely to be 36mm and the inside diameter 32mm. The outside diameter of the equivalent of a 1½in pipe is likely to be 43mm and the inside diameter 39mm. If in doubt, it is usually sufficient to ask the supplier for waste pipe fittings for a basin waste or – as the case may be – a bath or sink waste. Plain-ended plastic pipe is usually supplied in 3m (10ft) lengths, though a supplier will probably cut you off a shorter piece.

Joining solvent-weld types

Solvent-weld fittings are neater and less obtrusive than push-fit ones and they offer the facility of pre-fabrication before installation. However, making them does demand a little more skill and care and – unlike push-fit joints – they cannot accommodate the expansion (thermal movement) that takes place as hot wastes run through the pipe. A 4m (13ft) length of PVC pipe will expand by about 13mm (½in) when its temperature is raised above 20°C (70°F). For this reason, where a straight length of waste pipe exceeds 1.8m (6ft) in length, expansion couplings must be introduced at 1.8m intervals if other joints are to be solvent-welded. This rarely occurs in domestic design, however, and use of push-fit or solvent-weld is a matter of personal preference.

Although the instructions given by the different manufacturers vary slightly, the steps to making solvent-weld joints follow very similar lines. Of course, the first rule is to measure up all your pipe lengths carefully. Remember to allow for the end of the pipe overlapping the joint. When you've worked out pipe lengths cutting can start.

JOINING SOIL PIPES

These are joined in the same way as plastic waste pipes but are much bigger – about 100mm (4in) in diameter – so they take longer to fit. They also have some different fittings, such as a soil branch for use where the outlet pipe joins the stack, and access fittings with bolted removable plates for inspection. There are also special connectors to link to the WC pan, via a special gasket, and to link to the underground drainage system which is traditionally made of vitrified clay.

The accurate moulding of the fittings and the ease of assembly means that you can confidently tackle complete replacement of a soil system.that you can confidently tackle complete replacement of a soil system.

1 Soil pipes are joined in the same way as their narrower waste counterparts, but as they're bigger take special care with cutting and chamfering.

2 You have got a lot more area to cover with the solvent cement so you must work speedily – but don't neglect accurate application.

3 The soil branch pipe has a swept entry into the main stack fitting. This is one of the most important joints in the system, so make sure you get it right.

4 When you finally push the pipe into the fitting socket make quite sure that it goes right home against the pipe stop inside the fitting.

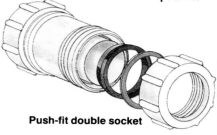

Cut the pipe clean and square with a hacksaw or other fine-toothed saw. A useful tip to ensure a square cut is to fold a piece of newspaper over the pipe and join the edges beneath it. The paper will then act as a template.

Remove all internal and external burrs or roughness at the end of the pipe, then use a file to chamfer the outside of the pipe end to about 45°. Not all manufacturers recommend this, but it does provide an extra key for the solvent.

Insert the pipe end into the fitting and mark the depth of insertion with a pencil. Using medium grade abrasive paper, or a light file, lightly roughen the end of the pipe, as far as the pencil mark, and also roughen the interior of the socket. Thoroughly clean the roughened surfaces of the socket and the pipe end using a clean rag moistened with a spirit cleaner recommended by the manufacturer of the fittings.

Select the correct solvent cement (PVC pipes need a different solvent cement from ABS ones; once again, buy all the materials needed at the same time from the same supplier). Read the label on the tin and stir only if instructed.

Using a clean paintbrush, apply the solvent cement to the pipe end and to the inside of the fittings, brushing in the direction of the pipe. It is usually necessary to apply two coats to ABS pipes and fittings. The second coat should be brushed on quickly before the first has dried.

Push the pipe fully home into the fitting (some, but not all, manufacturers suggest that this should be done with a slight twisting action). Remove excess solvent cement and hold the assembled joint securely in position for about 30 seconds. If hot water will be flowing through the pipe, don't use it for 24 hours to give time for the joint to set completely.

Joining ring-seal types

Preparation for ring-seal or push-fit jointing is similar to that for solvent welding. The pipe end must be cut absolutely squarely and all the burr removed. You should draw a line round the cut end of the pipe 10mm from its end and chamfer back to this line with a rasp or shaping tool, then clean the recess within the push-fit connector's socket and check that the sealing ring is evenly seated. One manufacturer supplies sealing rings separately, and they should be inserted at this point. The pipe end should now be lubricated with a small amount of petroleum jelly and pushed firmly into the socket past the joint ring. Push it fully home and mark the insertion depth on the pipe with a pencil. Then withdraw it by 10mm (⅜in), which is the allowance made for expansion. The expansion joint that is inserted into long straight lengths of solvent-welded waste pipe consists of a coupling with a solvent-weld joint at one end and a push-fit joint at the other.

As with solvent-weld jointing, individual manufacturers may give varying instructions. Some, for instance, advise the use of their own silicone lubricating jelly. Where the manufacturer supplies instructions it is best to follow these exactly.

Fittings

PVC pipe can be bent by the application of gentle heat from a blow-torch, but this technique needs practice and it is best to rely on purpose-made fittings. Sockets are used for joining straight lengths of pipe, tees for right-angled branches, and both 90° and 45° elbows are usually available. If you need to reduce the diameters from one pipe to another you can use reducing sockets. These are really sockets within sockets which can be welded together, one taking the smaller diameter pipe and the other the larger. Soil outlet pipes from WCs are joined in the same way; they are merely bigger – usually 100mm (4in) – in diameter. Sockets work in the same way, but the branch-junction with the main soil stack must be of a specially 'swept' design.

HOW PLASTIC FITTINGS WORK

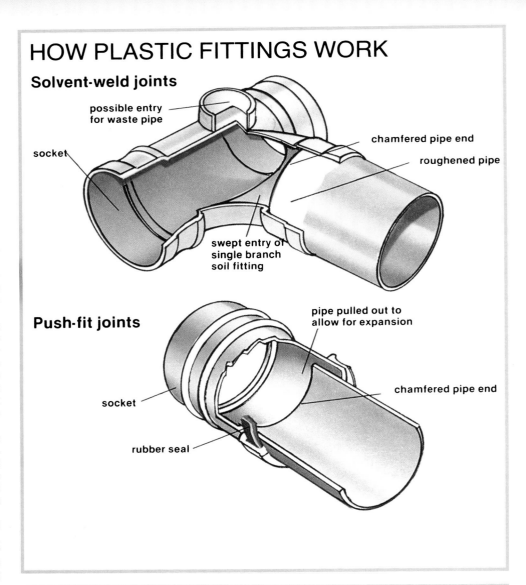

SPECIAL FITTINGS

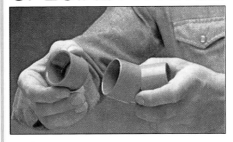

Special fittings are available when pipe fitting is not straightforward. This is a reducing adaptor for push-fit fittings where you need to join a

32mm pipe to a 40mm pipe. You join the relevant pipe to the mating part of the adaptor and then join the two adaptor parts together.

TYPES OF PIPEWORK

Lead and iron are no longer used as plumbing materials, having been replaced by copper and stainless steel. Now plastic pipework is the most commonly used material in domestic plumbing.

Virtually all **soil pipes** are now made from UPVC (1), which can be joined together using solvent welds or ring seals. Likewise, **overflow pipes** (2) are also made from UPVC, and lengths of these are connected with push-fit joins.

Waste pipes, made of UPVC and ABS plastic, are used for taking water away from baths, basins and sinks (3). Depending on the system they can be joined either by solvent welding or push-fit connections.

Plastic can also be used for water supply pipes. **Polybutylene pipes** (4) can take hot and cold water, the pipes being joined by compression fittings or special push-fit connectors. Similarly, **CPVC pipe** (5) can be used for hot and cold runs, but this is joined with solvent welds.

Black **polythene pipe** (6), the first plastic pipe to be used generally in domestic plumbing, is only suitable for cold water supplies, and consequently is mainly employed for garden and other outside water services.

Rainwater downpipes (7) are made from UPVC and have either circular or square profiles.

Half-hard temper **copper pipe** (8) is used for hot and cold distribution and central heating pipes, being easy to bend and join. **Stain-** less steel (9) has also been used, mainly because it can be joined to copper and galvanised steel without causing electrolytic action.

Flexible copper pipe (10), which can be bent simply in the hands, is ideal for making the awkward connections between tap tails and the supply pipes without having to alter the existing runs.

PLUMBING FITTINGS

Putting in hot and cold pipes means you'll need a lot of different fittings at the pipe junctions, elbows, tees, valves and so on. Here is a basic selection to show you what's available.

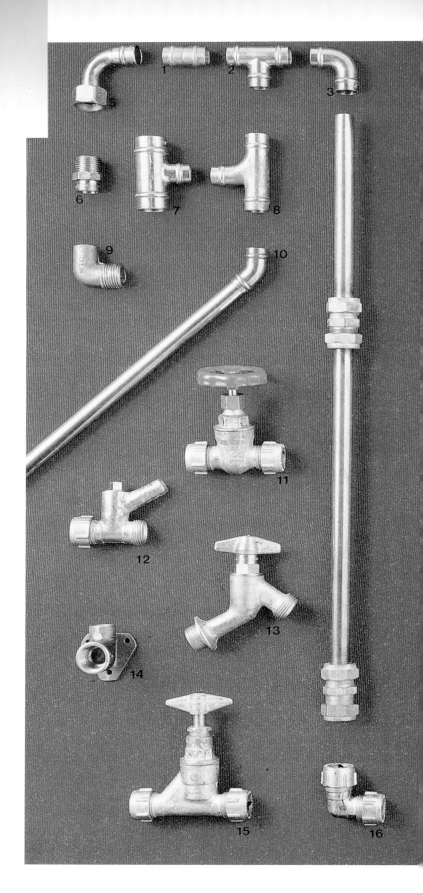

The most important skill required in any plumbing project involving hot or cold water pipe installation is that of making sound, water-tight joints between lengths of copper tubing and other pieces of plumbing equipment such as taps, ball-valves, and cold water cylinders. You will be required, for example, to take branches from existing water pipes and to make changes of direction in a pipe run.

To do all this, you need plumbing fittings, which make compression or soldered capillary joints (see pages 114 to 118). They are easily assembled using only a small tool kit. Type 'A' or non-manipulative compression joints are by far the more common. The other sort, type 'B' or manipulative joints are usually only used where the water authorities insist on them for underground pipe work.

It is possible to make Type 'A' compression fittings with only a couple of adjustable wrenches, a hacksaw and a metal file, but for a major project involving a number of joints, the purchase or hire of a wheel tube cutter is advisable; and to make soldered capillary joints some kind of blow-torch is also necessary, together with a pad of flame-proof glass fibre.

Compression joints and fittings

Compression joints and fittings are made either of brass or gunmetal, although brass is the more common. As brass is an alloy of copper and zinc, impurities in the water supply in some areas may produce a phenomenon called dezincification. This is an electro-chemical reaction which results in the extraction of the zinc from the alloy, leaving the fitting unchanged in appearance but virtually without structural strength. Where dezincification is likely to occur, gunmetal fittings are traditionally used. Gunmetal is an alloy of copper and tin. However, a more economical alternative these days is to use one of the recently developed corrosion-resistant ranges of brass fittings.

Sizes of compression fittings

Compression fittings are available for use with a number of sizes of copper or stainless steel pipe, but the only sizes likely to be required in domestic plumbing are 15mm, 22mm and 28mm. An existing plumbing system may well have imperial-sized pipe, and the imperial equivalents of 15mm, 22mm and 28mm are ½in, ¾in and 1in. The apparent difference between metric sizes and their imperial equivalents is accounted for by the fact that imperial-sized pipe is described by its internal diameter, and metric-sized pipe by its external diameter. You can use metric 15mm and 28mm compression joints and fittings to make connections with ½in and 1in imperial-sized pipe. When 22mm fittings are used with ¾in pipe, an adaptor is needed.

Compression fitting range

The copper-to-copper coupling is the basic compression joint. There are reducing couplings to enable 28mm or 22mm tubing to be joined to tubes of smaller diameter. There are equal-ended and reducing T junctions (usually simply called 'tees') to enable branch supply pipes to be taken from existing pipes. There are elbow bends and 135° bends.

There are also fittings with one end a compression joint and the other a threaded outlet for direct connection to cisterns, cylinders or pipes of other materials. Male outlets are threaded on the outside, female ones on the inside. Threaded joints of this kind are made watertight by binding the thread with plumbers' PTFE tape.

Soldered capillary joints

Capillary joints, which are neater and cheaper than compression joints, consist of a copper sleeve that fits fairly tightly over the tube ends so that solder may be run between the outside of the tube ends and the interior of the sleeve. 'Integral ring' or 'solder ring' capillary joints contain within the fitting sufficient solder to make the joint. With the cheaper 'end feed' fittings, solder has to be fed in separately from a reel of solder wire.

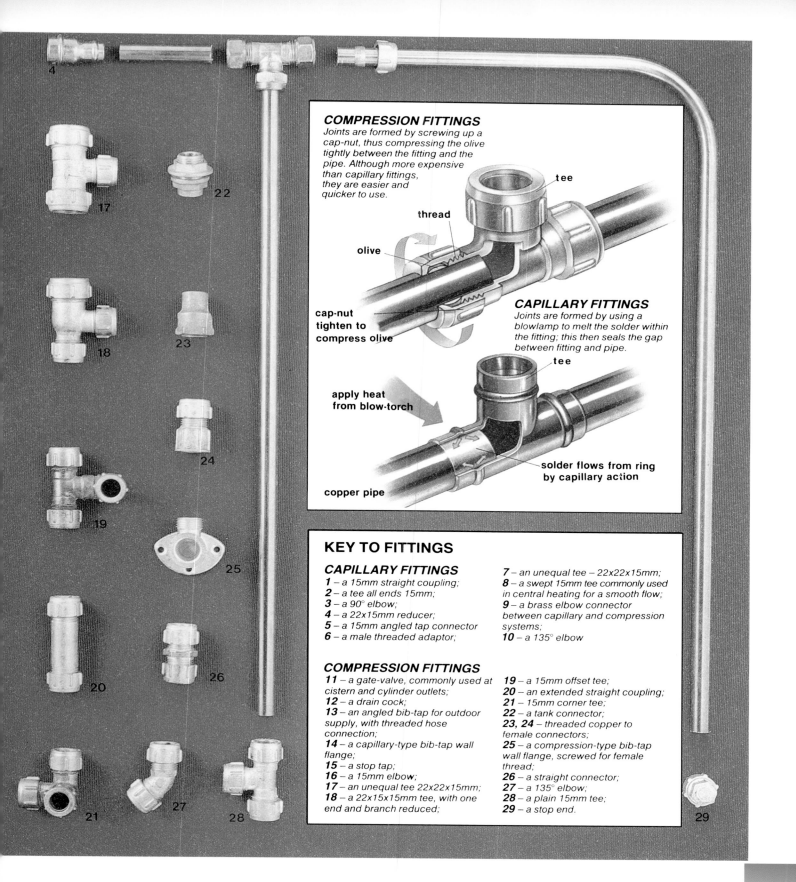

COMPRESSION FITTINGS

Joints are formed by screwing up a cap-nut, thus compressing the olive tightly between the fitting and the pipe. Although more expensive than capillary fittings, they are easier and quicker to use.

tee

thread

olive

cap-nut tighten to compress olive

CAPILLARY FITTINGS

Joints are formed by using a blowlamp to melt the solder within the fitting; this then seals the gap between fitting and pipe.

tee

apply heat from blow-torch

solder flows from ring by capillary action

copper pipe

KEY TO FITTINGS

CAPILLARY FITTINGS

1 – a 15mm straight coupling;
2 – a tee all ends 15mm;
3 – a 90° elbow;
4 – a 22x15mm reducer;
5 – a 15mm angled tap connector
6 – a male threaded adaptor;

7 – an unequal tee – 22x22x15mm;
8 – a swept 15mm tee commonly used in central heating for a smooth flow;
9 – a brass elbow connector between capillary and compression systems;
10 – a 135° elbow

COMPRESSION FITTINGS

11 – a gate-valve, commonly used at cistern and cylinder outlets;
12 – a drain cock;
13 – an angled bib-tap for outdoor supply, with threaded hose connection;
14 – a capillary-type bib-tap wall flange;
15 – a stop tap;
16 – a 15mm elbow;
17 – an unequal tee 22x22x15mm;
18 – a 22x15x15mm tee, with one end and branch reduced;

19 – a 15mm offset tee;
20 – an extended straight coupling;
21 – 15mm corner tee;
22 – a tank connector;
23, 24 – threaded copper to female connectors;
25 – a compression-type bib-tap wall flange, screwed for female thread;
26 – a straight connector;
27 – a 135° elbow;
28 – a plain 15mm tee;
29 – a stop end.

TOOLS FOR PLUMBING JOBS

You should always check you've got the right tools to hand before starting any work, and plumbing is no exception. Here's a list of the ones you're most likely to need, plus some essential items to help you cope with emergencies.

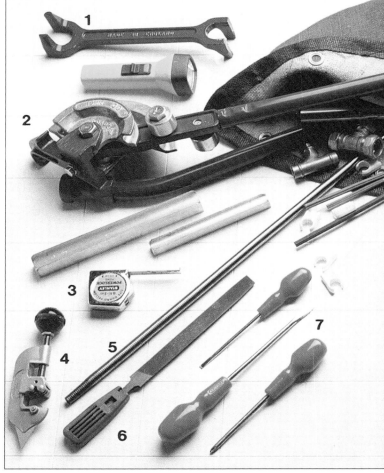

Anyone living in a fairly modern – or modernised – house with copper or stainless steel water supply pipes and a plastic waste water system can carry out all routine plumbing maintenance and repair work with only a minimal tool kit. In fact, many of the tools required for plumbing work will already be part of the general household or car tool kit. But, if you plan to do a lot of plumbing work you'll need a few specialised tools.

Before buying any expensive new tool ask yourself how often you will need to use it. If the honest answer is 'not more than once a year' then you should seriously consider hiring it instead.

Spanners
You'll need a couple of adjustable spanners for tightening up compression fittings – one to hold the fitting steady while you use the other to tighten it up. You'll need them for many other types of fittings too.

A useful tool which can make life easier is the 'crows-foot' spanner. It's used to undo the virtually inaccessible back-nuts that secure bath and basin taps in position. Unless you have a lot of room beneath the taps you'll find it almost impossible to undo these nuts with an ordinary spanner.

Wrenches
Only wrenches are capable of gripping and turning round objects such as pipes. There are two types used in plumbing. The pipe wrench looks like an adjustable spanner but its lower jaw is able to pivot slightly, and both jaws are serrated. As you use it, the lower jaw is able to open just enough to grip the pipe, then, as you turn it, the serrations dig in, pull in the jaws and grip even tighter. The harder you turn, the tighter they grip, so they're suitable for really stubborn jobs. Wrenches will only work in one direction; if you turn them the wrong way the jaws won't grip and the pipe will slip round.

The lockable wrench is slightly different. You adjust the jaw separation with a screw, then close them round the pipe, squeezing the handles to lock them on tightly.

Pipe cutters
You can cut pipes with a hacksaw quite successfully, but if you plan to do a lot of plumbing work you should consider buying a pipe cutter. The pipe is placed between two hardened rollers and a thin cutting wheel; the tool is then rotated round the pipe while the cutting wheel is screwed down into the metal. A pipe cutter always produces a perfectly square and smooth cut – there is none of the rough metal burr that you'd get with a hacksaw. Yet it does round the end of the pipe inwards a little and the metal flange must be removed with a reamer which is usually incorporated in one end of the tool. Since pipe cutters need to be rotated round the rube they can't be used to cut existing pipes fitted close to a wall. So you will need a hacksaw as well.

Pipe benders
Sharp bends in pipes are easiest to make with capillary or compression fittings. But you can bend pipe by hand it you want, and you'll have to if you want shallow curves. Copper pipe with a diameter of 22mm (¾in) or less can be bent using bending springs or in a bending machine. The purpose of both springs and bending machine is to support the walls of the tube so that they don't flatten or wrinkle inside the curve as the bend is made. A bending spring supports the tube internally, while the bending machine supports it externally. As you're unlikely to want to bend copper pipe that often, these are tools it's best to hire when they're required.

Thread sealers
Jointing compound and PTFE tape are both used to make a watertight – and gas-tight – seal on screwed fittings. Jointing compound is a sticky paste which you smear round the thread, and PTFE thread sealing tape is wound anticlockwise round the male fitting before the joint is assembled.

Flame-proof gloves
If you're using a blowlamp and doing a lot of soldering then you'd be wise to invest in a pair of flame-proof gloves. Copper pipe conducts heat very efficiently so the gloves could prevent many burnt fingers.

Torch
Very often you'll need to work at the back of sinks and baths or in dark, awkward corners or in the loft, so a torch is essential. Change the batteries as soon as the bulb dims.

Tape measure
You'll need a tape measure for accurate cutting of lengths of pipe and for positioning taps and fittings in the right place.

Files and steel wool
A file is essential for removing burrs left by a hacksaw. Emery paper and steel wool are both used to clean the ends of copper pipe ready for making soldered joints. They're also used to roughen plastic pipe to provide a key for adhesives.

Blowlamp
Unless you plan to use compression fittings for all your plumbing work you'll certainly need a blowlamp for making soldered joints. In most cases, a small blowlamp operating off a disposable canister of gas is easiest to use. Don't forget to keep a spare canister in your tool kit; they have a habit of running out at the most awkward moments.

Other tools
Apart from the tools described above, you'll also need a power drill for drilling holes for fixing screws and pipes, a set of screwdrivers and a pair of pliers.

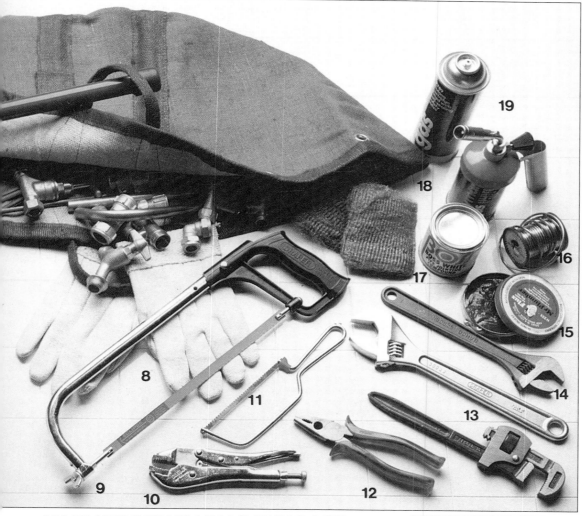

KEY

Tools for major plumbing work

1 *crowsfoot spanner (one end for bath taps, the other for basins)*
2 *pipe bender and formers for 15 and 22mm pipe*
3 *retractable tape measure*
4 *wheeled pipe cutter*
5 *bending spring (available in 15 and 22mm sizes)*
6 *half-round file*
7 *screwdrivers for slotted and cross-head screws*
8 *flame-proof gloves*
9 *hacksaw with spare blades*
10 *lockable wrench*
11 *junior hacksaw*
12 *pliers*
13 *pipe wrench*
14 *adjustable spanners*
15 *flux paste for soldered capillary fittings*
16 *solder in coil form for end-feed capillary fittings*
17 *jointing compound or for threaded connections*
18 *wire wool pads*
19 *butane or propane blowlamp with replacement gas canisters.*

In addition to the tools and items of equipment mentioned above, you are also likely to need:
● *power drill with a selection of different sized masonry, twist drills and wood-boring bits*
● *pipe clips in 15 and 22mm sizes*
● *wallplugs (the stick type that you cut to length are the most economical)*
● *screws for mounting pipe clips, radiator brackets and so on*
● *a torch*

AN EMERGENCY PLUMBING KIT

There's really no point in assembling a full plumbing tool kit if you never intend to do any plumbing work. But emergencies can always happen so it's wise to keep a small tool kit to hand to stop an accident turning into a disaster. This should include an adjustable spanner, a locking wrench, a screwdriver and a pair of pliers, plus equipment to cope with bursts and leaks.

If you hammer a nail into a pipe you can easily make a quick repair with a two-part pack of epoxy resin sold especially for plumbing repairs. The adhesive and hardener are worked together in the hands and the material is moulded round the hole. This makes a permanent repair for small holes or leaking joints, but a larger hole is repaired more securely by cutting out the damaged section of pipe and

inserting a straight compression coupling. So keep at least two of these in your tool kit – one each for 15mm and 22mm pipe.

Keep some penetrating oil for freeing jammed stop-valves or corroded nuts and, of course, an adjustable spanner to undo the latter. You'll also need a selection of tap washers – one for each type of tap, and some O-rings for the ball-valve. A few spare olives are always handy – compression fittings can be reused but you need a new olive each time. For clearing blocked waste pipes you'll need a 'force cup' or sink waste plunger, and a piece of flexible wire for clearing out blocked pipes and drains. Finally, mini-hacksaws are so cheap it's worth keeping one specially for your emergency tool kit. For more information see the following chapter.

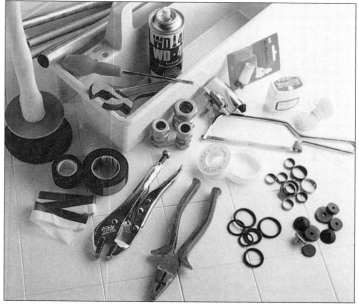

ROUTINE MAINTENANCE AND REPAIRS

Looking after your home's plumbing system is essential if you are to get the best from it, and every member of the family should know what to do in an emergency when the system springs a leak, so that it can be dealt with quickly and effectively.

DRAINING PLUMBING SYSTEMS

When you are carrying out repairs or alterations to your plumbing or wet central heating system, you will usually have to drain water from the parts you are working on. Here's what you'll have to do.

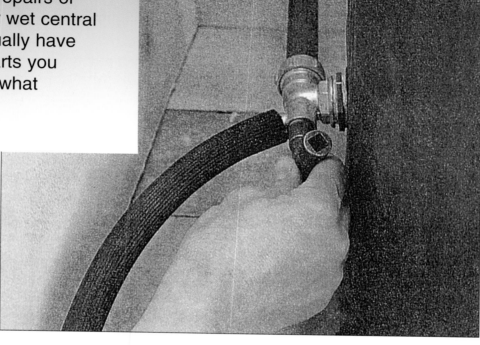

Virtually all major and many minor plumbing operations demand the partial or total drainage of either the domestic hot or cold water supply. If you have a 'wet' central heating system you'll also have to drain that before carrying out repairs or alterations. Before attempting this – long before the need for drainage arises, in fact – you should make yourself thoroughly familiar with the design and layout of these systems in your home. Here are some questions to which you should know the answers:

● Are all cold water draw-off points supplied direct from the rising main, or are the bathroom cold taps and the WC cistern supplied with water from a main cold water storage cistern (probably situated in the roof space)?

● Is the hot water system 'direct' or 'indirect' (see pages 103 to 107)?

● If the system is direct, is the domestic hot water heated solely by means of an electric immersion heater, solely by means of a domestic boiler (gas, oil or solid fuel), or are both means of heating available?

● If hot water is provided solely by means of an immersion heater, is there a drain-valve at the base of the cold supply pipe from the storage cistern to the hot water cylinder?

● If hot water is provided by means of a boiler, is there a drain-valve on the pipework beside the boiler, or possibly incorporated into the boiler itself?

● If the system is indirect, is it a conventional indirect system (indicated by the presence of a small feed-and-expansion tank in the roof space, feeding the primary circuit) or is it a self-priming indirect system such as the Primatic?

● Is there a 'wet' central heating system provided in conjunction with hot water supply?

● Where is the main stop-valve, and are there any other stop-valves or gate-valves fitted into distribution or circulating pipes in the system?

● Are there drain-valves at low points in the central heating circuit?

Draining down for simple repairs

Once you are thoroughly familiar with the contents and layout of your own plumbing and central heating systems, you will be able to work out for yourself how much draining-down will be necessary before you undertake any particular item of maintenance or any particular project. If, for instance, you wish to rewasher the cold tap over the kitchen sink (this is supplied direct from the rising main) or to tee into the rising main to provide a garden water supply, all that you need to do is to turn off the main stop-valve and to turn on the kitchen cold tap until water ceases to flow from it. You will then have drained the rising main to the level of the cold tap. In many modern homes a drain-valve is provided immediately above the main stop-valve to permit the rising main to be completely drained.

Rather more drainage is necessary when you wish to renew the washer on a hot tap, or on a cold tap supplied from a storage cistern, or to renew a ball-valve in a WC cistern that is supplied with water from a storage cistern. First of all, see if there are any stop-valves or gate-valves on the distribution pipes leading to the particular tap or ball-valve. There could be gate-valves on the main hot and cold distribution pipes just below the level of the main cold water storage cistern. There could even be a mini-stop-valve on the distribution pipe immediately before its connection to the tail of the tap or ball-valve.

In either of these circumstances you're in luck! All you have to do is to turn off the appropriate gate-valve or mini-stop-valve and then to turn on the tap or flush the lavatory cistern. You can then carry out the necessary repairs.

Avoiding unnecessary drainage

The chances are, though, that the main stop-valve will be the only one in the system, and that you'll have to contemplate draining the main cold water storage cistern and the appropriate distribution pipes before you can get on with your task, by turning off the main stop-valve and draining the cistern and pipes from the taps supplied by the cistern. This, however, will mean that the whole of the plumbing system is out of action for as long as it takes you to complete the job. It is generally better to go up into the roof space and lay a slat of wood across the top of the cold water storage cistern. You can then tie the float arm of the ball-valve up to it, so that water cannot flow into the cistern. Then drain the cistern by opening the bathroom taps. In this way the cold tap over the sink will not be put out of action.

Here's another useful money-saving tip: even if you are draining down to rewasher a hot tap, there is no need to run to waste all that hot water stored in the hot water cylinder, *provided that your bathroom cold taps are supplied from the cold water storage cistern.* Having tied up the ball-valve, run the bathroom *cold* taps until they cease to flow and only then turn on the hot tap you want to work on. Because the hot water distribution pipe is taken from above the hot water storage cylinder, only a little hot water – from the pipe itself – will flow away to waste and the cylinder will remain full of hot water.

For the same reason, unless you expect to have the hot water system out of action for a

WHERE TO DRAIN THE SYSTEM

On a well-designed plumbing system you should find that drain-valves have been installed at several points, so that partial draining-down is possible.

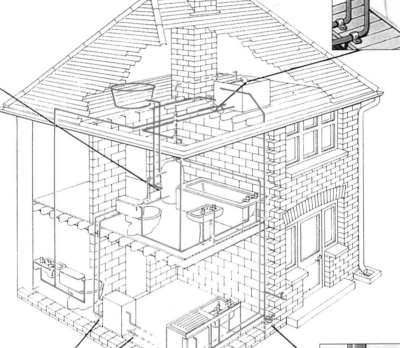

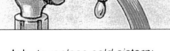

1 *A drain-valve at the point where the cold feed from the storage cistern in the loft enters the hot water cylinder means that you can empty the main body of the cylinder (at least, down to the level of the inlet pipe) in the event of it springing a leak. Here a T-shaped drain-valve spanner is being used to open the valve.*

3 *Drain-valves fitted beside the boiler allow you to drain the primary circuit and the central heating system.*

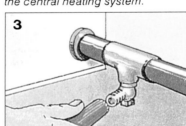

2 *If gate-valves are fitted on the outlets from the cold water storage cistern, all you have to do to drain a pipe run is shut the appropriate valve and open the taps. If they are not fitted, you will have to drain the cistern too. To stop it filling, tie the float arm up to a piece of wood resting across the cistern.*

4 *A drain-valve fitted above the rising main stop-valve allows you to drain the main and connect tees to it. The stop-valve saves you from having to tie up the storage cistern ball-valve when draining the cold supply pipes.*

Action checklist

Which part of the system you drain, and how you go about it, depends on the job you're doing. Here's a brief checklist of the sequence of operations in each case.

Job: *to rewasher/replace kitchen cold tap, tee off rising main for new supply pipe;*
● *turn off rising main stop-valve and drain rising main via drain-valve*
● *if no drain-valve fitted, open kitchen cold tap to drain main down to level of tee to kitchen sink.*

Job: *to rewasher/replace other cold tap, renew WC ball-valve, extend cold supply;*
● *if gate-valve fitted to outlet at cold cistern, close valve and open lowest appropriate cold tap; otherwise*
● *tie up arm of cold cistern ball-valve and drain cistern by opening cold taps.*

Job: *to rewasher/replace hot tap, extend existing hot supply;*
● *close gate-valve on outlet at cistern or tie up cistern ball-valve*
● *open cold tap until flow stops*
● *only then open hot tap.*

Job: *to replace hot cylinder;*
● *close gate-valve or tie up ball-valve arm*
● *turn off boiler or immersion heater*
● *empty cylinder via cylinder drain-valve*
● *close gate-valve on outlet from feed/ expansion tank, or tie up ball-valve*
● *drain primary circuit via drain-valve at boiler.*

Job: *to replace cold cistern;*
● *close rising main stop-valve*
● *drain cistern by opening cold taps (hot water will still run from cylinder).*

Job: *to replace boiler;*
● *on direct systems, turn off boiler or immersion heater and also heating system*
● *close rising main stop-valve*
● *open all taps, and drain boiler from drain-valve nearby*
● *on indirect systems, turn off boiler*
● *close feed/expansion tank gate-valve*
● *drain primary and central heating systems from drain-valves at boiler.*

prolonged period there is no need to switch off the immersion heater or to let out the boiler when carrying out a maintenance operation on the bathroom hot tap.

Problems with air locks

If your hot and cold water distribution systems are properly designed – with 'horizontal' runs of pipe actually having a slight fall away from the storage cistern or the vent pipe to permit air to escape – then the system should fill up with little or no trouble when you untie the ball-valve and permit water to flow into the cistern again. Should an air-lock prevent complete filling, try connecting one end of a length of hose to the cold tap over the kitchen sink and the other end to one of the taps giving trouble. Turn on first the tap giving trouble and then the one over the kitchen sink. Mains pressure from this cold tap should blow the air bubble out of the system.

Draining the whole system

Very occasionally – perhaps because of a major reconstruction of the system or because of that most traumatic of all plumbing emergencies, a leaking boiler – it may be necessary to drain the whole system. Let's assume, first of all, that you have either a direct hot water system or a self-priming indirect one.

Switch off the immersion heater and let out or switch off the boiler. Turn off the central heating system if this is operated from the self-priming cylinder. Close the main stop-valve and open up every tap in the house – hot as well as cold. Connect one end of a length of hose to the drain-valve beside the boiler or, if the cylinder is heated by an immersion heater only, at the base of the cold supply pipe entering the cylinder, and take the other end of the hose to an outside gully. Open up the drain-valve and allow the system to drain.

If you have an indirect system you should again turn off the boiler and central heating system. Then close the gate-valve leading from the feed-and-expansion tank, or tie up it's ball-valve, and drain the system from the boiler drain-valves.

How you proceed depends upon the reason for which you have carried out the draining-down. Your aim should be to get as much of the plumbing system as possible back into operation quickly.

Restoring partial supplies

The first step is to go up into the roof space and tie up the ball-valve on the main storage cistern as already described. Open up the main stop-valve and water supply will be restored to the cold tap over the kitchen sink.

It should also be possible to restore the bathroom cold water supplies. Trace the distribution pipe that takes water from the cold water storage cistern to the hot water cylinder.

COPING WITH AIRLOCKS

Clear supply-pipe airlocks by linking the affected tap to the kitchen cold tap with hose secured by worm-drive clips. Open the affected tap first, then the kitchen tap.

Avoid airlocks in primary or heating circuits by filling them upwards via a hose linking the kitchen cold tap and the boiler drain-valve. Close vents as radiators fill.

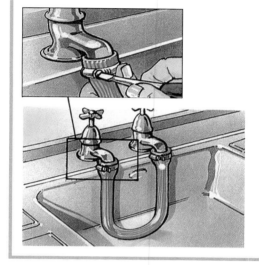
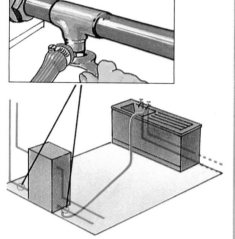

Find a cork of the correct size, lean into the cistern and push it into the pipe's inlet. Before doing so, it is a good idea to screw a substantial woodscrew part of the way into the cork to facilitate removal. You can then untie the ball-valve and allow the cistern to refill; no water will flow to the hot cylinder.

Draining heating systems

If you have a conventional indirect hot water system – perhaps installed in conjunction with a central heating system – you can drain the primary circuit, together with the radiator circuit if there is one, without draining the water from the outer part of the storage cylinder. Because of the increased risk of corrosion that arises from water and air coming into contact with steel surfaces, a radiator circuit should be drained only when absolutely essential. When this has to be done – to add additional radiators, perhaps – you should tie up the ball-valve serving the feed-and-expansion tank and drain from both the drain-valve beside the boiler and from any drain-valves provided at low points of the system. You must, of course, let out or switch off the boiler before attempting this.

When refilling the primary circuit (or when refilling a direct system with boiler) it may help to prevent the formation of air-locks if you connect one end of your garden hose to the boiler drain-valve and the other end to the cold tap over the kitchen sink. Open them both up and the system will fill upwards, with air being driven out in front of the rising water. As the central heating circuit refills,

open up all the radiator vents – and any other air vents that there may be in the system – and leave them open until water begins to flow through them. It is a good idea, when refilling a central heating system, to introduce a reliable corrosion-proofer into the feed-and-expansion tank to prevent future internal corrosion, but you can do this only if you fill the system from the top, not from the bottom.

Winter precautions

One final point: if you are leaving your home empty during the winter months, you should drain the main cold water storage cistern and, if you have a direct hot water system and will be away for more than two or three days, you should drain the hot cylinder, the boiler and its circulation pipes as well. Human memory is fallible. Having done so, leave a conspicuous notice on the boiler and by the immersion heater switch saying 'SYSTEM DRAINED – DO NOT LIGHT BOILER OR SWITCH ON HEATER UNTIL IT HAS BEEN REFILLED'.

Because of the risk of corrosion already referred to, the primary circuit and any central heating system connected to it should not be drained in these circumstances. If you have a central heating system that is capable of automatic control, leave it switched on under the control of a frost-stat. This is a thermostatic control, usually positioned in a garage or in the roof space, that will bring the heating into operation when a predetermined, near-freezing-point temperature, is reached.

STOPPING TAPS LEAKING

Although taps are in frequent use, they rarely need maintenance. But if one starts to leak don't ignore it. Leaking taps are not only annoying and wasteful, but also, if they are hot taps, expensive - you've paid to heat the water going down the drain.

A tap is a device for controlling the flow of water at an outlet point, and is opened and closed by turning a handle. This may be a 'tee' or 'capstan' type (so called because of the shape) fitted onto a spindle rising from the body of the tap. Or it may be a 'shrouded head', covering all of the upper part of the tap.

Turning the handle clockwise forces a jumper unit down onto a valve seating in the waterway of the tap and stops the flow of water. Because metal against metal doesn't make a very tight seal, a synthetic rubber disc — a washer — is attached to the base of the jumper so that it beds firmly onto the seating.

Turning the handle anti-clockwise raises the jumper from the seating and allows water to flow. An exception to this is the Supatap where the nozzle is rotated to control the flow. When you open a tap water pressure will also force water round the jumper unit and, unless there is some way of preventing it, this would escape from round the spindle.

To get round this problem some taps have 'O' ring seals fitted to the spindle while older taps have greased wool packed tightly in a gland around the spindle. More modern taps have rubber tube for packing.

Mixers work in exactly the same way as ordinary taps except that they have only one spout that combines the flow of water from the hot and cold supplies. On kitchen mixers particularly this spout can be swivelled so that it can be pushed to one side to give better access to the sink or can supply a double sink.

When a tap starts to leak, there's a strong temptation either to ignore it or to try to stop it by closing it as tightly as you can. Such action is invariably ineffective and could lead to the valve seating being permanently damaged.

Where leaks occur

Basically there are three places a tap can leak: at the spout, in which case the washer and perhaps the seating will need looking at; at the spindle when the tap is turned on, which means either the packing in the gland or the 'O' ring has failed; or at the swivel point at the spout of a mixer tap, which means that the 'O' ring is at fault. All these repairs are easy to deal with. But first you must know the type of tap and the terminology related to it

How washers are replaced

Conventional pillar tap This is the basic type of tap design and provides a good example of the procedure to follow when replacing a washer. These taps are commonly used for the hot and cold water supply over the kitchen sink and in this position they are probably the most frequently used taps in the house. It's quite likely that sooner or later the washers will need replacing.

To do this you'll first have to turn off the water supply either at the mains or, if you're lucky, at isolating stop-valves under the sink which when shut cut off the supply either to the hot or cold tap without affecting the rest of the system (see previous section and pages 171 to 172). Turn on the tap fully so it is drained before you start work.

Usually with a pillar tap the spindle rises out of a dome-like easy-clean cover, which you should be able to unscrew by hand. If this proves too difficult, you can use a wrench, but pad the jaws thoroughly with rag to avoid damaging the finish on plated taps.

With the tap turned on fully you can then raise the cover sufficiently to slip the jaws of a wrench under it to grip the 'flats' of the headgear — the main body of the tap which has a nut-shaped section to it. If you can't do this you'll need to take off the tap handle and easy-clean cover. First you'll have to remove the tiny grub-screw in the side of the handle which can then be lifted off. If this proves difficult a good tip is to open the tap fully, unscrew, then raise the easy-clean cover and place pieces of wood (a spring-loaded clothes peg will do) between the bottom of the easy-clean cover and the body of the tap. By turning the tap handle as if you were trying to close it the upward pressure on the easy-clean cover will force it off the spindle. However, you then have to replace it over the spindle just sufficiently to enable you to turn the tap on. When this is done take it off again and remove the easy-clean cover. While you are doing all this make sure

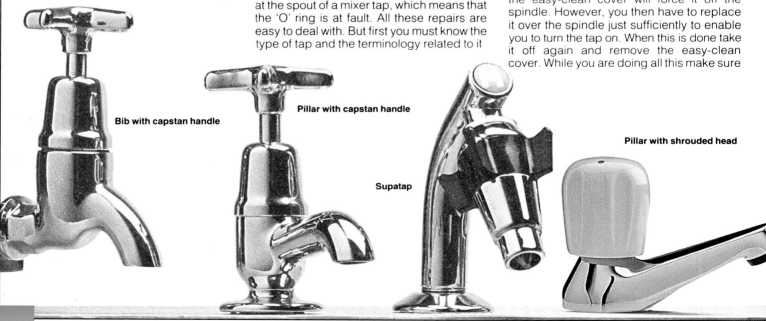

Bib with capstan handle

Pillar with capstan handle

Supatap

Pillar with shrouded head

you hold the tap steady. If the headgear is stiff and the entire tap turns you could damage the part of the sink into which the tap fits.

You can now put the headgear to one side. You should be able to see the jumper, with the washer attached, resting on the valve seating within the body of the tap (though sometimes it gets stuck and lifts out with the headgear). Often the washer is held in position on the jumper by a tiny nut which has to be undone with pliers before the washer can be replaced. This may be easier said than done, and rather than waste time attempting the all-but-impossible, it's probably better to fit a new washer and jumper complete rather than just renewing the washer. Once this has been done the tap can be reassembled, and as you do this smear the screw threads with petroleum jelly.

Tap with shrouded head This is basically a pillar tap where the spindle is totally enclosed by an easy-clean cover that also acts as a handle to turn the tap on and off. Some shrouded heads are made of plastic and care is therefore needed when using wrenches. But the mystery of this tap is how to get to the inside — and methods vary with the make of tap.

Some shrouded heads can simply be pulled off, perhaps after opening the tap fully and then giving another half turn. Some are secured by a tiny grub-screw in the side. But the commonest method of attaching the head is by a screw beneath the plastic 'hot' or 'cold' indicator. Prise the plastic bit off with a small screwdriver to reveal the retaining screw (normally a cross-headed screw). When the shrouded head has been removed you'll find that you can unscrew the headgear to reach the interior of the tap in the same way as with an ordinary pillar tap. Rewashering can then be done in the same way.

If the jumper is not resting on the valve seating in the body of the tap, but is 'pegged'

into the headgear so that it can be turned round and round but can't be withdrawn, it's slightly more of a problem to remove the washer-retaining nut. The easiest way is to fasten the jumper plate in a vice (although pliers will do) and turn the nut with a spanner. Some penetrating oil will help to free the thread. If after this you still can't loosen the nut, a good tip is to slip the blade of a screwdriver between the plate of the jumper and the tap headgear and lever it to break the pegging. A new jumper and washer can then be fitted complete, although the stem should be 'burred' or roughened with a file to give an 'interference fit' when it is slipped into the headgear.

Bib taps These taps are treated in exactly the same way as a conventional pillar tap. You might find with a garden tap that there's no easy-clean cover, so the headgear is already exposed.

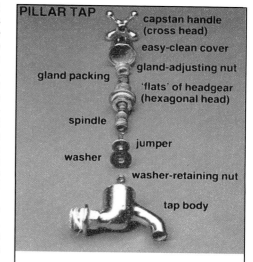

PILLAR TAP

- capstan handle (cross head)
- easy-clean cover
- gland-adjusting nut
- gland packing
- 'flats' of headgear (hexagonal head)
- spindle
- jumper
- washer
- washer-retaining nut
- tap body

New taps rarely need repairs – and the actuality is more likely to be taps like these which won't be bright and clean inside. In hard-water areas lime scale will have accumulated which can cause the tap to jam so remove it with wire wool when the tap's dismantled. This will also help you identify the parts.

TOOLS FOR TAP REPAIRS
- **thin screwdriver** is useful for prising off clipped on coverings, separating washer from jumper, removing 'O' rings, grub-screws
- **cross-headed screwdriver** might be needed for retaining-screw on some shrouded or mixer taps
- **adjustable wrench or spanner** is needed to remove the headgear.

SHROUDED HEAD TAP

- shrouded head
- gland-adjusting nut
- spindle
- gland packing
- jumper
- washer
- washer-retaining nut
- tap body
- screwed tail
- back nut

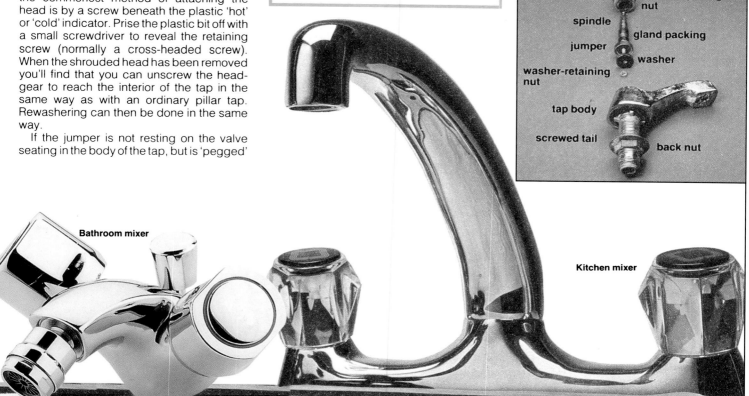

Bathroom mixer

Kitchen mixer

REPLACING A PILLAR TAP WASHER

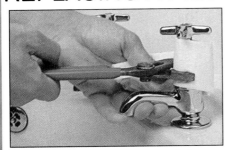

1 *Pillar taps should be opened fully after turning off the water supply. Now unscrew the easy-clean cover.*

2 *Lift up the easy-clean cover so you can slip an adjustable spanner or wrench in to undo the headgear.*

If there isn't enough space for the spanner or wrench, undo the grub-screw and then remove the handle.

If the handle won't come out, put a wedge under the cover and try to close the tap and force the cover up.

3 *With the handle fully opened, the headgear can be removed and the jumper unit pulled away.*

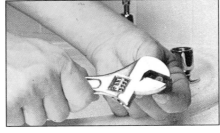

4 *Some taps have the washer fixed to the jumper unit by a nut; in others it has to be prised off.*

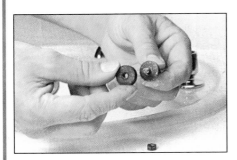

5 *Push a washer of the correct size over the end of the jumper unit. If held by a nut clean it with steel wool before replacing it.*

6 *Push the jumper unit back onto the headgear and replace in the tap. Turn the handle to half close the tap, then restore the mains supply.*

SHROUDED TAP

1 *With a shrouded head tap, you can either pull it off or prise off the indicator cap with a screwdriver after turning the water supply off and the tap on.*

2 *Undo the retaining screw (probably a cross-headed type so you'll need the right screwdriver) and then you will be able to pull off the head.*

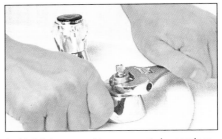

3 *Hold the spout to prevent damaging the basin while you unscrew the headgear either using a spanner or an adjustable wrench.*

4 *Unscrew the retaining nut, remove the old washer and replace with one of the correct size. Reassemble the tap, then restore the water supply.*

RE-WASHERING A SUPATAP

Although no longer available, changing a washer on this type of tap is a useful thing to know.

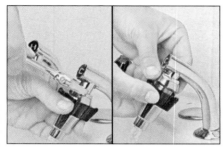

1 *Turn on the tap slightly and hold it while you undo the top nut. Open the tap fully, then turn the nozzle to unscrew it from the headgear.*

2 *As the nozzle comes away in your hand, a valve in the tap will automatically cut off the water so that you can make the repair.*

3 *Tap the nozzle on a hard surface so you can shake out the anti-splash device to which will be attached the jumper unit and the washer.*

4 *Prise the old washer and jumper unit from the anti-splash device and press in a new complete unit. Now you can reassemble the tap.*

Supataps Changing the washer on this type of tap can be carried out in minutes, without the need to cut off the water supply first. Before you begin, check that you have a replacement Supatap washer and jumper unit. Once you've undone the retaining nut at the top of the nozzle you have to open up the tap fully — and then keep on turning. At first the flow will increase, but then, just before the nozzle comes off in your hand, a check-valve inside the tap will fall into position and stop the flow. You can separate the anti-splash device, (containing the washer and jumper unit) from the nozzle by turning it upside down and tapping the nozzle on a hard surface — not a ceramic sink or basin. The washer and jumper unit then need to be prised from the anti-splash device — you can use a knife blade or the edge of a coin to do this. A new washer and jumper unit can then be snapped in. When reassembling the tap it's necessary to remember that the nozzle has a left-hand thread and so has to be turned anti-clockwise to tighten it.

Repairing a poor seating

Sometimes a tap will continue to drip although you've changed the washer. This is usually because the valve seating has become scored and damaged by grit from the mains, so the washer can't make a water-tight connection.

You can use a reseating tool to put the problem right. This entails removing the headgear after the water has been turned off, inserting the tool into the body of the tap and turning it to cut a new seating. It won't be worthwhile buying one of these tools for what is a once-in-a-lifetime job, but you may be able to hire one from a tool hire company.

An alternative method, and certainly one that's a lot easier, is to use a nylon 'washer and seating set'. Again with the water supply off, the headgear and the washer and jumper are removed from the tap end and the nylon liner is placed in position over the seating. The jumper and washer are then inserted into the headgear, which is screwed back onto the tap. The tap handle is then turned to the off position. This action will force the liner into and over the old seating to give a watertight joint.

You can also use a domed washer to cure a poor seating. It increases the surface area in contact with the waterway and so

LEAKAGE UP THE SPINDLE

1 *If the tap has a stuffing box round the spindle, first try to tighten the gland-adjusting nut.*

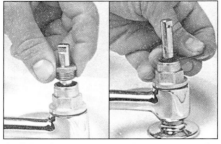

2 *If this fails to stop the leak, remove the nut and then pick out the old greased wool stuffing.*

3 *Smear petroleum jelly on a length of knitting wool, then wind it around the spindle, packing it down tightly.*

4 *Alternatively you may be able to use a rubber packing washer which just has to be slipped on.*

REPLACING 'O' RING SEALS

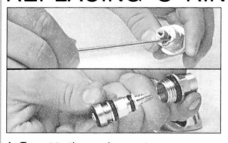

1 *To get to the seals on a tap, remove the headgear and prise off the circlip which holds the spindle in place.*

2 *Use a thin-bladed screwdriver to work off the worn 'O' rings and then replace them with new ones.*

3 *At the swivel point of a spout, first undo any grub-screw. Now twist the spout to one side and gently ease it from the mounting.*

4 *Prise off the worn seals with a screwdriver and then slip new ones into position. Replace the spout back in the mounting, restore water.*

effectively cuts off the flow when the tap is turned off even though the top of the valve seating may not be smooth.

Repacking a gland
This is necessary when you turn the tap on and water bubbles up the spindle towards the handle. At the same time the tap can be turned on and off far too easily — you might even be able to spin the handle with a flick of the fingers. This fault is a common cause of water hammer — heavy thudding following the closure of a tap or float-valve — that can result in damage to the plumbing system.

Leakage up the spindle is most likely to occur in rather old fashioned — but still very common — taps in which the spindle passes through a gland or 'stuffing box' filled with greased wool. It's inevitable that water containing detergent will be splashed onto the tap and this may result in the grease being washed out of the gland. The leakage can also be created if you run a garden or washing machine hose from the tap.

Fortunately, to make a repair you don't have to cut off the water supply to the tap, but you must be able to get at the gland-adjusting nut. This is the first nut through which the spindle passes.

Giving the gland-adjusting nut about half a turn may be enough to stop the leakage up the spindle, but eventually all the adjustment available will be taken up and you'll then have to repack the gland. When the gland-adjusting nut has been unscrewed and removed, the old gland packing material can be taken out and replaced with knitting wool saturated with petroleum jelly. The wool is wound round the spindle and packed down tightly before the gland-adjusting nut is put back and tightened until the tap handle can be turned fairly easily but without any leaks occurring.

Replacing an 'O' ring
Many modern taps have 'O' ring seals instead of a packed gland or stuffing box. If an 'O' ring fails the remedy is simply to undo the gland-adjusting nut, pick out the old 'O' ring and replace it with a new one. Leaks from taps with this fitting are rare. 'O' rings are also found at the swivel point of many mixer taps and if a leak occurs here you have to remove the spout to make the change – but this is usually only held with a grub-screw.

Older Supataps aren't fitted with an 'O' ring seal but if water leaks from the top of the nozzle you can fit a ring round the valve casing. Modern Supataps have an 'O' ring already fitted and if it needs replacing, it's a simple matter of slipping it off and pushing on another — but choose one that fits snugly and doesn't move about. If this doesn't cure the leak you'll have to replace the anti-splash device which could have become worn.

REPLACING TAPS

Changing the old taps on your basin is a bright and practical way of making your bathroom more attractive. It may also be a good idea if they are old and inefficient. Here's what is involved.

There may be a number of reasons why you wish to replace the taps supplying your sink, basin or bath. They may continually drip or leak, where new taps would give efficient, trouble-free service. Perhaps you want the advantages that mixers have over individual taps or perhaps it is simply that the chromium plating has worn off leaving the taps looking incurably shabby.

It is more likely, however, that appearance, rather than malfunction, will be your reason for changing. There are fashions in plumbing fittings as in clothing and furniture. Taps of the 1950s or 60s are instantly recognisable as out-of-date in a bathroom or kitchen of the 1980s. Fortunately, fashions in sinks, basins and baths have changed rather less dramatically over the past three decades. There is probably no more cost-effective way of improving bathroom and kitchen appearance than by the provision of sparkling new taps or mixers.

Choosing taps
When you come to select your new taps you may feel that you are faced with a bewildering choice. Tap size, appearance, the material of which the tap is made, whether to choose individual taps or mixers and – for the bath – whether to provide for an over-bath shower by fitting a bath/shower mixer: all these things need to be considered.

Size is easily enough dealt with. Taps and mixers are still in imperial sizes. Bath tap tails are ¾in in diameter, and basin and sink taps ½in in diameter. There are, however, a few suppliers who are beginning to designate taps by the metric size, not of the taps themselves, but of the copper supply pipes to which they will probably be connected. Such a supplier might refer to bath taps as 22mm and sink and basin taps as 15mm.

Most taps are made of chromium-plated brass, though there are also ranges of enamelled and even gold-plated taps and mixers. Although taps and mixers are still manufactured with conventional crutch or capstan handles, most people nowadays prefer to choose taps with 'shrouded'

heads made of acrylic or other plastic. In effect, these combine the functions of handle and easy-clean cover, completely concealing the tap's headgear. A still popular alternative is the functional 'Supatap', nowadays provided with plastic rather than metal 'ears' for quick and comfortable turning on and off.

There is also a very competitively priced range of all-plastic taps. These usually give satisfactory enough service in the home, but they cannot be regarded as being as sturdy as conventional metal taps, and they can be damaged by very hot water.

So far as design is concerned the big difference is between 'bib taps' and 'pillar taps'. Bib taps have a horizontal inlet and are usually wall-mounted while pillar taps have a vertical inlet and are mounted on the bath, basin or sink they serve.

Taking out old basin taps
When replacing old taps with new ones the most difficult part of the job is likely to be – as with so many plumbing operations – removing the old fittings. Let's first consider wash basin taps.

You must, of course, cut off the hot and cold water supplies to the basin. The best way of doing this will usually be to tie up the float arm of the ball valve supplying the cold water storage cistern so as to prevent water flowing in. Then run the bathroom cold taps until water ceases to flow. Only then open up the hot taps. This will conserve most of the expensively heated water in the hot water storage cylinder.

If you look under the basin you will find that the tails of the taps are connected to the water supply pipes with small, fairly accessible nuts, and that a larger – often

REMOVING OLD TAPS

1 *It's best to change taps by removing the basin completely. Loosen the two tap connectors carefully with an adjustable spanner.*

2 *Disconnect the waste trap connector using an adjustable wrench. Take care not to damage the trap, particularly if it is lead or copper.*

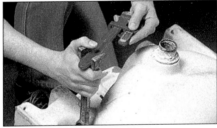

3 *Undo any screws holding the basin to its brackets on the wall, and lift it clear of the brackets before lowering it carefully to the floor.*

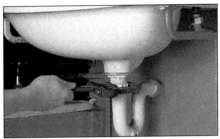

4 *Check the condition of the back-nuts, which may be badly corroded. It's a good idea to apply penetrating oil and leave this to work for a while.*

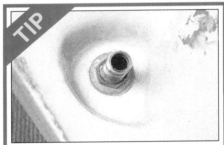

5 *Use the crowsfoot (with extra leverage if necessary) to undo the back-nut. If more force is needed, grip the tap itself with a wrench to stop it turning.*

6 *Remove the back-nut and any washers between it and the basin. Old washers like these should always be replaced with new washers.*

Ready Reference

EQUIPMENT CHECKLIST
For replacing existing taps, you will need the following tools and equipment:
- new taps of the right type and size
- an adjustable spanner
- a basin wrench ('crowsfoot')
- an adjustable wrench
- penetrating oil
- plastic washers (see below)
- plumber's putty
- PTFE tape

You may also need tap tail adaptors (if the new taps have shorter tails than the old ones) and new tap connectors (if your new taps have metric tails instead of imperial ones).

WHAT ABOUT WASHERS?
With ceramic basins, use a plastic washer above and below the basin surface (A) so you don't crack the basin as you tighten the back-nut. You can use plumber's putty instead of the upper washer.

On thin basins, use a special top-hat washer between basin and back-nut (B).

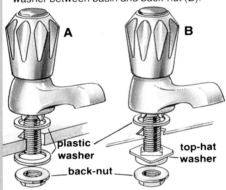

The lugs at the top of the tap tail are meant to stop it turning in square tap holes. Use special anti-rotation washers to stop new taps with smaller lugs from turning in old tap holes.

TIPS TO SAVE TROUBLE
- to undo stubborn back-nuts, add extra leverage to the crowsfoot by hooking a wrench handle into its other end
- if this fails, squirt penetrating oil around the back-nuts. Leave for a while and try again
- in really stubborn cases, remove the basin completely, and turn it upside down on the floor so you have more room to work
- grip the tap body with an adjustable spanner to stop it turning as you use the crowsfoot; otherwise the tap lugs could crack the basin

inaccessible – back-nut secures the tap to the basin. The nuts of the swivel tap connectors joining the pipes to the taps are usually easily undone with a wrench or spanner of the appropriate size. The back-nuts can be extremely difficult – even for professional plumbers!

There are special wrenches and basin or crowsfoot spanners that may help, but they won't perform miracles and ceramic basins can be very easily damaged by heavy handedness. The best course of action is to disconnect the swivel tap connectors and to disconnect the trap from the waste outlet. These are secured by nuts and are easily undone. Then lift the basin off its brackets or hanger and place it upside down on the floor. Apply some penetrating oil to the tap tails and, after allowing a few minutes for it to soak in, tackle the nuts with your wrench or crowsfoot spanner. You'll find they are much more accessible. Hold the tap while you do this to stop it swivelling and damaging the basin.

Fitting the new taps
When fitting the new taps or mixer, unscrew the back-nuts, press some plumber's putty round the tail directly below the tap body or fit a plastic washer at the top of the tail.

FITTING NEW TAPS

1 *Remove the tap and clean up the basin surround, chipping away scale and any old putty remaining from when the tap was originally installed.*

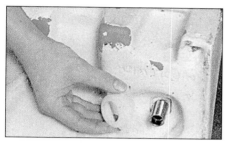

3 *Twist the tap so that it's at the correct angle to the basin and is firmly bedded on the putty. Then push a top-hat washer onto the tail.*

5 *Tighten up the back-nut until the tap assembly is completely firm, using the crowsfoot or an adjustable spanner. Repeat the process for the other tap.*

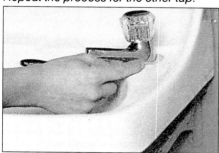

7 *When all is secure, remove any surplus putty from around the base of the taps, wiping it over with a finger to leave a smooth, neat finish.*

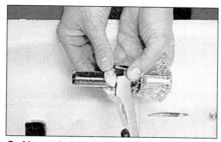

2 *Now take one of the new taps and fit a washer or plumber's putty around the top of the tail before pushing it into the hole in the basin.*

4 *With the top-hat washer firmly in place, take the new back-nut and screw it up the tail of the tap by hand.*

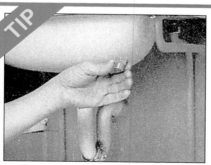

TIP

6 *Reconnect all the pipework. Use tap-tail adaptors if the new taps have shorter tails than the old ones.*

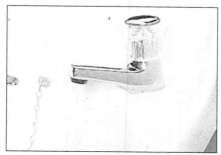

8 *Turn the water back on. Check that the flow from the taps is regular and that the waste trap is not leaking. If it is, tighten up its connectors slightly.*

Push the tails through the holes in the basin. Slip flat plastic washers over the tails where they protrude from beneath the basin, screw on the back-nuts and tighten them up. Make sure that the taps or mixer are secure, but don't overtighten them. To make tightening easier, (and undoing, if ever necessary) use top-hat washers.

All that remains to be done is to connect the swivel tap connectors to the tails of the new taps or mixer. You will see that a tap connector consists of a lining – with a flange – that is inserted into the tap tail and is then secured by the coupling nut. This nut is provided with a washer to ensure a watertight connection. When renewing taps you may well need to renew this small washer.

It is possible that when you come to connect the water supply pipes to the taps you will get an unpleasant surprise. The tails of modern taps are slightly shorter than those of older ones and the tap connectors may not reach. If the water supply pipes are of lead or of copper it is quite likely that they will have enough 'give' to enable you to make the connection but, if not, there are extension pieces specially made to bridge the gap.

Bib taps

If you're replacing existing bib taps with those of a more modern design, it's a relatively simple matter of disconnecting and unscrewing the old ones and fitting the new taps in their place. However, it's quite possible that you'll want to remove the bib taps altogether and fit a new sink with some pillar taps. This will involve a little more plumbing work. To start with, turn off the water supply and remove the taps and old sink. If the pipework comes up from the floor, you'll need to uncover the run in the wall to below where the new sink will go. You should then be able to ease the pipes away from the wall and cut off the exposed sections. This will allow you to join short lengths of new pipe, bent slightly if necessary, to link the pipe ends and the tap tails. Alternatively, if the pipes come down the wall you'll have to extend the run to below the level of the new sink and use elbow fittings to link the pipe to the tap tails. In either case it's a good idea to fit the taps to the new sink first and to make up the pipework runs slightly overlong, so that when the new sink is offered up to the wall you can measure up accurately and avoid the risk of cutting off too much pipe. Rather than having to make difficult bends you can use lengths of corrugated copper pipe. One end of the pipe is plain so that it can be fitted to the 15mm supply pipes with either a soldered capillary or compression fitting; the other end has a swivel tap connector.

STOP-VALVES AND BALL-VALVES

The valves that control your household water system aren't difficult to understand - or to fit or repair. So the next time one of yours goes wrong, be prepared to put it right yourself.

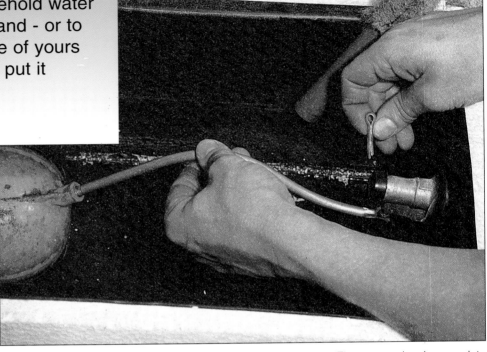

Stop-valves, gate-valves and ball-valves are all plumbing fittings that in different ways do precisely the same thing, which is to regulate the flow of water through pipes. Each of the three types of valve performs an important function in your water system, and it is therefore in your interest to know not only what they do and how they do it, but also how to put right any of the faults to which they are prone.

Stop-valves

Your main stop-valve is perhaps the single most important plumbing fitting in your house. In the event of almost any plumbing emergency the very first thing that you should do is turn it off. This will stop the flow of water into your house and reduce the extent of any damage. Looking like a very basic brass tap, your main stop-valve will be found set into the rising main not far from the point where this pipe enters your house. Often it will be located under the kitchen sink.

If your house is fairly old then it could be that it won't be provided with a main stop-valve. If this is the case, then you will have to use the local water authority's stop-valve instead. You will find it under a hinged metal flap set into your garden path or the pavement outside your property. This sort of stop-valve usually has a specially-shaped handle that can only be turned with one of the water authority's turnkeys. So that you can deal promptly with any emergency you should make sure that you either have one of these turnkeys, or at least that you have ready access to one. However, both for the sake of convenience and because specialist gadgets like turnkeys have a habit of disappearing when they're most needed, you may decide to install a main stop-valve yourself – not a difficult task if the rising main is made of copper pipe (see step-by-step photographs).

The internal construction of a stop-valve is identical to that of an ordinary tap, and so it is prone to the same types of faults (see *Ready Reference*). But one further trouble that may afflict your stop-valve – which doesn't crop up with ordinary taps – is that of jamming in the open position as a result of disuse. It's a problem cured simply by applying penetrat-

ing oil to the spindle. However, you can prevent this happening by closing and opening the stop-valve regularly, and by leaving it fractionally less than fully open – a quarter turn towards closure will do.

Gate-valves

Whereas stop-valves are always fitted to pipes that are under mains pressure, gate-valves are used on pipes that are only subject to low pressure. They are therefore found on hot and cold water distribution pipes and on those of the central heating system. Gate-valves differ from stop-valves in as much as they control the flow of water through them, not with a washered valve, but by means of a metal plate or 'gate'. You can distinguish them from stop-valves by the fact that their valve bodies are bigger, and by their wheel – as opposed to crutch – handles. Due to the simplicity of their internal construction gate-valves require little attention (see *Ready Reference*). Unlike stop-valves, which have to be fitted so that the water flowing through them follows the direction of an arrow stamped on the valve body, you can install a gate-valve either way round.

Mini stop-valves

Mini stop-valves are useful little fittings that you can insert into any pipe run. Their presence enables you to re-washer or renew a tap or ball-valve (see below) or repair a water-using appliance such as a washing machine without disrupting the rest of your

water system. They can also be used to quieten an excessively noisy lavatory flushing cistern that is fed directly from the rising main, since by slowing down the flow of water to the ball-valve you can reduce the noise without materially affecting the cistern's rate of filling after flushing. You usually fit a mini stop-valve immediately before the appliance that it is to control; and they can be turned off and on either with a screwdriver, or by turning a small handle through 180°.

Ball-valves

Ball-valves are really just self-regulating taps designed to maintain a given volume of water in a cistern. While there are a number of different patterns they all have a float – not necessarily a ball these days – at one end of a rigid arm which opens or closes a valve as the water level in the cistern falls or rises. There are basically two types of ball-valve: the traditional type, generally made of brass, in which the water flow is controlled by a washered plug or piston; and the type that has been developed more recently in which the flow is controlled by a large rubber diaphragm housed within a plastic body.

Croydon and Portsmouth ball-valves

The oldest of the traditional types of ball-valve is the Croydon pattern. You can easily recognise one of these by the position of its piston, which operates vertically, and by the fact that it delivers water to the cistern in two insufferably noisy streams. Due to their noisi-

FITTING A STOP-VALVE

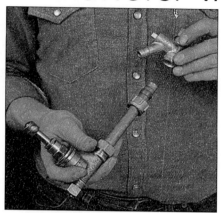

1 When installing a main stop-valve use the type that has compression fittings. If it isn't combined with a drain-cock then fit one separately.

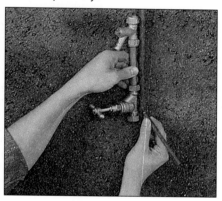

3 Take care when marking off the rising main. The extent to which the pipe will penetrate the fitting is indicated by a shoulder; use this as your guide.

5 Spring the stop-valve into the cut pipe so that the two ends meet the pipe stops within the fitting. The valve handle should be angled away from the wall.

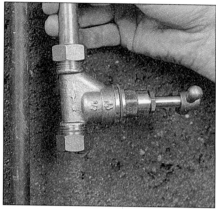

2 Make sure that you fit the stop-valve the right way round. The direction of the water flow is clearly indicated by an arrow stamped on the valve body.

4 Turn off the water authority's stop-valve and cut it at the mark with a hacksaw. Some water will flow out as you do this; be prepared for it.

6 Tighten up the nuts, restore the water supply at the water authority's stop-valve, then turn on the stop-valve and check the fitting for leaks.

Ready Reference

HOW A STOP-VALVE WORKS

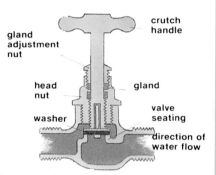

Because a stop-valve works in the same way as an ordinary tap its washer and gland are also subject to wear. You can:
● remove headgear to replace a worn washer (see pages 146 to 150), and
● deal with a worn gland by tightening the adjustment nut, or by re-packing the gland.

HOW A GATE-VALVE WORKS

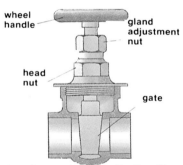

A gate-valve requires little attention. The only thing that may give trouble is the gland, which sometimes needs adjusting or renewing.

DEZINCIFICATION

In areas where the water supply is unusually acidic the zinc content of pipe fittings made of brass (an alloy of copper and zinc) can be dissolved by the water. This phenomenom is known as dezincification, and it results in the fittings losing their structural strength. When it presents a problem, fittings made of gunmetal (an alloy of copper and tin) are usually used though cheaper corrosion-resistant brass fittings are also available. These usually have CR stamped on the valve body.

155

VALVE TYPES

Apart from the float arm the only moving part on a diaphragm-type valve is a small plunger. When prompted by the float arm this plunger presses a large rubber diaphragm against the valve nozzle to close it.

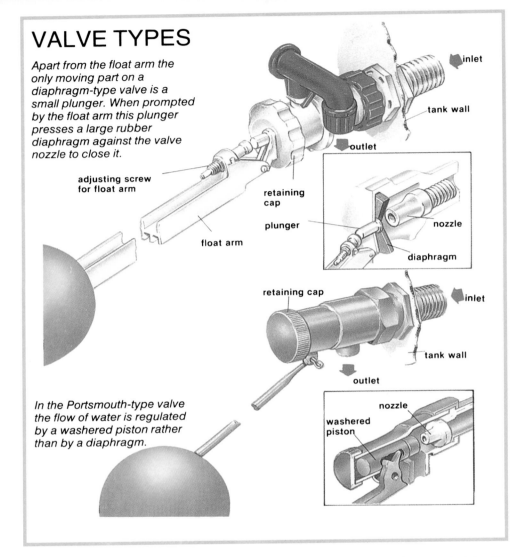

adjusting screw for float arm

retaining cap

plunger

float arm

nozzle

diaphragm

inlet

tank wall

outlet

retaining cap

inlet

tank wall

outlet

nozzle

washered piston

In the Portsmouth-type valve the flow of water is regulated by a washered piston rather than by a diaphragm.

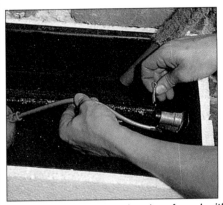

1 *The first thing you do when faced with a faulty Portsmouth valve is examine the piston. In order to get at it you will first have to remove the float arm.*

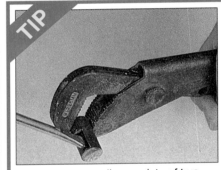

TIP

5 *A piston usually consists of two parts. If it's hard to unscrew, slip a screwdriver into the slot and turn the washer-retaining cap with a wrench.*

ness, Croydon valves are now by and large obsolete, and if you do come across one you will almost certainly want to replace it. The traditional type of valve that superseded the Croydon pattern was the Portsmouth valve (see illustration). You can distinguish it from the former type by the fact that its piston operates horizontally; and as it is still popular with plumbers despite the development of more sophisticated diaphragm type valves, it is a pattern that you may well find in your home.

When one of your ball-valves goes wrong the first thing you will notice is water dripping from an outside overflow pipe. If the valve is a Portsmouth pattern then it is likely to have developed one of three faults. First, it could have jammed partially open as a result of the build-up of scale or the presence of grit; or, secondly, it could need re-washering. In either of these cases this will necessitate you turning off the water supply so that you can either clean the ball-valve or fit a new washer

to it (see step-by-step photographs). Lastly, the valve could have been incorrectly adjusted to maintain the proper water level in the cistern – which should be about 25mm (1in) below the overflow pipe. Even modern Portsmouth valves are rarely provided with any specific means of adjusting the water level, so if you need to do so you will have to resort to bending the float arm.

Noise can be a problem with Portsmouth valves. It is caused either by the inrush of water through the valve nozzle, or by vibration created by the float bouncing on ripples on the surface of the water ('water hammer'). As silencer tubes are now banned by water authorities, you will have to try other methods to deal with this problem. Reducing the mains pressure by closing the rising main stop-valve slightly may help, and as vibration can be magnified by a loose rising main it is worth making sure that this pipe is properly secured with pipe clips. Another measure

you could take would be to improvise a stabiliser for the float using a submerged plastic flowerpot tied to the float arm with nylon cord. However, if all the above measures fail you will have to consider replacing the Portsmouth valve with one of the modern diaphragm types.

Diaphragm ball-valves

Diaphragm ball-valves, which are also referred to as BRS or Garston ball-valves, were specially developed to overcome the noisiness and inherent faults of the Croydon and Portsmouth valves. Since the moving parts of a diaphragm valve are protected from incoming water by the diaphragm (see illustration) there is no risk of them seizing as a result of scale deposits; and the problem of noisy water delivery is often overcome nowadays by an overhead sprinkler outlet which sprays rather than squirts the water into the cistern. Should you need to adjust the water

REPAIRING A BALL- VALVE

2 Then unscrew the retaining cap and push out the piston. Do this by inserting a screwdriver into the slot in the underside of the valve body.

3 If you can't get the piston out or if you suspect that your ball-valve needs a clean rather than a new washer, then you will have to remove the whole valve body.

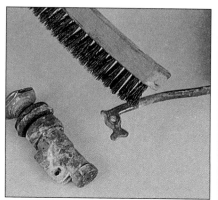

4 If a build-up of scale does turn out to be the cause of your problem, clean the valve and the end of the float arm with a wire brush.

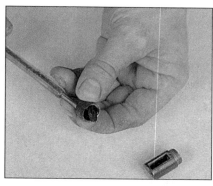

6 You'll find the old washer seated in the cap. Poke it out and substitute a new one. Smear the piston with petroleum jelly before replacing it in the valve.

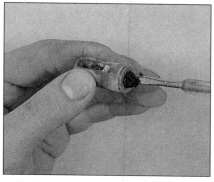

7 Rather than risk damaging a piston that refuses to unscrew, pick out the old washer with a point and force a new one back in its place.

8 Debris caught in the valve nozzle can interrupt the water flow. Cure this problem by dismantling the valve and removing the debris with a nail.

level in a cistern fitted with a diaphragm valve, then invariably you can by means other than bending the float arm. The only problems you are likely to encounter with diaphragm valves are jamming of the diaphragm against the valve nozzle, and obstruction of the space between the nozzle and diaphragm with debris from the main. You remedy these problems by unscrewing the knurled retaining cap and either freeing the diaphragm with a pointed tool or removing the debris.

High and low pressure water supply
The water pressure under which a ball-valve operates is an important factor, as the size of the hole in the nozzle of the valve will be either smaller or larger according to whether it is under high pressure (ie, mains pressure) or low pressure (ie, supplied by water from a storage tank). Older Portsmouth valves have either HP (high pressure) or LP (low pressure) stamped on their bodies, and will only operate

satisfactorily under the pressure for which they are designed. Modern valves, on the other hand, have interchangeable nozzles which allow you to convert them from low to high pressure or vice versa. If you fit a high-pressure valve (or nozzle) in a situation where a low-pressure one is required this will result in an agonisingly slow refill. A constantly dripping overflow may be the sign of a low-pressure valve that has been fitted to a cistern that is fed by the mains.

In some areas, mains pressure varies considerably throughout a 24-hour period. During the day, when demand is high, pressure will be low, whereas in the evening as demand falls off the pressure increases. These fluctuations in pressure don't affect low pressure valves but they do affect high pressure ones, which can perform erratically as a result. You can overcome this problem if it affects you by replacing your high pressure ball-valves with equilibrium valves.

Equilibrium ball-valves
You can buy Portsmouth and diaphragm equilibrium valves. These are both designed to allow a small quantity of water to pass through or round the washered piston (or diaphragm) into a watertight chamber beyond. Acting as it does on the rear of the piston, and being at the same pressure as the mains, the water in the chamber ensures that the piston is held in equilibrium. What this means in practice is that the valve is operated solely by the movement of the float arm, rather than by a combination of the movement of the float arm *and* the pressure of the incoming water as is the case in an ordinary high-pressure valve. In addition to re-filling your cistern promptly regardless of any fluctuations in mains pressure, equilibrium valves also eliminate the 'bounce' as the valve closes – a common cause of water hammer. A diaphragm equilibrium valve will give you a particularly rapid and silent refill.

REPLACING
A RADIATOR

If one of your existing radiators is malfunctioning in some way, or else just out of character with the decor of your home, why not replace it with a brand new one? You'll find this job straight-forward if you follow our instructions.

There are a number of reasons why you may want to replace an existing radiator in your home's central heating system. These can range from the aesthetic to the purely practical. At one time radiators were ugly and cumbersome, and if you have any still in use like this it's quite likely that they'll clash with the decor of your home. On the practical side, you may well find that a radiator in your system has developed leaks. This will mean both water and heat loss, as well as the inconvenience of cleaning up the mess. And, of course, you may simply feel that a modern radiator would produce more heat, and so improve the comfort in your home. Whatever your reasons for replacing a radiator, you'll have to choose a new one to go in its place, before actually removing the existing one.

Choosing a new radiator
Modern radiators are usually made of 1.25mm (about ¹⁄₁₆in) thick pressed steel, and are designed to be space-saving, neat and attractive. For a simple replacement job, size will be among the most important considerations. If the new radiator can be successfully connected to the existing fittings, you won't need to alter or modify the circulating pipes. Consequently, the job will be that much easier. Radiators are available in a wide variety of sizes, ranging in height from 300mm (12in) to 800mm (32in) and in length from 480mm (19in) to 3200mm (10ft 6in) – so you shouldn't have too much difficulty in finding one that will fit into the space left by the old one. Special low, finned radiators are also available. These are usually fitted along the skirting and are both neat and unobtrusive – yet can be turned into decorative features in their own right.

But size isn't the only important consideration. After all, a radiator's job is to provide heat, so you'll have to shop around and find the one which, for its size, will produce most heat. A radiator's heat output is measured in kW – kilowatts – so you should look for the one with the highest kW rating for its size. Remember, it's always possible to turn off a radiator that makes a room too warm; it's far less easy to increase heat output in a room which, with the radiator

THE FITTINGS

A typical panel radiator is fitted with a flow control valve (below), a lock-shield valve (bottom right), an air-bleed valve (right) and a blanking off plug (far right).

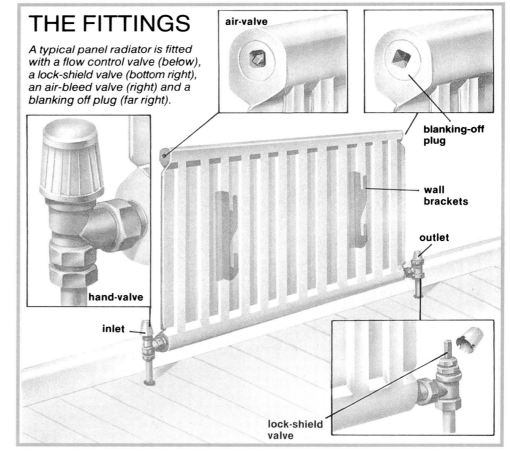

air-valve

blanking-off plug

wall brackets

outlet

hand-valve

inlet

lock-shield valve

REMOVING THE OLD RADIATOR

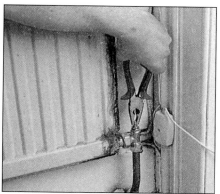

1 Turn off the flow control valve by hand, and the lock-shield valve by turning its spindle with pliers. Note how many turns are needed to close it completely.

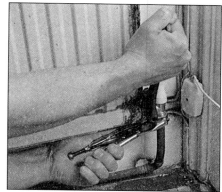

2 Hold the lock-shield valve body with a wrench so you don't bend the pipework, and undo the valve coupling carefully with an adjustable spanner.

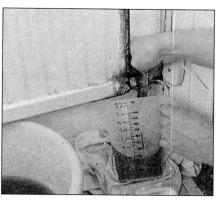

3 Open the air-bleed valve, pull the coupling away and allow the radiator to drain into a convenient container. Have rags and a larger bowl handy too.

4 Having drained most of the water, undo the other coupling, lift the radiator off its brackets and drain out the dregs. Then remove the old brackets.

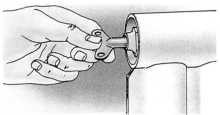
turned fully on, remains uncomfortably chilly.

However, one way of increasing heat output, while retaining the same sized radiator, is to install a double-panel radiator. This is, literally, an ordinary radiator with two panels for the hot water to fill instead of the usual one and therefore has virtually double the heat output. So, while a single panel radiator 675mm x 750mm (27in x 30in) will have a heat output of 0.68kW, a double panel one of the same size will be rated at 1.15kW.

Although modern radiators are likely to provide more heat than the older variety, they do have one drawback. Because of the thinness of their metal, they are more prone to internal corrosion and this will ultimately produce leaks.

Dealing with internal corrosion
Internal corrosion in modern radiators arises from an electrolytic reaction between the steel of the radiators and the copper circulating pipes of the central heating system. This results in the production of a corrosive black iron oxide sludge (magnetite) and hydrogen gas. In a similar fashion, if the original installation of your heating system was somewhat messily done, then copper swarf, produced when the pipes were cut, could have been retained within the circulating pipes. This will also corrode the steel at any point where the two come in contact – usually within a radiator. Because the raw material from which the sludge is produced is the metal of the radiators, eventually they will leak and need to be replaced. And as the sludge is also attracted by the magnetic field of the circulating pump, its abrasive qualities are a common cause of early pump failure.

Early indications of serious internal corrosion are a need to vent one or more radiators at regular intervals, and cold spots on their surfaces. If in doubt, the diagnosis can be confirmed by applying a flame to the escaping gas when the radiator is being vented. If it burns with a blue and yellow flame, you can be sure that hydrogen is in the system and will have been produced by the chemical reaction of the two metals. Once you've confirmed that corrosion is present within the system, you'll have to flush it through and introduce a reliable corrosion preventative chemical into the feed and expansion tank as you refill the system. That way you should be able to prevent further corrosion and so save your system.

Removing the old radiator

One of the great deterrents to anyone wanting to remove a radiator is the prospect of having to drain the whole system. However, this won't be necessary provided the radiator to be replaced has a valve at both the hot water inlet and the outlet. Once these are closed, you'll be able to keep virtually all the system's water isolated in other parts.

At the inlet end you're likely to find the hand-valve which is the control by which you open and close the radiator. At the outlet end you'll find what is termed the lock-shield valve. When you come to inspect your radiator, don't worry if their positions are reversed – they will still be equally effective.

The first thing to do when removing a radiator is to close these valves. The hand-valve is straightforward, but you'll have to remove the cover to get at the lock-shield valve. You'll be able to close this valve using a spanner or an adjustable wrench with which to grip its spindle.

As you turn it, it's a good idea to note carefully how many turns it takes to close. And you'll find this task slightly easier if you mark the turning nut with a piece of chalk before you begin. The reason for all this is to maintain the balance of the system. After it was first installed, your system would have been balanced. The lock-shield valves of all the radiators were adjusted to give an equal level of water through-flow so that they were all heating up equally. So, by noting the number of turns taken to close the lock-shield, when you come to fit the new radiator you can simply open it up by the same amount – so avoiding the somewhat tedious task of re-balancing the whole system.

Once you've closed both valves, you can unscrew the nuts which connect the valves to the radiator inlet and outlet. Do these one at a time after having placed a low dish under each end to collect the water and protect the floor. Use an adjustable wrench to undo the coupling nuts. It's wise to hold the circulating pipe securely in place with another wrench. Otherwise, if you apply too much pressure to the coupling nut you risk fracturing the flowpipe, and this would cause

FITTING THE NEW RADIATOR

1 *To ensure watertight connections to the new radiator, wrap PTFE tape round all threaded fittings and then smear on some jointing compound.*

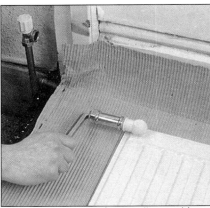

2 *Screw in the valve couplings with a hexagonal radiator spanner. Use extension pieces if the new radiator is slightly narrower than the old one.*

5 *Mark the height taken in **4** on the wall above each valve, and join up the marks at each end with a pencil line. This marks the level of the new brackets.*

6 *Transfer the measurements taken in **3** to the wall to indicate the vertical position of each bracket. Accuracy is not so vital here as in **5**.*

9 *Lift the radiator into place on its brackets. You can move it slightly from side to side to align the valve couplings with the inlet and outlet valves.*

10 *Wrap the coupling threads in PTFE tape and jointing compound, and do up the couplings. Again, use a wrench to support the valve body and prevent strain.*

3 Lay the radiator down in line with the two valves, and measure the distance from each valve coupling to the centre of the nearest bracket mounting.

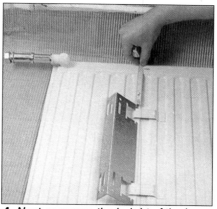

4 Next, measure the height of the base of the radiator brackets from a line joining the centres of the inlet and outlet valves.

7 Hold the bracket against the wall in line with the vertical and horizontal marks you've made, and draw in the positions for the fixing screws.

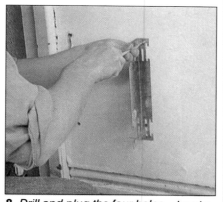

8 Drill and plug the four holes – two to each bracket – and fix the brackets in position. Make sure the wallplug is well below the plaster to avoid cracking.

11 After connecting up the couplings, use a bleed key to open the air-bleed valve slightly so that air can escape as the radiator fills with water.

12 Open the inlet valve, allow the radiator to fill and then close the air-bleed valve. Finally open the lock-shield valve by as many turns as you took to close it.

you a lot of extra work and expense to mend – as well as causing quite a mess. As you unscrew each nut, the water from the radiator will flow out. If the system has been previously treated with corrosion proofer, it's well worth saving the water. That way you can pour it back into the feed-and-expansion tank when the job is complete.

Once the water has drained out, remove the tail pieces and coupling nuts from each end. Then block up each hole with a rag and lift the radiator from the brackets that hold it to the wall. It's a good idea to get the radiator out of your home as soon as possible – just in case it leaks any remaining dirty water on to your carpet.

Fitting a new radiator

Your new radiator will probably have four holes or tappings – one at each corner – and each one will have a female screwed thread. How you connect the radiator up to your system depends on the way in which the old one was fitted. Nowadays it is usual for the flow and return connections to be made to the bottom two holes but, of course, if your system had the flow pipe at a higher level then you'll have to reconnect it in the same way.

Fit an air-valve into one of the top tappings. First wrap PTFE thread sealing tape anti-clockwise round the male thread of the valve and then use a radiator key that grips inside the body of the valve to screw it home. Unless your radiator has a top inlet the other top tapping must be plugged with a blanking off plug. This should also be wrapped with PTFE tape and screwed home in the same way as the air vent.

You'll then have to fit tail pieces and coupling screws (either new ones, or the ones from the original radiator if you can remove them) on to the new one. Again wrap each thread with PTFE tape before fitting them. It's a good idea to buy new wall brackets for your replacement radiator. After all, you can't be sure the old ones will be suitable. You should drill and plug the wall and then fix the brackets in place. Fit the radiator so that the air vent end is fractionally higher than the outlet valve. This will make venting easier. You can now fix the radiator in place and connect the coupling nuts to the hand-valve and lock-shield valve and screw them up tightly.

You'll have to open the air-valve at the top of the radiator so that the air in it can be displaced as it fills with water. All you do is slowly open the hand-valve and allow the radiator to fill. When water starts to flow from the air-valve you'll know all the air has been displaced and you should immediately close the valve. Finally, open the lock-shield valve by the same number of turns and part turns it took originally to close it.

INSULATING OLD TANKS AND PIPEWORK

Worried by the thought of your next heating bill? Concerned by the prospect of your pipes freezing in winter? If you have old pipework and an old water tank, proper insulation could be the answer - and what's more it's cheap and easy to install.

Insulation is important because it reduces heat loss, and when properly applied to your water system it benefits you in a number of ways. Firstly, it saves you money by slowing down the rate at which heat is lost from the pipes and tanks of your hot water system. Secondly, by reducing the heat loss from your cold water system (and even the coldest water contains *some* heat) it tends to keep your cold water warmer in winter, thereby minimising the risk of frozen pipes. Warmer cold water in winter also means that it takes less energy to heat it up to the desired temperature when it enters your hot water tank. In this respect, too, insulation saves you money.

So for all the above reasons you should consider properly insulating your pipes and tanks. The cost of the materials you will need is small and the potential savings great. And if you have already insulated your loft floor then this is one job you really must attend to. It has to be done because the temperature of your loft in winter will now be only marginally higher than that of the air outside, which means that the danger of any exposed pipework freezing in cold weather is greatly increased. Ideally you should therefore insulate your pipes and tanks before you tackle the loft floor. And don't forget that the risk of frozen pipes also applies to pipes in the cellar, and anywhere else where they might be subject to extremes of cold.

Before purchasing the insulation material for your pipes and tanks, work out how much you are likely to need. Most tanks will have their capacity and/or their dimensions marked on them somewhere – if yours don't then measure them yourself. You will also need to calculate the combined length of the pipes you intend insulating and establish what their diameter is – though this last measurement is only important if you plan to use split sleeve insulation (see below). As you'll want the insulation on your tanks to overlap that which you fit to any pipes that run into them, it's best to start by insulating your pipework.

Insulating pipes

Two types of pipe insulation are commonly available. The first is made out of a glass fibre or mineral wool material similar to that used for insulating loft floors, but supplied in bandage form (75 to 100mm/3 to 4in wide and 10mm/³⁄₈in thick) generally with a flimsy plastic backing. The second type comes in the form of split sleeves which are made from some sort of foamed material – usually plastic. Both types of pipe insulation have their advantages and disadvantages (see below) and both types are cheap. And since there is no reason why they can't be used side by side on the same pipe system, you'll almost certainly find that the easiest way to insulate your pipework is by using lengths of both.

Fitting bandage insulation

The bandage type is fitted by wrapping it around the pipe in a spiral, with each turn overlapping the previous one by at least 10mm (³⁄₈in). It doesn't matter which way round the plastic backing goes. Make sure that the bandage is sufficiently tight to prevent air circulating between the turns, but don't pull it too tight or you will reduce its effectiveness. When starting or finishing each roll, and at regular intervals in between, hold it in place using plastic adhesive tape or string. Tape or tie the bandage, too, on vertical pipe runs and on bends as these are places where the turns are likely to separate. And don't forget to lag any stop-valves properly – only the handle should be left visible.

Apart from being rather more time consuming to install than split-sleeve insulation the main drawback with the bandage type is that it is difficult to wrap round pipes in awkward places, such as those that run under floorboards. For pipes like these you will generally find that sleeves are more suitable since once fitted they can be pushed into position.

Fitting split-sleeve insulation

Split-sleeve insulation normally comes in 1m (3ft 3in) or 2m (6ft 6in) lengths. It is available in a variety of sizes to fit piping from 15mm (½in) to 35mm (1½in) in diameter. The thickness of the insulating foam is generally around 12mm (½in). Make sure that you buy the right size sleeve for your pipes – if the sleeves don't fit snugly round your pipework they won't provide satisfactory insulation.

INSULATING PIPEWORK

1 Start by wrapping the bandage twice round the end of the pipe next to the tank. Hold the turns in place securely with string or tape.

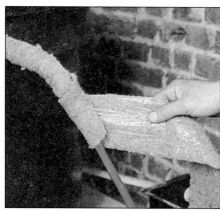

2 Wrap the bandage round the pipe in a spiral. Make sure that each turn overlaps the previous one by at least 10mm (³/₈in). Don't pull the bandage too tight.

3 Whenever you finish a roll of bandage and start a new one allow a generous overlap to prevent air circulating between the turns of the join.

4 Finish off the pipe in the same way that you started, with an extra turn of bandage. Lastly, check the pipe to make sure all the insulation is secure.

5 Fitting split-sleeve insulation is simple. You just prise apart the split and slip the sleeve over the pipe. Use tape to keep the sleeve in place.

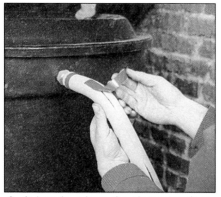

6 At bends, where the sleeve tends to come apart, tape the split lengthways. Tape the sleeves, too, whenever you join one to another.

7 At tees, first cut a 'notch' from the main pipe sleeve. Then shape the end of the branch pipe sleeve to fit and slot it into place. Tape the join.

8 Use split sleeve insulation on pipes that would be hard – or impossible – to fit with bandage. Slip the sleeve over the pipe and slide it into position.

TIP

9 Sleeve and bandage insulation can – and sometimes must – be used together. A stop-valve, for example, can only be properly lagged with bandage.

INSULATING COLD TANKS

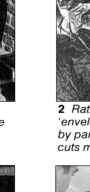

1 *Proprietary jackets will fit most cold water tanks. Start by flopping the jacket over the tank and pulling it roughly into position.*

2 *Rather than cut into the jacket's 'envelopes', try to accommodate a pipe by parting the seam between them. All cuts must be sealed with tape.*

3 *When installing blanket insulation start with the side of the tank. If you're using glass fibre blanket wear gloves and a face mask.*

5 *The tank must have a firm lid to prevent the water inside being polluted. Don't tie the lagging to the lid in such a way that it is impossible to undo.*

6 *Expansion tanks need insulating too. If using sheet polystyrene, remember to cut the panels so that their ends overlap when fitted to the tank.*

7 *Use tape, string, or glue to hold the side panels together. Fill the gaps left as a result of making cut-outs with wedges of waste polystyrene.*

Both flexible and rigid sleeves are available, but as the rigid type isn't much use for pipework that bends frequently, you'd probably be better off using the flexible variety.

Fitting the sleeves is very straightforward. You simply prise apart the slit that runs along the length of the sleeve and slip the insulation over the pipe. It's advisable to tape the sleeve at intervals, and you must do so at joins. At bends, where the sleeves will tend to come apart, you should tape the split lengthways.

Once sleeve insulation has been fitted, it can easily be slid along a length of pipe to protect a part of it that may be hard to get at. However, you should bear in mind that it won't be able to get beyond any pipe clips, very sharp bends or bulky joints it may encounter. You'll find that most flexible sleeves will readily slide round curves and even 90° bends made using soldered fittings, but whenever you run up against problems in the form of bulky compression elbows or

tee connectors the sleeves will have to be cut accordingly. However, in some circumstances you might well find that bandage insulation provides the better solution.

To fit round a 90° elbow the sleeve should be cut in two and the sleeve ends then cut at an angle of 45° before being slipped over the pipe. You should then tape over the resulting join. For the most convenient method of dealing with a tee fitting see the step-by-step photographs.

Insulating cold water storage tanks

When it comes to insulating your cold water storage tank and central heating expansion tank (if you have one), there are a number of options open to you. If your tank is circular you could cover it with a proprietary jacket consisting of a number of polythene or plastic 'envelopes' filled with insulant; or you could simply wrap it up in a layer of mineral wool or glass fibre blanket similar to – or even the

same as – that which is used to insulate loft floors. If, on the other hand, your cold water tank happens to be rectangular then you could construct a 'box' for it yourself out of expanded polystyrene, or buy a proprietary one ready-made.

A proprietary jacket couldn't be easier to fit: you simply pull it into position and then tie it in place – tapes are sometimes provided by the manufacturer. If you have to cut into the jacket to accommodate a pipe, make sure that you seal it up again with plastic adhesive tape to prevent moisture getting in and the insulating material from escaping.

Expanded polystyrene kits are also extremely easy to fit. Apart from having to fix the pieces of polystyrene together with tape, string or polystyrene cement, the only work you will have to do is to make cut-outs for the pipework. More work will be required should you decide to make your tank kit out of sheet polystyrene (see step-by-step photographs)

4 *If the blanket isn't as wide as the tank is deep, a second layer, which should overlap the first, will be necessary. Use string to hold the blanket in place.*

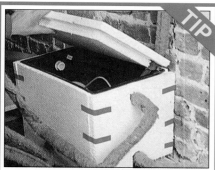

8 *Make a lid for your tank by gluing together two panels of polystyrene. The smaller (inner) panel should just fit inside the tank.*

UNLAGGED HOT WATER TANKS

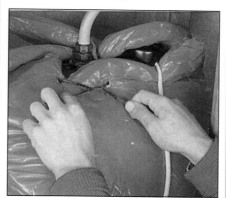

1 *When using a proprietary jacket to insulate a hot water cylinder, start by securing the polythene 'envelopes' round the hot water supply pipe.*

2 *The sides of the jacket are held in place with straps. Take care not to cover the capping and wiring of any immersion heater.*

Ready Reference

SLEEVING SIZES

To be effective, split-sleeve insulation must be the right size for your pipes. If they are modern – which usually means copper – most of your pipes will be 15mm (½in), though the main distribution ones are likely to be 22mm (¾in). Check any pipes that you aren't sure of.

TIP: PROBLEM PIPES

There are two areas where you must take extra care:
● when insulating a pipe that runs close to a wall – especially an outside wall – make sure that you protect the *whole* surface. To insulate only the more accessible side of the pipe would be worse than useless: the pipe would still be exposed to the cold wall but denied the heat of your house
● if the expansion pipe of the cold water tank you are insulating stops short of the lid then you'll have to devise some means of catching any outflow. The easiest way to do this is to use a plastic funnel. Bore a hole to accommodate the funnel through the lid and the insulation material, and fix it in place with plastic adhesive tape.

TIP: GOING AWAY

Insulation alone may not be sufficient to protect your pipes and tanks from the cold if you leave your house unoccupied for more than a few days in winter. So in your absence make sure that the heating is switched on briefly each day. If you can't trust your thermostat, ask a neighbour.

– but it would of course be a lot cheaper.

If you decide to use insulation blanket to lag your tank then try to buy the sort that is bonded with paper as you will find it much easier to handle. Buy a roll that is as wide as your tank is deep if you can, as this will save you the trouble of having to go round the side of your tank twice. The thickness of the blanket isn't critical, but blanket 50mm (2in) thick will give your tank adequate insulation and be easier to work with than a thicker one. However, it could well be that you have an odd roll or two of blanket left over from some previous insulation job; if you do, then use that rather than going to the expense of buying additional rolls.

The top of the tank to be insulated must have a firm covering to prevent the water inside being contaminated by fibres from the blanket you are fitting. So if it doesn't already have a lid, cut one out of hardboard, polystyrene or some other sheet material.

Lagging a tank with blanket insulation is simply a matter of common sense. You cut the blanket to size, drape it round the side of the tank, and having cut slits to enable the blanket to fit round the pipes, secure it with string. The lagging on the lid should overlap the side lagging by about 150mm (6in); and as you'll need to inspect the inside of your tank from time to time make sure it's easily removable.

Under normal circumstances the bottom of your tank should not be insulated, nor should the loft floor directly below. The reason for this is that it allows heat from the house to rise up through the floor and slightly increase the temperature of your cold water. The only circumstance in which you do insulate these places (and this applies regardless of what form of insulation you are using) is when, in order to increase the water pressure for a shower on the floor below, the tank has been raised more than a foot or so above the joists.

Insulating hot water tanks

Although you could in theory lag your hot water tank by adapting any of the methods that are used for cold water tanks, in practice you will nearly always find that you have no choice but to use a proprietary jacket. The fact that most hot water tanks are situated in airing cupboards means that blanket insulation is out of the question, and unless your tank is a rectangular one (which these days are very rare) you won't be able to use polystyrene.

Proprietary jackets for hot water tanks are made of the same materials as those used on cold water tanks and are just as easy to fit. The system used to fasten the jacket to the tank varies, but basically at the top you secure the 'envelopes' round the hot water supply pipe with a loop of cord, while further down you hold them in place with straps. The base of the tank is left uninsulated, as is the capping and wiring of any immersion heater.

CLEARING BLOCKAGES

There are few plumbing emergencies quite as unpleasant as a blocked drain or waste pipe. However, it's usually possible to cure the problem if you know what to do when you've tracked down the blockage, and you have the right equipment.

Professional plumbers rarely relish being called out to deal with a blockage. There *are* specialist drain clearance firms, but they can't always be contacted quickly in an emergency – and their charges reflect what can sometimes be the unpleasantness of the job. Drain or waste-pipe clearance is usually well within the capacity of the householder, and there are certainly few more cost-effective do-it-yourself jobs about the house.

Coping with blocked sinks

The outlet of the sink, usually the trap immediately beneath the sink itself, is the commonest site of waste-pipe blockage. Usually the obstruction can be cleared quickly and easily by means of a sink-waste plunger or force cup. This is a very simple plumbing tool obtainable from any do-it-yourself shop, ironmongers or household store. It consists of a rubber or plastic hemisphere, usually mounted on a wooden or plastic handle. Every household should have one.

To use it to clear a sink waste blockage, first press a damp cloth firmly into the overflow outlet, holding it securely with one hand. Then pull out the plug and lower the plunger into the flooded sink so that the cup is positioned over the waste outlet. Plunge it up and down sharply half a dozen or more times. Since water cannot be compressed, the water in the waste between the cup and the obstruction is converted into a ram to clear the blockage. The overflow outlet is sealed to prevent the force being dissipated up the overflow.

If your first efforts at plunging are unsuccessful, persevere. Each thrust may be moving the obstruction a little further along the waste pipe until it is discharged into the drain gully or the main soil and waste stack.

Should plunging prove unsuccessful you'll have to gain access to the trap. Brass and lead U-shaped traps have a screwed-in plug at the base. With plastic U-shaped and bottle traps the lower part can be unscrewed and removed – see *Ready Reference*. Before attempting this, put the plug in the sink and place a bucket under the trap; it will probably be full of water unless the blockage is immediately below the sink

WHERE BLOCKAGES OCCUR

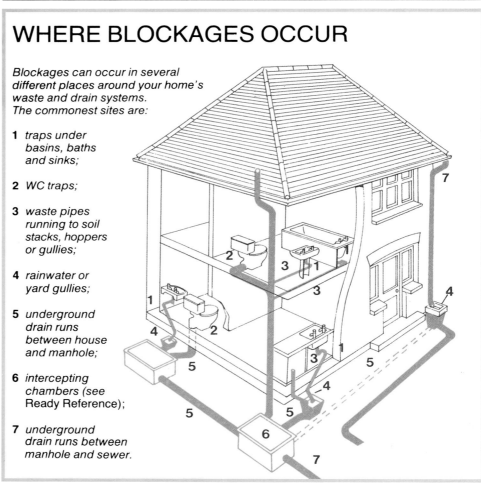

Blockages can occur in several different places around your home's waste and drain systems. The commonest sites are:

1 *traps under basins, baths and sinks;*

2 *WC traps;*

3 *waste pipes running to soil stacks, hoppers or gullies;*

4 *rainwater or yard gullies;*

5 *underground drain runs between house and manhole;*

6 *intercepting chambers (see Ready Reference);*

7 *underground drain runs between manhole and sewer.*

CLEARING BLOCKED TRAPS

1 Try using a plunger to clear blocked sinks, basins, baths or WCs. Cover the overflow with a damp cloth, then push the plunger down sharply several times.

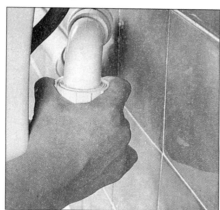

2 If the blockage persists, you will have to open up the trap. Put the plug in the basin and have a bucket handy to catch the trap contents.

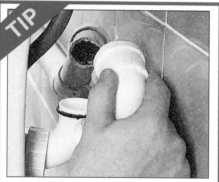

3 In a confined space like this, you may find it easier to remove the next push-fit elbow before tackling the connection to the waste outlet itself.

4 With the trap fully dismantled, wash each component thoroughly to remove the blockage and any scum clinging to the pipe sides. Leave the plug in.

5 Before reassembling the trap fully, check that the next section of the waste pipe is clear by poking a length of wire down it as far as you can reach.

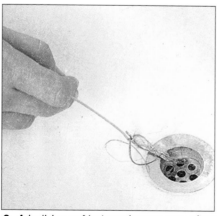

6 A build-up of hair and scum can often block basin wastes just below the outlet. Fish out as much as possible with a slim wire hook passed through the grating.

Ready Reference

TYPES OF TRAP
On old plumbing systems you may still come across lead traps, which have a removable rodding eye in the base. On more modern systems plastic traps will have been installed, and it is easy to unscrew part of the trap to clear a blockage.

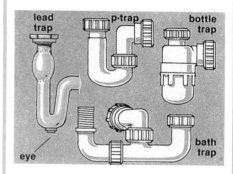

TIP: SUPPORT LEAD TRAPS
Lead traps are very soft, and may bend or split if you use force to open the rodding eye. To avoid this:
● insert a piece of scrap wood into the U-bend of the trap
● undo the rodding eye with a spanner, turning it in the direction shown while bracing the trap with the scrap wood
● reverse the procedure to replace it.

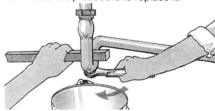

RODDING INTERCEPTING TRAPS
The manhole nearest the main sewer may be an intercepting trap, designed to keep sewer gases out of the house drains. To clear a blockage between it and the sewer,

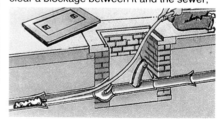

feed your rods into the rodding arm. To prevent the stoneware plug from being dislodged and causing a blockage, cement a glass disc in its place.

outlet, and the chances are that opening the trap will release it. Having done so, probe into the trap, and into the waste pipe itself. You can buy purpose-made sink waste augers for this purpose, but you'll find that a piece of expanding curtain wire, with a hook on the end, can be equally effective.

Blocked baths and basins

Basin and bath wastes are less likely to be totally blocked than sink wastes but, when blockages do occur, they can usually be cleared in the same way. They are, however, very subject to partial blockage. The waste water is often found to run from the bath or basin ever more slowly. This may be due to a build-up of scum, scale and hair on the inside of the waste pipe, and the use of a proprietary drain-clearing chemical will usually clear it. These frequently have a caustic soda base, so they should be kept away from children and handled with care, strictly in accordance with the manufacturer's instructions. Before spooning them into the bath or basin waste outlet it is wise to smear petroleum jelly over the rim of the outlet to protect the chromium finish, especially with plastic baths or fittings.

Partial blockage of a wash basin waste may often be caused by hair suspended from the grid of the outlet. This may be all but invisible from above, but probing with a piece of wire (the old standby of a straightened-out wire coathanger is useful) can often produce festoons. If you can't clear the hair by this means, unscrew the nut that connects the threaded waste outlet to the trap and pull the trap to one side. Now use a pair of pliers to pull the hair away from beneath the grid.

Overflows from gullies

Where waste pipes and downpipes discharge into gullies, the first signs of trouble may be when the gully overflows and the surrounding area is flooded as a result. The gully trap has probably become blocked, either by blown leaves or other debris, or by a build-up of grease and scum on the sides of the trap. Raise the gully grid if one is fitted (and get a new one if it's broken or missing). Then scoop out any debris with a rubber-gloved hand or an improvised scoop, scrub the gully out with caustic soda and flush it through with plenty of clean water before replacing the grid.

Blockages below ground

A blockage in the underground drains may be shown up by a WC which, when flushed, fills with water almost to the rim and then very slowly subsides, or by dirty water seeping from under a manhole cover. You'll need a set of drain rods to clear any underground blockage. It is best to hire these from a local

CLEARING BLOCKED GULLIES

1 *Both surface-water and yard gullies are easily blocked by wind-blown debris such as waste paper and dead leaves. First lift off the gully grating.*

2 *Try to scoop out as much debris as possible from the gully trap, either by hand or with an improvised scoop such as an old tin can.*

3 *If the blockage is cleared and the water flows away, scrub out the sides of the gully with detergent or caustic soda. Clean the gully grating too.*

4 *Finally, hose the gully out thoroughly with running water. If you are unable to clear the blockage, you may have to rod the drain run from a nearby manhole.*

tool hire firm if and when the emergency arises. A drain that blocks sufficiently frequently to justify the purchase of a set of rods undoubtedly has a major defect that needs professional advice and attention.

Raising the manhole covers will give you an indication of the position of the blockage. If, for instance, the manhole near your front boundary is empty, but the one beside the house into which the soil pipe and yard gully discharges is flooded, then the blockage must be between these two manholes. Screw two or three lengths of drain-rod together, add the appropriate accessory to one end and then lower it into the flooded manhole. Feel for the drain half-channel at its base and push the rod end along it and into the drain towards the obstruction. Screw on extra rods as necessary until you reach and clear the blockage. You may find it easier to push the rods into the drain — and to extract them

again — if you twist them as you do so. *Always* twist in a clockwise direction. If you twist anti-clockwise the rods will unscrew and one or more lengths will be left irretrievably in the drain.

Many older houses have intercepting traps. These traps, which were intended to keep sewer gases out of the house drains, are the commonest site of drain blockage. You can see if your drains have an intercepting trap by raising the cover of the manhole nearest to your property boundary before trouble occurs and looking inside. If there is an intercepting trap the half-channel of the gully will fall into what appears to be a hole at the end of the manhole; actually it is the inlet to the trap. Immediately above this hole will be a stoneware stopper. This closes the rodding arm giving access to the length of drain between the intercepting trap and the sewer.

A blockage in the intercepting trap is

RODDING BLOCKED DRAINS

1 *Raise manhole covers carefully. If the hand grips are missing, use an old brick bolster to lift one edge, and then slide in a piece of wood.*

2 *With the wood supporting one end of the cover, grasp it securely and lift it to one side. Bend from the knees so you don't strain your back.*

3 *Select one of the drain rod heads (a rubber disc is being fitted here) and screw it securely onto the threaded end of the first drain rod.*

4 *Screw a second rod onto the end of the first, and lower the head into the half-channel in the bottom of the chamber. Push the rods towards the blockage.*

5 *Screw on further rods as necessary and work the head in and out to clear the blockage. Never turn the rods anticlockwise, or they may unscrew and be lost.*

6 *When you have cleared the blockage, hose down the sides and base of the manhole with running water, and let water run through the drain for a while.*

indicated when all the drain inspection chambers are flooded. It can usually be cleared quite easily by plunging. To do this, screw a drain plunger (a 100mm or 4in diameter rubber disc) onto the end of a drain rod. Screw on one or two other rods as necessary and lower the plunger into the flooded manhole. Feel for the half-channel at its base and move the plunger along until you reach the inlet of the intercepting trap. Plunge down sharply three or four times and, unless you are very unlucky, there will be a gurgle and the water level in the manhole will quickly fall.

Very occasionally, there may be a blockage between the intercepting trap and the sewer, and the point must be made that this length of drain is the householder's responsibility, even though much of it may lie under the public highway. To clear such a blockage the stoneware cap must be knocked out of

the inlet to the rodding arm (this can be done with the drain rods but it isn't the easiest of jobs) and the rods passed down the rodding arm towards the sewer.

Intercepting traps are also subject to a kind of partial blockage that may go unnoticed for weeks or even months. An increase in pressure on the sewer side of the trap – due to a surge of storm water, for instance – may push the stopper out of the rodding arm. It will fall into the trap below and cause an almost immediate stoppage. However this will not be noticed because sewage will now be able to escape down the open rodding arm to the sewer. The householder usually becomes aware of a partial blockage of this kind as a result of an unpleasant smell, caused by the decomposition of the sewage in the base of the manhole.

The remedy is, of course, to remove the stopper and to replace it. Where the trouble

recurs it is best to discard the stopper and to lightly cement a glass or slate disc in its place. In the very unusual event of a stoppage between the intercepting trap and the sewer, this disc can be broken with a crowbar and replaced after the drain has been cleared – see *Ready Reference*.

After any drain clearance the manhole walls should be washed down with a hot soda solution and a garden hose should be used to flush the drain through thoroughly.

Blocked gutters
Roof rainwater gutters may become obstructed by leaves or other objects. An overflowing gutter isn't an instant catastrophe but, if neglected, it will cause dampness to the house walls. An inspection, removal of debris and a hose down of gutters should be a routine part of every householder's preparations for winter.

EMERGENCY PIPE REPAIRS

A leaking pipe is no joke. First you have to stop the water - so you need to know where to turn it off. Then you need to make some kind of emergency repair, even if it's just a holding operation.

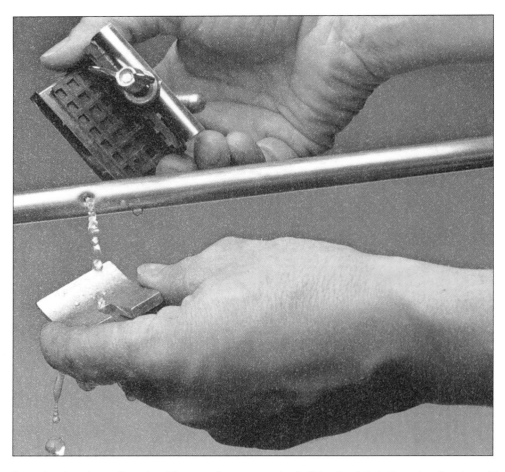

Leaks in domestic plumbing systems have a nasty habit of happening at the most inconvenient of times, often when it isn't possible to carry out a proper permanent repair. What you need is a plumbing emergency first aid kit, and there are now several proprietary products available that will at least enable you to make a temporary repair and get the water flowing again.

With any leak, the vital first step is to stop the flow of water. Even a small leak can create a surprisingly large pool of water in no time. Stopping the flow in any pipe is relatively easy provided that you know the locations of the various stop-taps or valves that isolate parts of your water system, or cut it off completely from the mains supply.

Water comes into the house through a pipe known as the rising main, and because

water in this pipe (and others leading from it) is under mains pressure, leaks from it will be particularly serious. It enters the house underground, and from there leads either to all the cold taps and a water heating system, or to just the cold tap in the kitchen and to a cold water storage tank.

Leaks can result from a number of causes. Pipework may have been forced or strained at some point, resulting in a leak at one of the fittings connecting the lengths of pipe together, or in a fracture at a bend.

Corrosion within pipes may lead to pinholes in pipe lengths, while frost damage can lead to bursts and splits in pipes and to leaks at fittings caused by ice forcing the fitting open. Whatever the cause, cutting off the water supply to the affected pipe is the first vital step.

Where to turn off the water

1 Cold water supply pipes connected directly to the mains: in the UK these pipes usually only supply the kitchen cold tap, the cold water storage tank and sometimes instantaneous water heaters. In many other countries, the pipes may supply *all* cold water taps and the hot water storage cylinder. The simple way of deciding whether any pipe or tap is supplied directly by the mains is by the pressure – taps supplied from a tank are what's known as gravity-fed and the pressure of water is relatively low compared to mains pressure.

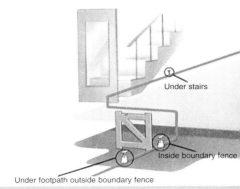

Under stairs

Inside boundary fence

Under footpath outside boundary fence

2 Cold water supply pipes from a cold water storage tank: in the UK these pipes usually supply the bathroom cold taps, the WC cistern and the hot water cylinder.

To close off the water supply in these pipes there's often a stop-valve immediately alongside the cold water tank where the pipe exits. Turn this off first and then open all cold water taps. They'll run dry almost immediately. If there isn't a stop-valve, you have to drain the whole tank. So first you stop water entering the tank by either turning off the mains (as above) or by tying up the ball-valve in the tank so that it remains closed. Then you open all the taps in the house.

3 Hot water pipes: these are all supplied from a hot water cylinder, which in turn gets its cold water either from the cold tank or from the mains.

Since hot water leaves the hot water storage cylinder from the top, it's only the pressure of water going in at the bottom of the cylinder that forces the water out. Turn off the supply of cold water (either at the cold water tank, or at the mains) and you stop the flow. In this sort of situation the hot water cylinder remains full. If for any reason you need to drain this as well, use the drain cock near the bottom. It's essential in this case to turn off either the immersion heater or boiler.

To turn off the water, look for the mains stop-valves. There may, in fact, be two: one inside the house where the mains pipe enters (under the kitchen sink, in the utility room, or even under the stairs); the other outside — either just inside the boundary of the property (near to a water meter, if you have one), or under the footpath outside the garden fence. Outdoor stop-valves may be set as much as a metre (3 ft) down beneath a hinged cover or metal plate, and you may need a special 'key' which is really just a long rod with a square socket on the end which fits over the tap to

turn it. In most cases, however, it's simply a matter of reaching down to turn it off by hand or with a wrench. Some outdoor stop-valves also control a neighbour's water supply, so do warn them if you're turning it off.

The stop-valve inside will either be a wheel type or an ordinary T-shaped type. The only possible complication is if it hasn't been touched for years and is stuck fast. A little penetrating oil and tapping it with a hammer will usually loosen it sufficiently. (It's worth closing the stop-valve now and again to see that it doesn't get stuck.)

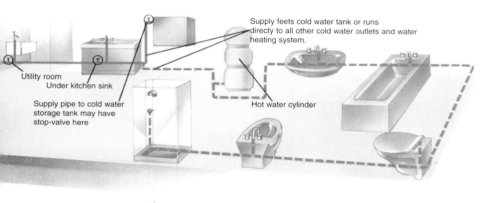

Supply feeds cold water tank or runs directly to all other cold water outlets and water heating system.

Utility room
Under kitchen sink

Supply pipe to cold water storage tank may have stop-valve here

Hot water cylinder

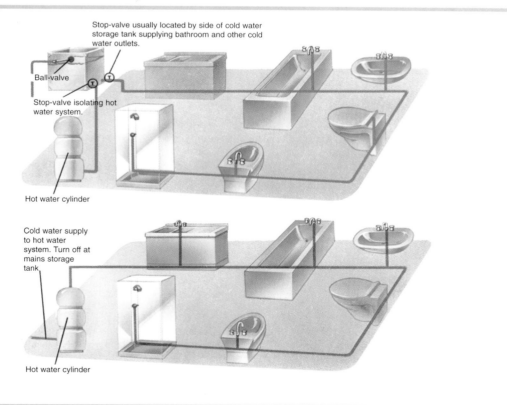

Stop-valve usually located by side of cold water storage tank supplying bathroom and other cold water outlets.

Ball-valve

Stop-valve isolating hot water system.

Hot water cylinder

Cold water supply to hot water system. Turn off at mains storage tank.

Hot water cylinder

Ready Reference

TURNING OFF THE STOP TAP

Make sure the family knows where the mains stop tap is.

● do not force the handle if it has seized up – it could break off
● use a hammer or wrench to tap the fitting while pouring penetrating oil down spindle.
● if you can't free it call the water authority emergency service — they can turn the water off where your supply pipe leaves the mains.
● don't reopen stop valve fully when turning on the supply until a permanent pipe repair is made. This reduces water pressure on a temporary seal.

TIP: MAKESHIFT REPAIRS

If you don't have the right materials to hand (see next page) try this:
● bandage insulating tape round the pipe and hole
● cover with a 150mm (6in) piece of garden hosepipe slit along its length and tie with wire at each end, twisting ends of wire together with pliers
● wrap more tape tightly over this

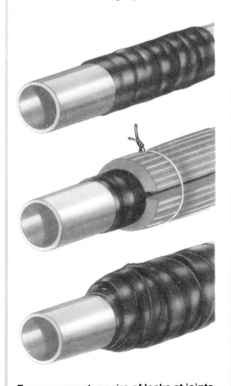

For permanent repairs of leaks at joints in copper pipe see pages 114 to 118.

EMERGENCY REPAIRS

● One type of repair kit is based on a two-part **epoxy resin plastic putty** supplied as two strips of differently-coloured putty in an airtight pack. When the strips are thoroughly kneaded together the putty is packed firmly round the pipe, where it will harden to form a seal. However, this hardening process takes up to 24 hours and the water supply will have to remain off for this period. (If you don't need to use all the pack in one go, reseal it immediately).

Equal amounts of putty should always be used and mixed together thoroughly until a uniform colour results, otherwise it won't harden properly. It's also essential that the pipe or joint is scrupulously rubbed down and cleaned with methylated spirit or nail polish remover. This will ensure a good bond between the putty and the metal.

● One of the most valuable aids is a multi-size **pipe repair clamp** which has the added advantage of being reusable. It consists of a rubber pad which fits over the hole (for this repair it's not necessary to turn off the water) and a metal clamp which draws the rubber tightly against the pipe when it is screwed in place.

Position the pad and one side of the clamp over the hole, and link the two parts of the clamp together, making sure that the pad is still in place. Tighten the wing nut fully. If the position of the hole makes this difficult, use blocks of wood to hold the pipe away from the wall. This method of repair cannot, of course, be used to mend leaks occurring at fittings.

● Another proprietary product uses a two-part **sticky tape** system which builds up waterproof layers over the leak — in the true sense this does form an instant repair. The area round the leak should be dried and cleaned and then the first of the tapes is wrapped tightly round the pipe, covering the leak and 25mm (1in) either side of it. Then 150mm (6in) strips of the second tape, with the backing film removed, are stuck to the pipe and stretched as they are wound round, each turn overlapping the previous one by about half the width of the tape. This covering should extend 25mm (1in) beyond either end of the first layer of tape. The job is completed by wrapping the first tape over all the repair.

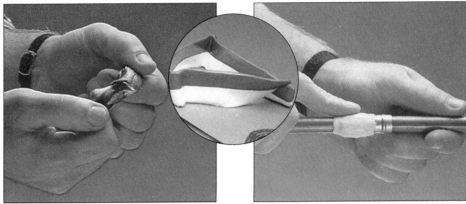

Plastic putty *Using your fingers, mix together equal amounts of the two putty strips. It's ready for use when the colour is even all through.*

Thoroughly clean area round the leaking pipe, then pack putty round fitting. It can be sanded smooth when it's completely hard.

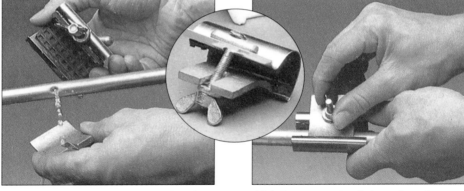

Pipe clamp *Place rubber pad and one side of metal clamp directly over leak in pipe. There's no need to turn off the water with this type of repair.*

Link the two parts of clamp together, being careful to keep it in position. Screw down wing nut to secure rubber pad against pipe.

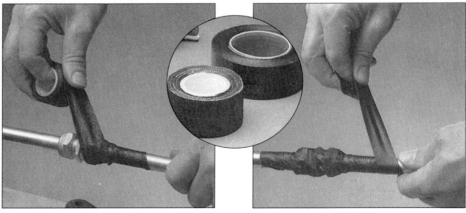

Sticky tape *Start winding first tape round pipe about 25mm (1in) from the leaking fitting. Continue over the joint and for 25mm on other side.*

Stretch and overlap 150mm (6in) strips of second tape round pipe. Continue 25mm (1in) either side of first tape. Finish off with layer of first tape.

HOME
CARPENTRY

CARPENTRY MATERIALS

The raw material of any carpentry project is wood – either one of the many species of natural timber, or man-made board. However, you will also need fixings to help you assemble whatever you are making, and some means of giving your workmanship an attractive and durable finish.

SOFTWOODS

The do-it-yourselfer uses enormous quantities of wood every year for projects of all sorts, and the bulk of it is properly termed softwood. But what is softwood, and what do you need to know about it to be able to buy and use it successfully?

1 **Parana pine** *is whitish yellow with occasional red streaks, straight-grained and usually has few knots, so is easy to cut and plane. Don't use it outdoors, and, since it tends to twist, for open shelving.*

S oftwoods come from coniferous (cone-bearing) trees such as pine, spruce, fir and larch – evergreens with needle-like leaves. These grow in a well-defined belt running round the northern hemisphere, with the greatest reserves being found in Canada, Scandinavia and Siberia. Some species of softwood also grow at high altitude in tropical regions, but in nothing like the same quantities.

The name 'softwood' is generally rather misleading: yew, for example, is technically a softwood, yet is dense and quite difficult to cut, while balsa is one of the softest woods there is and is classified as a hardwood (see pages 178 and 179).

How they're grouped
Softwoods are divided fairly arbitrarily into two groups.

The first group is commonly called redwood, pine, red deal or yellow deal. There is actually no such thing as a deal tree; deal originally meant a piece of sawn wood 9 inches wide, not more than 3 inches thick and at least 6 feet long. Red deal comes from the Scotch Pine, yellow deal from the Yellow Pine. The second group is called whitewood or white deal (Norway spruce – the traditional Christmas tree).

Both generally have a very pale colour and weak grain pattern, and these properties are more pronounced in timber grown recently, with the accent on fast-growing species. You can see this clearly by comparing a plank of recently-cut softwood with the timber used in, say, a Victorian house, which will have a deeper colour and a closer, more noticeable grain.

Softwood is comparatively strong in the direction of the grain, weak across it. It is easy to saw, plane, chisel and sand, and holds screws well (nails can cause the wood to split along the grain). The wood is fairly porous, and is generally not durable enough to be used out of doors unless protected by paint, varnish or preservative. Western Red Cedar is the one commonly-available

exception to this rule, its red colour weathering to a pleasant grey if exposed to wind, rain and sunlight. Most softwoods are easy to treat with preservatives, however, since their porous nature means that the preservative penetrates deep into the wood to protect it by keeping rot and wood-boring insects at bay.

How softwoods are used
By far the greatest use for softwoods is in building houses – for floor and ceiling joists, roofs, doors and windows, wall cladding, staircases, floorboards, skirtings and a whole range of other smaller features. For the do-it-yourselfer softwood is the perfect material for jobs large and small, from building extensions and outbuildings to making free-standing or built-in furniture.

Sawn or planed?
Softwood is converted (sawn) into a vast range of sizes – see overleaf. The most important thing to remember is that these are nominal sizes, not actual ones. The wood is sawn to the nominal size, but then shrinks during seasoning. It may then also be planed, which reduces the wood's actual size still further – by about 3mm (1/8in) on each dimension with smaller sizes, more on larger timbers. Such wood is known as planed all round (PAR) or dressed all round (DAR), but is still described by its nominal size.

Use sawn timber (which is cheaper) where the wood will be hidden – in partition walls, for wall battening and so on. You should also buy sawn timber to plane down yourself if you want to produce wood of a particular cross-sectional size that is not available PAR (DAR). Alternatively, you can order it planed to 'finished' size from the next available sawn size – more expensive than PAR wood.

Softwood is also machined into an enormous range of mouldings, rounds ('broomsticks') and matchings (profiled tongued-and-grooved boards for decorative wall cladding).

The metric foot
Timber now leaves the sawmill in metric lengths, and so to save wastage many timber merchants sell wood measured in a contrived unit of 300mm – the so-called metric foot, actually measuring 11¾in. So if you order '6 feet' of wood, you may be sold a piece 6 metric feet – 1800mm or 5ft 10½in – long. If you actually need a full 6ft (1830mm) of wood, you may have to pay for 7 metric feet (2,100mm/6ft 10in) and waste the off-cut.

The sawing processes
It is much easier to understand wood as a natural material if you know how it is 'converted' – turned from logs into usable rectangular planks. The secret of the sawmill lies in producing the largest quantity of good-quality wood from each log, with the minimum of wastage. Three methods are commonly used.

Plain sawing means cutting the log into parallel planks. It yields pieces with two different grain patterns, depending on their position in the log, and those cut from the edge tend to curl and warp badly. This can be avoided

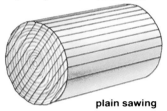

plain sawing

by *quarter* sawing – cutting the log along radial lines – and this also yields wood with a similar grain pattern throughout; it is,

2 **European redwood** *(deal) is a type of pine varying from dusty red to pale yellow. It can be used outside when preservative-treated. It's strong, hard and easy to work unless there's a lot of resin or knots.*

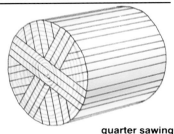

quarter sawing

however, more wasteful. The third method is *tangential* sawing, used to produce more wide planks from relatively small logs; wood sawn tangentially also has a plainer, more open grain pattern.

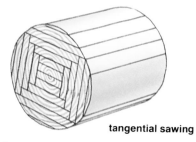

tangential sawing

Seasoning wood
Once wood is sawn, it has to be 'seasoned' at a controlled rate to dry out the sap and reduce the moisture content of the wood to around 10 or 12% – when felled wood can contain as much as twice its own weight of water. Seasoning makes the wood easier to work (anyone who has cut down a tree knows how difficult 'green' wood is to saw), lighter to handle and more

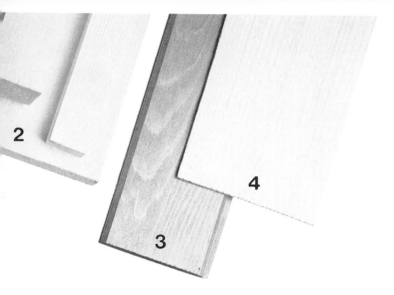

3 **Western Red Cedar** *is rather oily, fragrant and pinkish-red to reddish brown. It's the most common type of cedar available. It can be used outdoors untreated – the weather will turn it silver grey.*

resistant to attack by rot and insects. Carefully seasoned wood is also less prone to shrinkage and warping than unseasoned wood.

Faults in wood
Because wood is a natural material, it has its normal share of faults. One of the commonest is the knot, the cross-section of a branch exposed at the point where its starts growing from the trunk. Knots may be fresh (live) and tight-fitting, perhaps even oozing resin, or they may be dead, dark-coloured and loose – a sign that the branch was damaged before the tree was felled.

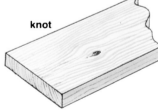

knot

Another common fault is the shake. Star shakes are caused by

end shake

4 **Spruce**, *also known as whitewood, is cream in colour. It's light and strong, physically easy to work and finishes well. It does not take preservatives well and so is restricted to interior use.*

the outside of the log drying and shrinking more quickly than the rest, resulting in splits running from the centre to the outside of the log. Cup shakes occur when the inner part of the log dries

warp

more quickly than the outside, causing the wood to split between the annual rings. End shakes are caused by too speedy drying during seasoning.
  Warping is caused by uneven drying during seasoning, and may

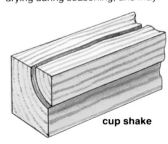

cup shake

occur across the grain (giving the wood a cupped cross-section) or along it as well (a twist, visible if you sight along the length).

Most softwoods bruise and mark easily; take care when using your woodworking tools to avoid damage. In particular, always protect the wood surface with an offcut of scrap wood when tapping joints together or when pulling out nails with a claw hammer.

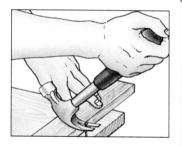

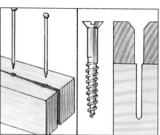

Splitting is likely to occur if you drive several nails in a row along the line of the grain – it's best to stagger them. Ideally you should use oval nails driven in with their flatter sides parallel to the wood grain. Drill clearance holes if using screws, countersinking if necessary to accommodate the screw heads.

When you are using a plane you should work with the grain to get a clean finish; you will find that the plane cuts much more easily in one direction than in the opposite one. Always sand wood along the grain too, never across it.

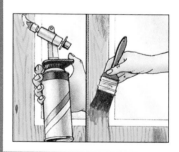

Some softwoods have a high resin content and this may show up in sticky pockets. You can seal small pockets by drawing out the resin with a blow-torch, then brushing on knotting. If pockets are large, they are best cut out – so always choose timber with care at the start.

You should look out for these faults when buying wood (except in the case of wood you want to be deliberately 'knotty') and reject any that is not sound and straight.

Quality control
Softwood is graded according to its quality when it leaves the sawmill in its country of origin. Wood from Scandinavia and Russia is divided into two broad categories called 'unsorted' (the better quality) and 'fifths'. Wood from Canada is usually sorted into 'clears' and 'merchantable' grades, with clears being somewhat better in quality than Russian or Scandinavian unsorted grade. Parana pine is

often graded into 'No 1' and 'No 2', both as good as the best Canadian wood.
  Softwood may be further sorted by timber merchants into three grades – 'best joinery', 'joinery' and 'carcassing' (or building) grade. Best joinery grade is top-quality wood, virtually free of knots and suitable for use where the wood grain will be visible. Joinery grade is used for most general woodwork, carcassing grade for rough structural work where the wood will eventually be hidden from view.
  Do-it-yourself shops usually sell only joinery grade wood. For other grades you will have to go to a timber merchant.

HARDWOODS

There's no mystery about hardwoods. Oak, walnut, mahogany, teak and many more well-loved timbers are readily available if you want to use their rich, varied shades and patterns in your home.

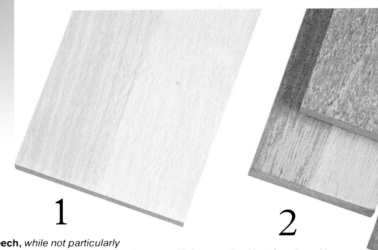

1

2

Most hardwoods really are harder than softwoods – but not quite all; the two classifications are named for botanical, not practical reasons, and hardwoods themselves vary widely in strength, toughness and weather-resistance. Their denseness can make accurate work easier, but it can also blunt tools faster; and you'll need to keep a sharp eye out for variable grain directions which make it hard to get an even surface with the plane.

Hardwoods do cost more, which is why softwoods are used for all rough house-carpentry. But your money buys a fascinating, inexhaustible variety of beautiful colours and grains. Once you have the confidence to work without paint to cover up your mistakes, and preferably with proper concealed joints rather than just screws and nails, you'll want to use hardwoods for all their subtle decorative possibilities, varnishing or polishing them to bring these out.

There are thousands of hardwoods, many strangely named and hard to get. Here we show only those you're most likely to find. But they give an idea of the tremendous range available. If your timber merchant shows you a piece of afzelia or jelutong, don't turn your nose up: it may be just what you want.

Many hardwoods are often used as thin sheets of veneer, to give the appearance without the cost. Sticking veneer down by

hand is a fairly specialised operation, unless you buy the 'iron-on' real-wood veneers which are available in some of the more common timbers. Ready-veneered chipboard, or plywood with a decorative top layer, is another option.

Hardwood sizes

You can't buy hardwoods in standard sizes like nails, screws or even softwoods. Dimensions available depend on the supplier – and the wood. No-one can cut wide planks from narrow trees, or long straight pieces from short, twisted trees.

However, two groups of basic cross-sections are generally obtainable. Squarish pieces, for table and chair legs, panel edges, etc, can usually be found in sizes between 25 x 25mm (1 x 1in) and 50 x 50mm (2 x 2in); and wider, flatter boards, eg, for wall cladding or joining edge-to-edge to make tabletops, from 6mm (¼in) to 25mm (1in) thick, and 150-300mm (6-12in) wide.

But visit your timber merchant, discuss your requirements and see what he's got. Although you may have to consider alternative woods, he'll often be willing to cut wood specifically to suit your measurements. In fact, since hardwoods come in so many different types and sizes, he may well have to. Be prepared, however, to modify your design if he suggests a more economical way of cutting the timber. His advice will save you money.

Beech, *while not particularly decorative, is strong, and easy to work and finish because of its straight, close grain. Not durable enough for outdoor use, it is used in furniture, especially for chair-frames, and is sometimes given a pinkish colour by steaming.*

Mahogany *is either American (the Honduras variety is on the right; Brazilian is also common) or African, left – not the same species, but closely related and just as good. Mahogany is widely used for reproduction furniture. Its attraction lies in its rich colour and lustre.* **Utile** *(on top), another fine African wood, is very similar.*

Oak *can be red or, more commonly, white. Varieties of white oak come from Europe, America (underneath in the picture) and Japan. English oak (on top), the hardest, strongest and most durable, was universally used for hundreds of years. Imported European oak is now commoner, while Japanese oak is the lightest in weight of the three. Oak is not richly coloured, but it can have an attractive figure.*

6

3

Ramin *is a plain wood whose straight grain and even texture, like those of beech, make it very useful, though it is lighter and less sturdy. It splits quite easily. Mouldings are often cut from it, and it is used in furniture. Like beech, it is easily stained to match its surroundings.*

4

Afrormosia *is just one of many African hardwoods which are unfamiliar to most people but nevertheless widely used. (Iroko is another.) Dense, richly coloured and durable, it is more than just a substitute for teak, with which it is often compared: it is even stronger, and not greasy.*

5

Elm *resembles ash except for its rather darker colour and often crooked grain – qualities which make it more ornamental but rather less generally useful. Devastation by Dutch elm disease has made it temporarily abundant in Britain, and varieties from Europe and Japan and also available.*

Teak *has long been celebrated for its great strength and extraordinary weather-resistance: it is ideal for all outdoor work. Its rich colour has been in demand for furniture in recent years, though it is not cheap. Its greasiness presents difficulties in glueing and for some finishing processes.*

Ash *is another strong, pale wood like beech, but with the coarse, open texture of oak. Its exceptional toughness and straight grain suit it for bending and for such things as tool handles. However, it is not a good outdoor timber.*

Walnut *was widely used in English furniture of the Queen Anne period. True walnut really comes from England (like the top piece in the picture) and other parts of Europe, as well as North America, but other similar woods are African (underneath), Queensland and New Guinea walnut. Its value lies in its depth and variety of colour and its nicely varied grain.*

Sycamore *is one of the most attractive types of maple, and has a lustrous creamy colour, sometimes nearly white. This, plus its compact grain and frequent rippling figure, give it a beauty of its own.*

7

8

9

10

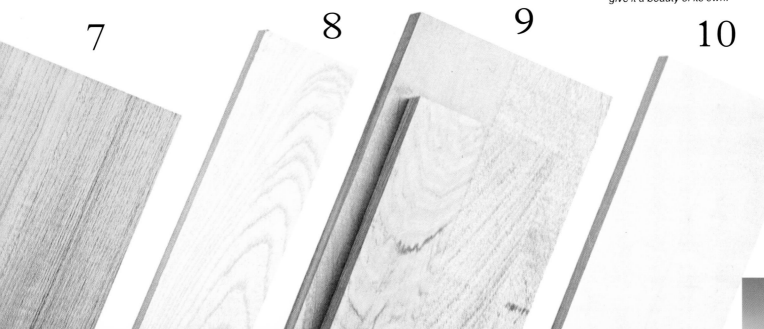

COMMON SIZES FOR SOFTWOODS

Planed or dressed timber is sold in the same nominal dimensions as sawn timber but it is in fact roughly 3mm (¹/₈in) smaller all round (the exact amount varies according to the cross-section). Thus the pieces of timber shown below are in fact slightly less in size than the dimensions by which they are sold. Not all planed timber sizes you can buy are shown here but the picture should give you some idea of the different sizes relative to each other.

The large sizes, eg 100 x 75mm (4 x 3in) or 150 x 75mm (6 x 3in) are used for structural work whereas the slim battens, eg 25mm x 12.5mm (1 x ¹/₂in) are used for decorative work or situations where strength is not a necessary requirement. You can also see how timber may be offered for sale split, warped, bowed or with knots and you should look out for these faults when buying.

The table below lists the range of sizes in which sawn and planed softwoods are sold and which you should find relatively easy to obtain. Softwoods are sold in other sizes by some stockists depending on the source of supply and the sawmill which processes the timber. You can also, of course, ask your stockist to plane a piece of timber for you from the next size up, though this is an expensive way of buying timber. All the PAR or DAR sizes listed here are available sawn but the reverse does not apply. A solid symbol means the size is available sawn or planed, an open one denotes a sawn size only.

Sawn and planed (dressed) sizes

thickness mm	width mm															thickness in
	12.5	16	19	25	32	38	50	75	100	125	150	175	200	225	300	
12.5	●					●	●	●			●					¹/₂
16		●				●	●									⁵/₈
19			●	●		●	●	●	●		●	●		●	●	³/₄
25				●		●	●	●	●	●	●	●	●	●	●	1
32					●		●	●	●		●	●		●	●	1¹/₄
38						●	●	●	●		●		●	●		1¹/₂
50							●	●	●		●	○	○	●	○	2
75								●	●		●	○	○	●		3
100									●				○	●	●	4
	⁵/₈	³/₄	1	1¹/₄	1¹/₂	2	3	4	5	6	7	8	9	12		
							width (in)									

CHOOSING HARDWOODS

To help you select hardwoods for particular jobs, their properties are summarized in this table. All the woods listed will make fine interior furniture and fittings, and can be finished with oil, polish or varnish (teak is an exception, for it is too oily to varnish successfully). Woods in **bold type** are those you're most likely to find.

	Walnut	Walnut (Afr)	Utile	Teak	Sycamore	Sapele	Rosewood	Ramin	Obeche	Oak	Meranti	Maple	Mahogany	Iroko	Idigbo	Elm	Cherry	Beech	Ash	Agba	Afrormosia
Shade Woods range from light to dark. 1 = palest	2	2	1	1	2	2	2	2	2	1	★	2	1	1	3	2	1	2	2	2	3
Richness Some timbers look bland, while others glow with a deep lustre when sealed. 1 = plainest	3	2	2	1	2	2	2	2	3	2	2	2	3	1	3	2	2	3	2	3	3
Figure Grain patterns vary from straight to swirling (sometimes depending on how the wood is cut). 1 = plainest	2	1	2	1	1	3	1	2	3	2	2	2	1	1	3	2	2	2	1	2	3
Durability Some timbers need preservative treatment for outdoors. 1 = most perishable	3	3	1	1	1	1	2	3	2	1	3	3	1	1	3	3	1	3	3	2	1
Density Timbers vary greatly in heaviness and hardness. 1 = lightest/softest	3	2	2	3	2	2	2	3	2	3	★	3	1	2	3	3	2	2	3	2	3
Cost Timber prices change constantly, and rarity value has to be taken into account. 1 = cheapest	3	1	1	1	2	★	1	1	★	2	1	★	1	1	3	1	3	3	2	2	3

★ *depends on variety*

hints

Hardwoods have an outer layer of 'sapwood', usually removed because it's paler and less insect-resistant than the inner 'heartwood'. A 'waney-edged' or 'unedged' (UE) piece still has both sapwood and bark. However, hardwoods also come square-edged (SE) and planed on one or more edges. As with softwoods, look out for distortions in shape – and for knots, though these are sometimes desirable on the grounds of appearance.

Remember that different and even unrelated species may have the same name – 'walnut' can mean English, European (French or Italian), American, African, New Guinea or Queensland walnut. Also the same species may have several names.

grain direction

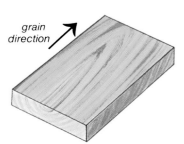

Since hardwoods are hard and dense, you must know the grain direction of your piece, and if possible plane 'with' it. Planing against the grain is difficult and at worst tears out the wood. Some species have 'interlocked' grain, which goes both ways at once! In such cases you just have to go carefully.

Hardwood must be conditioned for at least 72 hours in the environment where it will eventually be used – indoors if you're making fine furniture – to prevent shrinkage or swelling from marring the finished work.

With hardwoods the finish is all-important. Ensure it's perfect by using a cabinet scraper (right). This is a metal rectangle whose edge is squared on the oilstone, then turned over with a burr so

that it will remove shavings far finer than any plane. Use it with a pushing or pulling action (below). Finally clean off dust and grease with turps.

MAN-MADE BOARDS

Versatile, cheap and manufactured for uniform quality, man-made boards have become indispensable to all kinds of projects around the house. Here's a guide to differences between them and what each is suitable for.

Y ou only have to make some simple furniture or a few shelves from natural timber to realise just how expensive wood is. Man-made boards are the cheap alternatives. But they're not just substitutes for the real thing. In many situations, they have much more to offer than a low price. Most resist shrinking, swelling and warping better than natural woods. And because all are carefully manufactured for consistency in use, it's worth knowing exactly what each board can and can't do.

Fibreboards
Standard hardboard is the cheapest of all man-made boards and is produced by compressing wood fibre into hard, brown sheets. It is smooth on one side with a rough, mesh pattern on the other. Because it contains no adhesive, it's relatively weak, and if it gets wet it'll break up. But it's worth considering as a cladding, especially if you want something you can easily bend round curves.
● Thicknesses 2mm (5/64in) to 13mm (1/2in); 3, 5 and 6mm (1/8, 3/16 and 1/4in) are by far the most common.
Tempered hardboard is standard hardboard which has been treated to improve its strength and resistance to moisture, and is therefore suitable for use outdoors. It shouldn't be confused with oil-treated hardboard, which has only a short-lived and superficial moisture-resistance.
Decorative hardboards may be covered with PVC or melamine. They may also be factory-painted in a process known as 'enamelling'. Both types are easy to clean, but only their surfaces resist water. You can also get standard hardboard ready-primed for painting.
Moulded hardboards are often used as wall claddings. Some

even have a paint or plastic finish. You can buy them with embossed and textured designs – woodgrain, tile and brick being among the most popular. But you'll probably have to order the less common types.
Perforated hardboard has holes or slots in it. It comes in a range of designs, including plain 'pegboard' (with regular rows of small holes).
Duo-faced hardboard is smooth on both sides.
Medium board is softer and weaker than the others, and this is the main reason why it's used in thicker sheets – 6-13mm (1/4-1/2in). The denser type HM, also called 'panelboard', is used for cladding partitions in much the same way as plasterboard. The velvety grey/brown type LM is used for pinboards, etc. Both are available in versions made to withstand high humidity, and may also be flame-retardant, oil-treated, duo-faced or lacquered.
Softboard ('insulating board'), also made from fibres, is not compressed and is therefore even lighter and less dense than medium board. Apart from insulation, it too is used for pinboards.
MDF (medium-density fibreboard), is an extremely versatile material and can often be used instead of solid timber. It's far stronger than other fibreboards because it includes adhesive (like chipboard), and is highly compressed so that it's far denser than medium board. This means it not only does everything other man-made boards do, but also overcomes their two main problems – it doesn't flake or splinter, and when sawn it gives a smooth, hard edge which doesn't need disguising (it can even be stained to match a face veneer).
● Thicknesses 16mm (5/8in) to 35mm (1 3/8in).

Chipboard
Chipboard is made by bonding wood chips with plastic resin. It's quite strong, and one grade is tough enough to be used for flooring. However, it's difficult to work it neatly or to screw into it effectively: the thread breaks up the chips so the screw pulls out under load. Few chipboards can withstand moisture, though grades for external use are available.
● In the simplest type of chipboard, all the chips are approximately the same size – but usually those nearer the surface are finer. The surfaces mostly come filled and sanded, ready for decoration, and some are even primed for painting. Much chipboard is sold with a wood or PVC veneer, or a melamine laminate. Plastic-faced boards come in a limited range of colours and wood effects.
● Thicknesses range from 4mm (3/16in) to 40mm (1 1/2in); 12, 18, 22 and 25mm (1/2, 3/4, 7/8 and 1in) are commonest.

Plywood
Plywood is made by glueing wood veneers in layers. The grain of each veneer is laid at right angles to the ones on either side, the aim being to stop the sheet warping (though this isn't always completely successful). The sheet has an odd number of layers – hence the names, 'three-ply', 'five-ply' and so on. This ensures that the grains of the outside veneers always run in the same direction.
● Birch and gaboon are two of the main woods used for plywood.
Ideally, the veneers should be of the same wood and the same thickness. In fact, the outermost ones are always thin, and you'll often find thick veneers made of less dense timber in the centre.
● 'Stoutheart' plywood is the name given to a sheet where there is only one central thick veneer. This makes the edges of the sheet harder to work.
● Some plywoods have a decorative finish, which can range from a factory-applied paint or a plastic laminate to a particularly attractive wood veneer. Others are grooved to resemble match-board cladding.
● Two grading systems are used for plywood. The first indicates the number of knots, joins and other blemishes in the surface veneers. Its three grades are A (perfect), B, and BB for rough work. Where a board appears to have two grades (eg, B/BB), the first refers to one veneer the second to the other. The other system grades the

1 4mm (³/₁₆in) 3-ply
2 6mm (¹/₄in) stoutheart 3-ply
3 9mm (³/₈in) 5-ply
4 12mm (¹/₂in) 5-ply including oak veneer
5 12mm (¹/₂in) 7-ply, melamine-faced
6 18mm (³/₄in) multi-ply (13-ply)
7 12mm (¹/₂in) duo-faced blockboard
8 18mm (³/₄in) duo-faced blockboard
9 18mm (³/₄in) duo-faced blockboard
   including teak veneer

adhesive between the veneers. WBP (weather-and-boil-proof) will withstand severe weathering for at least 25 years; then, in order of durability, come BR, MR and INT, the last of which is only for dry internal use. The adhesive may outlast the veneers; but especially durable types of plywood (eg, marine plywood, used in boatbuilding) are also available.

● Thicknesses range from 3 to 6, 12 and 19mm ($\frac{1}{8}$, $\frac{1}{4}$, $\frac{1}{2}$ and $\frac{3}{4}$in), but thinner and thicker types are made.

Blockboard

Blockboard is a bit like stoutheart plywood. It has a thick core of softwood slats glued side by side, and two outer hardwood veneers, one of which may be decorative. The veneer grain runs at right angles to the core grain. In more expensive (double-faced or five-ply) boards, two outer veneers are used on each face, which makes

the core joins less likely to show through.

● Blockboard is very useful where you need a relatively light, inexpensive slab, eg, for a tabletop or door. However, it's hard to get the edges neat, especially those where the core endgrain shows: there are often unsightly gaps between the slats, too. Fixing into these edges can be a problem for the same reasons.

● Surface veneers and adhesives are graded as for plywood, but no blockboard is really suitable for external use. There's no WBP grade (see above), and anyway the board contains too much softwood to be truly durable.

Laminboard is a superior blockboard. Its core is made from thinner, more uniform slats with no gaps between them. But it's hard to get.

● Thicknesses range from 12mm ($\frac{1}{2}$in) to 32mm (1$\frac{1}{4}$in); occasionally up to 50mm (2in).

Buying boards

Say exactly what you want – name, grade, finish, thickness. A good timber merchant's catalogue helps a lot. Remember you can get a number of different veneers – from rosewood to oak – on chipboard, plywood and blockboard.

Think carefully how much you want. There are several 'standard' sheet sizes – commonest is 2400 x 1200mm (8 x 4ft). Buying a whole sheet is cheapest. If that's too much, or you have no power saw, small sheets may be available. Failing that, get it cut specially – but allow a little extra for trimming at home; shop sawing may not be very neat or accurate.

hints

EDGINGS FOR MAN-MADE BOARDS

For the best finish, edge man-made boards with a timber 'lipping'. Often this can be bought or planed to the same width as the board thickness so it

fits flush on both the face and the underside. Use panel pins and PVA adhesive to fix it in place, and mitre the ends at the corners for a clean edge all round.

Rectangular-section strip, pinned and glued in place

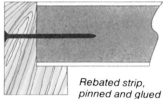

Rebated strip, pinned and glued

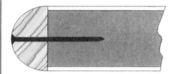

Half-round beading, pinned and glued in place

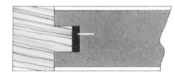

Tongue and groove – can be cut easily with power tools

Reeded moulding, pinned and glued

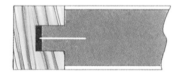

Another type of tongue and groove, slightly weaker

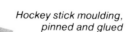

Hockey stick moulding, pinned and glued

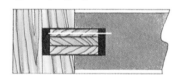

Loose tongue of thin plywood in two matching grooves

Plastic edging strip

1 4mm ($\frac{3}{16}$in) pegboard
2 3mm ($\frac{1}{8}$in) hardboard, melamine-faced one side
3 3mm ($\frac{1}{8}$in) standard hardboard
4 9mm ($\frac{3}{8}$in) medium board, type LM
5 12mm ($\frac{1}{2}$in) canite board, painted one side
6 15mm ($\frac{5}{8}$in) MDF
7 12mm ($\frac{1}{2}$in) chipboard
8 15mm ($\frac{5}{8}$in) chipboard, wood-veneered and edged
9 15mm ($\frac{5}{8}$in) chipboard, melamine-faced
10 18mm ($\frac{3}{4}$in) chipboard

FINISHES FOR FURNITURE

There are many products you can use to give your furniture and fittings a fine finish. The range includes polishes, waxes and oils as well as lacquers or varnishes of various types.

Once furniture has been assembled it must be finished to seal its pores, protect its surface against heat, liquid and scratches, and to give it an attractive appearance. Before doing so, however, you might have to give it some preparatory treatment.

Preparing the wood
Restorer and cleaner contains refined alcohol and gum spirit of turpentine to dissolve old finishes. It should be applied gently using fine steel wool. A further application will probably be necessary, but don't overclean as you could mark the wood. To remove just oil or wax, apply restorer with a clean rag.

Wood bleach literally turns wood lighter in colour and also removes stains. It can only be used on bare wood and comes in two parts. You can make up to four applications, but after that many you'll have to accept any remaining stains.

Reviver contains pure boiled linseed oil that sinks into wood that has had its finish removed and appears dry and unattractive. It will prevent further drying and cracking and give some surface protection. Allow it to soak in for 24 hours.

Finishing the wood
The finish you select will depend on two factors. Firstly, the amount of protection the surface requires from water, heat and so on, and secondly, the degree of shine you want it to have.

French polish will give a superb finish with a mirror-like gloss provided it is correctly applied. However, the finish won't provide any real protection. It is made from the finest quality shellac and industrial alcohol, and you can use white or transparent polish to keep the wood a light colour, or flake orange or garnet for a darker finish. The secret of success lies in the application and the building up of several layers to get a beautiful, reflective surface.

White polish is french polish with bleached white shellac added. It is designed for use on light-coloured woods where the true natural appearance is to be maintained. It can also be used for sealing wood before waxing.

Button polish is applied like french polish but produces a harder, more orange-coloured finish.

Wax polish can be applied on its own, but it also makes an excellent surface covering for other finishes. It is not resistant to heat or scratches and needs frequent re-application. It is available in traditional wax blocks or as a liquid or spray.

Varnish (often called synthetic lacquer) provides a durable matt, eggshell or gloss finish that is highly water-resistant and can also cope well with spills and heat. It cannot be applied to wood that has been waxed or oiled unless all trace of the previous finish has been removed.

It comes in both one and two-part forms and can be sprayed, brushed or rubbed on. Follow the manufacturer's instructions closely as some lacquers require rapid application of coats to give amalgamation between layers, while others need 24 hours between each coat.

Plastic coating is a modern alternative to french polish that provides resistance to heat, liquids and scratches. It is available in clear, black or white, while other shades can be obtained by adding a small amount of wood stain. It requires a two-part treatment and can be given a matt finish by gentle rubbing down with wax polish and 0 or 1 grade steel wool. For a mirror finish, rub down with glass paper and apply a burnishing cream.

Using oil
Wood can also be sealed with oil but the treatment is best used only on hardwoods – softwoods become dirty and discoloured very quickly. The finish gives good resistance to moisture, but not to spills or heat. Rub the oil well in to the grain and repeat the application. Allow drying time between the coats and finish with fine grade steel wool, wax polish and a clean cloth.

Teak oil contains 'drying agents' to speed up the drying process, and gives an attractive seal to most hardwoods. It gives a minimal sheen.

Danish oil will not dry to a gloss if used on wood that has been already oiled. It gives a natural, open-grained lustrous finish, and can be lacquered over (unlike the other oils).

Linseed oil is slow-drying and forms a poor film. Heat-treated linseed oil, called boiled oil, is a better bet, and is easier to apply if mixed first with equal parts of turpentine.

Olive oil should be used to seal wooden articles, such as a chopping board, that will be used in food preparation.

NAILS AND SCREWS

To ensure the success of all your carpentry projects, be sure to choose the right nails and screws for the task.

Nails come in many guises for all sorts of different jobs, though some are easier to find than others. Before looking at them all, a few general points are worth considering.

The first is strength. Friction is what makes a nail grip, so long thick nails provide a better grip than short thin ones. Another factor is the shape of the nail's shank; on the whole, nails with specially shaped shanks are strongest, and cut nails are stronger than wire nails.

Cut nails cause fewer splits than wire nails because, being blunt, they break the wood fibres and create their own holes, while wire nails merely force the fibres apart.

Nails aren't very attractive. The standard method of hiding them is to punch their heads below the surface of the wood and fill the resulting hollows with stopping. But if you're securing such things as carpet, fabric or roofing felt, the large head found on most tacks and roofing nails is essential to hold the material in place.

Finally, think about rust. In most indoor work ordinary mild steel nails are fine but outdoors, you need a nail with more rust resistance. Normally this means a galvanised nail, but other rust-resisting finishes are available – and you can also get nails made entirely from metals that don't rust at all, such as brass, copper and even bronze.

Buying nails
When buying nails, remember they're described by length rather than diameter. Also, though it may be sensible (if more expensive) to buy small amounts in packets and boxes, it's more economical to buy loose nails sold by weight, not quantity.

General-purpose nails
Round wire nails (12) are used only for rough carpentry. They're available plain (12) or galvanised (15), in lengths from 20 to 150 mm (¾ to 6in).

Oval wire nails (14) are used in all types of general woodwork. Lengths are as for round wire nails; galvanised types are also available.

Lost head nails (16) are often used instead of ovals. Lengths range from 12mm (½in) to 150mm; you'll find plain or galvanised finishes.

Cut floor brads (11) are traditional fixings for floorboards. Lengths range from 20 to 150mm; they have a plain finish.

Cut clasp nails (17) are used for rough fixings in wood, and in masonry if it's not too hard. Lengths range from 25mm to 100mm (1 to 4in).

Masonry Nails (4) are specially hardened to make a reasonably strong fixing in brickwork and the like. Twisted shanks grip better than plain ones. They come in various gauges (thicknesses) and in lengths from about 12 to 100mm (½ to 4in).

Plasterboard nails used for fixing plasterboard to ceilings and stud walls, are similar but have a jagged shank for extra grip.

Panel pins (6) are slim versions of the lost-head nail, used in fine work for fixing mouldings and the like. Lengths range from 12 to 50mm (½ to 2in).

Moulding pins (9) and **veneer pins** (7) are still thinner lost-head nails and are used for fixing thin lippings and mouldings. Lengths range from 12 to 25mm (½ to 1in).

Specialised nails
Hardboard pins (8) are for fixing hardboard. Their diamond-shaped heads burrow into the surface as the pin is driven home. Most have a coppered finish; lengths are from 10 to 38mm (⅜ to 1½in).

Sprigs (5), also called cut brads, are mainly used for holding glass in window frames. Normally plain, lengths range from 12 to 19mm (½ to ¾in).

Cut tacks (2) have large flat heads for holding fabric and carpet in place. Finishes are blued, coppered or galvanised; lengths range from 6 to 30mm (¼ to 1¼in).

Roofing nails are used for fixing corrugated roofing sheets. One (1) is used with curved washers; the other has a special sprung head. Both are usually galvanised. Lengths range from 63 to 112mm (2½ to 4½in).

Staples (3) are used to fix wire fencing, upholstery springs and the like, and are either galvanised or plain. Lengths range from 12 to 40mm (1½ to 1⅝in).

Annular nails (10) have ribs along the shank to prevent them pulling out, and are used for fixing sheet materials. Lengths range between 25 and 75mm (1 to 3in); finishes are plain steel or coppered.

Clout nails (13) have extra-large heads which make them ideal for fixing roofing felt, slates, sash window cords and so on. Lengths range from 12 to 50mm (½ to 2in); most are galvanised.

To be able to pick exactly the screw you need for a particular purpose, it helps to know what each part of the screw does.

The thread is the spiral that actually pulls the screw into the wood and holds it there. Most have the same profile, but chipboard screws combat the material's crumbly quality with their shallower spiral; some screws have a double thread, which means the screw won't wander off-centre and can be driven more quickly. Most wood screws have about two-fifths of their length unthreaded, forming the shank, but chipboard screws are threaded all the way up to head for better grip.

Screw heads come in three main shapes. Countersunk is the commonest. The name describes how the screw head fits into the surface of what you're fixing – into a hole with sloping sides. This hole is made in wood with a special countersink bit; many metal fittings such as hinges have their screw holes already countersunk.

The raised countersunk head looks more handsome, and is often used with exposed metal fittings. The round head is used for fixing metal fittings without a countersink to wood.

On wood screws the Pozidriv recess has now given way to the similar-looking Supadriv type. Each has its own screwdriver shape, but you can use a Pozidriver for both.

Screws for special purposes include the clutch-head screw, which can't be undone once driven. The coach screw, used for heavy framing work, has a square head and is tightened with a spanner. The mirror screw is inserted in the usual way; then a chrome-plated dome is screwed into the head, making it a decorative feature.

Sizes and materials
How big is a screw? Its length ranges from 6 to 150mm (¼ to 6in). The gauge – the diameter of the shank – has a number from 0 (the smallest) to 32; 4, 6, 8, 10 and 12 are the commonest. Remember that you can have the same screw length in different gauges and the same gauge in different lengths.

And what are screws made of? Steel is the commonest and cheapest material, but isn't very good-looking and rusts easily. Luckily there are several alternatives. Steel itself comes with various coatings, from nickel plate to black japanning. Of other metals, brass (available plain or chromium-plated) is fairly corrosion proof but weak. Aluminium (also weak), stainless steel and silicon bronze are virtually corrosion-free. Stainless steel is the strongest of the three, but is expensive.

Remember when buying screws to give all the relevant details – length, gauge number, head type, material, recess type and finish.

HEADS AND THREADS
1 The commonest head profile is countersunk, with a flat top and sloping sides.
2 Raised countersunk heads have a slightly domed top, and are used with metal fittings.
3 Round-head screws are used to fix metal fittings without countersunk screw holes.
4 The screw thread usually extends to about three-fifths of the screw length, but chipboard screws are threaded all the way up.
5 Most screws have a slot in the head.
6 Supadriv recesses need a special screwdriver.

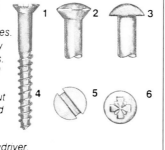

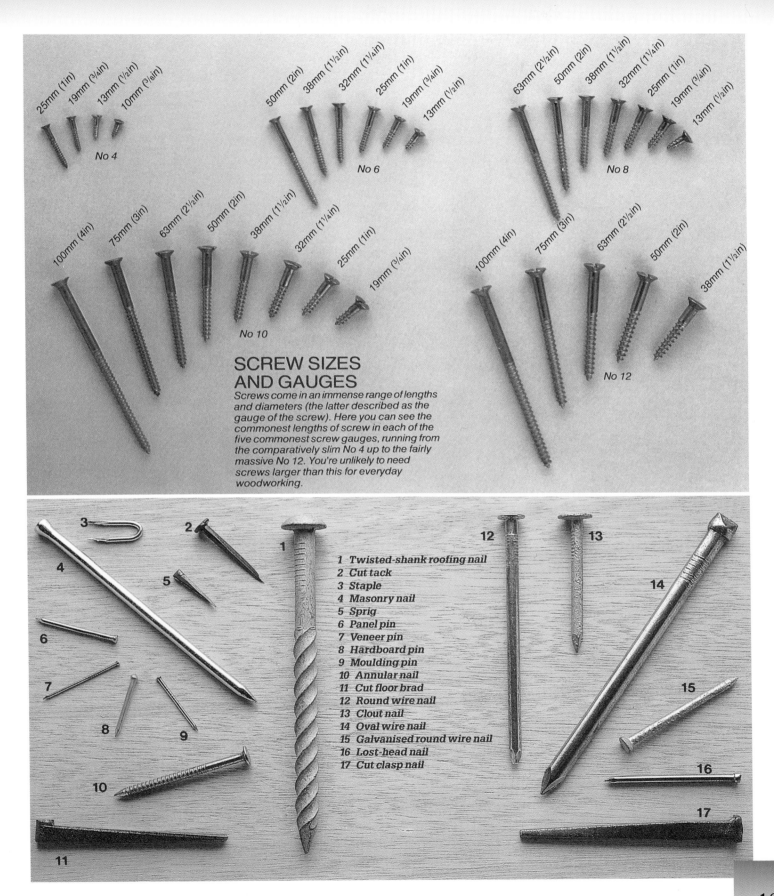

25mm (1in)   19mm (¾in)   13mm (½in)   10mm (⅜in)

No 4

50mm (2in)   38mm (1½in)   32mm (1¼in)   25mm (1in)   19mm (¾in)   13mm (½in)

No 6

63mm (2½in)   50mm (2in)   38mm (1½in)   32mm (1¼in)   25mm (1in)   19mm (¾in)   13mm (½in)

No 8

100mm (4in)   75mm (3in)   63mm (2½in)   50mm (2in)   38mm (1½in)   32mm (1¼in)   25mm (1in)   19mm (¾in)

No 10

100mm (4in)   75mm (3in)   63mm (2½in)   50mm (2in)   38mm (1½in)

No 12

SCREW SIZES AND GAUGES

Screws come in an immense range of lengths and diameters (the latter described as the gauge of the screw). Here you can see the commonest lengths of screw in each of the five commonest screw gauges, running from the comparatively slim No 4 up to the fairly massive No 12. You're unlikely to need screws larger than this for everyday woodworking.

1   Twisted-shank roofing nail
2   Cut tack
3   Staple
4   Masonry nail
5   Sprig
6   Panel pin
7   Veneer pin
8   Hardboard pin
9   Moulding pin
10   Annular nail
11   Cut floor brad
12   Round wire nail
13   Clout nail
14   Oval wire nail
15   Galvanised round wire nail
16   Lost-head nail
17   Cut clasp nail

HINGES

There's a very wide range of hinges available, in all sorts of sizes and materials. Some are general purpose types, while others are designed to do just one specific job, so it's important that you select the correct one.

When choosing a hinge, the first essential is to know what kind of door or flap you're fitting – what it's made of, and whether it's lay-on or inset (see Adding doors to basic boxes).

The second is to know how wide a choice you have. For most applications there are three or four suitable hinges. In all, there are scores of variations: here we show the main types you're likely to use.

Most hinges are made of steel, brass and white nylon, singly or in combination. Chromium and nickel plate, and brown plastic, are also used.

Butt hinges

Butt hinges, the traditional type, are still used constantly. They consist of two rectangular *leaves* (except on a flush hinge, these are the same shape), joined by a *knuckle* with a pin through it. Butt hinges come in sizes from 25mm (1in), for use on furniture, to in excess of 100mm (4in) long for hanging room doors. Materials include steel, brass and nylon.

● Some butt hinges (usually brass) have ornamental *finials* at each end of the knuckle; on some of these, such as the **loose-pin** type (4), the finials unscrew so you can tap out the pin. This makes fitting them a lot easier, because you can fasten one leaf each to door and frame separately before hanging the door by assembling the two.

● A **piano hinge** (8) is simply a narrow butt hinge sold as a continuous length of up to 1800mm (6ft), and originally designed to hinge the keyboard cover on a piano. You can easily cut it with a hacksaw to any length you need.

● The **back flap hinge**'s wide leaves (5) equip it for the task of holding table and desk flaps.

● **Rising butts** (6) are widely used on room doors. They enable the door to be lifted off at any time

– and the spiral in the knuckle pulls the door closed automatically. You may have to remove the inner top corner of the door to prevent it catching on the doorstop as the door swings home.

● The **flush hinge** (7) isn't strictly a butt hinge, because one leaf closes within, rather than against, the other. It's unsuitable for heavy doors, but – unlike ordinary butt hinges – it doesn't need to be recessed. Instead, its leaves are simply screwed onto the meeting surfaces – the smaller one to the door. The thickness of the leaves equals the clearance around the door.

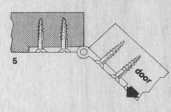

pin
leaves
knuckle
length

Butt hinges
Probably still the commonest type, these come in many varieties. When fitting, it's important to get them in line vertically.

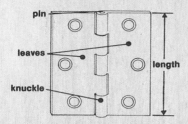

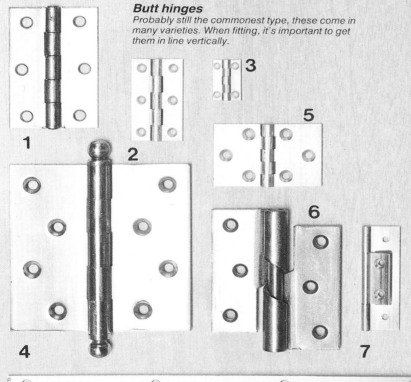

1 2 3 4 5 6 7

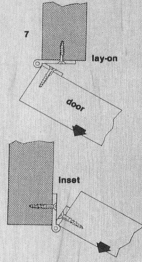

7
lay-on
door
inset

Fitting butt hinges
Butt hinges usually fit in pairs of chiselled rectangular recesses. They work on both lay-on and inset doors.

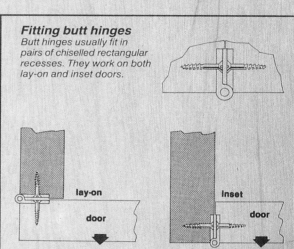

lay-on
door
inset
door

8

Decorative hinges

These hinges, also surface-fixing (9, 10 and 11), are of course used for their ornamental effect. Note that the front frame or edges of the cabinet must be fairly wide to accommodate them.

There's also a much smaller and less ornamental type of surface-fixing hinge which looks rather like (14) and is suitable for light doors.

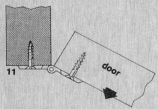

Pivot hinges

Pivot hinges are so called because all or part of each leaf lies in a horizontal plane and so needs only a small pivot, rather than a long knuckle, to connect it to the other.

● **Centre hinges,** the traditional type (12), can only be used on inset doors. A door hung with these has one hinge on its top edge, and one at the bottom; one leaf of each hinge is recessed into the door, one into the cabinet.

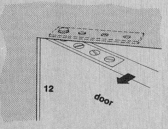

This hinge is hidden when the door is closed – and it's handy if for any reason you can't attach butt hinges to the door or cabinet or both.

● The more modern type (sometimes confusingly called 'semi-concealed') is *double-cranked.* On a cranked hinge, one leaf is bent into a right angle. On a double-cranked hinge this is true of both leaves.

Either way, the door swings from a different point to that on a non-cranked hinge – ideal for a lay-on door, because it will open fully (ie, to 90°) without passing beyond the cabinet side. If the cabinet is beside a wall, or next to

another cabinet of the same or greater depth, this is essential.

The other good point about cranked hinges is that they're easier to fit accurately, because their angles locate over the edges of timber or board.

The cranked pivot hinge shown here (13) requires a small saw cut to be made in the edges of the door and cabinet to take its neck. Other types are simply fitted to the top and bottom edges of the door, without the need for cuts. All can be bought for left- or right-hand opening doors.

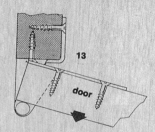

● Not shown is the **lift-off pivot hinge,** for lightweight lay-on doors, half of which screws bodily into the door and half into the cabinet. One half incorporates a pin and the other a socket, so you can hang the door after fitting them, as with a loose-pin hinge. (Lift-off butt hinges are also available.)

Cranked hinges

The main family of cranked hinges have knuckles rather than pivots. They give you several further options for fitting lay-on doors. Their main disadvantage is that they're highly visible on the edge of the door.

● The **cranked surface-fixing hinge** (14) will only take light weight doors because it isn't recessed. The one shown accommodates 6mm (¼in) thick plywood.

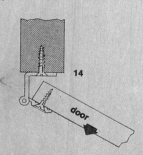

Decorative hinges

Because they're surface-fixing, and the knuckle is short compared to the leaves, these are useful where the meeting edges of door and cabinet aren't straight.

● The **lift-off cranked hinge** (15) combines the advantages of a cranked hinge with the ease of fitting given by separable leaves. It is recessed like a butt hinge.
● 16 is similar except that it lacks the lift-off facility. This particular model is very solidly made in brass.

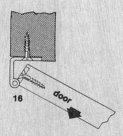

Cranked hinges

Always try these out (like pivot and concealed hinges) on scraps of timber or board before buying, to see how they work.

Pivot hinges

Traditional pivot hinges have two flat leaves. Modern types, which are cranked, differ in being especially easy to fit.

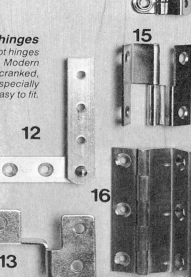

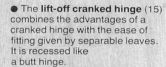

Invisible hinges

Invisible hinges are especially neat little devices. Although completely hidden when the door is closed, they have intricate mechanisms which allow it to open to 180°. They work on both inset and lay-on doors.

● The **cylinder hinge** (17) simply fits into a pair of drilled holes.
● The mechanism of the **Soss** or **invisible mortise hinge** (18) fits into a mortise, while its face plate sits in a shallow recess like the leaf of a butt hinge.

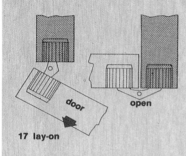

17 lay-on

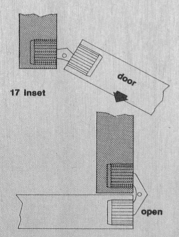

17 inset

Concealed hinges

An enormous amount of work has gone into the development of concealed hinges, and many different models are available.

While most are designed, like cranked hinges, to allow lay-on doors to open within the overall width of the cabinet, some will fit inset doors, and some both – those for lay-on doors varying according to the amount of overlap they give. Often the thickness of timber or board is important. You'll also find variations in how far the hinges open. And some concealed hinges, such as the two shown here, have a positive spring action which serves instead of a catch to keep the door closed.

The concealed hinge can't be seen, because it's fixed entirely inside the door and cabinet. As a rule, the part fixed to the door includes a threaded cylindrical section which fits into a wide, shallow circular recess bored in the surface, where it's held in position by screws.

● This recess is readily and accurately milled out by industrial machines, but less so by the home woodworker. That may lead you to choose a surface-fixing type like (19), which fixes in the easiest possible way – by screwing onto both surfaces.

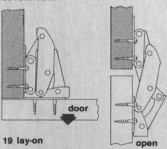
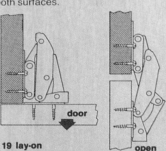

19 lay-on

open

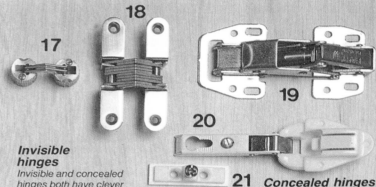

Invisible hinges

Invisible and concealed hinges both have clever mechanisms which pull the door clear of the cabinet instead of letting it swing. With invisible hinges this is completely hidden.

Concealed hinges
The great attraction of these is their adjustability and variety. Many models, too, don't require a separate catch to be fitted.

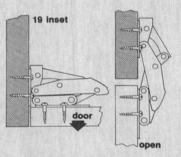

19 inset

door

open

This model also has a spring to keep the door firmly open, as well as closed. The action is so sure that it will even hold up a light flap without the need for a stay.

● (20) is the **recessed** type, (21) is its **mounting plate**, which is screwed inside the cabinet; the thin end of the hinge is screwed, in its turn, to the plate. This arrangement, like that of a lift-off or loose-pin hinge, makes for easy door hanging; but it's also unique in allowing easy adjustment of the door's position after it's been fitted.

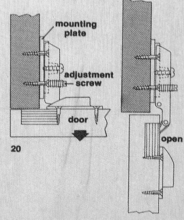

mounting plate

adjustment screw

door

20

open

FITTING HINGES

In essence, the fitting procedure is the same for all hinges.
1 Make sure the door fits.
2 Work out exactly how the hinges will be positioned, including the dimensions of any recesses.
3 Mark out the hinge positions on the door, plus recesses if any.
4 Fix the hinges to the door.
5 Position the door accurately, and fix the hinges to the cabinet.

All doors need at least two hinges, unless you're using a piano hinge. The very tallest and heaviest need four; intermediate ones need three.

There are no rules about the spacing of hinges. However, with butt and similar types, the top hinge is often placed a distance equal to its own length down from the top of the door and the bottom one up from the bottom by the same or twice the distance. On framed doors, the upper end of the top hinge is often lined up with the lower edge of the top rail in the frame, and the lower end of the bottom hinge with the upper edge of the bottom rail.

All hinges will work in any material. But they have to take a lot of stress, so you need to make sure they're secure. Don't use small, light hinges for a large, heavy door. Recesses usually make for greater strength than surface fixing, provided the hinges fit into them tightly.

But surface fixing is stronger in veneered or plastic-faced chipboard, because breaking through the facing weakens the material. If using butt hinges in this type of board, get round the problem by recessing them to twice the depth in the other material.

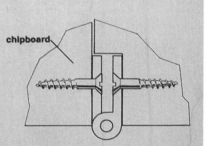

chipboard

In chipboard, too, you should use chipboard screws. Fixing into its edges is not, however, to be recommended.

BASIC
WOODWORKING
TECHNIQUES

Whether the woodworking job you are planning to carry out
is a simple or a complicated one, you will not get far
without first mastering the basic
carpentry skills.

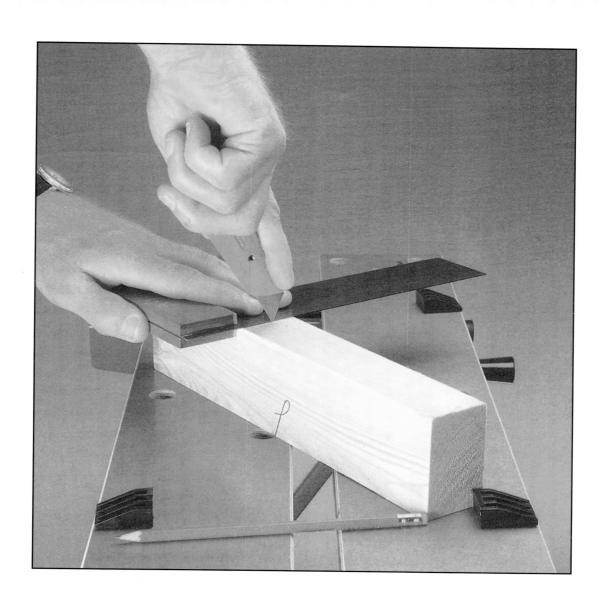

WOODWORK JOINTS

If there were no joints, there could be very little woodwork. They come in a great many varieties. This guide helps to remove the confusion from picking the right joint for the right job.

C arpentry without joints is a miserable affair, depending solely on adhesive, nails, screws, bolts and other fittings.

Though all these have their places, and are often needed for reinforcement, proper joints provide a wholly different source of strength and stability. Made by shaping the pieces themselves, they frequently (and traditionally) need no fixing hardware at all. Because of this, they usually contribute neatness too, and sometimes save money. They can even supply ornament.

General principles

Accurate cutting is absolutely basic to good jointing. Apart from looks, it's often vital for strength, since components which meet squarely and snugly help adhesives to do their work (especially PVA, which isn't much good at filling gaps).

Some joints, especially in building carpentry, need no adhesive, relying instead on weight and/or on being part of a large, solid structure. For the rest, the rule is that larger glued areas mean more strength. A mortise-and-tenon joint, for example, is stronger than a halving joint largely because it has two pairs of main meeting faces instead of one. Shoulders, too, aid location and rigidity.

Remember, however, that cutting any joint exacts its own price in

L-JOINTS FOR FRAMING

A mitred front (2) makes a halving joint (1) look neater; you can also include it in a corner bridle joint (3).

Haunches (4 and 5) stop a tenon piece from twisting.

A plain mitre (8) is quite weak. Keys (9) or a spline (10) reinforce it; both are planed flush after assembly. The spline can be of either thin plywood or solid timber. In the latter case the grain should run across it, for strength, instead of along it as you'd normally expect.

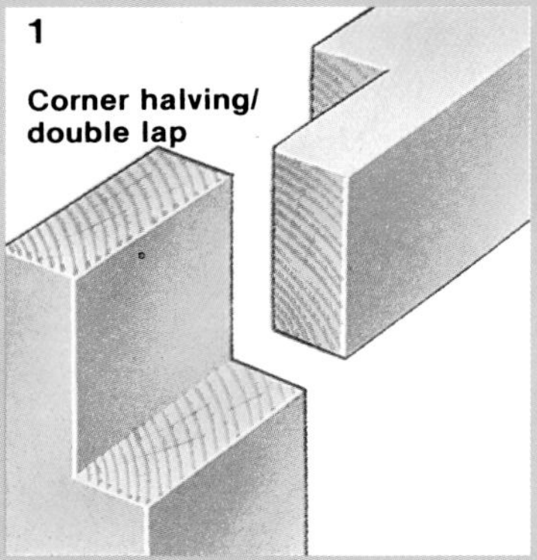

1 Corner halving/double lap

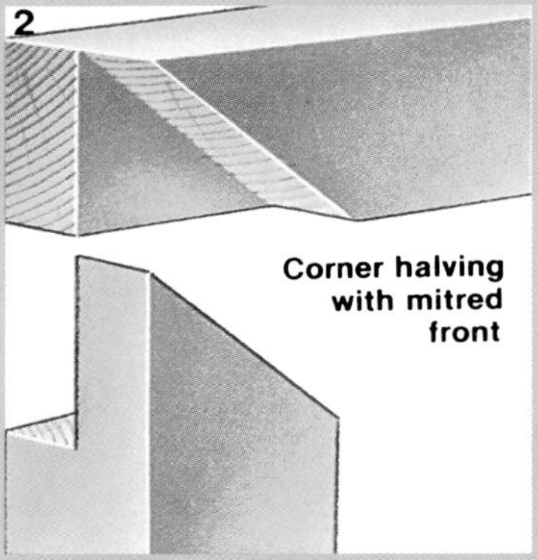

2 Corner halving with mitred front

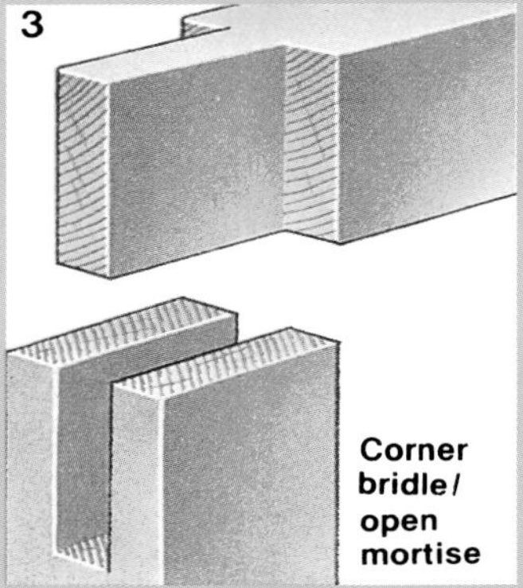

3 Corner bridle/open mortise

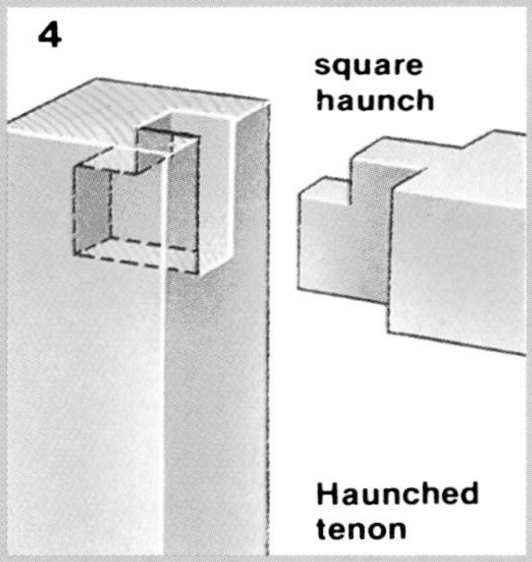

4 square haunch — Haunched tenon

5 Secret-haunched tenon — secret haunch

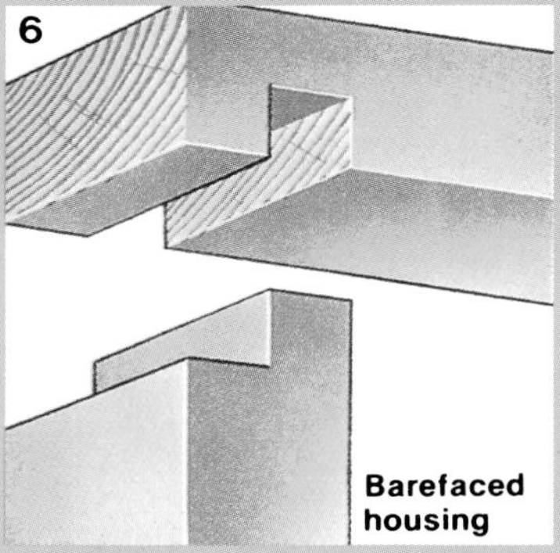

6 Barefaced housing

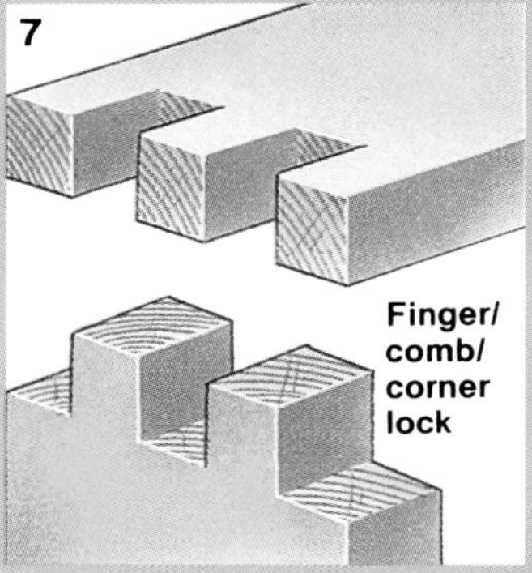

7 Finger/comb/corner lock

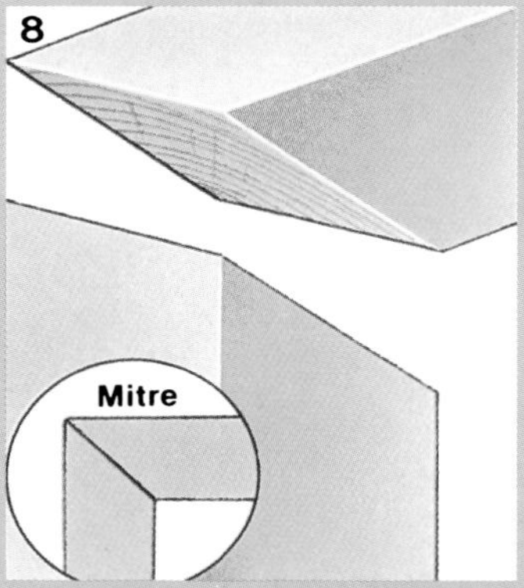

8 Mitre

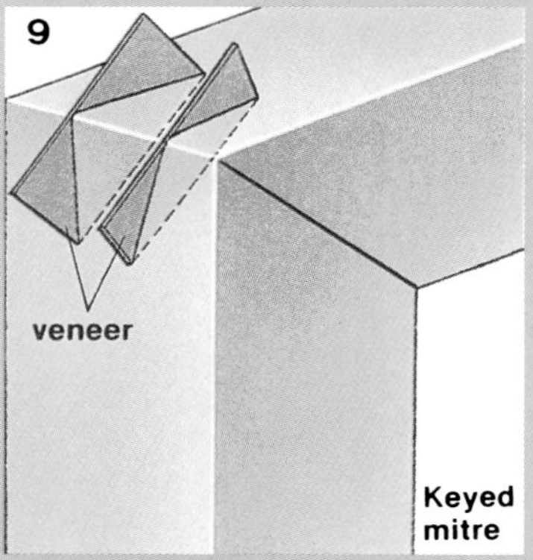

9 veneer — Keyed mitre

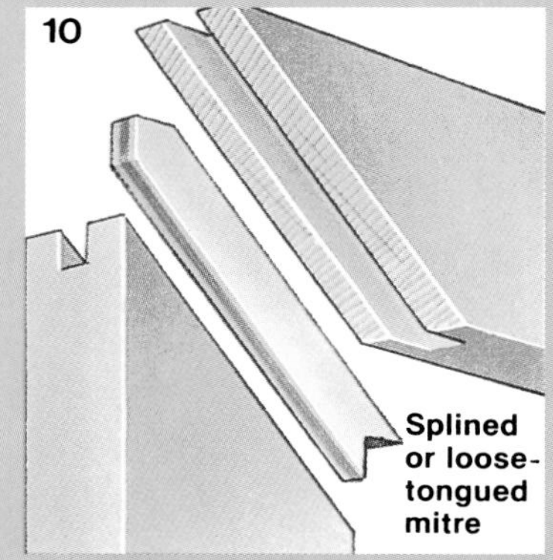

10 Splined or loose-tongued mitre

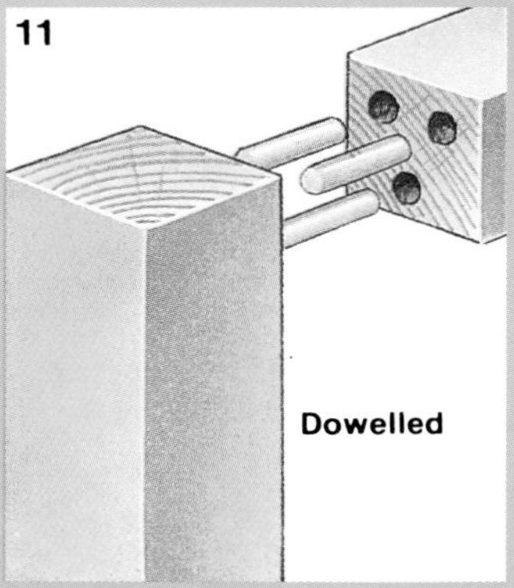

11 Dowelled

terms of strength. A halving effectively reduces (say) a 50x50mm (2x2in) piece to a 50x25mm (2x1in) piece. This point is often forgotten. The second piece, tight-fitting and well glued though that may be, won't lessen the fact. You must be sure your choice of joint justifies any overall reduction in size and therefore strength.

Choosing joints

Framing joints are used with lengths of timber, both softwood and hardwood. Board joints are for flat pieces, often of man-made materials. Broadly speaking, the two groups are separate, though some joints (eg, the finger joint) can be used in either situation. Both groups include corner joints, T-joints and a few X-joints. Three-way framing joints are usually combinations of simple corner joints.

Note that there's another category we don't show, namely 'scarf' joints. These join timber end-to-end. Though many ingenious patterns have been devised, they take some cutting, and none is as strong as a piece of wood which is long enough to start with. In new work that's not hard to come by, and the scarf joint is usually used only for localised repair work where a complete length of timber cannot be easily replaced.

On the whole, the joints in common use – of which a good selection appears here – are popular for good reasons, and serve most purposes. Common sense and growing familiarity with them will reveal these in more detail. Very often, of course, there's more than one joint for a particular task – and different people have their own favourites. In many cases, further information about individual joints is given in other sections of this book.

But, whatever you do, don't think that these illustrations tell the whole story. Probably thousands of other joints have been used at one time and another – and there's still

nothing to stop you from inventing your own variants if you want and need to. But it's wise, first of all, to check that an ordinary joint won't do. This may save you trouble – and the search for one will concentrate your mind on the exact qualities you're looking for. Usually strength, appearance and ease of cutting are what it all boils down to.

Consider, too, exactly what you want the joint to do. In which direction, or directions, is each piece likely to sag, twist, be pushed or be pulled? Make sure you combat exactly the stresses you expect – and not others which are unlikely, or you risk making the joint unnecessarily complicated.

L-JOINTS FOR BOARDS

On wider pieces like these, the grain must always run the same way on both halves of the joint, so they can shrink and swell freely across it even when glued. For the same reason, use a glued spline (16) only with man-made boards.

Joints 12 to 16 are all best made with a router – or on a saw table, tilting the blade for the mitre cuts. You could use a rebate plane for the first four, but power tools are pretty well essential for 16 (a neat, strong joint).

20 represents the ultimate in Western joints. As its name implies, its complex innards are entirely hidden. Don't attempt to cut it unless you're very keen indeed – even many tradesmen would have difficulty.

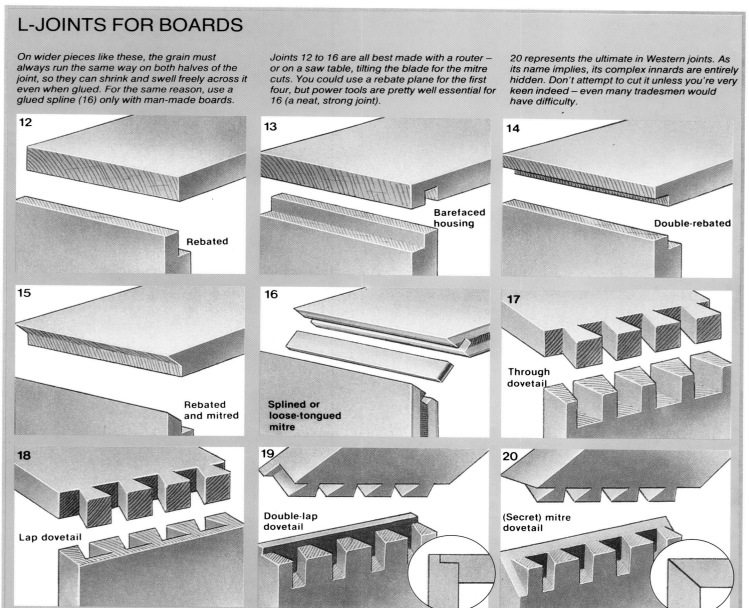

12 Rebated

13 Barefaced housing

14 Double-rebated

15 Rebated and mitred

16 Splined or loose-tongued mitre

17 Through dovetail

18 Lap dovetail

19 Double-lap dovetail

20 (Secret) mitre dovetail

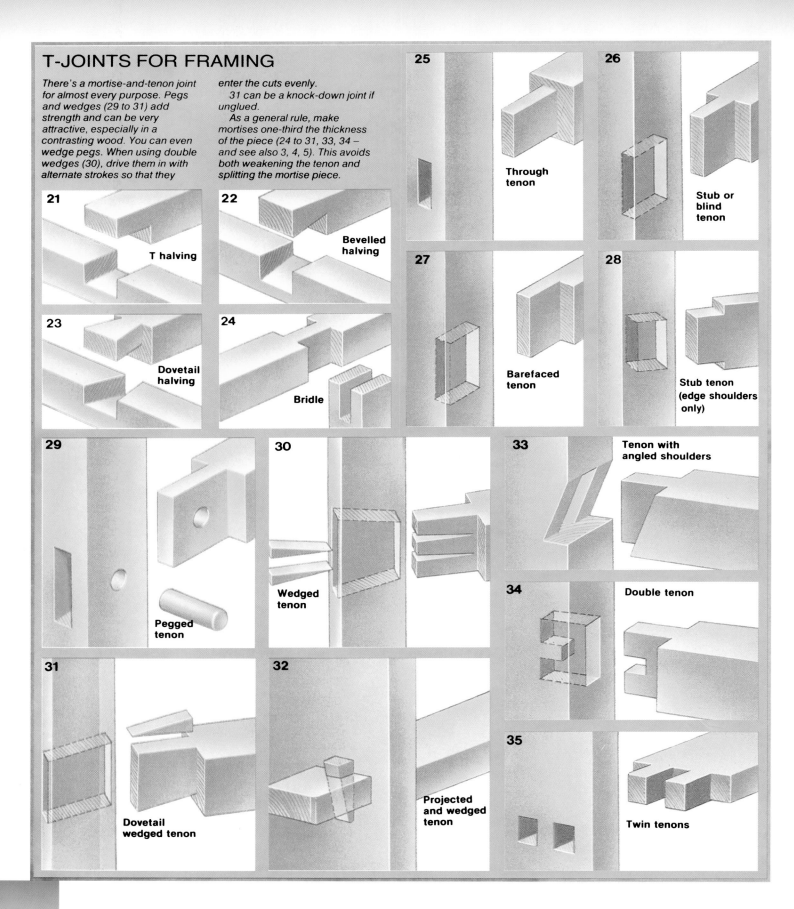

T-JOINTS FOR FRAMING

There's a mortise-and-tenon joint for almost every purpose. Pegs and wedges (29 to 31) add strength and can be very attractive, especially in a contrasting wood. You can even wedge pegs. When using double wedges (30), drive them in with alternate strokes so that they enter the cuts evenly.

31 can be a knock-down joint if unglued.

As a general rule, make mortises one-third the thickness of the piece (24 to 31, 33, 34 – and see also 3, 4, 5). This avoids both weakening the tenon and splitting the mortise piece.

21 T halving

22 Bevelled halving

23 Dovetail halving

24 Bridle

25 Through tenon

26 Stub or blind tenon

27 Barefaced tenon

28 Stub tenon (edge shoulders only)

29 Pegged tenon

30 Wedged tenon

31 Dovetail wedged tenon

32

33 Tenon with angled shoulders

34 Double tenon

35 Twin tenons

Projected and wedged tenon

SIMPLE JOINTS

It's often thought that only elaborate joints give good results in woodwork. It isn't true. There are simple ways to join timber, and one of the simplest is the butt joint. It's easy to make, and can be used on natural timber or man-made boards.

The great thing about butt joints is their simplicity. You can use them on any kind of timber or man-made board, provided it isn't too thin – not under 6mm ($\frac{1}{4}$in). The only problem you will run into is where you are joining chipboard. A special technique is needed here to get the screws to grip, as is explained later.

Although it is possible simply to glue two pieces of wood together, unless you add some kind of reinforcement the result won't be very strong. So in most cases, the joint should be strengthened with either screws or nails. The question is which? As a rule of thumb, screws will give you a stronger joint than nails. The exception is where you are screwing into the endgrain of natural timber. Here, the screw thread chews up the timber to such an extent that it has almost no fixing value at all. Nails in this case are a much better bet.

Choosing the right adhesive
Even if you are screwing or nailing the joint together, it ought to be glued as well. A PVA woodworking adhesive will do the trick in most jobs, providing a strong and easily achieved fixing. This type of adhesive will not, however, stand up well to either extreme heat or to moisture; the sort of conditions you'll meet outdoors; or in a kitchen, for example. A urea formaldehyde is the glue to use in this sort of situation. It isn't as convenient – it comes as a powder that you have to mix with water – but your joints will hold.

Choosing the right joint
There are no hard and fast rules about choosing the best joint for a particular job. It's really just a case of finding a joint that is neat enough for what you're making, and strong enough not to fall apart the first time it is used. And as far as strength is concerned, the various kinds of butt joint work equally well.

Marking timber
Butt joints are the simplest of all joints – there's no complicated chiselling or marking out to worry about – but if the joint is to be both strong and neat you do need to be able

to saw wood to length leaving the end perfectly square.

The first important thing here is the accuracy of your marking out. Examine the piece of wood you want to cut and choose a side and an edge that are particularly flat and smooth. They're called the face edge and face side.

Next, measure up and press the point of a sharp knife into the face side where you intend to make the cut. Slide a try-square up to the knife, making sure that its stock – the handle – is pressed firmly against the face edge. Then use the knife to score a line across the surface of the timber. Carry this line round all four sides of the wood, always making sure that the try-square's stock is held against either the face edge or the face side. If you wish, you can run over the knife line with a pencil to make it easier to see – it's best to sharpen the lead into a chisel shape.

Why not use a pencil for marking out in the first place? There are two reasons. The first is that a knife gives a thinner and therefore more accurate line than even the sharpest pencil. The second is that the knife will cut through the surface layer of the wood, helping the saw to leave a clean, sharp edge.

Ready Reference

MARKING AND CUTTING TOOLS

For butt joints:
measuring tape
sharp handyman's knife
try square
tenon saw

TIP: MARKING OUT

● use a try-square and sharp knife to mark cutting lines on all four faces
● press the stock of the try-square firmly against the wood, or the last line will not meet up with the first

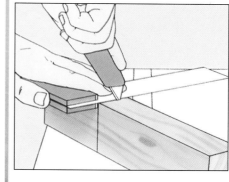

Sawing square

One of the most useful – and easiest to make – aids to sawing is a bench hook. It'll help you to grip the wood you want to cut, and to protect the surface on which you are working. You can make one up quite easily, by gluing and screwing together pieces of scrap timber (see *Ready Reference*).

You also need the ability to control the saw, and there are three tips that will help you here. Always point your index finger along the saw blade to stop it flapping from side to side as you work. And always stand in such a way that you are comfortable, well balanced, and can get your head directly above the saw so you can see what you are cutting. You should also turn slightly sideways on. This stops your elbow brushing against your body as you draw the saw back – a fault that is often the reason for sawing wavy lines.

Starting the cut

Position the piece of wood to be cut on the bench hook and hold it firmly against the block furthest from you. Start the cut by drawing the saw backwards two or three times over the far edge to create a notch, steadying the blade by 'cocking' the thumb of your left hand. Make sure that you position the saw so that the whole of this notch is on the waste side of the line. You can now begin to saw properly using your arm with sort of piston action, but keep your left (or right as the case may be) hand away from the saw.

As the cut deepens gradually reduce the angle of the saw until it is horizontal. At this point you can continue sawing through until you start cutting into the bench hook. Alternatively, you may find it easier to angle the saw towards you and make a sloping cut down the edge nearest to you. With that done, you can saw through the remaining waste holding the saw horizontally, using the two angled cuts to keep the saw on course.

Whichever method you choose, don't try to force the saw through the wood – if that seems necessary, then the saw is probably blunt. Save your muscle power for the forward stroke – but concentrate mainly on sawing accurately to your marked line.

Cleaning up cut ends

Once you have cut the wood to length, clean up the end with glasspaper. A good tip is to lay the abrasive flat on a table and work the end of the wood over it with a series of circular strokes, making sure that you keep the wood vertical so you don't sand the end out of square. If the piece of wood is too unmanageable, wrap the glasspaper round a square piece of scrap wood instead and sand the end of the wood by moving the block to and fro – it'll help in keeping the end square.

DOVETAIL NAILING

This is a simple way of strengthening any butt joint. All you do is grip the upright piece in a vice or the jaws of a portable work-bench, and glue the horizontal piece on top if it – supporting it with scrap wood to hold the joint square – and then drive in the nails dovetail fashion. If you were to drive the nails in square, there would be more risk that the joint would pull apart. Putting them in at an angle really does add strength.

The only difficulty is that the wood may split. To prevent this, use oval brads rather than round nails, making sure that their thickest part points along the grain. If that doesn't do the trick, try blunting the point of each nail by driving it into the side of an old hammer. This creates a burr of metal on the point which will cut through the wood fibres rather than parting them.

Once the nails are driven home, punch their heads below the surface using a nail punch, or a large blunt nail. Fill the resulting dents with wood stopping (better on wood than ordinary cellulose filler) and sand smooth.

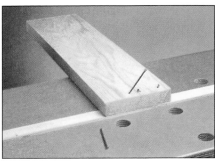
1 *Drive nails at angle: first leans to left; next to right, and so on.*

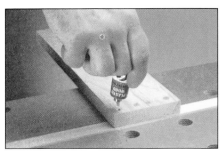
3 *Fill resulting dents with stopping compound to cover up nail heads.*

THE OVERLAP

This is the simplest of all and is one you can use on relatively thin timber. The example shown is for a T-joint, but the method is the same if you want to make an X-joint.

Bring the two pieces of wood together as they will be when joined, and use a pencil to mark the position of the topmost piece on the one underneath. To reinforce the joint, countersunk screws are best, so mark their positions on the top piece of wood, and drill clearance holes the same diameter as the screw's shank – the unthreaded part – right the way through. The screws should be arranged like the spots on a dice (two screws are shown here, but on a larger joint where more strength is needed five would be better) to help stop the joint twisting out of square. Enlarge the mouths of these holes with a countersink bit to accommodate the screw heads, and clean up any splinters where the drill breaks through the underside of the wood.

Bring the two pieces of wood together again using a piece of scrap wood to keep the top piece level. Then make pilot holes in the lower piece using either a bradawl or a small drill, boring through the clearance holes to make sure they are correctly positioned. Make sure the pilot holes are drilled absolutely vertically, or the screws could pull the joint out of shape. Finally, apply a thin coating of adhesive to both the surfaces to be joined (follow the adhesive manufacturer's instructions), position the pieces of wood accurately and, without moving them again, drive home the screws.

1 *Bring pieces squarely together. Mark position of each on the other.*

2 With nail punch or large blunt nail, hammer nail heads below surface.

4 When stopping is dry, sand flush with surface of surrounding timber.

CORRUGATED TIMBER CONNECTORS

Another simple way of holding a butt joint together is to use ordinary corrugated timber connectors. Simply glue the two pieces of wood together, and hammer the connectors in across the joint. Note that they are driven in dovetail fashion – the fixing is stronger that way.

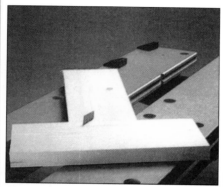

For strength, hammer in connectors diagonally rather than straight.

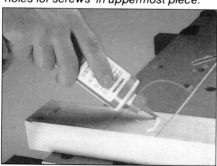

2 Drill and countersink (inset) clearance holes for screws in uppermost piece.

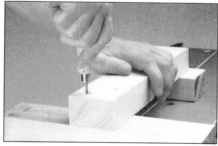

4 Apply woodworking adhesive to both pieces and press them together

3 Reassemble joint and bore pilot holes in bottom piece with bradawl.

5 Carefully drive in screws. If they're tight, remove and lubricate with soap.

Ready Reference

MAKING YOUR OWN BENCH HOOK

This a very useful sawing aid to help grip the wood when cutting. Hook one end over the edge of the workbench and hold the wood against the other end. Make it up from off-cuts and replace when it becomes worn.

You need:
● a piece of 12mm (½in) plywood measuring about 250 x 225mm (10 x 9in)
● two pieces of 50 x 25mm (2 x 1in) planed softwood, each about 175mm (7in) long. Glue and screw them together as shown in the sketch. Use the bench hook the other way up if you're left-handed.

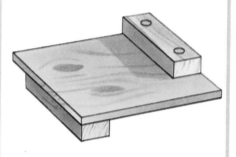

TIP: SAWING STRAIGHT

● hold wood firmly against bench hook and start cut on waste side of cutting line with two or three backward cuts
● decrease angle of the saw blade as cut progresses
● complete cut with saw horizontal, cutting into your bench hook slightly

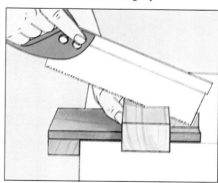

TIP: TO SMOOTH CUT END

● rub with a circular motion on glasspaper held flat on the workbench, so you don't round off the corners
● on large pieces of wood, wrap glasspaper round a block of wood and rub this across the cut end

HALVING AND MITRE JOINTS

Getting joints to fit snugly is one of the
major objectives in carpentry, and
nothing introduces the techniques
so well as the halving joint. As
for the perfect finish, that's
the role of the mitre.

There are many situations in woodwork
when you need a joint that's fast and
simple, but also neat and strong. And this is
where halving joints come into their own.
Despite their simplicity, they're very effective
joints because the two pieces of wood are
cut so they interlock together, either face to
face or edge to edge, making the joint as
strong as — if not stronger than — the timber
itself. They are used almost exclusively for
building frameworks, joining the rails (side
pieces) either at a corner or in a cross
absolutely flush. You end up with a frame
that's neat enough to be on show and sturdy
enough to need no reinforcement.

Mitre joints, though not strictly speaking
considered halving joints as there's no
interlocking, are halved to make up a perfect
90° angle. In this section, only the simple
mitre is dealt with — the more complicated
forms (eg, mitred secret dovetails) are
covered in another section.

Strength of joints

There are three things that affect the
strength of a halving joint — the size of the
timber, the quality of the timber, and any
reinforcement you add.

The size of timber is important because it
governs the amount of adhesive in the joint;
the greater the areas glued together, the
stronger the joint will be. Usually problems
only arise when you are trying to join thin
pieces of timber together — it's almost
impossible to get the joint to stay rigid.
Regarding timber quality, hardwoods rarely
present a problem, but with softwoods, splitting can occur which will seriously weaken
the joint. You should, therefore, reject timber
containing knots, cracks and other potential
weak spots.

In many cases, the correct adhesive is all
the reinforcement you need — use a good
quality PVA woodworking adhesive, or, if the
joint will be subjected to heat or moisture, a
urea formaldehyde woodworking adhesive.
If still greater strength is required — this is
more likely on corner halving joints than on
cross halvings — you should drive screws
through the overlaps, or, for a more natural
look, drill a hole right through and glue in a

length of dowel. Both the dowels and screws
are set like the spots on a dice to stop the
joint twisting.

Simple butt joints (see pages 195 -197)
must be reinforced in some way to have
strength, but with mitred butt joints this
would defeat the decorative aim. Because of
this, they are normally reserved for situations
where strength is not required — picture
frames and decorative edgings, such as
door architraves for example.

Marking corner halving joints

Having sawn the ends of the two pieces of
wood to be joined perfectly square (see
pages 195 -197) place one piece on top
of the other, and mark the width of the top
piece on the one below. Carry this mark right
round the timber using a knife and a try-
square, then repeat the process, this time
with the bottom piece of wood on top.

Next divide the thickness of the timber in
two. You need a single-tooth marking gauge
for this: it consists of a wooden shaft with a
sharp metal pin called a spur near one end,
and a block of wood (the stock) which can
be moved along the shaft and be fixed at any
point with the aid of a thumbscrew.

Position the stock so that the distance
between it and the spur is roughly half the
timber's thickness, and place it against one
edge of the wood. Use the spur to dent the
surface of the timber, then repeat with the
stock against the other edge. If the dents co-

incide, the gauge is set correctly. If they
don't, reset the gauge. Don't try to make
small adjustments by undoing the
thumbscrew and moving the stock — you'll
go on for ever trying to make it accurate.
Instead, with the screw reasonably tight, tap
one end of the shaft sharply on a hard surface. Depending which end you tap and how
hard you tap it, the setting will increase or
decrease by the merest fraction.

With the setting right, wedge one end of
the timber into the angle of a bench hook,
place the stock of the gauge firmly against
the timber's edge and holding it there, score
the wood from the width line to the end. You'll
find this easier if, rather than digging the
spur right into the wood, you merely drag it
across the surface. Score identical lines on
the other side and the end.

Use a pencil to shade the areas on each
piece of wood that will form the waste (the
top of one, the bottom of the other), then grip
the first piece upright in a vice. The lower
down you can get it the better. If you can't
get it low, back it with a piece of scrap wood
to reduce vibration. Using a tenon saw, carefully saw down until you reach the width line
— the first one you marked. The golden rule
of sawing any kind of joint is to saw on the
waste side of the marked line (it's *always*
better to saw or chisel off too little rather than
too much since you can always take off a
little more but you can never put it back).
And remember that the closer the fit, the

MAKING A CORNER HALVING JOINT

1 *First mark the width of each piece of wood on the other. Then, using a knife and square, continue these width lines round all four sides of each piece.*

2 *To mark the thickness line, set a marking gauge to half the thickness of the wood and, holding the stock firmly against one edge, scribe the line.*

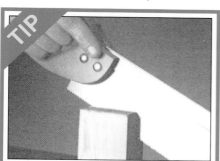

TIP

3 *It's easier to start sawing at an angle, then gradually bring the saw to the horizontal. Keep the wood gripped firmly in the vice until you're finished.*

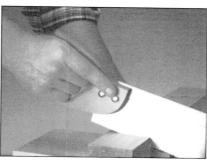

4 *Transfer the wood to a bench hook and cut down along the width line to remove the waste wood. Be sure to cut on the waste side of the guide line.*

5 *Smooth both parts to be joined with glasspaper and apply adhesive. Clamp together with a G-cramp until dry, protecting the wood with scrap timber.*

6 *When the adhesive has set, drill holes for reinforcing wood screws or dowels. If using screws, countersink the hole to take the screw head.*

stronger the joint will end up. Basically, it should fit like a hand in a glove.

Remove the wood from the vice, put it on a bench hook and cut down along the width line to release the waste wood. Again make sure you cut on the waste side of the line and be prepared to make final adjustments with a chisel. Treat the second piece of wood in exactly the same way, then bring the two together and check the fit.

You can use either a chisel or a piece of glasspaper to take off any unevenness in the timber, although it'll be quicker to use a chisel to clear out the edges so that the corners are absolutely square. When the pieces finally fit neatly, spread adhesive on both faces of the joint and hold them in place with a G-cramp (protecting the wood's surface with scrap timber) until the glue has set. Remove the cramp, and add any re-

Ready Reference

WHERE TO USE HALVING JOINTS

Halving joints are usually used for making frameworks. Here you can see which joint to use where, and how each one is assembled.

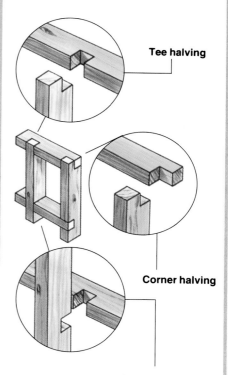

Tee halving

Corner halving

Cross halving

TOOLS FOR HALVING JOINTS

For measuring and marking: use a *handyman's knife* rather than a pencil for marking; use a *marking gauge* on each face of the joint – it'll be more accurate than using a tape measure; a *try-square* ensures accurate squaring off.
For cutting: use a *tenon saw* and a broad-blade *chisel* (25mm/1in) for cutting out cross halvings.

TIP: LABELLING JOINT PARTS

Avoid mixing up the pairs of joints by labelling the two parts with a letter and a number as soon as you cut them.

MAKING A CROSS HALVING JOINT

1 *First mark out the waste area to be removed, then cut down the width lines with a tenon saw.*

2 *Hold the timber in a vice or against a bench hook and remove the waste by chiselling at a slight upward angle.*

3 *Do the same on the other side until there's a 'pyramid' of waste in the middle. Gradually flatten this.*

4 *When nearing the thickness line, hold the cutting edge at an angle to the wood grain. Trim*

The next step is to turn the wood round and slope the other edge to leave a sort of pyramid of waste. With that done, pushing the chisel through the wood rather than hitting it, gradually flatten off the pyramid until you have brought it level with the half-way lines. You'll get a neater finish here if, in the final stages, you work with the chisel's blade flat but at an angle to the grain of the wood. Finally, again pushing the chisel, remove any ragged fibres lodged in the angles of the housing.

Once you've sawn and chiselled out the housing in the second piece of wood, the next step is to try fitting the two together. Don't try forcing them if they don't quite fit — you're in danger of splitting the wood. Instead, carefully chisel off a fraction more wood, bit by bit, until you can fit the pieces together without undue force. If, on the other hand, you've cut the housing too wide so the fit is very loose, you'll have to add some re-inforcement like screws or dowels, and fill in the gaps with a wood filler, stopping or a mixture of fine sawdust and PVA adhesive. It's not worth trying to add a wedge unless the gap is very wide (over 6mm/¼in) because the result can be very messy.

Making a mitre joint

With wood that's square or rectangular in section, the first job is to make sure that both pieces are absolutely squarely cut. Use the try-square to check this — if they're not, it's better to cut another piece of wood than attempt to make adjustments. Next, place one piece on top of the other to form a right angle. Mark an internal and external corner on both, then take them apart and carry the marks across the edge with a knife and try square. Join up the marks on each piece of wood — this will give sawing lines at 45°. Mark the waste side of each with a pencil.

Wood that is raised on one side (eg, mouldings for picture frames) cannot be marked in the same way as the pieces won't sit flat on each other. The easiest way is to mark the

inforcing screws or dowels that may be needed, drilling pilot holes first.

Making cross halving joints

The difference between cross halving joints and corner halving joints is that you cannot remove the waste using only a saw. You have to make a 'housing' and for this you need a chisel (see pages 260-209 for more details of halving joints).

Saw down the width lines to the halfway mark and make additional saw cuts in between to break up the waste — these can

be the same width as the chisel blade to make chipping out easier. Grip the work in a vice, or on a bench hook, and now use the chisel to remove the waste. This is done in four stages. Guiding the chisel blade bevel uppermost with one hand and striking the handle with the palm of your other hand — for this job your hand is better than a mallet — reduce the edge of the timber nearest to you to a shallow slope ending a fraction above the halfway line. Don't try to remove all the wood in one go or it will split. Remove just a sliver at a time.

MAKING MITRES

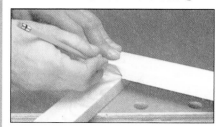

1 *With square or rectangular wood, cut ends absolutely square and stack to form a right angle. Then mark the inner and outer corners on both pieces.*

2 *Carry lines down each edge with knife and try square, and score a line between corner marks to create an angle of 45°. Shade waste in pencil.*

3 *Press the wood against the bench hook and keep the saw at a shallow angle. Cut the diagonal, using the line on the edge to keep the saw vertical.*

THE SIMPLE MITRE

1 *The ends of two battens are cut to 45° and, when fixed together, make a 90° angle in this simplest of mitre joints, ideal for picture framing.*

2 *With thick timber frames, use corrugated steel fasteners driven into the back of mitre joints, where they will not be seen from the front.*

3 *Another method of strengthening a fairly thick mitre joint from behind is to pin triangles of plywood across the corner, out of sight.*

4 *Ready-made angle brackets with pre-drilled, countersunk screw holes make a quick, rigid and hidden fixing for two mitred battens in a frame.*

point of the mitre (the corner point) and then to use a simple *mitre block* to cut the angle. A mitre block not only helps you support the piece of wood (like a bench hook) but also has saw cuts at 45° in the back face to guide the saw. Then you only have to line up the mitre point on the wood with the saw now set at the correct angle. You can make a mitre block yourself — see *Ready Reference*.

Mitre aids

There are other devices available to help you cut mitres accurately. A proprietary *jointing jig*, for example, guides the saw either at right angles or at 45°; a *mitre box* is like a mitre block but has an extra side so that the whole length of the saw is kept in line.

Without these devices, getting the angles right isn't easy — but if necessary you can use a bench hook, driving in two nails so the wood is held against the block and the line of cutting is free of the bench hook. This is not as easy as using one of the other methods. Mark the wood so you know the sawing line, then place it in the mitre block, box or jig, to line up with the appropriate groove to guide the saw. If the wood you are cutting is very thin, put some blocks of scrap wood under the device to bring it up to a reasonable height. Insert a tenon saw into the guide slot and, holding it level, saw away.

There are only two things that can go wrong. If the block is old, the 'guide' cut may have widened, resulting in an inaccurate cut. A larger tenon saw may help, but really the only answer is to hold the saw as steady as possible. The other common error when cutting mouldings and the like is to cut two mitres the same — that is two right-handed or left-handed angles, instead of one of each. This can be avoided by always marking the waste on the wood, and checking that the saw is in the correct guide slot before you begin.

Clean up the cut ends with glasspaper, taking care not to alter the angle, and glue and cramp the joint together. For frames, special mitre cramps are available, but you again make up your own. From scrap wood, cut four L-shaped blocks, and drill a hole at an angle through the point of each L. Feed a single piece of string through the holes of all four blocks, position the blocks at the corners of the frame and tie the string into a continuous loop. To tighten up, twist the string around a stick, and keep twisting the stick to draw the blocks together. You can then wedge the stick against the frame to stop it untwisting until the adhesive has set.

There are three ways to strengthen mitres — with timber connectors, plywood triangles or metal angle repair irons. For frames they should be fitted from behind, either by glueing, or glueing and pinning (see the photographs above).

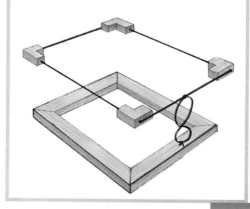

DOWEL JOINTS

Called wood pins or pegs, dowels are lengths of hardwood with an important role to play in simple carpentry. They can be a decorative part of joints, or be there for strength alone. Few tools are needed but the secret of success lies in using them accurately.

There are two basic ways in which you can use dowels in woodworking joints. You can drive a dowel through such joints as a half lap instead of using a nail or screw, or you can use them to make joints in their own right by drilling holes in one piece of wood, glueing in dowels, and then slotting these into corresponding holes in the second piece.

The dowel joint proper is used mostly in furniture making where it provides a neat joint of great strength without intricate cutting and without the need for unsightly reinforcement. Dowels can also be used to repair furniture.

In any joint, the size of the dowel is very important. Use a small one in a big joint and it won't have sufficient strength; use one that's too large and the holes you drill to accommodate it will weaken the wood. Ideally you should choose dowels which are no more than one third the thickness of the timber into which they will be fixed.

The thickness of the wood must be considered, too, for the dowels must have sufficient space between them and at each side otherwise when they're hit home or pushed into their corresponding holes the wood will split. So follow the carpenter's 'one third rule' and mark the width as well as the thickness into three (ie, a 9mm/³⁄₈in dowel will need at least the same amount on both sides of it). And don't forget that planed wood can be up to 5mm less all round than the dimensions you ordered, and three into this size might not give you enough room for a successful joint.

Types of joints

There are different types of dowel joint. The simplest and easiest to make is the *through* dowel joint in which the dowel peg passes right through one piece of timber and into the other, sometimes passing through this as well if it's thin enough. Because in either case the ends of the dowels show, they are often used as a decorative feature of the article you're making.

If you don't want the ends of the dowels to be seen, you must make a *stopped* joint. In

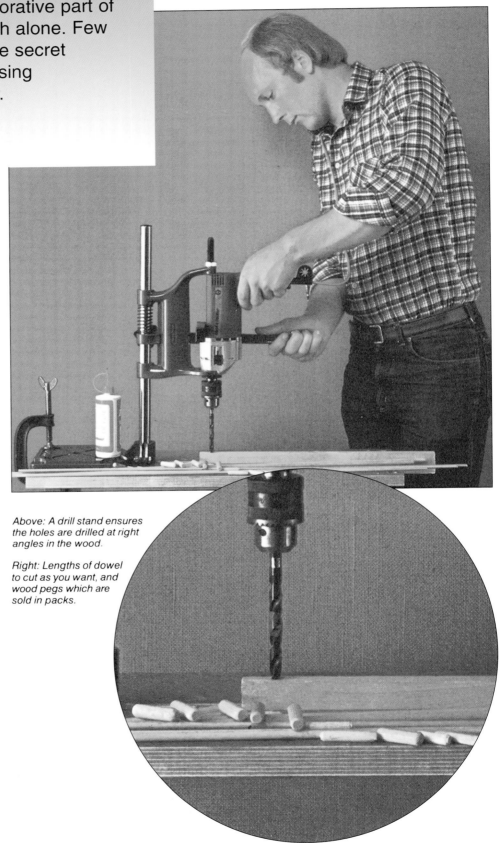

Above: A drill stand ensures the holes are drilled at right angles in the wood.

Right: Lengths of dowel to cut as you want, and wood pegs which are sold in packs.

JOINTS MADE WITH DOWELS

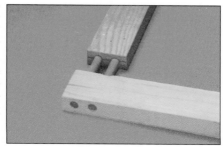

The through dowel joint ready for assembly. The dowels are firmly embedded in one piece and will pass right through the other.

When assembled the through joint shows up the dowels. Cut them a little longer so after cramping they can be planed flush with the wood.

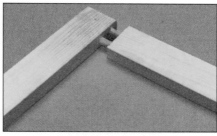

The stopped joint has dowels in one piece which will go into the other far enough to ensure rigidity but won't be seen on the other side.

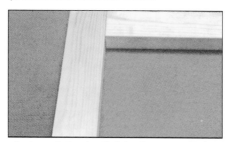

A close fit for the finished stopped joint. When drilling the holes they should be slightly deeper than the dowel to hold any excess adhesive.

Mitred dowel joints can be tricky to make as you can't use the 'pin' method (see next page) for marking up because of the 45° angle.

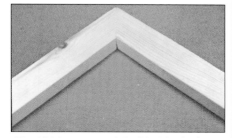

The hidden strength in this joint is the two different lengths of dowel. Very effective for frames where you don't want reinforcement to be seen.

A halving or half lap joint made at a corner can either be glued and screwed or, if it will be on show, made secure with dowels which fit into holes placed like spots on a dice.

The completed dowelled halving joint gives one overall look of wood. The same effect can be achieved by topping countersunk screws with dowel pellets cut from an offcut of the wood.

Ready Reference

BUYING DOWELS

Dowel lengths from timber merchants are sold in these diameters:
- 6mm (¼in)
- 9mm (⅜in)
- 12mm (½in)

Larger diameters – 16mm (⅝in) and 19mm (¾in) – can be softwood rather than hardwood.

TIPS TO SAVE TIME

- Buying grooved dowel saves you having to groove it yourself.
- **Pre-packed dowels** are bought in packs containing short lengths of diameters such as 4mm, 8mm and 10mm. They are fluted (finely grooved) and the ends are chamfered.
- **Dowel pellets** finish woodwork where screws have been countersunk. They should fit the hole exactly but be fractionally deeper so they can be planed back when the adhesive has set. Buy pre-packed, or cut your own from offcuts using a special plug attachment for an electric drill.

TOOLS

- **try-square and marking gauge** are essential for accurate marking up
- **electric drill** held in a drill stand for perfectly plumb holes
- **mallet** for tapping in the dowels
- **block or ordinary plane** for finishing a through joint
- **cramp** to hold the joint until the adhesive has set

CHAMFER DOWEL ENDS

If cutting your own dowels rub the cut ends with medium-grade glasspaper to give a gentle chamfer (it makes the dowel go in more easily).

Apply woodworking adhesive to the meeting faces of the wood as well as brushing or squirting it into the holes.

MARKING UP

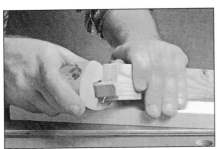

1 With wood that's rectangular or square in section, use a marking gauge to make the central line on the edge where the dowels will go.

3 Lightly tap small panel pins into the wood at the two centre points. Snip off their heads leaving about 3mm (1/8in) protruding.

2 Divide this central line into three, then draw two lines at right angles.

4 Holding the second piece of timber firmly against a bench hook or edge of the try-square, press the pins in to mark the drill positions (inset).

this the peg doesn't go right through either piece of timber. This is perhaps the most common dowel joint.

Joint shapes

Dowels can be used to make joints of various types, including L-joints, T-joints and X-joints between rails or boards, and three-way joints between rails and posts, as in furniture-making. They can also be used to reinforce edge-to-edge joints between boards, for example when making a drawer.

Cutting dowels

Cut dowels to length with a fine-toothed tenon saw, holding the dowels in a bench hook or a vice. For through joints, cut one dowel slightly longer than the combined thicknesses of the timbers, so that the ends can be trimmed flush after the joint is assembled. For stopped joints, cut the dowels slightly shorter than the combined depths of the holes into which they fit, and lightly chamfer the ends using glasspaper, a chisel or a proprietary dowel sharpener (which works just like a pencil sharpener).

Dowels need a shallow groove cut in their sides to allow excess adhesive to squeeze out as the joints are assembled. With much

practice you can do this with a chisel or tenon saw (having cramped it lengthways in a workbench), but it is probably easier to buy grooved dowel in the first place – in lengths you cut to size yourself, or for small jobs as pre-packed pegs. If buying pegs make sure you choose ones that correspond with the bit size for your drill.

Marking hole positions

First, use a try-square to check that the meeting faces or ends of the timber to be joined are cut perfectly square and are of the same thickness. You can then mark the positions for the dowel holes. Set a marking gauge to half the width of the timber, and mark a line down the middle of the end of one length of timber. Determine exactly where on this line the centre of the holes will be – the ideal is that they should be from 25mm (1in) to 50mm (2in) apart and never nearer than 19mm (3/4in) from the edges. Using a try-square, draw lines across the gauge line to mark the exact centres of the holes.

To mark matching holes in corresponding positions on the second piece of timber use the following method to ensure accuracy. Drive small panel pins into the first piece at the positions you've marked for the holes.

Leave the pins slightly proud of the surface and snip off their heads with pliers. Bring the two pieces of wood together in the correct joint position, and the heads of the pins will mark where the holes are to be bored in the second piece of timber. Remove the pins with pincers before drilling.

Where you are joining two horizontal rails to an upright at a corner, you should stagger the holes, otherwise the dowels will clash inside the upright.

Cutting holes

Holes for the dowels can be made either with a hand drill or an electric drill. In each case, obviously, the bit used must match the diameter of the dowel. The main difficulty is that you must ensure the bit is truly at right angles to the timber you are drilling, or a dowel that protrudes from one hole will not fit snugly into the hole in the matching timber.

You can use an electric drill held in a drill stand to guarantee that the bit is truly at right angles to the timber. Or where the timber is too large for this you can use a dowelling jig to ensure accuracy. Where you are cutting a through dowel joint, you can avoid this problem by cramping both pieces of wood together in a vice and boring through both.

For stopped joints, the hole you bore should be slightly deeper than the depth to which the dowel penetrates, to leave a small reservoir for any excess glue that is not squeezed out along the groove. A depth gauge ensures this. Various types for both hand and electric drills are available but you can improvise by making your own. Either stick a bit of tape on the bit's shank, carefully positioned so that the distance between its lower edge and the end of the drill exactly equals the depth of the hole required. Or you can take a length of timber – 25mm (1in) or 38mm (1½in) square according to the diameter of the dowel – and bore a hole right through its length. Cut this timber to length so that when it is slipped onto the bit's shank, the part of the bit left protruding will cut a hole of the right depth. In both cases you should take your measurement to the cutting end of the drill only – not to any threaded or shaped lead-in point.

For a stopped dowel joint, drill holes so the dowels will penetrate each piece of timber by between one-half and two-thirds of the timber's thickness.

Fixing and finishing dowels

Always check first that the joint is a good fit and is accurately square before applying PVA adhesive. You can then squirt adhesive into the holes, but since you risk applying too much this way, it is better to brush the

DRILLING HOLES

1 To ensure that holes will be in exactly opposite positions on a through joint, drill both pieces of wood at the same time.

2 The depths you have to go to for a dowel joint can be marked on the bit with a piece of tape, allowing a little extra at both ends for glue.

3 Another way of making sure you don't go too deep is by making a depth gauge from a scrap of timber. Or you can buy a proprietary gauge.

4 A dowelling jig has holes for different sized bits. When you cramp it over the wood use spare timber to prevent the screw marking the wood.

adhesive onto the dowel before tapping it into place with a mallet — you can use a hammer but you should protect the dowel with a block of wood. You should also apply adhesive to the meeting faces of the timber.

The glued joints should be cramped until the adhesive has set.

With through joints and halving joints, you now saw off the bulk of the protruding dowel

and use a block plane to trim the end flush. You can use an ordinary plane for this, but it must be set for a very fine cut. Smooth off any remaining roughness with glasspaper.

If using dowel pellets, hit them into place over the countersunk screws (with the ones you've cut yourself make sure the grain follows that of the wood). Plane off excess after the adhesive has dried.

MAKING THE JOINT

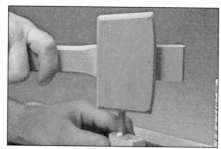

1 First check that the dowel fits snugly, but not too tightly. Then apply adhesive and gently tap it into place with a mallet.

2 After cramping to allow the adhesive to set, finish off a through joint by planing away the excess along the side of the wood.

Ready Reference

RULES FOR DRILLING HOLES
● make them the same diameter as the dowels
● they should be a little deeper than the dowel's length
● slightly countersink these where the pieces of wood meet

TIP: DOWELLING JIG
With a drill use a dowelling jig so the holes will be straight and square.

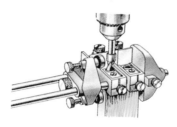

WHAT CAN GO WRONG?
The most common problems are:
● the dowels being too tight. Forcing the joint together causes the wood to split – so always check the fit first
● the joint being forced out of alignment because the holes were drilled out of line with one another – always check the alignment before finally applying the adhesive

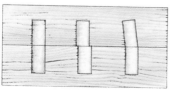

MITRED DOWEL JOINTS
● use a mitre box for accuracy
● place mitred pieces together in a cramp and mark them at the same time
● the dowel at the outer corner should be shorter than the one at the inner corner

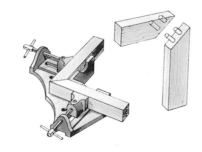

HOUSING JOINTS

If you're putting together a bookcase or installing shelves, or any other sort of furniture, then housing joints are the ones to use for attaching the shelves to the uprights. Here's how to make them.

Housing joints are very useful in constructing drawers, door frames and partition walls, among other things: but they're indispensable for fixing shelves neatly into uprights. The joint gets its name because the end of the shelf fits into a square-bottomed channel or 'housing' across the upright. A basic housing joint is as simple as that, and very easy to cut and assemble. What's more, it's ideal for supporting the weight of a shelf and its contents – it resists twisting, and it looks much more professional than the metal brackets or other fittings which can do the same job.

Such fittings are readily available and often easy to use, but if your design is modern, they'll tend to spoil its clean lines; and if it's traditional, they'll naturally be inappropriate. They will never give the unobtrusive and craftsmanlike finish which you can obtain from carefully designed and made housing joints.

Types of housing joint
There are a few variations, and each has its own purpose. A 'stopped' housing joint is completely invisible; you can't see the connection between shelf and upright at all, because (unlike the basic 'through' housing joint) its housing stops about 20mm (¾in) short of the front of the upright. You can also cut out a step in the front of the shelf to allow it to fit flush with the upright just as in a through housing joint, and so get the best of both worlds.

A 'barefaced' housing joint is a little more complicated. You still slot the shelf into the upright – but this time you also cut away a step or 'rebate' across the end of the shelf to form a sort of tongue (with one 'bare face'). So the housing into which it fits has to be correspondingly narrower than the shelf thickness. This type of joint is used at corners, where you can't cut an ordinary housing; and its stepped shape helps to keep the structure rigid. It can also be used with the rebate in the upright where you want unbroken woodgrain across the top surface of the horizontal.

Strongest of all is the dovetail housing joint. For this one, the housing has sloping (undercut) sides, and the end of the shelf is shaped to fit – which means it can't be pulled out sideways. This is an attraction where you expect furniture to come in for rough treatment, (eg, being dragged across the floor). However, it's tricky to cut without power-tool assistance, and in practice the do-it-yourselfer will seldom find it really necessary.

It's worth saying here that even the best-made housing joint is only as strong as the shelf. If you're planning shelf storage, you have to think about what the shelf is made of, its thickness, its length and how much weight you want it to carry. A thin shelf bends easily, and it's unwise to try to span a gap of more than 1,200mm (4ft), at the very most, without some support in the middle. Even then, a full load of books will cause sagging.

Making a housing joint
Even with hand tools, housing joints are among the easiest to cut. For a basic through housing joint, you don't need to touch the shelf at all. You just mark out the position of the housing in the upright, cut down the housing sides with a tenon saw, and pare away the waste with a chisel and wooden mallet (see pages 198-201 for details). The only difficulty, as in all carpentry, is to make sure that your marking, sawing and chiselling are always careful and accurate.

A stopped housing takes a little longer to cut, but only because you need to hollow out its stopped end first, to make sawing easier. You may also need to remove a small notch or 'shoulder' from the shelf, which is easily done with a tenon saw and perhaps a chisel too.

For a barefaced housing joint, the housing is cut in the same way as a basic housing. Cutting the rebate in the shelf is another job for tenon saw and chisel.

Using power tools
A power router is an integral tool with a chuck that accepts a wide range of special bits for cutting grooves and mouldings quickly and accurately. It saves a lot of time when making housing joints, and eliminates both sawing and chiselling. Or you can use a circular saw, setting it for a very shallow cut and running it across the upright where you want the housing to be – first clamping on a batten to act as a guide. Because the saw-

BASIC HOUSING JOINT

1 Use your knife and try-square to square a mark across the inner face of the upright where the top of the shelf is to go.

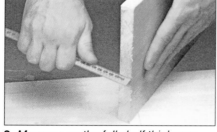

2 Measure up the full shelf thickness with a carpenter's rule or a flexible tape measure. As always, try for absolute accuracy.

3 Mark this distance on the upright, working down from the first line to give the housing width; square the mark across in pencil only.

4 Place the shelf between the two lines to check them. If necessary, re-draw the second. When that's right, go over it with knife and try-square.

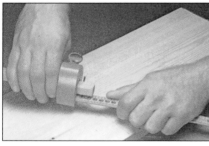

5 Use a rule to set your marking gauge to 1/3 the thickness of the upright, which is the usual depth of a housing for a strong and rigid joint.

6 With the gauge, mark the housing depth on the upright's edges. Then use a knife to square the marks for the housing sides to depth across the edges.

7 When cutting the sides to depth, cramp on a batten to prevent the saw from wandering sideways.

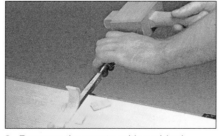

8 Remove the waste with a chisel, working from both ends on long housings. Pare along the sides if necessary to clean them up.

Ready Reference

WHICH HOUSING GOES WHERE

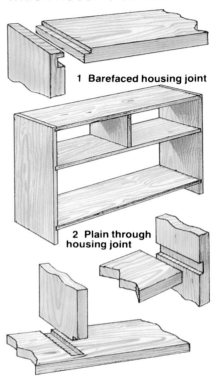

1 Barefaced housing joint

2 Plain through housing joint

3 Stopped housing joint with shoulder

THE TOOLS YOU'LL NEED

A tenon saw: for cutting the sides of housings, rebates and shoulders.
A bevel-edged chisel: the same width as the housing, plus a wooden mallet.
A hand router: is useful for smoothing the bottom of the housing.
Marking gauge, knife, pencil and try-square: for accurate setting-out.

POWER TOOL OPTIONS

A power router: ideal for cutting all types of housing quickly and easily.

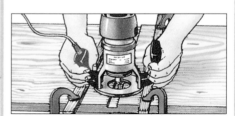

A circular saw will cut an ordinary housing very well – but you'll need to make several passes with it across the timber to cut the housing.

STOPPED HOUSING WITH SHOULDER

1 *After marking out the housing on the upright (except on the front edge), mark where it stops, about 19-25mm (³/₄-1in) inside the front edge.*

2 *With the marking gauge still at the same setting, mark the shoulder depth across the shelf end and a little way down each of its faces.*

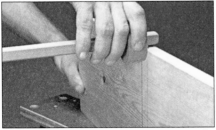

3 *Set the gauge to ¹/₃ the thickness of the upright, and mark the housing depth on its back edge only. Bring the side marks down to meet it.*

4 *Use the same setting to mark the shoulder width on the front edge and both faces of the shelf, meeting the marks you've made for the depth.*

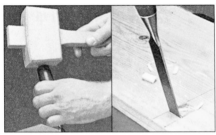

5 *Roughly chisel out the first 25mm (1in) or so of the stopped end of the housing – across the grain and up to the sides, then back towards the end.*

6 *Cut the sides of the housing with a tenon saw. You'll need to use short careful strokes so as not to bang against its inner end.*

7 *Clear out the housing with a mallet and chisel, inching forwards at an angle if the chisel won't reach all the way in when held flat.*

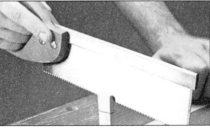

8 *Saw down into the front edge of the shelf until you reach the marked depth of the shoulder, being careful not to overshoot.*

9 *Chisel into the endgrain to remove the waste and complete the shoulder; or you can use a saw – but again, don't cut too deep.*

blade is narrower than the housing you're cutting out, you'll need to make several parallel, overlapping cuts.

Putting it together

When you assemble the joint before glueing, to see if it fits, you may think that it's too tight and you need to pare away wood from the housing or the shelf.

But be sure not to overdo this – and be careful where you remove it from. A shaving off the wrong place can allow the end of the shelf to rise or fall so that it's no longer level.

If, on the other hand, the joint turns out to be very loose, you'll need thin slivers of wood or veneer to pack it out.

For maximum tightness, strength and squareness, a housing joint should really be glued, then cramped together while the adhesive sets. Where a shelf or shelves fit between a pair of uprights, as usually happens, your best plan is to glue and cramp the whole structure up at once, so as to get it all square in one go. Use sash cramps (long bars of steel with two adjustable jaws) and simply place the structure between them, with the shelf running along their length, and blocks of scrap wood positioned on the outside of the uprights to protect them from the pressure of the jaws. You'll probably have to borrow or hire the sash-cramps. When using them, you need to

check the structure constantly for squareness, as cramping, unless done correctly, can cause distortion.

You can always reinforce a housing joint by nailing through the outside of the upright and into the endgrain of the shelf, concealing the heads by punching them in and plugging the holes with wood filler.

On the whole, screws are best avoided, since they grip badly in endgrain; but for a chipboard shelf you can use special chipboard screws – or ordinary wood screws each driven into a special plastic plug, or 'bush', which is pressed into a pre-drilled hole in the end of the shelf. You can disguise screwheads with plastic covers.

BAREFACED HOUSING JOINT

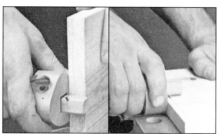

1 *At 1/3 the shelf thickness, mark the rebate depth along its end and across its edges; likewise mark across the upright's edges and inner face.*

2 *At 1/3 the upright thickness (very likely the same as the shelf thickness), mark your rebate width across the top face and both edges of the shelf.*

3 *Saw out the rebate depth across the shelf with a tenon saw, using careful strokes to keep it the right side of the line.*

4 *Chisel out the rebate width along the endgrain. You'll get a more accurate result if you do it in several goes rather than all at once.*

5 *Measure the full shelf thickness and set your marking gauge to that measurement by holding it against the rule.*

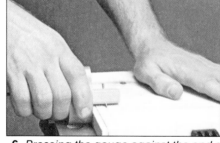

6 *Pressing the gauge against the end of the upright, mark across its face and edges where the bottom of the shelf will be positioned.*

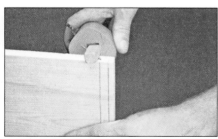

7 *Mark the depth of the housing on the back edge of the upright, only 1/3 of the way across: any further and you'll weaken the joint.*

8 *Cut the housing just like the basic one, taking care not to break off the end. After glueing, nail through into the tongue for extra rigidity.*

Ready Reference

TIPS FOR BETTER HOUSINGS
- a cramped-on batten is useful as a saw guide
- a third saw-cut down the centre of a wide housing will help the removal of waste

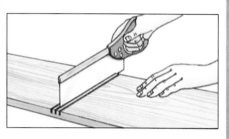

- for short housings in narrow wood, set the piece on edge and chisel vertically for greater accuracy

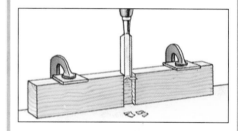

- use a rule or try-square to check that the housing has a level bottom

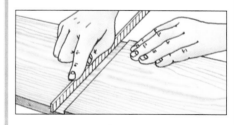

- for pairs of uprights, use the housings in the first to mark out those in the second; this will ensure a level shelf

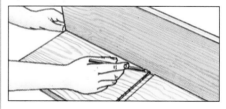

- a chipboard shelf can be secured with chipboard screws driven into special plastic plugs.

ADVANCED WOODWORKING TECHNIQUES

Once your confidence has grown, you can begin to extend your repertoire by acquiring some of the more advanced woodworking skills.

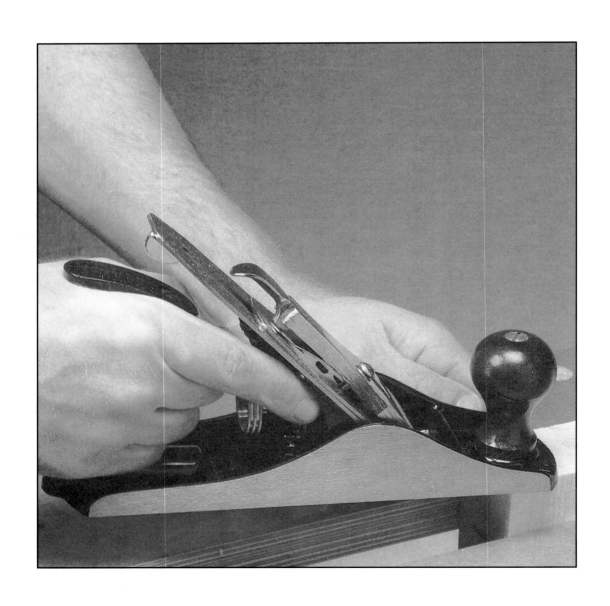

MORTISE AND TENON JOINTS

Mortise and tenon joints are indispensable if you're making furniture that's both strong and good-looking, and are particularly useful for making the most popular pieces of furniture - tables and chairs.

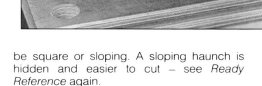

Take a piece of wood, shape the end to form a 'tongue', then fit the tongue into a matching slot in the side of another piece, and you've made a mortise-and-tenon joint.

The tenon is the tongue and the mortise is the slot, and the joint has proved its usefulness over centuries in all kinds of wooden frameworks because of its strength and resistance to movement. It's the best joint for fixing horizontal pieces of wood – 'rails' – into uprights such as table and chair legs.

Once you've got the knack of cutting it cleanly, you've mastered a joint which will stand you in very good stead. Whenever you're joining two lengths of wood in a T or L shape, and you want something stronger and more elegant than a halving joint, go for a mortise and tenon joint. The only time it won't work is on thin, flat pieces – boards, planks and panels: use housing joints instead.

There are numerous types of mortise-and-tenon joint at your disposal. Think carefully about the job the joint has to do before deciding which to use.

Choosing the right joint
A *through tenon* passes right through the mortise piece (which makes it easier to cut the mortise). Because you can see its endgrain, it's used in rougher work or as a decorative feature. It can also be wedged from the outside for strength and/or visual effect.

A *stub tenon* is one which doesn't pass right through, but fits into a 'blind' mortise – a hole with a bottom. The most familiar kind, especially in furniture, has shoulders all round which conceal the joint.

A *barefaced tenon* has the tenon cut with only one side shoulder instead of two – useful if the tenon piece is already very thin; or the tenon may be reduced in width by having edge shoulders cut in it – see *Ready Reference*.

A *haunched tenon* is a compromise often used at the corner of a frame to keep it from twisting. The haunch – an extra step between the tenon and the piece it projects from – can

be square or sloping. A sloping haunch is hidden and easier to cut – see *Ready Reference* again.

A *double tenon* is just a pair of tenons cut on one piece of wood – used if the piece is very wide and you don't want to cut a single enormous mortise to take one wide tenon.

An *offset tenon* is simply one which isn't in the centre of the tenon piece.

Making the joint
Let's assume you're making a basic stub tenon joint. It doesn't really matter whether you start by making your mortise or your tenon; the important thing is to get them to fit together. However, cutting the tenon first means you can mark off the mortise from it, possibly getting a better fit. This is easier than the other way round. Either way, play safe by making the tenon a little too large (or the mortise a little too small), rather than the reverse. You can always cut off a bit more.

Marking and cutting the tenon
Begin by scoring round the tenon piece with a knife and try-square to mark the length of the tenon, using the width of the mortise piece as a guide. A through tenon should be a little bit over-long to allow for planing it flush to give a neat finish; a stub tenon should go about halfway through, and be about 3mm (⅛in) shorter than the mortise to leave room for any excess adhesive.

A mortise gauge is very useful for the next stage. Choose a mortise chisel which has a blade about one third the thickness of the tenon piece (under rather than over, though you can use a wider one if the tenon piece is

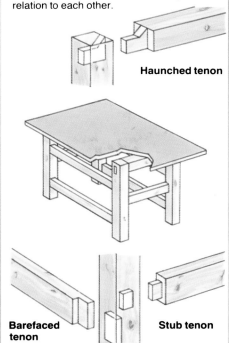

MARKING THE TENON

1 *Lay the mortise piece on the tenon piece and mark where the tenon starts. Leave a through tenon over-long, as shown, for later trimming.*

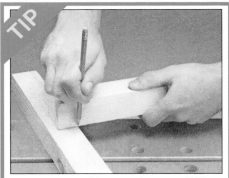

2 *If you're making a stub tenon, it'll be easier to mark the tenon length if you lay the tenon piece on top of the mortise.*

3 *Square the mark round all four sides of the tenon piece by scoring across them with your marking knife against a try-square.*

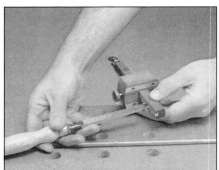

4 *Set your mortise gauge to the exact blade width of your mortise chisel, or to the diameter of your drill auger bit if you have one available.*

5 *Use the gauge to score out the tenon width down the sides and across the end of the piece, stopping at the length marks you have already made.*

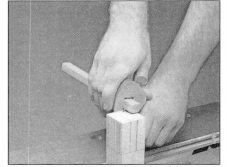

6 *If you are cutting edge shoulders as well, use an ordinary marking gauge to score lines the other way for each of the shoulders in turn.*

much thinner than the mortise piece), and set the gauge's twin spurs that distance apart. Then set the stock so as to place the resulting 'tramlines' in the centre of the timber thickness – unless you're deliberately off-setting the tenon – and try it from both sides, adjusting the position of the stock till the two sets of tramlines coincide.

Now you can score the edges and end of the tenon piece to mark where the tenon will be cut. If you don't have a mortise gauge, use an ordinary single-spur marking gauge and mark the tramlines separately.

For a straight tenon, that's all the marking-up you need. If you're cutting shoulders in the width as well, set a marking gauge to one sixth the width of the tenon piece and mark down both faces and across the tramlines on the end.

If you're including a haunch, use the gauge to mark its width across the end and down the faces; then mark its depth with a knife and try-square. For maximum strength, the haunch should be not more than one third the tenon's width, and its depth not

more than one quarter the length (or 12mm/½in long, whichever is smaller). We will be dealing with these joints in more detail in another section.

To cut a tenon you need, not surprisingly, a tenon saw. All you have to do is grip the piece upright in a vice and saw down each side of the tenon; then lay the wood flat and saw off the shoulders. The vital thing is always to keep your saw-cuts on the waste side of the lines.

Marking and cutting the mortise
At this stage, you can lay the tenon on the mortise piece and mark the mortise length on it. Then score its width with the gauge.

To cut the mortise, cramp the timber in position. If working near the end of a piece, leave extra length – a 'horn' which you saw off later – to prevent the wood from splitting as you chisel into it. If you have a carpenter's brace or a power drill, you can start by drilling holes close together along the length of the mortise. Make quite sure you keep the drill vertical – a drill stand will help.

Then chop and lever out the waste with the mortise chisel, and cut the recess for any haunch. Lastly, clean off the sides and ends with a bevel-edged chisel.

If you have no drill, use a mortise chisel by itself, keeping the bevel away from you and working from the centre of the mortise towards the ends – stopping just short of them so as not to bruise them when you lever out the waste before going deeper. On a through mortise, chisel halfway and then work from the other side. Clean up with a bevel-edged chisel.

Assembling the joint
Now you can fit the pieces together. Don't be tempted to force them, or you may split the wood; if the joint is impossibly tight, carefully shave the tenon with a chisel and glass-paper checking all the time. When it's a neat, close fit, glue it, cramp it and leave it to set.

Ideally, you need sash cramps – long steel bars with one fixed head and another which you tighten – plus some pieces of scrap wood to protect the work.

CUTTING THE TENON

1 *After marking off the waste areas, clamp the piece upright and start to cut the tenon. Be sure to keep the saw on the waste side of the lines.*

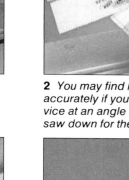

2 *You may find it easier to work accurately if you clamp the piece in the vice at an angle of about 45° while you saw down for the next few strokes.*

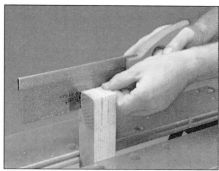

3 *Finish off the cut with the piece upright again. It's easy to overshoot when sawing along the grain, so be careful as you approach the depth marks.*

4 *Make identical cuts along the grain, down to the same depth marks, for each of the edge shoulders if you have marked any.*

5 *Firmly hold or clamp the piece down flat on the workbench as you cut away each of the tenon's face shoulders by sawing across the grain.*

6 *Lastly, turn the piece over on to its side and make similar cross-cuts to remove the edge shoulders, if any are included. This completes the tenon.*

Ready Reference

STRENGTHENING THE JOINT

For extra strength and decorative possibilities, consider wedging or pegging the joint once it's fitted. Hardwood wedges go either into previously made saw-cuts in the end of a through tenon (A), or into the mortise above and below it (B). The mortise needs to be slightly tapered. Pegging is done with one or more dowels inserted into holes drilled sideways through the joint.

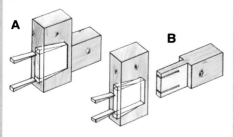

TIPS FOR BETTER JOINTS

● a through tenon should be cut too long, and made flush once the joint is assembled
● some people find it easier to start cutting the tenon while holding the piece upright, then to re-position the wood and saw at 45°, and to finish off with it upright again
● set your mortise gauge from the exact width of your mortise chisel
● if mortising near the end of your timber, leave it over-long to prevent splitting, and cut off the extra bit later
● to keep drill or chisel vertical, stand a try-square on end beside the tool as you're working

● leave it till last to pare down the mortise ends, so as not to risk bruising them while levering out the bulk of the waste
● to stop yourself drilling too deep when starting a mortise, fit a depth stop (an item you can buy) or wrap masking tape round the bit as a depth indicator.

MARKING AND DRILLING THE MORTISE

1 If you're working near the end of the mortise piece, mark off a short length or 'horn' as waste, for removal once the joint is assembled.

2 Lay the tenon on the mortise piece, allowing for any horn, and mark there the tenon's width.

3 Square these two length marks across the inner side of the mortise piece.

4 With the gauge at its existing setting, score down the mortise piece, between the last two marks, to give the mortise's width.

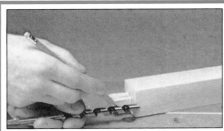

5 For a stub mortise-and-tenon joint, mark out the tenon length on your drill bit, if you have a bit of the right diameter.

6 Drill holes to remove the bulk of the mortise. For a stub joint the tape at the mark on the bit warns of the depth.

CHISELLING OUT THE MORTISE

1 Instead of drilling, you can chop and lever out the waste with a mortise chisel, starting halfway down the length of the mortise.

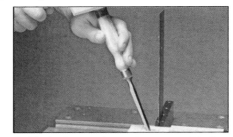

2 Work along to its ends as you chisel deeper. For a through mortise, chop halfway through, then work from the other side of the piece.

3 For a stub mortise and tenon joint it pays to mark off the length of the tenon on the chisel as a depth guide, just as you would for a drill bit.

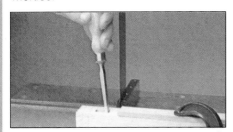

4 Then you can wind sticky tape round it next to the mark, again as a depth indicator, for use when you chisel out the bottom of the mortise.

5 After removing most of the waste, use a bevel-edged chisel to pare down each end of the mortise, shaving off any irregularities.

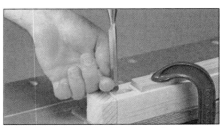

6 Work on the sides likewise. As you're cutting along the grain, you'll need greater care, to avoid splitting out more wood than you want.

ASSEMBLING THE JOINT

1 Try the pieces together to see if they fit – but without forcing the tenon all the way in. Carefully sand or pare away as needed.

2 A through joint can be strengthened with small wedges cut from scrap hardwood and inserted in or next to the tenon after assembly.

3 A stub joint will need to be glued, and cramped. If working at a corner, leave the horn on until this is done.

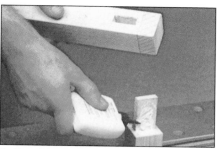

4 For either type, start by spreading adhesive all over the tenon and shoulders. Use a wet rag to wipe off any excess after assembly.

5 Once the through tenon is fully home, insert any wedges you are using and drive them carefully into place with a wooden mallet.

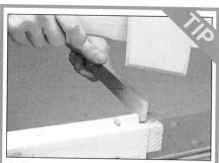

6 To get wedges tight, you'll probably need a piece of scrap wood to help drive them fully home past the projecting end of the tenon.

7 Saw off the excess length of the tenon and any wedges so that they're almost flush with the surface of the mortise piece.

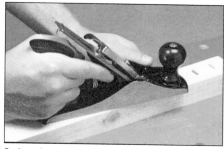

8 Lastly, turn the assembly round and complete the operation by planing across the end of the joint to give it a smooth finish.

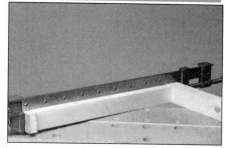

9 A wedged joint can now be left alone while it sets, but any other (whether it's through or stub) will need cramping during this stage.

10 After the adhesive has set, saw off any horn that you may have been leaving at the end of the mortise piece while making the joint.

11 Now plane the end you've just sawn, to get it smooth. Work inwards, as shown, to avoid splitting from the mortise piece.

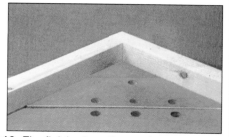

12 The finished mortise-and-tenon joint is both strong and neat. A corner version is shown here, but a T shape is equally possible.

DOVETAIL JOINTS

Dovetail joints are not only beautiful, they're very strong. Once you know the right way to cut them, it only takes practice to get a good fit every time.

Most pieces of wooden furniture are built as either frames or boxes. The mortise and tenon, as the principal framing joint, is common in chairs and tables. But in box construction the dovetail has traditionally reigned supreme.

True, modern storage furniture often uses screws, dowels, assembly fittings, and edge joints cut with power tools. But you only have to look at a set of dovetails to see that they make the perfect corner joint between flat timbers such as box sides – including the top and side panels of furniture 'carcases'.

In fact, dovetails are impossible to pull apart. That's why they're found joining drawer sides to drawer fronts and sometimes backs. Every time you open a drawer, you're trying to pull the front off – and the dovetail joint withstands this tendency as no other joint can. Note, however, that it only locks in one direction. If you use it the wrong way round where its strength matters, its unique properties are wasted.

There's one other major point to remember. Chipboard is far too weak a material in which to cut dovetails – although, at a pinch, they'll work in plywood and good-quality blockboard.

The dovetail joint is always admired and even respected. But there's really no mystery about it. While no one could pretend that well-fitting dovetails are easy for a beginner to cut, the only secret of success is practice; and you'll find things go a lot more smoothly if you stick closely to the time-tested procedure described here.

Anatomy of a dovetail joint

Dovetails themselves are fan-shaped cutouts in the end of one of the pieces being joined – fan-shaped, that is, when you look at the face of the piece.

The sides of each tail slope along the grain at an angle of between 1 in 5 (for a 'coarse' but strong joint, suitable for softwood and man-made boards) and 1 in 8 (generally considered the best-looking, and usually used with hardwoods). If you make them any coarser, they may break; any finer, and they may tend to slip out under strain.

Between the tails, when the joint is assembled, you can see the 'pins' cut in the other piece. These, of course, follow exactly the same slope or 'rake' as the tails – but across the endgrain, so you can only see their true shape when looking at them end-on. Note that there's always a pin at either end; this helps to secure both pieces against curling up.

The spacing of the tails is another factor in the joint's appearance. In general, the wider they are (and therefore the further apart the pins are) the better – but this too affects the strength if you overdo it.

Marking out the tails

The first step in making a dovetail joint is to get the ends of both pieces square (they needn't be the same thickness). Particularly if it's your first attempt, you may find it wise to leave a little extra length as well – say a millimetre or two.

After that, it's customary to start with the tail piece (which is the side, not the front, in the case of a drawer). First decide on the slope of your dovetails – say 1 in 6 – and mark it out on a scrap of wood or paper. That's just a matter of drawing two lines at right angles to each other, then making a mark six units along one, and another mark one unit up the other. Join up the marks with a diagonal, and set a sliding bevel to the same slope.

Now you need to work out where each tail should come. However, there's no need for fiddly calculations. First decide the width of

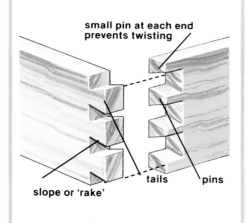

MARKING OUT THE TAILS

1 Plane both pieces to exactly the same width, and check that the ends are dead square. Correct with a block plane if necessary.

2 Square the end pins' width along the tail piece, then slant a measure between the lines to give handy divisions for the pin centres.

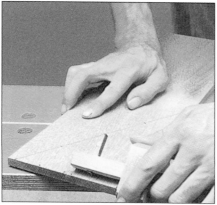

3 Use a gauge to extend these centre marks from the slanting line down to the end of the piece, where the tails will be cut.

4 Make another mark 3mm (1/8in) either side of each centre mark. This will give you the widths of the tails at their widest.

5 Set a sharp marking gauge, or preferably a cutting gauge, to the exact thickness of the pin piece or a bit more – but no less.

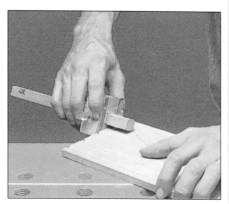

6 Score a neat line all round the end of the tail piece with the gauge. It's usual to leave this visible in the finished joint.

7 Set a sliding bevel (or make a card template) to a slope of 1 in 6 – ie, six units in one direction and one unit in the other direction.

8 Use the bevel or template to mark out the slope of the tails, working inwards from the marks which denote the tail widths.

9 Square the width marks across the end of the piece, then mark the slope again on the far side with the bevel or template.

TYPES OF DOVETAIL JOINT

Coarse and fine dovetails
For general work, tails and pins are equally spaced and steeply raked (below left) – unlike fine work (below right).

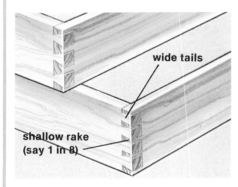

wide tails

shallow rake (say 1 in 8)

Carcase dovetails
A coarse dovetail joint traditionally joins sides to top on solid timber cabinets. An added top panel hides it.

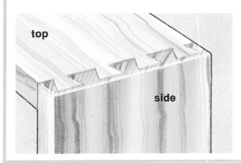

top

side

Lap dovetails
Concealed by an overlap, unlike through dovetails (shown in Ready Reference), these are traditional in drawers.

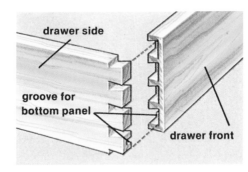

drawer side

groove for bottom panel

drawer front

Framing dovetails
A large dovetail can provide useful strength in a frame where its locking properties are especially vital.

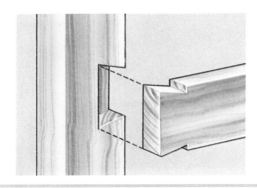

Dovetail housings
The dovetail housing is the odd man out – it's not a corner joint. The tail runs across the width.

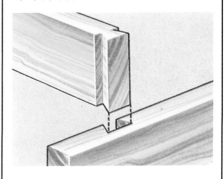

Cut like other housing joints (see pages 40-43), it can be plain (above) or barefaced (below). The latter will usually do.

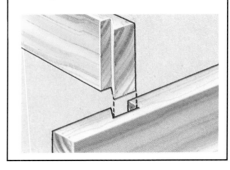

the pin at each end, and square that along the grain. Then place a tape measure diagonally between the squared lines, and swing it round to give a figure easily divisible into equal parts. Mark off these equal divisions, and square them along to the end of the piece. These are the centres of the gaps between your tails.

Then make a mark 3mm (⅛in) either side of each centre mark, and draw a line sloping inwards from it along the face – using the sliding bevel as your guide. Square these marks across the end, and then repeat them on the other face.

Lastly, set a marking or cutting gauge to the exact thickness of the pin piece, and scribe a line all round the end of the tail piece. If you've been allowing for extra length, add that to the scribed thickness. This will make the tails slightly too long; when the joint is complete, trim them flush with a block plane.

At this stage, a very wise precaution is to hatch in – or mark with an X – all the bits you're going to cut out.

Cutting the tails and pins
The next essential is to have the right saw. An ordinary tenon saw is too heavy; you need the lighter version actually known as a dovetail saw, or the still finer gent's saw. But even one of these, especially if new, will have too much 'set' – the teeth will project too far sideways, giving too wide and inaccurate a cut. You can remedy this by placing the blade on an oilstone, flat on its side, and very lightly rubbing it along. Do this once or twice for each side.

To make your cuts, cramp the tail piece in a vice. (If making, say, two identical sides for a box, you can cut more than one piece at the same time.) Align the timber so that one set of sloping marked lines is vertical. Cut along all these, one after the other, before tilting the piece the other way and cutting those on the opposite slope.

Saw immediately on the outside of each marked line, and begin each cut with the saw angled backwards, steadying its blade with your thumbnail. Once you've got the cut

established, tilt the saw forwards to make sure you're keeping to the line on the other side. Lastly, level the saw up as you finish the cut. Whatever you do, don't cut down past the gauged line!

The next step is to use your gauge to mark the thickness of the tail piece in turn on the pin piece.

A neat trick follows. Hold the pin piece in a vice, and cramp the tail piece over its end in exactly the intended position. Then, inserting the saw in the cuts you've just made, use it to score corresponding marks on the endgrain of the pin piece. Square these across its faces.

At this point you can remove the waste from between the tails. Begin by sawing out the little piece next to each of the two outer tails; then use a chisel. (Some people like to get the bulk of the waste out with a coping saw first.) Drive the chisel down into the face each time, keeping well in front of the gauge line, then tap the blade into the endgrain to get the chips up and out. Turn the piece over and do the same on the other side.

EXTERIOR MAINTENANCE

EXTERIOR PAINTING

The main reason for decorating the outside of your house
is to protect it from the elements. But paint can also
transform the appearance of your house and
increase its value, so it's a job
worth doing well.

EXTERIOR PAINTING: THE BASICS

The outside of every house needs to be protected from the elements. But when is the best time to do it? and in what order should things be done? Here we look at when it is best to do the work, and how to tackle those tricky parts.

The outside of your house is under continuous attack from rain, frost, heat and light from the sun, dirt and pollution. Properly applied paint or varnish is the best way of protecting the fabric of the house, and it should last for about five or six years before it needs renewing. If the outside hasn't been touched for several years it's probably looking rather shabby by now and you should start to think about repainting.

Modern paints come in a very wide range of colours and are very easy to apply. A little time spent preparing and painting your house now can transform a drab old building into a desirable residence; and increase the value of the house with very little outlay.

The main parts of the house that have to be painted are the woodwork, metalwork, and possibly the walls. Plastic gutters and pipes do not need to be painted. It's up to you whether you paint the walls or not. Brick, pebbledash, stone and rendering can all be left in their natural state, but if the walls are in need of repair or are porous, stained and dirty, a good coat of paint will both protect the surface and brighten up the house.

The first thing to do is to take a long, critical look at your house to assess what needs to be done. Search for any defects that may affect the final paintwork. A common fault on older houses is leaking gutters. These can leave unsightly stains on the wall or cause woodwork to rot. They can be easily sealed or even completely replaced with new gutters. Other common faults are flaking and peeling paint, rotten window sills and cracked rendering. The illustrations on the next page show many different defects that need repairing. It's unlikely you'll find all of these faults on one house, but you'll probably find a few. It is very important that you remedy every fault you find before you begin to paint or the paint won't be able to do its job and your house will only deteriorate further. This preparation will usually be the most time consuming part of the decoration and will often be quite hard work. But it has to be done if you want your new paintwork to last. Details on how to prepare each different type of surface – wood, metal, brick, render etc – will appear in a later article.

When to paint

Outside painting should only be done in dry weather and after at least two days without rain, fog or frost. The ideal time is late summer when the wood has had a good time to dry out and the weather is usually quite settled. Even a small amount of moisture trapped under a new paint film will vaporise, causing blisters and peeling. For the same reason you should wait an hour after sunrise to let the dew dry out, and stop work an hour before sunset. On the other hand, don't paint under the full glare of a hot sun as this will dry out the surface too quickly, leaving relatively soft paint underneath which may cause wrinkling as it dries in turn. The ideal practice is to follow the sun, and only paint when it has dried one part of the house and passed on to another. Unfortunately this advice is often difficult to follow in practice as some walls may never see the sun, so you'll have to look for the best compromise.

What to paint first

There is a logical sequence of painting which holds for nearly all houses. In general it's best to start at the top and do larger areas before smaller ones. So if you're going to paint the whole of your house try to follow this order: do the fascia boards and barge boards first, followed by the gutters. The rendering (if any) comes next, then the windows and doors and finally the downpipes. The reason for doing it in this order is that splashes of paint dropped onto a wall beneath a fascia or gutter, even if wiped off immediately, will leave a mark; but subsequent painting of the wall will cover them up. Also, since windows and doors are smaller in area than the rendering, it will be easier to 'cut in' (that is, leave a finer edge) when painting them, so giving a much neater finish.

You will need to follow this sequence three times in all, first to do the preparation, then to apply primers or under coats, and finally to paint on the top coat. If this sounds like far too much work to do all at once there's no reason why you shouldn't split it up and do just a part each year. You could, for instance, do the walls this year, the woodwork next year and the gutters and downpipes the year after. It may even be better to do it this way, spread over several years, as you'll be more aware of the condition of the paintwork and will be able to touch up bits and make small repairs as you go along, when the first signs of wear show. (But remember that this will restrict you to using the same colour as you have at present. It's going to look odd if you change the colour only gradually.)

COMMON SURFACE DEFECTS

Before painting your house, give it a thorough going over to find out where any faults and defects may lie. You're certainly not likely to find all the faults shown here, but the drawings do point out the problem areas. All faults must be put right before you start to paint, otherwise you are likely to achieve a poor result and will waste much time and money in the effort.

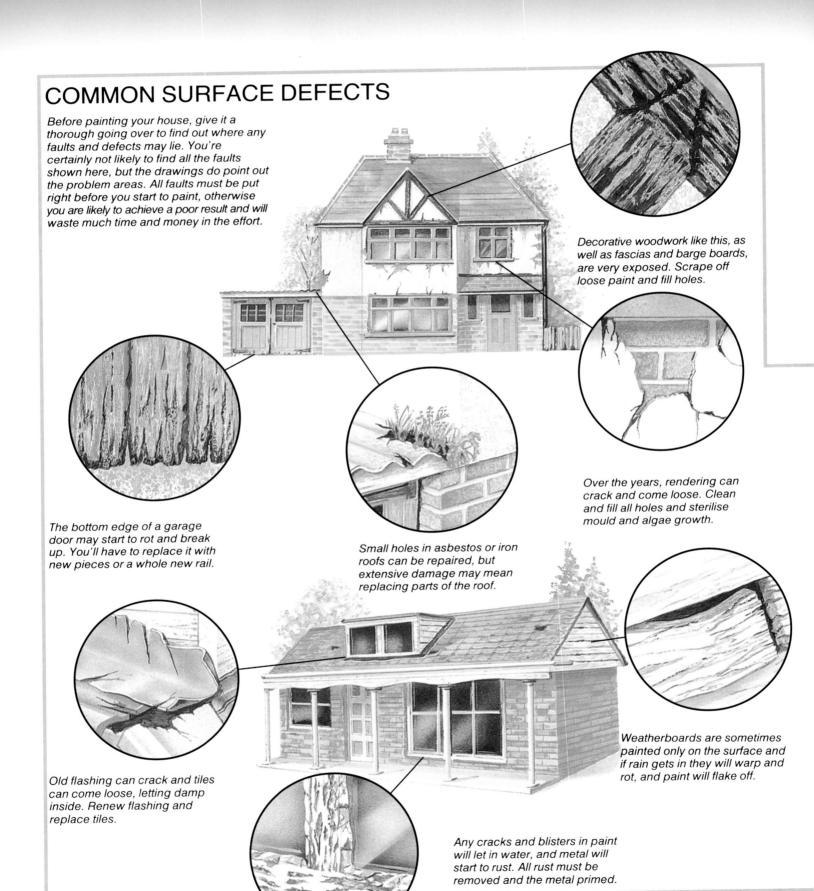

Decorative woodwork like this, as well as fascias and barge boards, are very exposed. Scrape off loose paint and fill holes.

Over the years, rendering can crack and come loose. Clean and fill all holes and sterilise mould and algae growth.

The bottom edge of a garage door may start to rot and break up. You'll have to replace it with new pieces or a whole new rail.

Small holes in asbestos or iron roofs can be repaired, but extensive damage may mean replacing parts of the roof.

Weatherboards are sometimes painted only on the surface and if rain gets in they will warp and rot, and paint will flake off.

Old flashing can crack and tiles can come loose, letting damp inside. Renew flashing and replace tiles.

Any cracks and blisters in paint will let in water, and metal will start to rust. All rust must be removed and the metal primed.

TESTING A PAINTED SURFACE

1 Try this easy way of testing your paint surface to see if it's suitable for repainting. First, score a double cross in the paint with a sharp knife.

2 Stick a piece of adhesive tape over the length of the cross cuts and press it down firmly. Then pull the tape away from the surface slowly.

3 If the tape is clean, the paint surface is sound and safe for painting. If flakes of paint are pulled off you must strip off the old paint first.

A blocked gutter can overflow, joints can leak and iron gutters can rust – causing damp patches and stains on the wall.

The white deposit (efflorescence) is caused by damp; it should be brushed off and the source of damp treated.

Old, dry putty can fall out and must be replaced; knots should be stripped and treated; rotten wood must be cut out and holes filled.

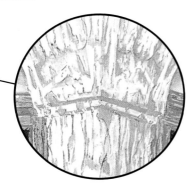

Flaking paint on render should be scraped off and the render brushed down. Fill holes and, if the surface is powdery, apply a stabiliser.

WORKING SAFELY AT HEIGHT

Ladders are an easy and convenient way of reaching heights, but since most domestic accidents involve ladders, it's worth taking time to secure them safely.

Always lean the ladder at a safe angle so that for every 4m of height, the base is 1m from the wall. Always tie it securely at the top or bottom to stop it slipping, and overlap an extension ladder by at least three rungs.

You'll need a roof ladder if you want to paint or repair the chimney or the dividing wall between two roofs. If your house has overhanging eaves, use a ladder stay to hold the ladder away from the wall.

Right: if you have a wide clear area round your house a tower platform is the safest way of getting up high. Make sure it stands perfectly level.

Left: often the gap between two houses is too narrow to put up a ladder at the correct angle. The only answer is to use a special narrow tower.

Special brackets fit on a pair of ladders to provide a long working platform which is useful for reaching the area over a bay window. A third ladder is needed to gain access to the platform.

Tower platforms can be assembled in a cantilevered structure to bridge an outbuilding or a bay window. Protect the roof with sacking and blocks of wood, or use sandbags if the roof is very steep.

Working in safety

To paint the outside of your house in comfort and safety you need the right tools and equipment. There's nothing worse than balancing dangerously on a makeshift working platform with a paint pot in one hand, trying to reach into an awkward corner with the other. But as long as you follow a few simple rules you should be able to work easily and safely. Always work from a step-ladder or an extension ladder and make sure it stands on a firm and level surface. If the ground is uneven, push wedges under a board until the board is level then stand the ladder on this. You'll have to put down a board on soft ground too. If you're working on grass there's a danger of the board slipping, so drive in two stakes on either side of the ladder and rope the ladder to these. On a slippery surface put down some canvas or sacking, and put a board on soft ground. Don't use plastic sheeting as a dust sheet, because the ladder could slip on it.

If you're working high up it's best to tie the ladder to something solid at the top. Don't tie it to the gutter or downpipe as these are not designed to take the extra weight and wouldn't support a ladder if it started to slip. The best way is to fix big screw eyes into sound woodwork such as a window sill, fascia or barge boards and tie the ladder to these. Or, if convenient, you can tie the ladder to the centre mullion of an open window. If there's no sound woodwork, it's advisable to drill and plug the wall to take the screw eyes. Fix them at intervals of about 2m (6ft) and leave them in place when you've finished so they're ready the next time you have to decorate.

Be sure to position the ladder square against the wall so it won't wobble, and lean it at the correct safe angle of 4 to 1, that is, for every 4m of height the bottom should be 1m out from the wall.

When you're working on a ladder don't lean out too far as it's all too easy to loose your balance. Never work from the very top of a step ladder as you'll have nothing to hold on to. A paint kettle, to hold your paint, is an essential piece of equipment as you can hook it on to a rung of the ladder, leaving both hands free.

A safer alternative to a ladder or step-ladder is a tower platform which you can hire from most hire shops. The tower comes as a set of interlocking sections which you build up to the required height; you then lay boards across to provide the platform. A handrail fits around the top and there is plenty of room for tools and paint. The towers can be extended over bay windows or round chimneys so you can reach all parts of the house in safety. If you have a wide, flat area around your house, choose a tower with locking castors so you can move it along more easily. Always lock the castors before using the tower, and always climb up on the inside. NEVER on the outside.

THE TOOLS YOU'LL NEED

It saves a lot of time and trouble to have the right tools to hand before you start any job. The tools shown here are the ones you'll need to prepare and paint the outside of your house – the walls, metalwork and the woodwork. Some large items (not shown here) which you'll also need are a dust sheet, a large bucket and a ladder or tower platform.

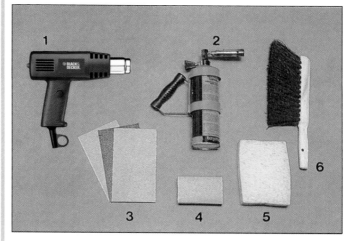

1 Hot air electric stripper for stripping unsound paintwork.
2 Gas blow lamp may be preferred as it saves trailing wires about.
3 A selection of fine, medium and coarse grades of sandpaper for woodwork, and emery paper for metal.
4 Sanding block to hold sandpaper.
5 Sponge for washing down woodwork.
6 Stiff brush for removing dust from masonry.

1 Small trowel for repointing brickwork and repairing holes.
2 Combination shavehook for scraping paint from mouldings.
3 Scraper for flat areas of woodwork.
4 Filling knife for filling holes and cracks.
5 Narrow filling knife for tricky areas round window frames.
6 Putty knife for re-puttying windows.
7 Wire brush for removing rust and paint from metal.

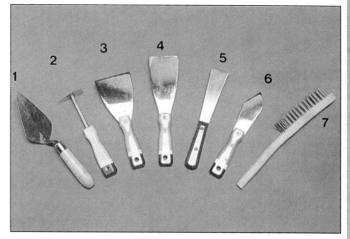

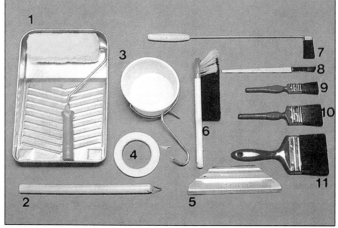

1,2 Long pile roller with extension handle and tray for large areas of masonry.
3 Paint kettle and hook to hold the paint when working on a ladder.
4,5 Masking tape and shield protect areas you want unpainted.
6 Banister brush for painting rough textured surfaces.
7,8,9,10 A selection of brushes for wood and metalwork.
11 Wide brush for smooth surfaces.

EXTERIOR PAINTING: PREPARATION

Whether you like it or not, preparing the outside of your house before painting it is a job that has to be done. If you provide a sound surface the paint will last much longer.

If your house is in good order and has been decorated regularly, then the paintwork may need no more than a quick wash down and a light sanding before it's ready for re-painting. But if your house is in a rather worse state than this, take some time now to make a really good job of the preparation and you'll have a much easier time in the future. The preparation may seem rather time-consuming, but don't be tempted to miss out any of the steps. Properly applied, paint will protect your house for several years, but it won't stick to an unsound surface.

The most convenient order of working is to start at the top of the house and work down, and to do all the preparation before you start to paint so that dust and grit won't fall on wet paint. When working at a height, make sure the ladder or platform is firm and secure.

Gutters and downpipes

Gutters manage to trap a surprising quantity of dirt and old leaves, so clear this out first. It's a good idea to check that the gutter is at a regular slope towards the nearest downpipe. You can easily check this by pouring a bucket of water into one end and seeing if it all drains away. If puddles form, you'll need to unscrew some of the gutter brackets and adjust the level of the gutter until the water flows away freely. Check all the joints for leaks and if you do find any, seal them with a mastic compound applied with a gun.

Plastic gutters need little maintenance, and they don't need painting. But if you want to change their colour, simply clean them thoroughly and wipe them over with a rag dipped in white spirit or turps to remove any grease spots before starting to paint. There's no need for a primer or undercoat, but you may need two top coats for even coverge.

Metal gutters and pipes need more attention as all rust has to be removed. Scrape off flaking paint first, then use a wire brush and emery paper to remove the rust. A wire brush attachment on an electric drill would make the cleaning easier (but wear a mask and goggles while using one). You can buy an anti-rust chemical from paint shops which is useful for badly rusted metalwork. It works by turning iron oxide (rust) into phosphate of iron which is inert and can be painted over. In any case, prime all bare metal immediately with either a red lead primer or a zinc chromate metal primer. Metal primers contain a rust-inhibitor which protects the metal against further corrosion, so don't miss them out. If the gutters and pipes are in good condition with no sign of rust, simply wash them down and sand the surface lightly to key it ready for repainting.

Fascias and barge boards

Fascias and barge boards run along the top of a wall just below the roof. Fascias support the guttering below pitched roofs and edge flat ones, while barge boards are fitted beneath the roof tiles on gable ends. Because they are so high up, don't worry too much about their appearance; the main consideration is protection as they are in such an exposed position. Clean out well behind the gutters as damp leaves or even bird's nests can be lodged there. Then, using a wide scraper, remove all loose flaking paint, sand down the whole board surface and prime the bare patches. Fill holes and cracks with an exterior-grade filler or water-proof stopping and smooth it level while still damp using a filler knife. You can prime the filler when it's dry.

Walls

The main surface materials and finishes used on the outside of your house are brick, stone, wood and render.

Walls of brick and stone, especially when weathered, have a beauty all of their own and don't really need painting. But the surface can become cracked and dirty and a coat of paint will cover up repairs that don't match the original surface, and protect the wall from further damage. Examine the pointing and, if it has deteriorated, rake out the damaged parts and re-point with fresh mortar. Use a mixture of about 1 part cement to 4 parts of fine sand, or buy a bag of ready-mixed mortar. Use a small trowel and try to match the original pointing in the surrounding brickwork. Don't worry about hairline cracks as these will easily be covered by the paint. The white crystalline deposit which sometimes appears on brickwork is known as efflorescence. It is caused by water-soluble salts in the brick being brought to the surface, and should be brushed off with a dry brush. Don't try to wash it off as this will only make it worse.

The main types of render are plain, roughcast and pebbledash. Plain render can be applied to give a smooth, finish or a textured 'Tyrolean' finish, for example. Roughcast consists of pebbles mixed with mortar before application, and with pebbledash the pebbles are thrown on while the mortar is still wet. Pebbledash deteriorates more quickly than the other types of render as, over the years, differences in rates of expansion between each pebble and the surrounding mortar may result in small surface cracks causing the pebbles to become loose and fall out. Paint will bind in the pebbles and protect small cracks.

PREPARING THE WALLS

1 Before painting an exterior wall, brush it down well to remove any loose material. Start at the top and use a fairly stiff brush.

2 Kill mould and algae with a solution of 1 part bleach to 4 parts water. Leave for two days, then wash down and brush off.

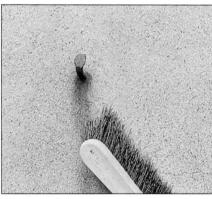

3 Rusty metal and leaky gutters can easily cause stains, so cure the leaks and clean and prime all metal first. Sterilise the stain and brush down.

4 Holes in the wall are often created when old downpipe brackets are removed. Brush them out well and damp the surface with a little water.

5 Fill the hole with a sand and cement mixture using a small trowel. Small bags of ready-mixed mortar are ideal for jobs of this size.

6 If the wall is powdery or highly porous, or if a cement-based paint has been used previously, seal the surface with a stabilising primer.

Ready Reference

CHOOSE THE RIGHT PRIMER
Different materials require different primers; be sure to choose the right type.

Wood

softwood &	wood primer or
hardwood	acrylic primer
resinous wood	aluminium wood primer

Metal

iron and steel	calcium plumbate primer, zinc chromate primer or red lead primer
galvanised iron	
(new)	calcium plumbate primer
(old)	calcium plumbate or zinc chromate primer
aluminium	zinc chromate primer
brass, copper and lead	none necessary: allow new lead to weather

Masonry etc

brick, stone,	stabilising primer
concrete & render	alkali-resisting primer, acrylic primer

Other materials

asbestos	stabilising primer, alkali-resisting primer or acrylic primer
bitumen-coated wood	aluminium wood primer
bitumen-coated metal	aluminium spirit-based sealer

PROPERTIES AND COVERAGE
Where there is a choice of suitable primers, it's often helpful to know something more about each type. For instance, many primers are toxic and you should choose a non-toxic one if you're painting anything in a child's room.
● Acrylic primer – white or pastel shades, water-based, quick drying, non-toxic, 13-18m^2 (140-190sq ft) per litre.
● Alkali-resisting primer – needs two coats on very porous surfaces, non-toxic, 3-10m^2 (30-110sq ft) per litre.
● Aluminium wood primer – dull metallic grey, self-knotting, non-toxic, 16m^2 (170sq ft) per litre.
● Calcium plumbate primer – off-white, rust inhibiting, toxic, 8-12m^2 (90-130sq ft) per litre.
● Lead-free wood primer – white or pink, non-toxic, 10-12m^2 (110-130sq ft) per litre.
● Red lead primer – bright red, rust inhibiting, only for exterior use, toxic, 12-17m^2 (130-180sq ft) per litre.
● Lead-based wood primer – white or pink, only for exterior use, toxic, 12-14m^2 (130-150sq ft) per litre.
● Zinc chromate primer – yellow, rust inhibiting, non-toxic, 11m^2 (120sq ft) per litre.

PREPARING THE WOODWORK

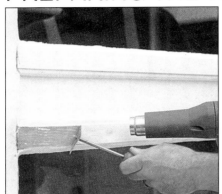

1 Start preparing the woodwork by scraping off all the loose flaking paint. Large areas of unsound paint are better if stripped completely.

2 Sand and prime all the bare wood, taking care to work the primer well into cracks and any exposed end grain, then leave the surface to dry.

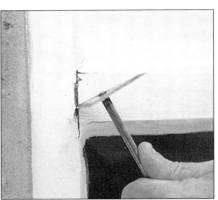

3 Where joints have opened up, scrape off the paint and rake out the gap with a knife or shavehook. Clean out all the loose debris.

4 Small cracks can be filled with putty, but use exterior-grade filler or waterproof stopping for larger cracks and holes.

5 Gaps often appear between the window frame and the wall. Fill these with a mastic compound to provide a continuous water-tight seal.

6 Make sure the drip groove underneath the window sill is clear of paint, then thoroughly sand down the whole of the window frame.

REPLACING OLD PUTTY

1 Old, damaged putty must be raked out. Scrape old paint from the glass, and clean the glass with methylated spirit to remove any grease spots.

2 Work the putty in your hands until it has an even consistency. If it's too oily, roll it on newspaper first. Press it firmly into the gap.

3 Smooth the new putty level with the old using a putty knife, then run a soft brush over it to make a water-tight seal with the glass.

TREATING KNOTS

1 *Active knots like this ooze out a sticky resin which quickly breaks through the paint surface, leaving a sticky and unsightly mess.*

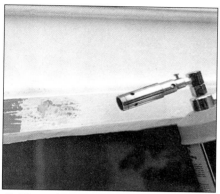

2 *The paint must first be stripped off to expose the knot. Use any method of stripping, and scrape the paint off with a shavehook or scraper.*

3 *Use a blow-torch to heat the knot until the resin bubbles out. Scrape off the resin and repeat until no more of it appears.*

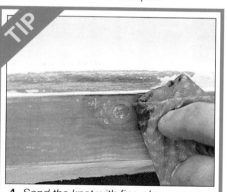

TIP

4 *Sand the knot with fine glasspaper, then wipe over the area with knotting applied with a soft cloth. Prime the wood when it has dried.*

When repairing any of these surfaces, try and achieve the same finish as the original, or as near as you can, so that when it's repainted the repair won't be too noticeable. Stop up cracks with mortar, using a mix of 1 part cement to 5 parts sand. Chip away very wide cracks until you reach a firm edge, then undercut this to provide a good key for the new mortar. Dampen the surface, then stop up with a trowel. Use a float if the surface is plain, or texture the surface to match the surrounding area. Where the rendering is pebble-dash, throw on pebbles with a small trowel while the mortar is still wet, then press them into the mortar lightly with a flat piece of wood.

Mould and stains

If there's any sign of mould or algae on the wall, treat this next. Mix up a solution of 1 part household bleach to 4 parts water and paint this on the affected area. Be generous with the solution and cover the area well. Leave for 48 hours for the bleach to kill off all the

growth, then wash off thoroughly and brush down with a stiff brush.

Rusty gutters, pipes and metal fittings can all cause stains if rusty water drips down the wall. So cure any leaks first and clean and prime all metal to ensure there's no trace of rust. Mould and algae thrive on damp walls; even if you can't actually see any growth on a damp patch, there may be some spores lurking there, so you should make absolutely sure that you sterilise all stains with the bleach solution just to make sure.

Dusty or chalky walls

All walls, whether dusty or not, should be brushed down thoroughly to remove any loose material. But if, after brushing, the wall is still dusty or chalky, if a cement-based paint was used previously to decorate it, or if the wall is porous, you'll have to brush on a stabilising solution. This will bind together loose particles to allow the paint to stick, and it will seal a porous surface and stop paint from being sucked in too much. The

stabiliser also helps to waterproof the wall and you can paint it on as an extra layer of protection whether it's really necessary or not. Most stabilisers are colourless, but off-white stabiliser/primers are available and this would be a good choice if you were planning to paint your house in a light colour, as it could save one coat of the finishing colour. These off-white stabilisers, however, are not recommended for use on surfaces painted with a cement-based paint.

Stabilisers must be painted on a dry wall and should be left to dry for 24 hours before painting on the top coat. Don't paint if rain is expected. Clean your brush in white spirit or turps as soon as you stop work.

Timber cladding

If the cladding or weatherboarding is bare and you want to leave the natural wood surface showing, it should be treated with a water-repellent wood preservative to give protection against damp penetration and decay. The preservative is available clear or pigmented with various colours.

If the wood has been varnished, scrape off the old varnish and sand down well, following the grain of the wood. Fill cracks and holes with plastic wood or a tinted stopper to match the colour of the wood.

If you wish to paint the surface you'll have to wait a year or so for the water-repellent agents in the preservative to disperse before priming with an aluminium wood primer.

Woodwork

If the paintwork on the windows is in good condition all you need do is give them a wash and a light sanding. If the paint is cracked and flaking, a little more preparation is needed. To check if the paint surface needs stripping, lay on a piece of sticky tape and see if it lifts off any paint. Occasional chipped or blistered portions can be scraped off and cut back to a firm edge. As long as the edge is feathered smooth with glasspaper, it shouldn't show too much. If previous coatings are too thick for this treatment, build up the surface with outdoor grade hard stopping until it is just proud of the surrounding paint, then sand level when it's dry. Don't allow the stopping to extend too far over the edge of the damage or it'll be difficult to sand it smooth.

There comes a time, however, when the condition of the old coating has become so bad that complete stripping is advisable.

A blow-torch or an electric hot air stripper are the quickest tools to use. Start at the bottom softening the paint, and follow up immediately with a scraper. Hold the scraper at an angle so the hot paint doesn't fall on your hand, and don't hold it above the flame or it may become too hot to hold. Try not to concentrate the flame too long on one part or you're likely to scorch the wood,

PREPARING METAL

1 Metal pipes and gutters are often in a very bad state of repair and need a lot of preparation. Scrape off all the old flaking paint first.

2 Brush well with a wire brush to remove all traces of rust. Badly rusted pipes should be treated with an anti-rust chemical.

3 Hold a board or a piece of card behind the pipe to keep paint off the wall, and paint on a metal primer, covering every bit of bare metal.

4 A small paint pad on a long handle is a useful tool for painting behind pipes, especially when they are very close to the wall.

though this rarely matters on exterior wood-work which will be over-painted again. Always be extremely careful when using a blow-torch, and keep a bucket of water or sand nearby in case something does catch fire. A chemical paint stripper is the best method to use near glass in case the glass cracks under the heat of a blow-torch.

Knots, putty and holes

Check the woodwork for any live knots which are oozing out resin. If you find any, strip off the paint over them and then play a blow-torch or electric hot air stripper over them to burn out the resin. Sand lightly and treat with knotting, then prime when dry.

You should also check the putty fillet round each pane of glass, and if any has disintegrated, rake it out with an old knife. Then sand and prime the wood and bed in new putty using a putty knife. Use linseed oil putty on wood and metal glazing or all purpose putty on metal-framed windows. Smooth the putty with a damp cloth and leave it for about a week before painting.

Rake out any cracks in the wood and cut back wood which is starting to rot. If a large amount of wood is rotten – usually along the bottom edge of a sash window – a larger repair is needed. This could involve replacing a section or all of the window. Prime the bare wood, working the primer well into cracks and end grain as this is where the weather gets in. Small cracks can be filled with putty, but larger ones should be filled with exterior grade hard stopping or filler. Sand level when dry and spot-prime. Gaps between the window frame and wall should be filled with a flexible, waterproof, mastic compound applied with a special gun.

Finally, sand down the whole of the wood-work to make it ready for repainting.

New doors and windows

New wooden windows and doors may already have a coat of pink primer applied at the factory, but it's best not to rely on this for complete protection. Knots, for instance, will rarely have been properly treated, and the primer film will have been damaged here and there in transit. So sand down the whole surface, treat any knots with knotting compound and apply another coat of wood primer overall. It may be advisable to paint doors while they're lying flat; certainly it's vital to paint the top and bottom edges before you hang them in place. It's very important to paint the bottom as rain and snow can easily penetrate unpainted wood causing it to swell and rot. Paint also protects the wood against attack from woodworm.

Metal and plastic windows

Metal doors and windows should be treated in the same way as metal pipes and gutters. So sand them down and make sure all rust is removed before priming. Aluminium frames can be left unpainted, but if you do want to paint them you must first remove any surface oxidation which shows as a fine white deposit. Use a scraper or wire brush, but go very gently and try not to scratch the surface. Prime with a zinc chromate primer. Plastic window frames should not be painted.

Galvanised iron and asbestos

You're likely to find galvanised iron used as corrugated iron roofing, gutters and down-pipes. The zinc coating on galvanised iron is to some extent 'sacrificial', so that if a small patch becomes damaged, the surrounding zinc will, in time, spread over to cover the damage. But this weakens the coating and an application of paint will prolong its life. If the galvanising is new and bright, simply clean it with a rag dipped in white spirit or turps to remove any grease, and apply a calcium plumbate primer. If it's old and grey-looking, first remove any existing paint by rubbing lightly with a wire brush, trying not to scratch the surface. Then clean with white spirit or turps and apply zinc chromate primer.

Asbestos is often used for guttering, fascia boards, as walls on out-houses and as corrugated sheeting for roofs. Asbestos is a very dangerous material and for this reason great care should be taken when dealing with it. It'll probably need cleaning before painting and the only safe way is to wet it thoroughly first and scrub it down with a scrubbing brush. Be sure to wear rubber gloves and a face mask. Leave it to dry, then prime it with a stabilizing primer, an alkali-resisting primer, or simply a coat of thinned-down emulsion paint. Asbestos is very porous, so always paint both sides of any asbestos sheet to prevent damp penetrating from the back.

EXTERIOR PAINTING: COMPLETION

The first two parts of this article described how to prepare the outside of your house to make it ready for repainting. This last part shows you the best way to paint the walls, pipes, windows and doors to give a professional look to your home.

If you have completed all the cleaning, repairs and preparation on the outside of your house, and if the weather has been dry for the past couple of days and looks settled for a while, you are now ready to start painting. Tackle the painting in more or less the same order as the preparation, starting at the top and working downwards.

Gutters, fascias and barge boards

If you have plastic gutters and want to paint them, simply apply a thin coat of gloss paint to the outside surface. This is the only case outside where paint is used purely for decoration rather than protection. Iron gutters can be painted on the inside with a bituminous paint as this will provide a waterproof coating and protect the iron. Paint the outside of gutters and downpipes with the usual gloss paint system. You'll need a small paint pad or crevice brush to get into the narrow gaps at the back of gutters and pipes. Protect the fascia with a piece of board held behind the guttering. Don't miss out these awkward bits as this is where the rust will start up again. You can use bitumen paint on the inside of asbestos gutters too, but it's best to use

TEXTURED WALLS

1 *Use a 'banister' brush or 'dust pan' brush for painting rough-textured finishes such as pebbledash or a randomly-textured finish.*

2 *Paint brickwork with a well-loaded old brush. Small cracks are bridged by the paint, but larger cracks have to be filled first with exterior filler.*

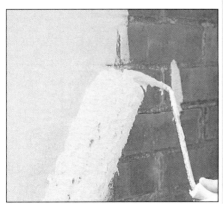

3 *Alternatively, use a roller on brick to give a thicker coat of paint and a slightly textured finish. Special rollers give even deeper textures.*

emulsion paint rather than solvent-based gloss ones on the outside. Asbestos is porous and needs to be able to 'breathe'. Gloss paint would trap moisture within the asbestos, and this would eventually cause the paint to blister.

Fascias and barge boards are so exposed that it's best to give them an extra coat of gloss. You'll need your crevice brush or paint pad again to paint behind the gutters.

Walls

There is a wide range of paints available for exterior walls, and full information is usually available from suppliers. As for tools, a 100mm (4in) brush is the easiest size to handle; anything larger would put too much strain on the wrist. An alternative is a long-pile roller which has the advantage of being much quicker to use – about three times quicker than a brush. An extra long-pile roller is needed for roughcast or pebbledash; choose one with a pile 32mm (1 ¼in) deep, or use a banister brush instead. Use a cheap disposable brush or roller for cement paints as they are almost impossible to clean afterwards.

A large plastic bucket or paint kettle is essential when working up a ladder. Stir the paint thoroughly first, then pour some into the bucket until it's about one third full. If you're using a roller, use a special roller tray with a large paint reservoir, or else stand a short plank in the bucket (see step-by-step photographs, page 233) to allow you to load the roller evenly.

Hook the bucket or tray onto a rung of the ladder with an S-hook to leave both hands free. Lay a dust sheet below to catch any drips and you're ready to start.

Application

Start at the top of the wall and paint a strip across the house. Work from right to left if you're right-handed, and left to right if you're left-handed. Be sure to secure the ladder to prevent it slipping and allow a three-rung overlap at the top.

Use a brush to cut in under the eaves or fascia boards and to paint round obstacles, then fill in the larger areas with a brush or roller. Paint an area only as large as you can comfortably manage and don't lean out too far, your hips should remain between the ladder's stiles at all times.

If you have an awkward area which is too far away to reach, push a broom handle into the hollow handle of the roller, or buy a special extension handle. Protect pipes by wrapping them in newspaper, and mask any other items you don't want to paint. Leave an uneven edge at the bottom of each patch so the join won't be too noticeable, then move the ladder to the left (or right) and paint another strip alongside the first. The principle is always to keep working to the longest wet edge so the joins won't show. When you've done the top series of strips, lower the ladder and paint another series across the middle. Lower the ladder again or work from the ground to do another series along the bottom. Working across the house like this means you have to alter the ladder height the least number of times.

Woodwork

You can choose either a non-drip gloss or a runny gloss for the exterior woodwork. The non-drip jelly paints combine the properties of undercoat and finishing coat so a separate undercoat is not required. But this single coat won't be as long-lasting as the undercoat-plus-runny-gloss system and you'll have to apply two or three coats to build up a thick enough paint film to give adequate outside protection. Inside, however, one coat of non-drip paint would be quite sufficient.

The sequence of painting all jointed woodwork – windows, doors and frames – is determined by the method of construction. In nearly all cases the rails (horizontal bars) are tenoned into mortises cut into the stiles (uprights). Therefore, you should paint the rails and cross bars first, then deal with the stiles. By painting in this way, any overlaps of paint from the rails and bars are covered up and leave a neater finish. An even edge on the glass is best achieved freehand, but if you doubt the steadiness of your touch, use a paint guard or masking tape. Bring the paint onto the glass for up to 3mm (⅛in) to protect the edge of the putty. If you are using masking tape, remove it shortly after painting round each pane; the paint may be peeled off if it is left to harden completely before the tape is removed.

When a visitor calls at your house, he'll stand face to face with your front door and have nothing to do but examine it while he awaits your answer. So it's here you should put in your best work. Remove all the door furniture such as knobs, knockers, locks, keyhole covers and letterbox. Prepare the woodwork carefully and wipe it down with a tackrag (a soft cloth impregnated with a sticky varnish) to collect any remaining dust. Tackrags are obtainable from any good paint shop. Use a perfectly clean brush, preferably one that has been used before so that no loose bristles will come adrift. Wedge the door ajar and cover the floor with a dust cloth or old newspapers. Use paint which doesn't need straining, and pour about 50mm (2in) into a small container or paint kettle.

All coats of paint should follow the grain of the wood. Don't attempt to cross-hatch – that is, apply a primer in one direction, undercoat at right angles and finishing coat in the direction of the primer. If you do, you'll get a criss-cross effect when the paint dries which produces a poor finish.

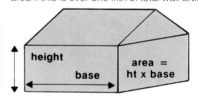
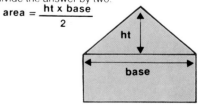

PAINTING WALLS

1 A roller is much quicker to use than a brush, but make sure you have a large enough bucket to dip the roller in. Fill this about ⅓ full.

2 Cut a short plank of wood to the same width as the roller and put it in the bucket so you can load the roller evenly by pressing against it.

3 When painting the house wall, start at the top right hand corner (if you are right-handed) and use a brush to cut in round the edges.

4 Using the roller, cover a strip on your right-hand side. Don't lean over too far and only make the strip as long as you can easily manage.

5 Move the ladder to the left and paint another strip by the first, without overlapping too much. Touch in round obstacles with a brush.

6 Using the brush again, carefully paint round the window. Try to leave a neat edge with the woodwork and wipe off any splashes with a damp cloth.

7 Continue painting a strip at a time from right to left, then lower the ladder and paint a further series of strips until the wall is covered.

8 Protect pipes by wrapping old newspaper round them and securing it with adhesive tape. Use a brush to paint the wall behind the pipes.

9 Be very careful when painting the bottom edge of the wall, and don't load the brush too thickly or paint will run onto the path.

Ready Reference

HOW MUCH GLOSS PAINT?

The coverage of a litre of gloss paint depends on several factors, including the smoothness of the surface and whether it is interrupted by edges and mouldings. Also, a lot depends on the painter's technique. However, as a general guide, for one litre of paint:
- runny gloss covers 17m² (180sq ft)
- non-drip gloss covers 13m² (140sq ft)

CALCULATING AREAS

It would be very difficult to calculate the area of every bit of wood and metal you wanted to paint. But you need to make a rough estimate so you'll know how much paint to buy. The following examples are intended as a rough guide and they should give you an idea of how much paint you'll need, assuming you're using **runny gloss** and you give everything **two coats of paint**. If you're using non-drip gloss you'll have to buy about 25% more paint:
- a panelled front door will take ⅓ litre (½ pint)
- a flush door will take about ⅕ litre (⅓ pint)

 panelled door

 flush door

3 doors/litre   **5 doors/litre**

- a sash window, about 2x1m (6ft 6in x 3ft 3in) with an ornate frame will take about ⅙ litre (¼ pint)
- a modern picture window of the same size with a plain frame will take only ⅛ litre (⅕ pint)

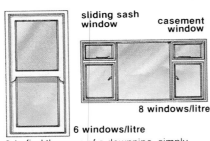

sliding sash window   casement window

8 windows/litre

6 windows/litre

- to find the area of a downpipe, simply measure round the pipe and multiply by the height, then add a little for clips and brackets. For two coats of paint, one litre will cover 18m (60ft) of 150mm (6in) diameter pipe and 27m (90ft) of 100mm (4in) pipe.

PAINTING WINDOWS

1 *Start to apply undercoat at the top of the window. Prop the window open, tape up the stay and paint the frame rebates first.*

2 *Paint the rebates on open casements next. If you get paint on the inside surface, wipe it off immediately with a cloth dipped in white spirit or turps.*

3 *Close the window slightly and paint the area along the hinged edge. You may need to use a narrow brush (called a fitch) to reach this part.*

4 *A neat paint line on the glass is best achieved free-hand, but if you find this too difficult, use a paint shield or apply masking tape.*

5 *The general order of painting is to do the cross bars (rails) first, followed by the uprights (stiles) and then the window sill.*

6 *When the undercoat is dry, sand it down with a fine grade glasspaper, then apply the top coat in the same order as the undercoat.*

PAINTING SEQUENCES

Windows and panelled doors are tricky areas to paint properly but you shouldn't have any trouble if you follow the correct sequence of painting shown here.

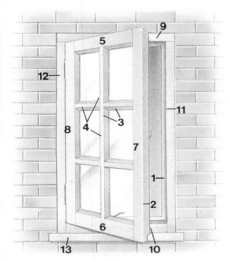

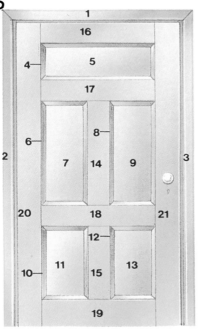

Start with the rebate on the frame (1), then paint the outside edge of the window (2). Do the putty (3) next, followed by the glazing bars (4) and the rails and stiles (5 to 8). Paint the frame (9 to 13) last.

Wedge the door ajar and paint the frame (1 to 3), the hinged edge of the frame and door. Do mouldings and panels next (4 to 13) followed by the muntins (14,15), the rails (16 to 19) and finally the stiles (20, 21).

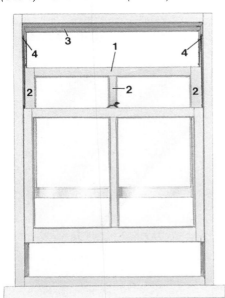

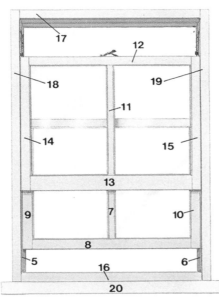

Sliding sash windows need to be painted in two stages. Pull down the top sash and paint the top rail of the inside sash (1) and the sides as far as you can go (2). Do the runners at the top of the frame (3) and a short way down the outer runner(4). Almost close the windows, then paint the bottom runners (5,6), and the remainder

of the bottom sash to meet the other paint (7 to 10). Paint the whole of the top sash including the bottom edge (11 to 15) and finally the window frame (16 to 20). This view shows the interior of the window: for the exterior the sequence is identical except of course, that you start with the top sash.

Deal with the door frame first (the top, then the sides) so that any splashes can be wiped off an unpainted surface immediately. Then do the door itself, following the sequence of painting shown on this page. Don't put too thick a coat on the inner edge of the door frame because although gloss paint dries fairly quickly, it won't oxidise (ie, thoroughly harden) for about a week. So in that period, when you close the door, paint may 'set-off' from the frame onto the door, producing a vertical streak an inch or so from the door's edge. A good idea to prevent this is to insert a thin strip of polythene sheeting round the door's edge after the paint has become touch dry, and leave it until the paint has thoroughly hardened.

If you want to apply two finishing coats, wait at least 12 hours but not more than a week between coats. There's no need to sand down between coats because the solvent used in modern gloss paints is strong enough to dissolve the surface of the previous coat and so to ensure a firm bond between the two layers.

Weatherboards

Weatherboards and timber cladding can be left in their natural state as long as you treat them with a wood preservative, and you can use wood stains to enhance or change their colour. If you prefer a glossy finish, use a suitable external varnish such as an oil-resin varnish (marine varnish), rather than a one-pack polyurethane varnish which can prove brittle and difficult to over-coat in future. If you wish to paint the wood you'll have to apply one coat of wood primer, followed by an undercoat and two finishing coats of gloss.

Galvanised iron and asbestos

Because it is waterproof, bituminous paint is best for galvanised or asbestos roofs. In addition to the customary black it can be obtained in shades of red, green or brown to simulate or match tiles. These colours are more expensive than black and may have to be ordered specially from a builders' merchant. Bitumen soon loses its gloss and its surface tends to craze under a hot sun. But that doesn't matter as roofs are not usually visible.

Paint the walls of asbestos outhouses with outdoor-grade emulsion in a colour to match the rest of the house. Thin the first coat to allow for the porosity of the asbestos and follow this with a normal second coat. Apply emulsion on the interior surface as well to minimise moisture absorption. Galvanised iron on vertical surfaces should be painted with gloss paint.

When painting corrugated surfaces, give the high parts a preliminary touch-up with paint, leave it to dry and then paint the whole lot. If you apply paint all over in one go it will tend to flow from high to low parts, giving an uneven coating.

SPRAYING EXTERIOR WALLS

Painting the exterior walls of your home with a brush or roller can be fairly time consuming. But with a properly used spray gun you can finish the job.

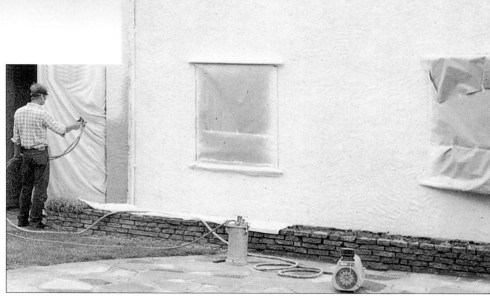

P ainting the exterior walls of your house with a brush is hard and tedious work; even if you switch to a roller, things will not be a lot simpler. To avoid this drudgery, you can use an alternative method: you can spray the paint onto the walls. It's quicker, easier and, because it tends to give a more even coverage, should give more durable results, particularly on rough surfaces where brushes and rollers tend to leave tiny gaps through which moisture can penetrate to undermine the paint film.

If the only experience you have had of spray painting is retouching scratches on a car with an aerosol, then spraying houses may seem very novel. But it isn't a new idea. Specialist contractors have been doing it for years, though their advertising has tended to concentrate on the fact that they use special, very durable paints. In fact you'll find that you don't need special paint; so long as it's of a type suitable for exterior use.

Types of spray gun

Although you don't need special paint, you do need costly special equipment: you need a spray gun. Fortunately, these are widely available at a modest rental from good local tool hire shops. The important thing is that you choose the right kind of spraying equipment for the paint you wish to use. Choosing the gun can, in fact, be rather complicated – there are so many different kinds available – so you could tell the hire shop what you want to spray and leave the decision to them.

The simplest type of spraying equipment you are likely to be offered is called an airless spray unit. It is a straightforward pump which takes paint from a container (any container will do) and then squirts it out through a spray nozzle. It is very efficient in terms of labour and use of materials and very fast. It is capable of delivering up to 2.25 litres (4 pints) of paint per minute (a practised operator would normally cover about 240sq m/262sq yd in an hour). This type of gun does, however, have a few drawbacks. To begin with the paint must be thinned before it can be sprayed, which may mean applying an extra coat in order to achieve the required coverage and colour density. Also, with the pump at

ground level, problems may arise when you are working on buildings higher than about two storeys. The machine may not be powerful enough to pump the paint that distance. In addition, this type of unit will not handle paints containing fillers.

An alternative is a machine that works a bit like an old-fashioned scent spray: the air flow is provided by a compressor which may or may not be rented out as a separate item (if you do have to hire the compressor separately, make sure it is sufficiently powerful for the application you have in mind). Reaching heights with a machine of this type should not be a problem. The only limitation is the length of the hose between the compressor and the spray gun, but many hire shops supply 10m (30ft) hoses. A point here: not all compressor-operated units are the same and you should check that you are using a suitable type. At the bottom end of the scale, you'll find small portable units primarily designed for spraying cars and the like. So long as you use a paint that does not contain fillers, these can be used to spray walls, but since the integral paint container normally has a capacity of less than a litre (1½ pints), you will spend a lot of time running up and down to refill. Larger 'industrial' versions using more powerful compressors are available and these are faster and have feed cups of around 1 litre (1½ pints). They too will only handle ordinary resin- and water-based paints.

If you want to spray on a reinforced paint there are a number of options, with different suppliers calling them by different names. Those able to cope with most ordinary filled exterior paints may have a shoulder-carried, or back-pack style, paint container. Those capable of spraying anything from reinforced paint to very heavy, plaster consistency materials tend to be fed from a gravity feed hopper on top of the spray gun, or from a separate pressurised tank – see step-by-step photographs.

Whatever you decide on, do double-check that the gun is suitable for the material you wish to spray; even if the basic equipment is right for the job a different nozzle may be required. Also make sure you get adequate instructions on using and cleaning the equipment before you take it home. If you damage it or return it dirty, you may lose some or all of your deposit. Again, bear in mind that some compressors are electric and some petrol-driven, but the smaller units are almost always electrically operated (check that you get a 240V model, not a 110V one).

Choosing access equipment

Since the main virtue of spray painting walls is speed, it's only sensible to choose a means of reaching the heights that allows you to get up, down and along with the minimum of fuss. This means that a scaffold tower, even one on castors, although excellent when you are preparing the surface, is not a particularly

PREPARING THE WALLS

1 *Most exterior wall paints will fill hairline cracks when sprayed on. Rake out and fill larger cracks and holes with mortar or exterior-grade filler.*

2 *The paint will not adhere properly to a dusty, crumbly surface. Go over areas like these with a stiff brush to remove dirt and any loose material.*

3 *Where old paint has begun to crack and flake off, use a scraper to remove it from affected areas of the wall. Prime bare areas with paint before spraying.*

4 *Look out for green spots, which are a sign of mould growth. To prevent any further outbreaks, brush on a solution of bleach or apply a proprietary fungicide.*

good choice for spraying unless you have a suitable flat, hard 'road' running right round the area you wish to paint. A step ladder (or possibly two, spanned by a scaffold board) for the lower levels, and a lightweight, aluminium extension ladder for the rest is generally a better bet.

Having said that, you should not, of course, allow speed to take precedence over safety. It's probably true that as there is no physical contact with the wall, you are less likely to push yourself off balance than you would be if using a brush or roller and that as spraying is quick and easy you are less likely to over-stretch in order to reach that extra little bit before climbing down and moving the ladder along. But don't take any chances. Always make sure that the ladder is set at the correct angle on a firm, level footing and that it is roped in place at the top. If necessary, spend an hour or two fixing stout hooks at

intervals into the top of the wall to make roping off easier. You'll find they come in handy wherever you need to scale a ladder.

Preparing the site
You should thoroughly prepare the surface so it is clean, dry and sound. In particular, fill any cracks which are wider than about a millimetre with mortar, and check that all rendering is securely adhering to the surface underneath. Also, you should treat dusty surfaces with stabilising primer and kill off any mould or algae using a proprietary fungicide or algicide.

Masking off will normally be your next step (see *Ready Reference*). This can take time and you may feel it rather cancels out the benefits of spraying. This is true to some extent, but wielding a heavy brush can hardly be compared with snipping away at a length of sticky tape. However, it is possible to do

MASKING OFF

1 Masking off takes some time, but it's essential that you do it properly. Cover drainpipes with newspapers, working from the bottom up.

2 For larger areas such as windows it's easier to use larger sheets (paper is cheaper than polythene). Tape all edges and joins carefully for the best results.

3 To prevent the spray from falling over surrounding areas, it's a good idea to protect the ground at the bottom of the wall with dust sheets.

SETTING UP THE EQUIPMENT

1 Make sure you've got all the equipment you need. Then assemble the components; here, start with the gun and paint hose.

3 Fill up the paint tank to the level recommended by the hire company. If thinning is necessary, do it now and then stir the paint thoroughly.

5 Next, pressurise the container by pumping with the integral pump. Don't exceed the recommended pressure level shown on the gauge.

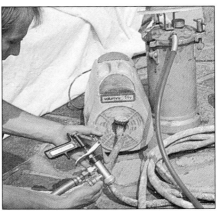

2 Link the other end of the paint hose to the pressurised paint tank. Then connect the air hose to the turbine and the gun. Tighten all connections fully.

4 Fit the lid of the tank back on. When you are sure it's correctly placed, screw it down so the tank is properly sealed and can be pressurised.

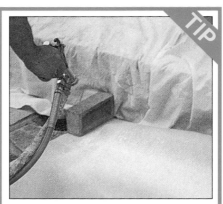

6 Test the gun by spraying paint onto an old board, and adjust the nozzle on the front of the gun as necessary to give a uniform spray pattern.

SPRAYING THE WALLS

1 If you are right-handed, begin at the top right-hand corner (or the top left if you are left-handed). Spray towards a natural break such as a downpipe.

2 As soon as you've completed one band of paint you can begin work on the next. Here, the two windows neatly define the next area to be tackled.

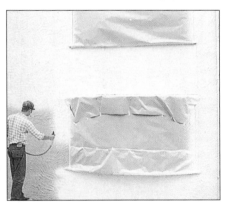

3 Keep the gun at right angles to the wall surface when you are spraying. Spray over the edges of the masked-off areas; the paper will protect them.

4 Before you reach the end of the wall, make sure that you have covered up any adjacent areas which you don't want to be splotched with paint.

5 Remove the masking tape before the paint dries. Otherwise it would be more difficult to remove and you also risk peeling off the paint.

6 If your masking-off has been effective there should only be small areas left for you to fill in by hand. A small brush is best for cutting-in work.

away with masking; though you will still need to protect the ground. All you do is stop spraying when you get too close to whatever it is you don't want painted; normally within 300-600mm (1-2ft). These 'safety zones' can then be painted in using a brush or roller. Do be warned though: a sudden puff of wind or a momentary loss of concentration could have disastrous consequences. If you intend using this technique you should be prepared to have to paint the woodwork and metalwork soon after and to keep some white spirit (turps) or water (according to the type of paint) handy to wipe off any spray that strays onto the window panes.

Spraying technique

The basic technique for spraying walls is to aim to cover the surface with a series of barely overlapping stripes. You should keep the gun moving a constant distance from the surface at a constant speed: slow enough to ensure good coverage and fast enough to avoid the runs that result from applying too much paint. If you don't get a perfect result at the first attempt you can put things right by applying another coat.

Keep on working as blockages may occur if you stop spraying. When you have to stop clean the equipment thoroughly.

Order of work

As when you are brushing on paint, you should follow the sun round the house so your new paintwork won't be exposed to the full blistering heat of the sun until the next day.

It's certainly worth dividing the area into manageable sections using features such as drainpipes and window bays to provide sensible boundaries. This not only gives natural cues for rest breaks but also helps boost morale. Having completed a section, you'll feel you're really getting somewhere.

Similarly, for the sake of comfort and efficiency, tackle each section working down and across, starting at the top right if you are right-handed, top left otherwise. Overstretching is dangerous so climb down and move the ladder.

You'll have to take the weather into account. Don't work in the rain, or if rain is likely within the next few hours, and don't start work if the surface is wet with rain or dew; give it time to dry out. The heat of the sun can damage new paint and will exacerbate the problem of paint drying in the gun so avoid working when the weather is really scorching.

And don't forget the wind. The stiller the day the easier it will be to spray accurately and the less paint you will waste. With a reasonably powerful modern gun, you should be alright working in anything up to a gentle summer breeze, possibly a bit more. But if you have trouble when you first start work, take a rest and try again later.

DRAINAGE AND OUTDOOR PLUMBING

Plumbing jobs need not necessarily be confined to indoors; there are many jobs that require plumbing skills outdoors as well. Foremost among these, is the maintenance and repair of the rainwater system - the gutters and downpipes. Another problem area outdoors is the gullies into which rainwater downpipes, and the waste pipes from downstairs sinks and appliances, discharge.

REPAIRING AND REPLACING GUTTERING

The chances are you won't realise there is anything wrong with your home's guttering until it leaks. Note where the water is coming from, and once the rain has stopped, get up a ladder and see what's wrong.

The gutters on your home are supposed to capture all the rain falling on the roof and channel it to one or more downpipes. In turn these downpipes take the water into the main drain, a storm drain, or to a soakaway in your garden. This efficient removal of rainwater is important to keep your outside walls sound. Any missing, damaged, or blocked guttering will result in water cascading down the face of your wall, leading to dampness, and eventually mortar and brick decay. You may be able to repair it; or you may be faced with having to replace whole sections or the complete system.

Until the mid-1940s most guttering was made of cast iron, although asbestos enjoyed a brief popularity. Cast iron had the disadvantage of being very heavy to work with – as you'll find if you take some of it down. It is also prone to rusting if not properly maintained. Asbestos was heavy, looked rather bulky in appearance and was easily damaged. When plastic piping and guttering was introduced, it became an obvious choice. It is light to work with, doesn't need painting and its smooth surface allows water to flow through it more effectively. In any case, cast iron is very expensive these days, and not particularly easy to obtain.

Blockages
You should check why a blockage has occurred in the first place. This may be due to sagging, or poor installation preventing a free run for the water. Or the blockage may be combined with a faulty joint which may be possible to repair. But if cast iron guttering is at all cracked it needs replacing.

If your gutter overflows during heavy rain, the chances are that it's blocked with leaves.

PREPARING FOR WORK

1 Access is always a problem when working on guttering – a convenient garage roof made this job a lot easier. Scaffold towers are useful on high roofs.

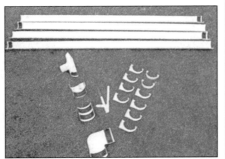

2 Before you start work assemble all the components you will need. You can check them off against the existing guttering.

REMOVING OLD GUTTERING

1 Gutter sections are usually bolted together and these bolts won't come out easily. Saw through the nut.

2 When the nut has been detached try to hammer the bolt out but don't use too much force as the gutter itself may crack and collapse dangerously.

3 You may need to use a hammer and chisel to get the joints moving. Loosen the joints before unscrewing the gutter sections.

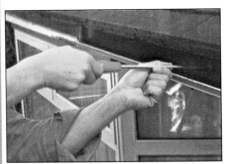

4 Cast iron guttering is supported by brackets or screws depending on its profile. You can lift it off brackets, or in this case unscrew it.

5 Start to take down the guttering at the point closest to the down pipe – it should come free quite easily even if it's attached directly to the pipe.

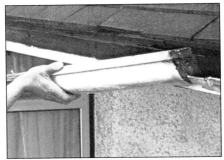

6 Detach and lift off each succeeding section in turn – remember that cast iron is heavier than it looks. Be careful not to overbalance.

7 Always carry pieces of guttering down to the ground, never throw them down – you may cause the cast iron to splinter dangerously.

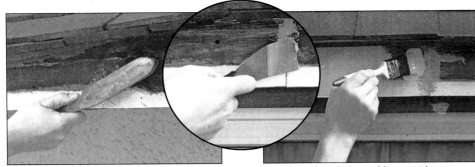

8 Thoroughly brush down the fascia board to remove dirt and cobwebs, then fill any holes using a filler suitable for outside work.

9 If the fascia board has not been painted, use this opportunity to do the work. Sand down first and then apply primer and topcoats.

You can use an old dustpan brush to clean it out, scraping the debris into piles and scooping them out with gloved hands. But prevent any bits from getting into the down-pipe or this may get blocked as well.

Coping with sags

If a section of guttering has sagged, making it lower than the top of the downpipe, the water will not drain away properly. And you will be able to see this from puddles of water collecting in the guttering itself. You must decide whether to raise the sagging section, or lower the mouth of the downpipe to bring everything back into line. If you flex cast iron guttering more than about 25mm (1in) you'll break the seal on the joints, causing a leak. So choose the option that involves moving the guttering least.

In order to reset the guttering to the correct gradient you'll need to fix a piece of string taut between two nails hammered into the fascia board. You can then use this as a guide as you reposition each gutter support in turn.

Leaking joints

Joints in cast iron gutters are made by over-lapping the two lengths of gutter, and bolting them together with a layer of sealant in between to form a watertight seal. As this sealant begins to deteriorate with age, the joint starts to leak.

To make the repair, first remove the bolt holding the joint together. Often this is too rusty to undo, so hacksaw off the bolt between the nut and the guttering, or drill out the rest of the bolt. Lever the joint apart with an old chisel, and scrape away all the old sealant. Clean up the joint with a wire brush, then apply a finger-thick sausage of new sealant and bolt the sections back together using a new nut and bolt and a couple of washers. Scrape off any sealant that has oozed out before giving the repair a coat of bitumen-based paint on the inside of the gutter.

Dealing with rust
If one bit of guttering has rusted right through, it won't be long before the rest follows suit, so you may as well save yourself a lot of trouble and replace it all. If meanwhile you want a temporary repair, there are several suitable repair kits on the market. They consist of a sort of wide metal sticky tape which you apply inside the guttering and over the holes with bitumen adhesive.

Choosing a replacement
Assuming you won't be using cast iron again – you'll have a job getting hold of it and even more of a job putting it up, apart from the fact that it's expensive – your choice is between aluminium and plastic. Plastic guttering is made of UPVC (unplasticised polyvinyl chloride). It's probably the better choice for a do-it-yourself installation: it is far more widely available than aluminium, and has the edge in terms of cost and durability.

Two different cross-sections are commonly available – half-round and 'square'. The latter is often given a decoratively moulded face similar to the more ornate ogee cast iron guttering. In addition, a semi-elliptical guttering is available – it looks a bit like half-round but is deeper and more efficient. This, together with some brands of conventional profile, can be camouflaged by being boxed in with a clip-on fascia panel. Which type you choose is largely a matter of personal taste, but try to choose something that blends into the style of your home.

More important than looks is the size of the gutter. Too small, and it will be forever overflowing; too large, and you will have paid more for the installation than is necessary. It's all to do with relating the amount of water the guttering can carry to the amount of water likely to come off the roof during a heavy rainstorm. These calculations are complicated, but you can assume that they were done when the guttering was originally installed. Just measure the existing

guttering at its widest point to find its size, and buy the same again. The most commonly available sizes are 75mm (3in), 100mm (4in), 112mm (4½in), 125mm (5in), and 150mm (6in). If in doubt, consult the manufacturer's literature.

The actual cross-section of the gutter may vary from brand to brand; this can make it difficult to join with existing guttering: for example, the guttering belonging to a neighbour on a semi-detached or terraced house. Most firms offer adaptors to link their product with cast iron guttering, or with a different size from within their range. However, they tend not to offer adaptors to tie in with the equivalent size from another brand, so if possible stick to one brand throughout the installation. If you have to link up with a neighbour's gutter, find out which brand was used, and try to use the same.

There are many different fittings as well as lengths of guttering available on the market. Before you start buying your new guttering get hold of a manufacturer's brochure from the stockist you use and carefully check to ensure you have all the fittings you will need. Make sure you understand how the particular system works before you buy anything.

Taking down old guttering
Cast iron guttering is heavy, and may also be rusted into place, so removing it can be tricky. But there is no need to be gentle with it: it doesn't matter if it breaks. The important thing is to work in safe conditions. If you are wrenching things apart, do it in a controlled way so you don't fall off the ladder, and so that great chunks of gutter don't fall down. Try not to drop cast iron guttering to the ground: it shatters easily, and, if it lands on a hard surface, dangerous fragments can fly off. If you toss the guttering clear of the house you might overbalance and fall off the ladder, so aim to lower larger sections gently to the ground with a rope.

Begin with the section linking gutter and downpipe. Cut through the old bolts holding the sections together. Then, if you lift the gutter slightly, you should be able to pull it free from the downpipe. Once it's out of the way, unmake the joints between the sections of gutter (as if you were repairing them), and lift the guttering off its supporting brackets. It may, of course, be screwed directly to the fascia board.

You can now turn your attention to the brackets themselves. These are usually screwed to the fascia board just beneath the eaves of the roof, and can either be unscrewed or levered off with a claw hammer. In older houses the brackets may be screwed to the tops or sides of the roof rafters, to support the weight of the iron guttering. If there is a fascia board to which

PUTTING UP PLASTIC GUTTERING

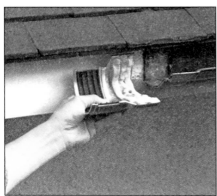

1   If you are joining onto your neighbour's gutter you'll need a special adaptor. Line it with a lump of mastic and bolt it into place.

2   Fix a string at the level of the top of the adaptor or end furthest from the downpipe. Hammer a nail into position to hold it in place.

3   Pull the string taut and fix it with a nail at the other end of the gutter run. Make sure it is horizontal, then lower it enough for the correct fall.

4   Fix the brackets to the fascia board at intervals of about 1m (39in), making sure their tops are aligned with the string.

5   You can now put in the first section of guttering so that it is resting on the brackets, and connect it to the end piece or adaptor.

6   Each manufacturer has a different system for making joints. Here the next section rests in the previous one and is then firmly held with a clip.

7   You will very likely have to cut a section of guttering. Measure it exactly at roof level, then cut it squarely.

8   In this system, once a section is cut, new notches must be made in the end for the clip. To do this you can use a proprietary notch cutter or a wood file.

9   The final corner piece and downpipe fitting is made up on the ground which is the easiest procedure when dealing with small sections.

you can fit the new gutter, the ends of the brackets can be hacksawed off. Otherwise, you will have to lift off some of the roofing to remove them.

When all the old guttering has been removed, inspect the fascia board to make sure it is sound and securely fixed. If it is, fill the old screw holes and paint it before fixing the new guttering. If it isn't, it will have to be replaced.

Fixing new guttering

The obvious first step is to assemble the various bits and pieces you need, and you can use the old guttering system as a model to decide what's required. It's best to measure up the length of the guttering itself, allowing a little extra to be safe.

At the end of the run furthest from the downpipe, fix a gutter support bracket as high up the fascia as possible, and about 150mm (6in) from the end. The fixings here, and elsewhere, are made with 25mm (1in) screws. Choose ones that are galvanised to stop them rusting. Insert a nail into the fascia board level with the top of the bracket.

At the other end of the run, 150mm from the downpipe, fix another nail, tie a length of string tightly between the two, and use a spirit level to check that this string is level. When it is, lower the second nail by the amount needed to ensure that the guttering runs downhill towards the outlet. This 'fall', as it's called, varies according to the type of guttering, so check the manufacturer's recommendations. Usually, it is in the region of 5mm (¼in) for every metre (3ft) of gutter run. Once you've found the right line for the gutter, fix another bracket level with the lowest nail.

The next job is to fix the next bracket 1m (39in) from the one at the downpipe

end of the run, using the string as a guide to set it at the correct level. Use these two brackets to support a length of gutter with the downpipe outlet attached.

Exactly how you join the gutter to the outlet – or indeed make any other joins in the guttering – will vary from brand to brand. With some, you slip the ends of the components into a special jointing piece called a union, and clip the whole lot together. With others, one of the components will have a union built into its end.

Now work your way along, building up the gutter run as you go and adding additional support brackets as required, again using the string as a guide. In most cases, you will need a bracket every metre, plus one on each side of every join – though some ranges contain combined unions and support brackets. Check the manufacturer's recommendations.

The only problem you may run into is when you have to cut the guttering to length, either to go round a corner, or to finish the run with a stop end. Do the cutting on the ground using a hacksaw, making sure that you cut the end square. Any roughness left by the saw should be cleaned up with a file. If you want to turn a corner, fix the corner piece before cutting the straight piece of gutter to length. You can then use it to work out exactly how long the straight gutter length needs to be. When cutting to finish at a stop end, it is usual to leave about 50mm (2in) of gutter projecting beyond the ends of the fascia.

When you've finished the job and checked to see that all the joints are properly connected, take a bucket of water to the highest point of the gutter and pour it down. If the gutter doesn't drain all the water then go back and check your work.

10 The made-up section is fixed in place taking care to locate the down-pipe end into the hopper head. Any pipe connection needs a sealant joint.

11 When the whole system is up, you should check that it will work by pouring water in at the point furthest from the downpipe.

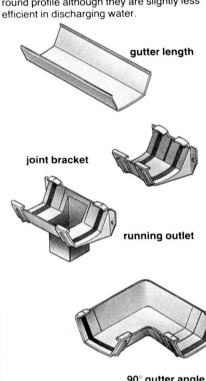

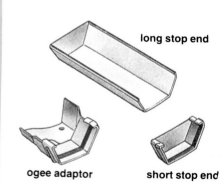

REPLACING DOWNPIPES

If your downpipes are blocked, damaged or badly fixed, the overflowing rainwater can damage your house, and soak passers-by! Routine maintenance is half the battle, but complete replacement may ultimately be the only solution.

The rainwater that falls on your house cannot be allowed to run off freely over the sides of the roof. If it were, it would soak the walls below, flood the ground all about, and drench anybody unlucky enough to be walking underneath. So it is taken away harmlessly by what is known as a rainwater disposal system. This consists of gutters that collect the water flowing off the roof, and convey it to downpipes which carry it to the drains. At one time most gutters and downpipes were made of cast iron. But although this is a tough material, gutters and downpipes made from it suffer from two big disadvantages: in use they are prone to attack by rust, a big drawback in something that comes into such close contact with water; they need to be kept well painted to ensure that corrosion is held at bay; and during installation (or removal) they are heavy and cumbersome to handle.

Because of this, alternative materials were sought for gutters and downpipes, and for a time they were made in asbestos. This was, however, a rather bulky material and is now recognised as a potential health hazard. So, when the full potential of plastics became apparent during the late 1940s, the opportunity was seized to manufacture rainwater systems in a plastic material – UPVC (unplasticised polyvinyl chloride). As a result, iron systems have just about disappeared from the scene and it's difficult to buy at all. When a rainwater disposal system nowadays is being renewed in whole or part, it is invariably plastic goods that are used.

Plastic gutters and downpipes have many advantages. They seem to be everlasting (unless broken); they don't need painting, though they take paint if you don't like the colours in which they are available; they are light to handle, and easy to cut with a hacksaw. In fact, their only drawback is that they are not as rigid as cast iron, and can sag under such things as ladders.

Maintenance

The trouble you get with downpipes are not the same thing you get with gutters. For example, you may occasionally get

a blockage, caused by dirt, leaves or other debris being washed off the roof. You should clear this out as soon as possible, otherwise the surrounding wall of your house will get soaked with escaping water, and damp could find its way inside the house. You will see at a glance in which section of a downpipe the trouble has occurred because the joins between various lengths are not sealed. Thus when during a downpour water bubbles out of a join, you will know that the trouble lies in the section below.

The fact that the sections are just loosely joined also means that a blocked one can be taken down for clearance. You merely lift it up and pull it away, rather like a sliding door that operates in a groove.

On a straight run, you can usually push out the blockage with a long stick, although in stubborn cases you might have to tie a wad of rags to the end of the stick to make a sort of plunger. Bends will have to be poked clear with a length of wire or cane. Then clean them thoroughly by pulling through a piece of rope with a rag tied to the end of it.

Should the system have a hopper head, scoop debris out with a trowel. You should wear protective gloves as you do this. Take care not to push anything down the pipe; in fact, it's a wise precaution to push a rag bung into the top of the pipe as you work. When everything has been cleared up, fit netting to

the top of the pipe so that the trouble will not occur again.

Another fault that sometimes develops is that one or more of the clips holding the pipe to the wall may become damaged or displaced in some way, and the pipe then becomes loose at the joint. The remedy is obvious: refix the clip securely (or replace it if it is badly damaged) and push the pipe back into place. Sections of pipe, too, may be badly damaged, or missing altogether. Again, you should replace them although minor damage on cast iron can be repaired with a glass fibre repair kit.

If you have cast iron downpipes, then a lot of these faults may arise because of rust, for unless you keep them well painted, they will eventually corrode. Even householders who are meticulous about regularly re-painting the exterior of the house tend to neglect the back of the downpipes because they cannot be seen, and it is difficult to treat them without getting paint all over the wall. There is one simple solution to this last problem: protect the wall with a scrap piece of card or hardboard as you work. Obviously, corrosion can take place just as readily at the back as at the front, so it is as well to be meticulous when you paint.

When one length of old downpipe becomes defective, you can replace it with a new one, and there is no problem about inserting a

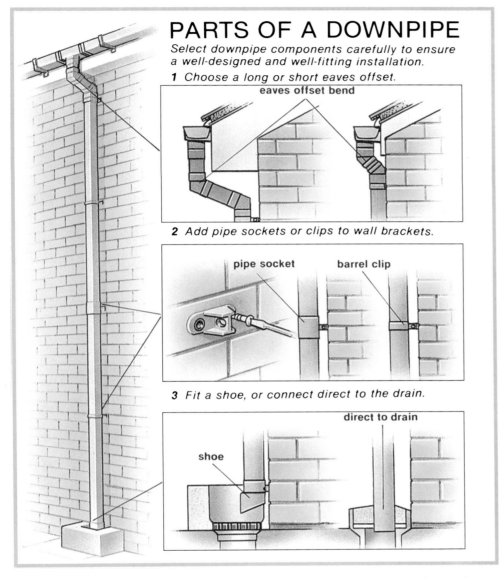

PARTS OF A DOWNPIPE

Select downpipe components carefully to ensure a well-designed and well-fitting installation.

1 *Choose a long or short eaves offset.*

eaves offset bend

2 *Add pipe sockets or clips to wall brackets.*

pipe socket   barrel clip

3 *Fit a shoe, or connect direct to the drain.*

direct to drain

shoe

moving. Insert the screw-driver blade in the slot of the screw, then give the handle a short sharp blow with a mallet (if it's wooden). This should free the screw so you can turn it. Alternatively, the brackets may be held in place by large galvanised nails cemented into the mortar. These will have to be prised out. If all else fails, cut everything loose with a hacksaw.

The pipe itself comes in a series of standard lengths and you'll probably have to join two or more sections together with a special socket, or cut one down to size, to make up the required run. You should leave an expansion gap of 10mm (3/8in) at the end.

Plastic pipes are held to the wall by a series of small clips. These may come, according to the make, as one unit, or in two parts – a separate back-plate and clip. A clip should be placed at each joint socket, and at the manufacturer's recommended spacings in between – possibly every 2m (6ft 6in). Incidentally, there is no need to go to the trouble of drilling holes in brickwork to take the plugs for the screws that hold the clips in place. The pipes are so light that you will get a fixing by drilling the holes into the mortar.

On a simple structure, such as a garden shed, the gutter outlet may well be fitted directly into the top of the pipe without being sealed, and this makes it easier to locate and to deal with blockages. However, houses have eaves, which means the gutters won't be flush with the wall on which the downpipe is situated. So some form of fitting is needed to make the connection: this is known as an offset or 'swan neck'. You can make one of these yourself from an offset socket, an offset spigot, and a short length of pipe – perhaps an offcut from one of the main lengths – as shown in the diagram overleaf. The joins between the gutter outlet and the offset socket and spigot should be solvent-welded, for these do need to be watertight. The same is true of any section of the system that is not vertical.

Once you've made up the offset you can position it to work out where you can fix the downpipe. And this will also allow you to site the clip that holds the socket which connects the offset to the downpipe itself.

With this clip in place, you can plumb the drop of the pipe and mark the positions of the clips on the wall with chalk, so that they will all be directly underneath each other. Then fix these clips in place, and fit the pipe sections.

If your downpipes discharge into an open gully at the bottom, a curved or angled end, known as a shoe, is fitted. A clip will, of course, be needed here, as at every other joint. The shoe should be pointing away from the house wall, and should be only 50mm (2in) or so higher than the grating, so that splashes will not get onto the wall. Should the connection be direct to the drain, a special adaptor is required.

length of plastic pipe in a cast iron system. It merely sits loosely in place, so you do not have to worry about sealing joints, as you do with gutters.

However, if one section of pipe corrodes, it is a good bet that all are coming to the end of their useful life. And, of course, if the whole system becomes ramshackle, it is time to replace the lot. This is especially true if you are fitting new gutters.

Putting in new pipes
There are a number of brands to select from, but little to choose between them, so settle for one which is available from a convenient store. If you are fitting new gutters, the pipes should be of the same brand to ensure that you can link the two at the eaves. With only a short length of guttering, consider replacing the whole gutter and downpipe system.

Begin by getting a manufacturer's catalogue. With this in one hand, inspect your existing downpipe system, and note down the exact replacements you will need. The pipes come in three common diameters – 75mm (3in) for extensions and the like, 100mm (4in) for most normal houses, and 150mm (6in) for very large roofs. Your pipes must, of course, match the gutters in size.

You have to begin the work by what is really the only troublesome part of the job, and that's taking down and getting rid of the old metal or asbestos pipes. Once you've freed each section you can lower it gently to the ground. Don't drop it as it may shatter. The clips holding the pipe to the wall can now be removed. If held by screws, there's a fair chance they will have rusted into place and will be virtually impossible to turn. However, there is a trick you can use to start the screw

REPLACING A HOPPER

Most drainage systems operate without trouble year in, year out. But if your system incorporates hopper heads to collect rainwater, or upstairs wastewater, then these may need your attention from time to time.

A hopper head is simply a funnel-shaped container with a vertical outlet in its base that is used for collecting water from different sources. Indeed, its original purpose was to receive water draining from two roofs, perhaps at different levels, so that this could be conducted away in one main downpipe. In short, hoppers made for a neater simpler drainage system.

The introduction of two-pipe drainage gave hopper heads another use. With this system, the waste from sinks, baths, basins and showers – anything, in fact, except the waste from a WC, urinal and slop-sink – had to enter the underground drainage system via a trapped yard gully. This didn't present any problems for fittings situated on the ground floor, but dealing with the upstairs waste water was not as straightforward. To get round the need for individual downpipes casting an unsightly web over the wall of the house, plumbers seized on the idea of using a hopper head to collect all the waste water at one point on the outside wall and then to take it via a downpipe to a yard gully.

This arrangement remained in vogue for many years before being superseded by single-stack drainage in the 1940s, although there are hundreds of thousands of homes where the two-pipe drainage system is still functioning perfectly adequately. However, because of the age of these systems and their inherent design drawbacks, particularly concerning the hopper head itself, it's likely that they have begun to cause trouble.

Problems with hoppers

The original iron hopper was, and is, a common source of nuisance. It has a rough interior surface that tends to hold back any debris or scum the waste water discharges into it. Inevitably, this dries and decomposes to produce unpleasant smells in the vicinity of the bathroom window. Furthermore, during cold weather, if you leave a bathroom tap dripping overnight it can quickly fill the hopper with ice, so blocking the outlet and possibly causing a flood in the morning when more waste water is discharged. In a similar manner, the open top of a hopper provides a

WHERE HOPPERS ARE USED

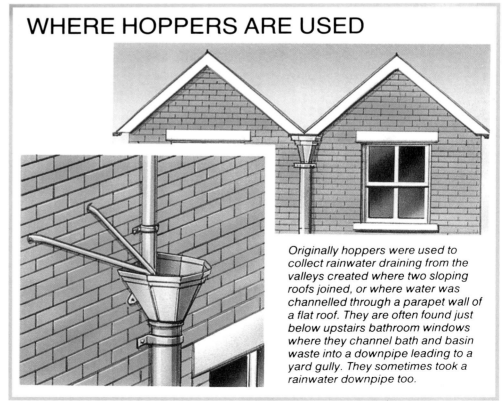

Originally hoppers were used to collect rainwater draining from the valleys created where two sloping roofs joined, or where water was channelled through a parapet wall of a flat roof. They are often found just below upstairs bathroom windows where they channel bath and basin waste into a downpipe leading to a yard gully. They sometimes took a rainwater downpipe too.

FITTING A NEW HOPPER

1 The hopper head will be fixed to the wall with bolts or screws – often rusted securely in place. Unscrew them if possible or lever them out.

2 Lift the hopper head clear of the downpipe. Cast iron ones are heavy and there may be sharp rusted edges, so take care and lower it carefully to the ground.

3 Use a filling knife or trowel to fill the holes left by the old fixing bolts with a small amount of mortar or some exterior-quality filler.

4 Hold the new hopper in place and mark the position of the new fixing holes which go through the back wall. Check that they're level then drill and plug them.

5 Choose No. 10 round-headed screws about 38mm (1½in) long. They will need to be rust-proof so use zinc-plated or sherardised ones.

6 There will probably be a poor fit between the hopper and downpipe so seal this with some bitumen mastic. The sort applied by a gun is most convenient.

convenient receptacle for falling leaves, which in turn can cause blockages even in the downpipe itself. Corrosion can also be a problem and metal hoppers should be protected by regular painting. But so often the interior surfaces are ignored, and if this is the case, rust is the inevitable outcome.

All this makes the hopper head seem like an unsavoury fitting, yet many of the drawbacks can be alleviated by regular maintenance. Cleaning the inside with caustic soda and coating the surfaces with paint aren't daunting or time-consuming jobs. And some chicken wire fixed over the top will prevent leaves blocking the outlet.

If, however, the hopper has deteriorated beyond repair, then more drastic action is needed. You may think that this is as good an opportunity as any to convert your existing drainage into a single-stack system (as described on pages 250 to 253) rather than replacing the hopper. Admittedly, this gets round the problems of the hopper, but it's not as simple as it seems. The existing soil pipe, for example, may not be suitable for single stack use and the length of the gradient of the bath and basin wastes may make it impossible to take them to a single stack without realignment. You may even need to reposition the bath or basin. So before you take the plunge remember that a well-designed and satisfactorily functioning two-pipe system is far better than a bad conversion to a single-stack one.

For this reason, often the simplest answer is just to replace the hopper itself. Metal ones are still available to match old metal downpipes, but it's advisable to fit a modern streamlined hopper made of UPVC or similar plastic. This won't need any decoration or protection from corrosion. Its internal surfaces are smooth and far less likely to hold back debris from bath or basin water. And there is less likelihood of frost damage. However, if you choose this option you'll probably have to replace the downpipe as well (see the previous section) even if it's in good repair as it may look unsightly to have a plastic hopper set on an old metal pipe.

A new plastic hopper head will probably be about 280mm (11in) wide, 150mm (6in) deep from front to back, and 280mm (11in) from rim to outlet. Normally, there are two pre-drilled fixing holes just below the rim on the back of the hopper. Ideally, these holes should coincide with a mortar joint when the hopper is being fitted, but often this won't be possible especially if the downpipe isn't being replaced at the same time. In any event, make sure you plug the drill holes and use zinc-plated or sherardised steel screws. Also remember that cast iron hoppers are heavy so be extra careful when taking one down. Make sure you secure your ladders in position and have all the necessary tools to hand.

REPLACING
AN OUTSIDE
SOIL STACK

You can't make new connections into an
old cast iron soil pipe. So changing
your indoor plumbing system will
mean fitting a new soil
stack too.

If your house was built before the mid-1950s
it will almost certainly have a 'two-pipe'
above-ground drainage system made of
cast iron. This system was originally devised
by Victorian sanitary engineers in a
determined effort to keep 'drain air', which
was believed by the public health experts of
the time to be the cause of virtually all human
disease, out of the home. The system made
a distinction between 'soil appliances' –
WCs – and 'waste appliances' – basins,
sinks, baths, etc. Soil was sent down one
pipe to the underground drain, and waste
was sent down another (although it
eventually reached the same drain). Drain
smells were, and still are, prevented from
spreading inside the house by the use of
water traps at the outlet of each appliance.

Modern homes are provided with 'single
stack' above-ground drainage systems
using PVC or similar plastic waste pipes. In a
single stack system no distinction is made
between soil and waste appliances. All discharges go into one main stack which, as with
the old soil pipe, terminates open-ended
above eaves level. To make these systems
safe they must be in strict accordance with
the regulations.

In most cases it is possible to replace an
obsolete two-pipe system with a modern
single stack one, but the local council's
Building Inspector must be consulted about
your plans in advance, and very careful
attention should be paid to the design of the
new system if it is to be both efficient and
safe. In new houses the single stack is often
located inside the house, in a boxed service
duct, but this isn't a legal requirement and
replacement of an existing external soil
stack by a single stack in the same position
is perfectly acceptable.

Single stack requirements
In order to prevent water from siphoning out
of the traps of baths and basins which have
pipe connections to a single stack, deep-
seal 75mm (3in) traps must be used. For the
same reason, branch waste pipes from
baths and basins have to be laid with a very

small angle of fall to the stack and should be
as short as possible. This is particularly
important with the basin waste, because, if
the trap should siphon out, very little water
is left after the main discharge to reseal it.
The basin branch waste should preferably
be no longer than 1.7m (5ft 7in). If a greater
length is unavoidable, you should install a
patent anti-siphon trap or use a branch
waste-pipe 38mm (1½in) in diameter,
instead of the usual 32mm (1¼in). This
means that if an old system has shallow
traps – often 50mm (2in) in depth – long pipe
runs and steep angles, any replacement of
the stack will mean considerable
replumbing inside.

The branch soil pipe from the WC suite
must be connected to the main soil and
waste stack by a swept joint in the direction
of the soil flow. To prevent waste outlets from
baths, basins or bidets from being fouled or
obstructed by discharges of soil from the
WC, no connection may be made to the
opposite side of the main stack within
200mm (8in) of the centre point of the
connection of the soil branch. Special boss
sockets are available which allow connections to be made at apparently the same
level as the lavatory outlet. In fact, inside the
boss the waste is deflected downwards to
flow into the stack itself below the level of the
soil pipe entry.

The main soil and waste stack, which must

have an internal diameter of at least 100mm
(4in), must connect to the underground
drain with a bend of at least 200mm (8in)
radius. In some cases this will mean that, as
well as replacing the old soil pipe, it will be
necessary to replace the – usually short –
length of underground drain between the
foot of the soil-pipe and the drain inspection
chamber. This job is not too difficult but must
be done with great precision to ensure
efficient drainage.

Although the single stack is now the most
popular system for the drainage of
appliances on first floors and above, there is
little, if anything, to be gained by converting
ground floor drainage to a single stack
system. Ground floor WCs may quite
conveniently be connected direct to the
nearest inspection chamber by means of a
branch from the underground drain, and
there is no objection to ground floor sinks,
baths and basins discharging over a yard
gully. These discharges should however
enter the gully above the water level but
below the level of the gully grid. Slotted grids
are available to allow existing gullies to be
adapted in this way.

Assembling the new system
Get an illustrated catalogue of plastic
above-ground drainage components from
your local builder's merchant, or send away
for one. Using this, have a look at the existing

REMOVING THE OLD PIPEWORK

1 *Start on the old waste pipe; use a club hammer and chisel to loosen the brackets supporting the pipe and lever them out.*

2 *The pipe should now come free from the hopper head connection. If you can't move it easily, then tap gently downwards with a club hammer.*

3 *When you've got the waste pipe out of the way, remove any other inflows, including the old bath overflow pipe which is illustrated here.*

TIP

4 *The top part of the soil stack, with an eaves level vent, needs a lot of care. If you can't lift it free, try and break up the pipe.*

5 *When you have cracked the old pipe, lift the section clear. It will be quite heavy, so be careful how you lower it to the ground.*

6 *Move further down the stack and break each joint in turn. Lift each section clear and carry it carefully down to the ground.*

7 *When you get to the old outlet from the WC pan, lever it gently out through the wall. Try not to dislodge any bricks in the wall.*

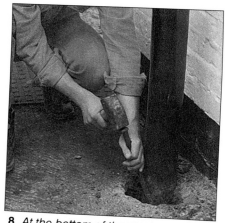

8 *At the bottom of the stack, gently chip away the concrete round the base of the pipe, until it starts to loosen and come free.*

9 *Lift the pipe free of the drain socket connection. Ensure that no pieces of broken concrete and debris fall into the opening.*

ASSEMBLING THE STACK

1 *Carefully clean out the old underground drain connection. It may need replacing if the bend is too tight; check the Regulations.*

2 *Install new outlet connections so that they emerge flush with the outside wall surface. Don't fix them rigidly in place yet.*

3 *Using a drain connector and access branch, start to make up the base of the stack. Use push-fit or solvent-weld fittings.*

4 *Mortar in the drain connector to the underground drain joint, using a quick-dry mortar. Check that the pipe is truly vertical.*

5 *When the mortar joint is firm, start to extend the stack upwards, using sockets according to the connections you want to make.*

6 *Support the stack with brackets about every 2m (6ft 6in). These are easily fixed by drilling into the wall and using wall plugs.*

7 *...vermost connection to ...the appropriate ...g technique. Here an ...n is being fitted.*

TIP

8 *Make sure the connections to the stack are firm, and don't finally fix the through-wall connections (see 2) until these are made.*

9 *In the case of solvent-weld jointing (as used here), further connections should only be made when the previous ones are completely firm.*

COMPLETING THE STACK

1 Attach the swept branch for the WC/soil pipe connection; check that you have fulfilled all the Regulations regarding these connections.

2 Make the soil pipe bend connection to the pipe emerging through the wall. Check that the angle of the soil pipe is correct.

3 Connect the soil pipe to the stack and then continue the stack upwards, installing any other branch connections that are necessary.

4 Fix the remaining connections, still making sure that no movement takes place in those lower down, and that the stack remains vertical.

5 Make up the top section of the stack. Don't forget to fix the balloon grating in place; this is required by the Regulations.

6 Fix the top section of the stack, and attach any necessary support brackets to the wall. Again, check that the stack remains vertical.

drainage system and work out what components you will need. You must stick to the products of one manufacturer throughout. When you have a clear idea of the new system you want to install, draw out some plans and go to see the local Building Inspector and get his approval for your proposals (and his advice, if you need it).

Dismantling the old pipe stacks needs a lot of care. If you have to work at any great height you should seriously consider hiring a scaffold tower. Try and take the old stacks apart by levering out the fixing brackets and pulling out each section of pipe, starting from the top. If this is difficult you'll have to break up the pipe with a club hammer, but be careful of splinters. Then either lower each piece to the ground with a length of rope or carry it down.

When you've taken out all the old pipework clean and tidy up carefully the underground drain connection. Start the new installation by connecting the new stack to the underground drain (unless the bend needs replacing). The drain connector should be fixed in place with quick-setting mortar, and should be supported to make sure that it remains firmly vertical during setting. When this connection is in place you can continue upwards using brackets at roughly 1m (39in) intervals to support the stack against the wall. Depending on the pipe system you are using, the joints will be either push-fit or solvent-welded. You may have to fit new deep-seal traps to basins and sinks, and run plastic pipe from the trap outlets to the bosses provided in the boss-branch of the main stack.

The job is easier if you can use the existing cast-iron branch soil pipe from the WC. You can do this if the stack is made of UPVC by slipping a neoprene sealing ring over the spigot of the iron pipe. Insert the spigot, with the ring round it, into the UPVC socket, the gently heat the socket with a blow torch un it shrinks round the spigot with its neopre ring seal. If you have to replace the soil pi it may even mean a new WC pan if connection is mortared in.

When you get to the top of the stack must finish it off with a balloon grating to debris, in particular birds' nests, from f in. This is in fact a requirement c Regulations. Put the balloon onto th section of the stack before you fix it in

When you have finished erectir whole system check carefully for lea may then receive a visit from the P Inspector to make sure that all is in there are any problems with the nev he will be able to suggest the cat what you should do about them.

INDEX